I0882101

Governing Interests

In the present period of globalization *Governing Interests* presents new research on the impact of internationalization on the organization and representation of business interests through trade and employer associations. By exploring ongoing, gradual but nevertheless profound changes in the structures and functions of business interest associations, the book develops a more precise understanding of the relationship between the national and the international.

Focusing on national business associations and the ways they are adjusting to the changing composition and interests of their membership, and to the shift in functions of economic governance to levels above the nation state, the essays in this volume cover a selection of OECD countries, paying special attention to Britain, Germany, the Netherlands, Switzerland and Sweden. Unlike much of the current top-down research on European integration, the volume contains both theoretical and empirical papers studying internationalization from the bottom-up, adopting the perspective of national actors facing new challenges and opportunities in their international environment.

Wolfgang Streeck is Director at the Max Planck Institute for the Study of Societies in Cologne. **Jürgen R. Grote** is a Senior Research Fellow and Stand-in Chair in Public Sector Reform in the Department of Public Policy and Administration at the University of Konstanz. **Volker Schneider** is a Professor of Political Science at the University of Konstanz, where he has held the Chair of Empirical Theory of the State since 1997. **Jelle Visser** is Professor of Sociology at the University of Amsterdam, where he directs the Amsterdam Institute for Advanced Labour Studies.

Routledge studies in international business and the world economy

1 **States and Firms**
Multinational enterprises in institutional competition
Razeen Sally

2 **Multinational Restructuring, Internationalization and Small Economies**
The Swedish case
Thomas Andersson, Torbjörn Fredriksson and Roger Svensson

3 **Foreign Direct Investment and Governments**
Catalysts for economic restructuring
Edited by John H. Dunning and Rajneesh Narula

4 **Multinational Investment and Economic Structure**
Globalization and competitiveness
Rajneesh Narula

5 **Entrepreneurship in a Global Context**
Edited by Sue Birley and Ian Macmillan

6 **The Global Structure of Financial Markets**
An overview
Edited by Dilip K. Ghosh and Edgar Ortiz

7 **Alliance Capitalism and Global Business**
John H. Dunning

8 **Multinational Enterprises from the Netherlands**
Edited by Roger van Hoesel and Rajneesh Narula

9 **Competition, Growth Strategies and the Globalization of Services**
Real estate advisory services in Japan, Europe and the United States
Terrence LaPier

10 **European Integration and Foreign Direct Investment in the EU**
The case of the Korean consumer electronics industry
Sang Hyup Shin

11 **New Multinational Enterprises from Korea and Taiwan**
Beyond export-led growth
Roger van Hoesel

12 **Competitive Industrial Development in the Age of Information**
The role of co-operation in the technology sector
Edited by Richard J. Braudo and Jeffrey G. MacIntosh

13 **The Global Restructuring of the Steel Industry**
Innovations, institutions and industrial change
Anthony P. D'Costa

14 **Privatisation and Liberalisation in European Telecommunications**
Comparing Britain, the Netherlands and France
Willem Hulsink

15 **Multinational Corporations**
Emergence and evolution
Paz Estrella Tolentino

16 **Foreign Direct Investment in Emerging Economies**
Corporate strategy and investment behaviour in the Caribbean
Lou Anne A. Barclay

17 **European Integration and Global Corporate Strategies**
Edited by François Chesnais, Grazia Ietto-Gillies and Roberto Simonetti

18 **The Globalisation of Corporate R & D**
Implications for innovation systems in host countries
Prasada Reddy

19 **Globalization of Services**
Some implications for theory and practice
Edited by Yair Aharoni and Lilach Nachum

20 **A Century of Foreign Investment in the Third World**
Michael J. Twomey

21 **Global Capitalism at Bay**
John H. Dunning

22 **Foreign Direct Investment**
Research issues
Edited by Bijit Bora

23 **Ford and the Global Strategies of Multinationals**
The North American auto industry
Isabel Studer Noguez

24 **The World Trade Organization Millennium Round**
Freer trade in the next century
Klaus Deutsch and Bernhard Speyer

25 **Consultancy and Innovation**
The business service revolution in Europe
Edited by Peter Wood

26 **Knowledge Economies**
Clusters, learning and co-operative advantage
Philip Cooke

27 **The Role of Resources in Global Competition**
John Fahy

28 **Globalization, Employment and the Workplace**
Diverse impacts
Edited by Yaw A. Debrah and Ian G. Smith

29 **Transnational Corporations**
Fragmentation amidst integration
Grazia Ietto-Gillies

30 **Growth Theory and Growth Policy**
Edited by Harald Hagemann and Stephan Seiter

31 **International Business and the Eclectic Paradigm**
Developing the OLI framework
Edited by John Cantwell and Rajneesh Narula

32 **Regulating Global Trade and the Environment**
Paul Street

33 **Cultural Industries and the Production of Culture**
Edited by Dominic Power and Allen J. Scott

34 **Governing Interests**
Business associations facing internationalization
Edited by Wolfgang Streeck, Jürgen Grote, Volker Schneider and Jelle Visser

Governing Interests

Business associations facing internationalization

Edited by Wolfgang Streeck, Jürgen R. Grote, Volker Schneider and Jelle Visser

Routledge
Taylor & Francis Group
LONDON AND NEW YORK

First published 2006
by Routledge
2 Park Square, Milton Park, Abingdon, Oxon, OX14 4RN

Simultaneously published in the USA and Canada
by Routledge
711 Third Avenue, New York, NY 10017

First issued in paperback 2012
Routledge is an imprint of the Taylor & Francis Group

Transferred to Digital Printing 2009

© 2006 Wolfgang Streeck, Jürgen Grote, Volker Schneider and Jelle Visser selection and editorial matter; the contributors their contributions

Typeset in Garamond by Wearset Ltd, Boldon, Tyne and Wear

All rights reserved. No part of this book may be reprinted or reproduced or utilized in any form or by any electronic, mechanical, or other means, now known or hereafter invented, including photocopying and recording, or in any information storage or retrieval system, without permission in writing from the publishers.

British Library Cataloguing in Publication Data
A catalogue record for this book is available from the British Library

Library of Congress Cataloging in Publication Data
A catalog record for this book has been requested

ISBN13: 978-0-415-64809-7 (PBK)

ISBN13: 978-0-415-36486-7 (HBK)

Contents

Contributors

Pieter Bouwen works in the European Commission's Directorate-General for Enterprise and Industry. He holds a doctoral degree in Political and Social Sciences from the European University Institute in Florence and is professor at the Free University of Brussels. Previously, he was a research fellow at the Université Catholique de Louvain, the Max Planck Institute for Research on Collective Goods in Bonn and the Max Planck Institute for the Study of Societies in Cologne. Pieter Bouwen obtained a degree in economics at the Katholieke Universiteit Leuven and equally holds degrees in political science, international relations and international political economy from respectively the Université Catholique de Louvain, the Johns Hopkins University and the London School of Economics. He has published several articles in international peer-reviewed journals such as the *Journal of European Public Policy*, the *Journal of Common Market Studies* and the *European Journal of Political Research*.

William D. Coleman holds the Canada Research Chair on Global Governance and Public Policy and is Founding Director of the Institute on Globalization and the Human Condition at McMaster University, Hamilton, Ontario, Canada. He has written four books: *The Independence Movement in Quebec, 1945–1980* (Toronto: University of Toronto Press, 1984), *Business and Politics: A Study in Collective Action* (Montreal: McGill-Queen's University Press, 1988), *The State, Business and Industrial Change in Canada* (with Michael M. Atkinson; Toronto: University of Toronto Press, 1989) and *Financial Services, Globalization and Domestic Policy Change: A Comparison of North America and the European Union* (Basingstoke: Macmillan, 1996). He has also edited three books in the public policy field, the most recent being *Regionalism and Global Economic Integration: Europe, Asia and the Americas* (with G. R. D. Underhill; London: Routledge, 1998).

Jürgen R. Grote is a Senior Research Fellow at Konstanz University (Department of Politics and Management). He has been assistant professor at Konstanz and has previously worked and held positions at the EUI Florence, the MZES Mannheim, and the LSE. Besides his current field of research ('Organizational Change in National Business Associations under Conditions of Europeanization and Globalization'), he has been involved in a number of projects on regional and European forms of governance. His main subjects are comparative politics, European Union politics, and network analysis. Among his publications are (with J. Greenwood and K. Ronit) *Organized Interests and the European Community* (London: Sage, 1992) and (with B. Gbikpi) *Participatory Governance. Political and Societal Implications* (Wiesbaden: Leske und Budrich, 2002).

Hanspeter Kriesi is Professor of Political Science at the University of Zurich (since 2002). Before, he was teaching at the Universities of Amsterdam and Geneva. He has published widely in the area of social movements, comparative politics and Swiss politics. He was a visiting scholar at Cornell in 1995/1996 and at the Wissenschaftszentrum Berlin in 2000/2001.

Dirk Lehmkuhl holds a PhD from the European University Institute, Florence. He is now a Senior Research Fellow at the University of Zurich. He is co-author (with Adrienne Héritier, Dieter Kerwer, Christoph Knill, Michael Teutsch, and Anne-Cécile Douillet) of *Differential Europe. EU Impact on Domestic Policies.* He also has published articles in *Current Politics and Economics in Europe, European Journal of Political Research, Governance, Zeitschrift für Rechtssoziologie* and *West European Politics.*

Victor A. Pestoff was educated in Long Beach, California, Stockholm, Paris and Oslo. He received his PhD in political science in 1977. Pestoff has taught at the Departments of Political Science (1978–1984) and then the School of Business (1982–1996) at Stockholm University. He became Professor of Political Science at Södertörns Högskola and is now Head of Department at Mid-Sweden University in Östersund. He is the author of several books including: *Voluntary Associations and Nordic Party Systems; Between Markets and Politics: Cooperatives in Sweden*; and *Beyond the Market and State: Civil Democracy & Social Enterprises in a Welfare Society.*

Karsten Ronit is Associate Professor at the Department of Political Science, University of Copenhagen. He has for many years studied the relationship between business and politics in a wide field of sectoral and territorial contexts. Apart from books and articles published on the Danish case, he has edited: *Organized Interests and the European Community* (with J. Greenwood and J. R. Grote), *Evolution of Interest Representation and Development of the Labour Market in Post-Socialist Countries* (with O. K. Pedersen and J. Hausner) and *Private Organizations in Global Politics* (with V. Schneider). In recent years he has analysed the development of consumer policy in domestic and international settings.

Volker Schneider is Professor of Political Science at Konstanz University (since 1997) where he holds the Chair for Empirical Theory of the State.

He received his PhD at the European University Institute in Florence in 1986, and his *Habilitation* at the University of Mannheim in 1995. From 1986 to 1997 he was a Research Fellow at the Max Planck Institute for the Study of Societies in Cologne. Recent book publications include: *Private Organizations in Global Politics* (2000; with Karsten Ronit), *Die Transformation der Telekommunikation. Vom Staatsmonopol zum globalen Markt* (2001) and *Entgrenzte Märkte, grenzenlose Bürokratie* (2002).

Wolfgang Streeck is Director at the Max Planck Institute for the Study of Societies in Cologne, Germany. From 1988 to 1995 he was Professor of Sociology and Industrial Relations at the University of Wisconsin-Madison. He is author of *Social Institutions and Economic Performance* (1992). He edited *Germany: Beyond the Stable State* (with Herbert Kitschelt; 2003); *The End of Diversity? Prospects for German and Japanese Capitalism* (with Kozo Yamamura; 2003); *The Origins of Nonliberal Capitalism: Germany and Japan* (with Kozo Yamamura; 2001); *Political Economy of Modern Capitalism: Mapping Convergence and Diversity* (with Colin Crouch; 1997) and *Works Councils: Consultation, Representation, Cooperation in Industrial Relations* (with Joel Rogers; 1995). He was President of the Society for the Advancement of Socio-Economics in 1998/1999.

Franz Traxler is Professor of Industrial Sociology at the University of Vienna. He worked as a consultant to the OECD and the ILO. His research focuses on comparative industrial relations and interest groups. Book publications include *Organized Industrial Relations in Europe* (with Colin Crouch; 1995) and *National Labour Relations in Internationalized Markets* (with Sabine Blaschke and Bernhard Kittel; 2001).

Jelle Visser is Professor of Empirical Sociology and of Sociology of Labour and Organization at the University of Amsterdam, where he directs the Amsterdam Institute for Advanced Labour Studies (AIAS). He worked as consultant to the OECD, the European Commission and the ILO. He was a member of the EU High-level Group on Industrial Relations and Change and has been appointed Chief Editor for the 2004 Industrial Relations in Europe report of the European Commission. He is (co-) author of several books and some 100 refereed articles on industrial relations, trade unions, labour markets, working time and organizations. His recent books in English include: *Trade Unions in Western Europe Since 1945* (with Bernhard Ebbinghaus; 2000) and *A Dutch Miracle. Job Growth, Welfare Reform and Corporatism in the Netherlands* (with Anton Hemerijck; 1997).

Arnold Wilts received his PhD at the University of Amsterdam. He is lecturer at the Department of Public Administration and Organisation at the Free University of Amsterdam. He was a post-doctoral research fellow at the Max Planck Institute for the Study of Societies in Cologne and at the Department of Sociology at the University of Amsterdam.

Preface

This book has a long history – longer, perhaps, than is warranted in times of rapid social change and political turmoil. Initial drafts of some of its chapters were already available in 2000.

Volker Schneider and Jürgen R. Grote, with financial support from the Fritz Thyssen Foundation and with the cooperation of Philippe Schmitter, first brought together a number of scholars studying business associations under Europeanization and globalization. The conference, which took place in June 2000 at the European University Institute in Florence, assembled more than two dozen participants and produced an almost equal number of papers. At its end, the view was unanimous that, after more than a decade of relative silence in the field of comparative research on business associations, there was a need for a new publication summarizing the insights of recent research. To bring this about, a number of potential authors met again in May 2002 at the Institute for Advanced Labour Studies in Amsterdam. Most of the contributors to this volume were present. Arguments were conceptually straightened out, and chapters were arranged under more specific headings. At a meeting at the Max Planck Institute for the Study of Societies in Cologne, almost a year later, the editors finally selected the chapters to be included and added a number of new contributions that had meanwhile been written.

Many people have contributed to bringing this enterprise to a successful conclusion. Our gratitude, first of all, goes to Philippe Schmitter, the great inspirer of modern research on interest politics. We also would like to thank the many colleagues who have submitted papers, by now published elsewhere, and contributed to the stimulating discussions we had in Florence and Amsterdam. These were, in particular, Mirella Baglioni (Parma), Robert Bennett (Cambridge), Tom Burns (Uppsala), David Coen (London), Axel Hauser-Ditz (Düsseldorf), Rainer Eising (Hagen), Justin Greenwood (Aberdeen), Patrick Kenis (Tilburg), Luca Lanzalaco (Milan), Alberto Martinelli (Milan), Johan Nylander (Uppsala), Jörg Teuber (Cologne) and Frans van Waarden (Utrecht). Last but not least, we thank Petra Küchenmeister, Astrid Dünkelmann and Cynthia Lehmann at the Max Planck Institute for the Study of Societies for expert assistance with the final editing, of both text and tables, and for their patient management of an ever more complex set of files and of the often confusing signal traffic between four editors and their authors.

Wolfgang Streeck
Jürgen R. Grote
Volker Schneider
Jelle Visser

1 Introduction

Business associations, associative order and internationalization

Volker Schneider and Jürgen R. Grote

Interest representation and associative order

Modern politics is interest politics. Interests, as the old saying goes, govern the world – which implies that they are both a driving and a guiding force. Since the seventeenth century the mediating and rationalizing role of interest orientations in individual and collective behaviour has been viewed as a distinct advantage. According to another old proverb, interests don't lie. Behaviour defined by interest is more predictable than behaviour that is driven by sentiments, passions and other human idiosyncrasies (Hirschman 1977).

This is not to say that there are no problems with interests. Interests are complex entities whose alignments do not merely emerge from within themselves, but also are affected by the institutional and structural embeddedness of relevant actors. Interests can be defined in short-sighted or far-sighted, narrow or comprehensive terms. If we essentially agree that the political process is determined to a greater extent by interests than by ideas or feelings, we still have to identify and analyse those structures and social forces that define and guide the perception, manifestation and implementation of interests in the institutionally structured political process.

Even if we do endorse the observation that private interests constitute the principal driving force behind human actions, we cannot assume that interests as such are objectively given and clearly structured. What individuals perceive to be their interest varies with and depends on the horizon in which they navigate the network of direct and indirect independencies and behavioural effects that link the realization of the interests of one actor to those of others. A well-understood or enlightened personal interest may come close to collective or common interests – a possibility that de Tocqueville (1953) found to be a general conviction in America more than 170 years ago:

> The Americans . . . are fond of explaining almost all the actions of their lives by the principle of self-interest rightly understood; they show with complacency how an enlightened regard for themselves constantly prompts them to assist one another and inclines them willingly to sacrifice a portion of their time and property to the welfare of the state.

Under certain conditions, even altruistic motives can be supported by enlightened personal interests. While this idea is quite old, modern institutionalism has been able to identify institutional contexts and mechanisms that mould and structure the perceptions and articulation of interests at the individual and collective level. Social orders such as a community, the market, the state and associations (Streeck and Schmitter 1985) can be understood from this perspective as institutional rule systems which affect how individual and collective actors perceive, define and pursue their interests in complex surroundings. Indeed any social order ultimately implies differentiated rule systems on the basis of which interests are structured and mediated to allow for conflict resolution and social integration.

More specifically, in *communities* individuals are made to subordinate their private interests to a common interest or to a collectivity by means of diverse forms of soft and hard sanctions. In a *market*, individuals and organizations are induced to narrow their interests to pure self-interest, at the risk of their economic demise. State and associational orders are more complex because they are founded upon precarious equilibriums of personal and collective interests. The *state* order is based on the principle that individuals delegate the pursuit of their common interests, ultimately irreversibly, to a collective power that is explicitly or implicitly authorized to assert such interests, if necessary by means of physical force. Today this principle is embodied worldwide in nation states that exercise a monopoly of physical force on a given territory. Finally, *associations* resemble the state in that they organize the pursuit of common interests. However, here the delegation of powers and the authority to act is reversible, and the organization can be more easily abandoned. Especially where there is voluntary membership, associations are constantly engaged in a precarious balancing act in which the compliance contributed by their members must be compensated with benefits for them.

A further insight of institutional analysis is that models of social order – including the governance of interests – generally depict idealized forms that never exist in reality. No social order functions solely by state force, market exchange, communitarian identification or voluntary association. Viable markets demand a minimum degree of regulation of ownership rights where state power must be present at least in the background. State power, however, cannot merely be founded on force, and in the long run it cannot survive without social and associational 'stabilizers'. Both Schumpeter (1976) and Habermas (1973), for instance, point out the key role that traditional common values play in legitimizing state power. In the discussion on neo-corporatism in particular, the legitimizing and reinforcing effects of associative elements for the state order have been frequently emphasized (Lehmbruch and Schmitter 1982; Schmitter and Lehmbruch 1979; Streeck and Schmitter 1985). State structures are more efficient when they can depend on the support of interest associations. This also functions vice versa: associative orders evolve in a more stable and effective fashion when they are supported by a state. The contributions of interest associations to the governance of more or less modern societies have been thoroughly documented in a broad literature on the subject matter (Berger 1981; Streeck and Schmitter 1985; Campbell *et al.* 1991; Hollingsworth *et al.* 1994; Hollingsworth and Boyer 1997).

With few exceptions – which ultimately failed – in which associations were suppressed by the state (in radical liberalism) or state structures were subservient to associative structures (as in syndicalism), a long-term relationship of co-evolution can be recognized in the development of both orders, in which state and associations enhanced each other through their mutual relations (Streeck and Kenworthy 2004). As a result of this co-evolution of interest group and state structures, associative orders were established in almost all nation states in the twentieth century. Not only were these accepted by state decision makers, but they were often actively promoted by them. Of course, although associations exist in almost all countries, distinct differences can be recognized in terms of the form and intensity of their relations to the state. National varieties exist with respect to both the intensity of the symbiosis between state and association and the relative dominance of the different forms of order (Crouch 1993; Streeck and Kenworthy 2004). A loose and more one-sided relationship between state and associations exists in *pluralistic arrangements* in which the state benefits from the articulation and aggregation of group interests. Associations participate only in the initial phases of the policy cycle, if they are included in public policy making at all. In return for their representation of interests, the state offers associations acceptance and the selective allocation of access to specific decision-making points. But the position of associations in this exchange relationship remains weak, and they never become capable of exerting effective control over their members and the multitude of competing interest associations.

In *corporatist arrangements*, by comparison, strong reciprocal relations prevail in which interest associations are involved in many if not all phases of public policy making. Of central importance is the fact that associations are particularly active in implementation, and in some cases even provide for self-regulation of their domains or sectors, mostly in the shadow of public meta-regulation ('regulated self-regulation'). Following Lehmbruch and Schmitter (1982), we can distinguish between state (or authoritarian) and liberal corporatism. Under state corporatism, relations between the state and interest associations are asymmetric: the associative order is dominated by the state and is instrumentalized for public purposes. In state-corporatist countries, interest associations are not only promoted but are also monitored by the state and frequently incorporated into its structure. In liberal corporatism, on the other hand, relations between the state and associations are more balanced as public policy is founded upon a sharing of public space between the state and relatively autonomous associations.

The effectiveness of an associative order in the production and implementation of social regulation depends on the structure of the associational system as well as on the specific character of state–society relations. In pluralistic competition, associations are propelled to keep their interest domain homogeneous and small, resulting in highly specialized and fragmented associational structures. In less competitive systems, interest domains can be more comprehensive as a small number of associations manage to integrate a variety of heterogeneous interests. In corporatist structures represented interests tend to be broad and comprehensive and are often geared towards general societal objectives.

Interest associations between the logics of influence and membership

If we exclude institutional configurations in which associations are either suppressed and isolated or incorporated in the state, associations can be regarded as *intermediary organizations*. They function like brokers in networks where they operate in numerous environments simultaneously. Of particular significance for associations are their *members* on the one hand and their *political target structure* – where they try to assert their influence – on the other.

Associations are membership organizations and in most cases their members are the most important environment from which they extract resources. Therefore associations must prove to their members that with them their interests are in good hands. This implies that interests are defined and bundled so that members can recognize their needs, concerns and identities. Even if associations may sometimes know earlier than their members what is good for them, they must remain open and responsive to their members' demands and concerns. The interaction between associations and their members is modelled in the relevant literature as driven by 'logic of membership' (Schmitter and Streeck 1999 [1981]).

An association can be attractive only to the extent that it effectively defends and enforces the interests of its members in the political process. Here, the logic of membership intersects with the 'logic of influence', which governs the relations between associations and their political interlocutors. Most interest associations must compete with other actors for the realization of their interests. Associations must demonstrate to their members that the interests they represent have access to the political decision-making process and are at least partially taken into account.

To some extent, that is to say, the logics of membership and influence mutually complement and even reinforce each other through positive feedback. An increase in membership enhances the power of an organization, and the attractiveness of an organization would seem to increase as a result of its influence. But whether the number of members actually translates into influence and vice versa greatly depends on the context. Mutual reinforcement may occur if the association represents homogeneous interests and can use its influence to provide benefits to a clearly limited group of members (club goods, categorial goods). However, if the influence of an association is used for the production of non-exclusive collective goods, the paradoxical effect may be that an increase in influence may diminish member support as members may prefer to be free-riders (Olson 1965). Then the leadership of the association may try to mobilize resources from other environments (e.g. from the state), or it may look for ways to make membership less voluntary. Both strategies would tend to increase the autonomy of the leadership from the members.

Moreover, a tense relationship can exist between the two logics as a too-intensive membership orientation can weaken the position of the association in its influence environment. An association that transmits unfiltered radical demands from its members to its political interlocutors may become politically marginalized. Similarly, heterogeneous interests at the membership level may hamper the capacity of associational leaders to act in a consistent way. Vice versa, strong associational leadership that gains autonomy from members can strengthen the influence of an association. Factors that play a role in this context include the existence of a professional staff, accumulation of technical expertise and the development of external resources.

The 'two logics' concept of Schmitter and Streeck (1999 [1981]) theorizing the intermediary position of interest associations between membership and influence environments has been applied by a great number of authors (e.g. Chiesi 1991; Lehmbruch 1994; Bennett 1999; Werle 2000; Grande 2003; Rosse 2003). Also, the conceptual framework was summarized in various recent contributions (Streeck and Hassel 2004; Streeck and Kenworthy 2004). It is therefore not necessary to go into details here with respect to the complex exchanges that the two logics make possible as well as require between interest associations and their key environments (for a visual representation see Figure 1.1). What is most important to keep in mind is that the position of intermediary organizations is always a precarious one between divergent demands that must be balanced for associations to survive and grow, and that associations may become autonomous social actors and gain strategic freedom precisely because of the contradictory claims that are often made upon them.

The profound social change triggered in past decades by economic and political internationalization raises the question of how interest associations cope with an increasingly complex environment, in terms of both membership and political decision-making institutions. What is the influence of globalization and regional political integration in Europe on the position and evolution of interest associations? Do economic liberalization and the transfer of political decision-making competencies to international or supranational agencies lead to a weakening, not just of nation states, but also of interest associations? Is an increasingly internationally oriented membership still interested in national interest associations? The present collection of chapters analyses recent changes in business associations at different levels, to determine how associations and associational orders in different contexts react to internationalization.

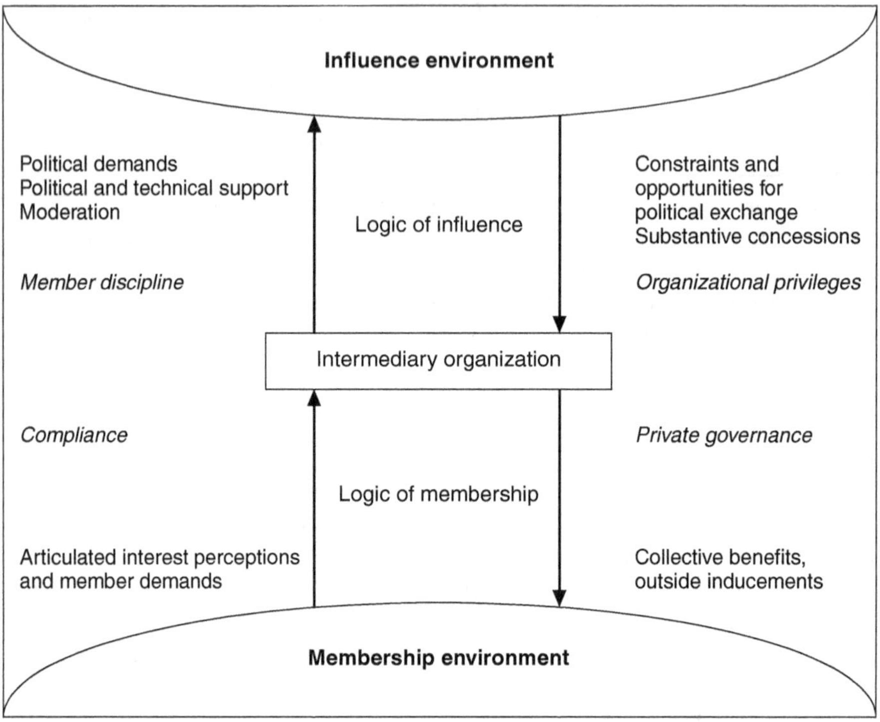

Figure 1.1 The logics of membership and influence.

Internationalization and interest associations

Before we expound on the different factors and dynamics that today affect the two logics, we should first attempt to pinpoint the sort of change in the environments of associations with which this book is dealing. Both Europeanization and globalization are variants of internationalization, which is the most general of the three concepts. Europeanization is internationalization in Europe, while globalization is internationalization on a world scale. Internationalization refers to an increase in cross-border relations (transactions, social and political linkages, cultural transfers, etc.) including its effects on the perceptions, motives and opportunity structures of individual or collective action. Cross-border relations may be of an economic, political, technical or cultural nature. Economic relations comprise trade, direct investment and similar transactions. Political relations pertain to diplomatic exchange, political–military cooperation and alliances, as well as participation in collective international decisional and problem-solving arrangements, through networks between nation states as well as through state and non-state international organizations. These represent the most diverse forms of collective political behaviour, from associations of European firms to federations of political parties, 'global public interest groups' and scientific–technical communities. Technical relations include cross-border infrastructural systems (Mayntz and Hughes 1988) such as communications and transportation links, as well as integrated logistics networks between multinational companies (Schneider 1994). Many of these relations exist within the European Union, but this does not imply that they are restricted to it.

Internationalization creates contacts that may eventually bring about convergence. There are different mechanisms that propel such convergence processes (Schneider 2002):

- *Competition*: The dismantling of national market barriers allows for the competitive selection of superior political, legal and cultural arrangements.
- *Coercion*: Through supranational jurisdiction in international organizations, it is possible to bring about harmonization and standardization by means of collective decisions. This holds in particular for the European Union. To a lesser extent, it also pertains to international organizations such as the Organization for Economic Cooperation and Development (OECD), the World Trade Organization (WTO), the International Monetary Fund (IMF) or the World Bank.
- *Diffusion*: The development and fortification of communication structures increases the potential for institutional imitation and learning. On the one hand it becomes easier to emulate the structures of other countries, while on the other hand the mistakes of other countries can be better observed.
- *Co-adaptation*: In system competition and diffusion, strategies of reciprocal assimilation may become widespread.

How do Europeanization and globalization as specific forms of internationalization affect associational systems and associative orders? In particular, what direct and indirect effects does internationalization impose on the logics of membership and influence?

Internationalization and the logic of membership

Economic internationalization, as it extends and intensifies cross-border transactions, has a direct effect on the interest structure of sectors by making the interests of firms more heterogeneous. On the one hand, increasing size of the market allows for greater specialization. On the other hand, international reach of market transactions gives rise to new cleavages between firms due to a greater variety of individual market conditions. Globally oriented firms have different interests from European or national firms. While national political interests do not necessarily vanish, they are balanced and indeed made more complex by transnational and international interests. Furthermore, in an age of liberalization and privatization, global firms can no longer rely on a position of national champion. Also, foreign multinational firms profit from infrastructural investment to the same extent as domestic ones.

One possible effect is that national economic interest groups may come under pressure as they now have to represent a broader spectrum of interests of increasingly multinational firms. Indeed the organizational capacity of nationally based business associations to expand into international contexts is limited. At the same time, multinational companies are becoming less dependent on national and international associations due to their size and reach. Their immense resources often enable them to represent their expanded spectrum of interests on their own and exert considerable influence on political decision makers by means of direct lobbying (Grant *et al.* 1989; Coen 1997; Cowles 1995; 2001; Schneider 2004). Alternatively, multinational firms may join international business associations, and indeed there is an increase in direct membership in associations whose domain is not confined to one nation state.

This, in turn, is likely to limit the capacity of national associations to incorporate multinational companies in collective commitments and collective discipline. Nevertheless, declining interest among 'global players' for national interest mediation does not necessarily mean that associations will lose them as members although declining support by affluent members may cause financial problems. Associations often react to this by means of rationalization or by the introduction of new services and selective incentives in an effort to remain attractive for their members. Still, to the extent that interest associations not only aggregate but also define interests, by selecting between the more narrow concerns of potential members, their role as an 'interest funnel' (Schmitter 1981) which individual concerns have to pass to become articulated has become less significant. Where associations had an established monopoly of interest definition, they tend to lose it.

Another effect of internationalization is that global firms increasingly maintain multiple memberships in national and international associations. Among other things, this makes for faster diffusion of new ideas, organizational routines and lobbying strategies. With global players among their members, national associations may learn from the experiences of associations in other national contexts in a more direct way.

Internationalization and the logic of influence

Internationalization causes a differentiation and shift of power in political decision making. Through increased and intensified cross-border economic and social relations, many political problems gain an international scope and require international treatment. This is the material base for the rapid growth of international organizations and regulatory regimes in recent decades, which ultimately led to vertical differentiation of public policy making at the national, European and global levels. In the emerging European multilevel system, shifts in power are the most pronounced. Many decisions are made in Brussels while national policies are often reduced to the mere implementation of European law.

National business associations are affected by this development in several ways. A transfer of competences to international bodies entails a loss of jurisdiction for national governments. While in a national context public policies used to be formulated by the government together with a smaller or larger number of associations, national governments are only one of many categories of diverse actors in the European framework.

In very general terms, one of the effects of more porous borders and of the internationalization of public policies is a broader spectrum of actors participating in policy making. The emergence of new kinds of actors in the influence dimension of interest politics corresponds to the decline of the associational monopoly over the definition of interests in the membership dimension. This has been emphasized among other things by research on policy networks. In particular, as has been mentioned, large firms that are represented as members of associations frequently in addition represent their interests directly. Moreover, alongside interest associations, new forms of collective action of firms have emerged, such as alliances and other forms of *ad hoc* cooperation, round tables of CEOs and various types of forums in which firms coordinate their political strategies among themselves and with public decision makers. Although these new forms of cooperation face fewer compliance problems, they are likely to lack legitimacy and accountability. It is not clear, therefore, whether they will remain attractive to public authorities in the long term.

In trying to cope with these changes national associations reorganize their strategic repertoire and develop new capacities. First, they must be able to survive the competition with other forms of representation. Second, they must learn how to make the interests of their members more noticeable in international policy arenas. This entails the organization of regional and international federations of interest associations. In some international policy arenas, however, this type of multilevel interest representation may not suffice. A third option, then, is for national associations themselves to move onto international or supranational terrain and establish national offices near the headquarters of international organizations.

In fact, due to the continuing embeddedness of economic interest groups at national level and their different associational 'cultures', it seems improbable that they will ever completely disappear and delegate their functions and power resources entirely to supranational federations. More likely national associations will become more internationally active on their own initiative and build the necessary expertise and political skills for doing so. In this they need not necessarily regard their multinational member firms as competitors, even if these are involved in direct lobbying. Instead they may develop complementary activities. International expertise in national associations can after all best be mobilized through multinational companies. As Coleman claims (in this volume), precisely those interest associations that have internationalized members will become more significant in the new international context of associational activity.

A further change in the influence environment of interest associations results from changes in the nation state itself that may be described as a transformation of statehood generally. Economic internationalization was accelerated among other things by the fact that markets were opened up and previous state monopolies were privatized. In many areas, the nation state withdrew from public infrastructures and instead attempted to secure long-term control over private provisions by means of regulatory policies. This may make traditional forms of associational self – regulation redundant, which may in turn erode the traditional support of associations by the state (Schmitter 1997).

Internationalization and associative order

Internationalization changes the logic of both membership and influence, and thereby transforms the conditions under which interest associations have to carry out their precarious balancing act between their two main environments. One aspect of associations' changing logic of influence in particular is the redefinition, caused by internationalization, of the conditions for *associative order*, i.e. for associations assuming functions of quasi-public governance in relation to their members. It seems useful for our argument to explore the connection between internationalization and the stability and form of associative order in more detail.

Internationalization is fundamentally a process by which mobile actors, or actors with mobile resources, are enabled to extend their range of action beyond national borders. The more that process advances, the more actors become capable of evading the control of national authorities. As actors' freedom of choice increases – to be sure, for some more than for others – their mutual relations become more a matter of their volition than of hierarchical direction; this is why, everything else being equal, internationalization tend to be accompanied by liberalization. International liberalization calls forth a variety of responses within the state system, the core elements of which are still national states (Figure 1.2). The transformation of the state system, in turn, goes together with, or sets in motion, a corresponding restructuring of associative orders. In other words, the impact of internationalization on associative order, which is one factor among others that transform associations' logic of influence, is mediated by the impact of internationalization on states and the state system.

State responses to internationalization can be crudely distinguished in three categories. First, national states in an internationalized economy experience growing interdependence with each other. To manage this inter-

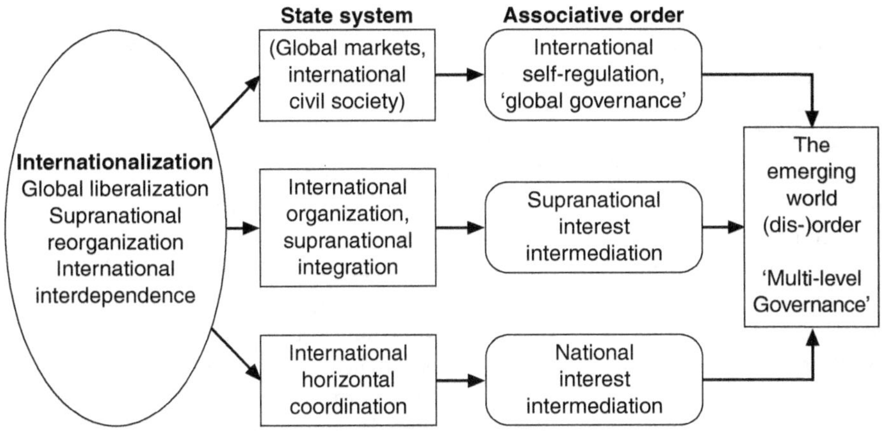

Figure 1.2 Internationalization, modes of governance and associative orders.

dependence and restore some sort of sovereign control over national actors and resources, national states may seek alliances with other national states, in more or less loosely-knit 'variable geometries' of issue-specific cooperation ('international horizontal coordination'). However, as students of European integration have been keen to point out, above a certain level of intensity bilateralism or multilateralism tends to become difficult to manage as 'transaction costs' skyrocket. In response and second, then, national states may transfer part of their authority, or even sovereignty, to an international organization charged with enforcing common rules upon its member states, which if intensified may result in some form of supranational integration ('international organization, supranational integration'; Figure 1.2). How far this can go is an open question. Undoubtedly, though, the European Union represents the, by far, most advanced form of supranational integration since the invention of the modern nation state, which may be taken as an indication that supranational integration is most likely to occur on a regional rather than on a global scale.

What, then, on the global system? Here individual nation states are particularly weak, apart from a hegemonic state like the United States. Also, supranational integration is highly improbable. Clearly at the global level, the erosion of statehood in the face of internationalization is likely to be deepest. As a result, economic internationalization, to the extent that individual states cannot prevent it, tends to be tantamount to liberalization. In the political vacuum above the regional level, hegemonic states and mobile economic actors operate in global power structures and global markets in which their behaviour is regulated, if at all, only by weak supranational organizations and a weakly organized 'international civil society'. The rise of the latter represents the third reaction of the state system to internationalization.

The effects of internationalization on the state system in turn affect the governance functions of organized interests inside associative orders. Concerning the national level, the prevailing view in the literature now seems to be that internationalization weakens corporatist arrangements between the state and organized interest groups in a variety of ways. Not only do governments use international negotiations or mandates from supranational bodies to protect themselves from the influence of domestic organized interests, which changes the balance of power and the character of the bargain between the two sides, they also need to be free of domestic pressure in order to be able to negotiate complex package deals with other states that they cannot afterwards submit to renegotiation in corporatist bargaining. International markets tend to be suspicious of what to outsiders tends to appear as closed, less than transparent and potentially unfair self-regulation by insiders, preferring more internationally accountable public regulation by independent authorities that can if needed be taken to national and international courts (Lütz 2003). The same preference seems to be built into European Union legislation which emphasizes the responsibility of governments for the correct implementation of European law, as opposed to implementation by interest associations with only quasi-public status.

Generalizations are always difficult, and certainly cases can be found of organized interest groups that have gained in corporatist status as a result of internationalization. Still, on the whole it would appear that at the very least, national interest intermediation tends to lose its clout at least in the same way and for the same reasons as the national state, and then perhaps even more as a side effect of the latter's attempts to recover control through ('horizontal') international coordination and ('vertical') supranational integration. It seems highly plausible that the recent phenomenal growth of supranational interest associations is due to parallel attempts by national interest groups also to recover some of the influence and status that has been eroded by internationalization at the national level. But in our terms, not only does, the logic of membership pose greater and different challenges in international settings than in national ones. Although international organizations and supranational authorities sometimes hold out promises of institutionalized influence in a supranational associative order, trying to build for themselves a constituency of interest groups that mirrors national corporatism, a recreation of the latter at the next-higher level seems on the whole highly unlikely, the glib talk of 'Euro-corporatism' notwithstanding. If it is true that stable interest intermediation requires state institutional support, it cannot emerge in a political arena devoid of unified statehood. Moreover, a supranational institution like the European Union based on refused statehood by its constituent member states, cannot achieve it through the support of a corporatist infrastructure that it could nourish only if it already had achieved state capacities. And as has been pointed out some years ago, in the unique polity of integrated Europe interest associations have to compete, not only with other organized interests, but also with nation states, regions and multinational companies for the attention of decision-making bodies, in a complex system of power and influence that is inevitably much more pluralist than any postwar European nation state ever was (Streeck and Schmitter 1991).

Finally, at the global level, free markets and competing national states face a weakly organized international civil society that is at best only in its infancy. In part this is undoubtedly because here, state support for organization is even less available than at the regional level in Europe. On the other hand, precisely because states and governments are as weak as they are in the global system, there may appear to be a space for regulation of social and economic transactions by other than state actors, i.e. by non-governmental organizations (NGOs) of all sorts. Whether or not organized interest groups, in particular business associations, are NGOs in the common meaning of the words is an interesting question; while literally they clearly are, one hesitates to include them precisely because of their close relations in corporatist national politics with states and governments. Moreover, they may seem too 'self-interested' to fit the altruistic image of a category of organizations that promote supposedly universal objectives like a clean environment or human rights. In any case, whether or not and what form of an associative order of collective self-regulation by organized groups from international civil society can and will fill the empty political space that exists at the global level of a globalizing world is an intriguing question on which, at least for much of the 'global governance' literature, the jury is still out.

Today, such associative order as exists in a period of internationalization is distributed over at least three levels; the national, the regional and the global (Figure 1.2). Increasingly the three seem to interact and influence one another, in particular the first two. In this they are embedded in the emerging multilevel governance system that includes national states without, however, absorbing them. It is in this context that the growing strategic complexity that faces the organization of business interests intersects with the even greater complexity of the constraints and opportunities for regulation and non-regulation in a layered and multipolar world polity.

Organization of this volume

By far the largest number of business associations represent the interests of *economic sectors*, i.e. of a multitude of firms producing similar products and, as a result, facing similar conditions in product and factor markets. Traditionally the domains of sectoral associations are demarcated, not just by products and production methods, but also by national boundaries: a sectoral interest association normally represents a sector only to the extent that the latter is located in a given national economy. The underlying assumption is that it is not only their economic but also their national–political location that shapes the interests of firms. Nationality becomes the predominant concern in those associations that organize firms regardless of sector, either directly or as federations of sectoral associations. Internationalization has produced, in addition to sectoral–national and intersectoral–national associations, both sectoral and intersectoral associations with international domains, where the latter may be federations of international sectoral or of national intersectoral associations or of both, as well as direct membership associations of large firms. In other words and as indicated above, internationalization has considerably complicated the menu of organizational forms for the representation of economic interests.

Nation and sector are the two dimensions of social structure around which this volume is organized. Following this introduction, Part I, under the general heading of *Nations*, features four chapters that explore the reactions of national business associations to various aspects of internationalization. Jelle Visser and Arnold Wilts, Hanspeter Kriesi and Victor Pestoff provide detailed qualitative case studies of recent transformations in the national systems of business interest representation in the Netherlands, Switzerland and Sweden, i.e. three prosperous and highly internationalized small European countries that seem eminently comparable. The fourth chapter, by Franz Traxler, reports a quantitative comparison of national federations of employers associations in 20 OECD countries – in other words, of a highly specialized type of business interest organization that, unlike trade associations, closely interacts with labour unions.[1]

Part II, then, is concerned with sectors, and especially with sectoral associations organized at the national level. The first two of its three chapters each compare the development, under the impact of internationalization, of sectoral trade associations in two countries. Jürgen Grote and Volker Schneider look at the chemical industry – which continues to be a core manufacturing sector – in Britain and Germany. Dirk Lehmkuhl compares the evolution of business associations in the Dutch and German road haulage sectors, where firms are vitally affected by European legislation under the common European transport policy. Finally, Pieter Bouwen reports findings on the role of national sectoral business associations in European policy making in the financial sector, in comparison with the role of other representatives of the sector's interests such as European-level associations.

Bouwen's analysis leads over to the third and final part of the book, which deals with *international systems*. Unlike Bouwen, both chapters, the first by William D. Coleman and the second by Karsten Ronit, address the question of the viability of associational orders beyond the nation state, in the absence of the sort of institutional support that is provided by the traditional resources of statehood. Coleman's chapter explores the impact of internationalization on national policy networks and finds these at risk of being undermined as issues and competencies migrate towards higher-level decision-making arenas. Coleman identifies three types of international policy environments (multilevel governance, intergovernmental negotiations and private regimes) and illustrates in two case studies their interaction with national associations and national associative orders. He finds that, while the latter may be destabilized or even collapse, to be replaced in favourable conditions with international associative regimes, the former are likely to develop capacities to intervene not just in national but also in international policy making. Next, Karsten Ronit discusses the prospects of self-regulation of business in global environments. He argues that while business associations remain important even in state-free international contexts, they must compete here with alternative forms of self-regulation, like agreements between large firms or the internal standards set by multinational corporations. Also, even where business associations continue to have a function, their structures may change under the impact of internationalization, depending on the character of the institutional environment they face in their respective policy-making sectors. Ronit concludes that the emerging global economy will definitely not be a place governed solely by market relations. As state capacities remain fragmented and state action remains limited to intergovernmental negotiations or sector-specific supranational governance, self-regulation of business, through associations or otherwise, will continue to be with us for a long time to come.

The volume ends with a concluding chapter by Wolfgang Streeck and Jelle Visser. The authors try to synthesize core insights of research assembled in the chapters of this book and elsewhere. National business associations, it seems, and with them the character of interest representation and associative self-governance, have been deeply affected in the last two decades by the internationalization of the economy and, in part, of the polity that governs it. But national associations have by no means disappeared, and neither have they become subservient to or absorbed by supranational federations or international direct membership associations. Supranational 'lobbying', while it undoubtedly exists and has assumed growing importance, is far from becoming the only game in the town of business interest politics. This, of course, is significant not only for the practitioners of business interest representation. To the political scientist it is one more indication that the current transformation of the national state and of national politics is far from amounting to a transfer of statehood to what was and remains the international arena. State capacities – at least those that in the past were sometimes strong enough to transform the representation of economic interests into their publicly disciplined self-government – apparently decline at the national level without being recreated at the international one. Given their ingrained preference for 'less state' and 'more market', national business associations, at least to the extent that they represent leading sectors, seem to cope surprisingly well with the erosion of traditional state power, by changing their operations domestically as well as reaching out beyond national borders. Here, unlike what was expected almost without question in earlier, with hindsight naive, scenarios of international integration especially in Europe, they are not absorbed in international organizations. To the contrary, they increasingly compete with them both for political influence and the support of member firms.

What is the future, then, of the representation of economic interests through business associations, and of organized interest politics in general? In Europe at least, it seems one observes what may be called a process of *nationally based Europeanization from below*, where national associations that can no longer rely on their established access to their traditional interlocutors pragmatically begin to extend their range of action beyond national borders, in order to regain at least some of their old clout in a new environment whose logic of influence is as yet only vaguely understood. At the same time, undefined and indeed in flux as the emerging institutional setting at international level may still be, what seems clear is that it is entirely unsuited to provide associations with the sort of support that enabled some of them in the context of the neo-corporatist nation state of the postwar period to establish themselves as private governments. New forms of associative order, if at all, are forming in a space that is by and large state free, and for this very reason they seem to be forming in ways and for purposes that differ significantly from previous, national experience. Whether the international order after the erosion of the nation state will be more of a disorder, and whether organized collective action will have a place in it, either providing 'neo-voluntaristic' regulation or defending the anarchy of free markets or both, is a question that will probably require different answers for different sectors, in a highly complex international polity with a myriad of independent players whose search for a centre is likely to be abortive for a long time to come.

Note

1 National coverage by the chapters of the book is broader than it might seem. Scandinavia, which in comparative politics is treated as a part of Europe different from the Continent, is strongly represented. Germany, Switzerland and the Netherlands are Continental-European countries, and the UK stands for the Anglo-American type of polity. Chapters 9 and 10 deal with international organizations and global contexts in which Britain and the United States play an important role. A core chapter (Chapter 6) compares Germany and Britain, the two polar types of interest political systems in Europe. The strong presence of Germany reflects the economic importance of the country, as well as the fact that its model of interest representation was long seen as a model for Europe as a whole. As the book makes clear, this is no longer the case and recent developments in Europe may well be described in terms of a movement away from the German tradition, or in any case a parallel transformation of all national traditions in an expanding European context.

References

Bennett, R. J. (1999) 'Explaining the Membership of Sectoral Business Associations', *Environment and Planning* A 31: 877–898.

Berger, S. (ed.) (1981) *Organizing Interests in Western Europe: Pluralism, Corporatism and the Transformation of Politics*, New York: Cambridge University Press.

Campbell, J. C., Hollingsworth, J. R. and Lindberg, L. (eds) (1991) *The Governance of the American Economy*, New York: Cambridge University Press.

Chiesi, A. M. (1991) 'The Logic of Membership in Chemical Business Interests Associations', in A. Martinelli (ed.) *International Markets and Global Firms*, London: Sage, pp. 114–144.

Coen, D. (1997) 'The Evolution of the Large Firm as a Political Actor in the European Union', *Journal of European Public Policy* 4 (1): 91–108.

Cowles, M. G. (1995) 'Setting the Agenda for a New Europe: The ERT and EC 1992', *Journal of Common Market Studies* 13: 501–526.

Cowles, M. G. (2001) 'The Transatlantic Business Dialogue and Domestic Business–Government Relations', in M. G. Cowles, J. Caporaso and T. Risse (eds) *Transforming Europe. Europeanization and Domestic Change*, Ithaca: Cornell University Press, pp. 159–179.

Crouch, C. (1993) *Industrial Relations and European State Traditions*, Oxford: Oxford University Press.

Grande, E. (2003) 'How the Architecture of the EU Political System Influences Business Associations', in J. Greenwood (ed.) *The Challenge of Change in the EU Business Associations*, Houndmills: Palgrave, pp. 45–59.

Grant, W., Martinelli, A. and Paterson, W. (1989) 'Large Firms as Political Actors: a Comparative Analysis of the Chemical Industry in Britain, Italy and West Germany', *West European Politics* 12: 72–90.

Habermas, J. (1973) *Legitimationsproblem im Spätkapitalismus*, Frankfurt am Main: Suhrkamp.

Hirschmann, A. O. (1977) *The Passions and the Interests: Political Arguments for Capitalism before its Triumph*, Princeton NJ: Princeton University Press.

Hollingsworth, J. R. and Boyer, R. (eds) (1997) *Contemporary Capitalism. The Embeddedness of Institutions*, New York: Cambridge University Press.

Hollingsworth, J. R., Schmitter, P. C. and Streeck, W. (eds) (1994) *Governing Capitalist Economies*, New York and Oxford: Oxford University Press.

Lehmbruch, G. (1994) 'Dilemmata verbandlicher Einflußlogik im Prozeß der deutschen Vereinigung', in W. Streeck (ed.) *Staat und Verbände*, Opladen: Westdeutscher Verlag, pp. 370–392.

Lehmbruch, G. and Schmitter, P. C. (eds) (1982) *Patterns of Corporatist Policy-Making*, London, Beverley Hills, New Delhi: Sage Publications.

Lütz, S. (2003) 'Convergence within National Diversity – A Comparative Perspective on the Regulatory State in Finance', Discussion Paper 03/7, Cologne: Max Planck Institute for the Study of Societies.

Mayntz, R. and Hughes T. P. (eds) (1988) *The Development of Large Technical Systems*, Frankfurt am Main: Campus.

Olson, M. (1965) *The Logic of Collective Action: Public Goods and the Theory of Groups*, Cambridge MA: Harvard University Press.

Rosse, J. (2003) 'Umweltorganisationen zwischen Mitgliedschaftslogik und Einflusslogik in der europäischen Politik', in A. Klein, R. Koopmans, H.-J. Trenz and L. Klein (eds) *Bürgerschaft, Öffentlichkeit und Demokratie in Europa*, Opladen: Leske und Budrich, pp. 141–158.

Schmitter, P. C. (1981) *Needs, Interests, Concerns, Actions, Associations and Modes of Intermediation*, Unpublished Paper, University of Chicago and Science Centre Berlin (WZB).

Schmitter, P. C. (1997) 'The Emerging Europolity and its Impact upon National

Systems of Production', in J. R. Hollingsworth and R. Boyer (eds) op. cit.: pp. 395–430.

Schmitter, P. C. and Lehmbruch, G. (eds) (1979) *Trend Towards Corporatist Intermediation*, London, Beverley Hills, New Delhi: Sage Publications.

Schmitter, P. C. and Streeck, W. (1981; 2nd edn 1999) 'The Organization of Business Interests: Studying the Associative Action of Business in Advanced Industrial Societies', MPIfG Discussion Paper 99/1, Cologne: Max Planck Institute for the Study of Societies.

Schneider, V. (1994) 'Multinationals in Transition: Global Technical Integration and the Role of Corporate Telecommunication Networks', in J. Summerton (ed.) *Large Technical Systems in Change*, Boulder CO: Westview, pp. 71–91.

Schneider, V. (2002) 'Europäisierung zwischen Markt und Bürokratie. Eine Einführung in die Problematik', in V. Schneider (ed.) *Entgrenzte Märkte – grenzenlose Bürokratie. Europäisierung in Wirtschaft, Recht und Politik*, Frankfurt am Main: Campus.

Schneider, V. (2004) 'Großfirmen in Politiknetzwerken: Zum Bedeutungsgewinn des "Corporate Lobbying" im Kontext von Europäisierung und Internationalisierung', in C. Henning and C. Melbeck (eds) *Interdisziplinäre Sozialforschung: Theorie und empirische Anwendungen*, Festschrift zum 65. Geburtstag von Franz Urban Pappi. Frankfurt am Main and New York: Campus.

Schumpeter, J. A. (1976) *Capitalism, Socialism, and Democracy*, 5th Edition, London: Allen and Unwin.

Streeck, W. and Hassel, A. (2004) 'Trade Unions as Political Actors', in J. T. Addison and C. Schnabel (eds) *International Handbook of Trade Unions*, London: Edward Elgar.

Streeck, W. and Kenworthy, L. (2004) 'Theories and Practices of Neo-corporatism', in T. Janoski, R. Alford, A. Hicks and M. Schwartz (eds) *Handbook of Political Sociology*, New York: Cambridge University Press.

Streeck, W. and Schmitter, P. C. (1985) 'Community, Market, State and Associations? The Prospective Contribution of Interest Governance to Social Order', in W. Streeck and P. C. Schmitter (eds) *Private Interest Government. Beyond Market and State*, London, Beverley Hills, New Delhi: Sage Publications, pp. 1–30.

Streeck, W. and Schmitter, P. C. (1991) 'From National Corporatism to Transnational Pluralism: Organized Interests in the Single European Market', *Politics and Society* 19 (2): 133–165.

Tocqueville, A., de (1953) *Democracy in America*, edited with an Introduction by Henry Steele Commager, Volume II, Section II, Chapter VIII. Repr. London, Cumberledge: Oxford University Press.

Werle, R. (2000) 'The Impact of Information Networks on the Structure of Political Systems', in C. Engel and K. H. Keller (eds) *Understanding the Impact of Global Networks on Local Social, Political and Cultural Values*, Baden-Baden: Nomos, pp. 159–185.

Part I

Nations

2 Reaching out and fitting in

Dutch business associations at home (and) in Europe

Jelle Visser and Arnold Wilts

Business associations in Europe are confronted with fundamental changes in their economic and political environments. The markets in which their members operate are internationalizing. The project of a Single European Market, now completed by single money, has been surpassed, and refracted, by several other developments in order to create a homogeneous 'home market' for European firms. Labour markets in Europe are still mostly national and quite diverse across countries due to different, and in part competing, models and visions of industrial relations, welfare state development and social policy. Although coordination in economic and social policy is not wholly absent at the European level, it has to make do with few legal instruments and rely mostly on voluntary cooperation through dialogue and non-sanctioned monitoring, combined with competitive peer pressure in both the economic and political market.

The distinctive organized versions of national capitalism, based on a stakeholder model of the firm and more or less articulated in a dense associative order of firm–firm and firm–union relationships underwritten by public law, have no equivalent at the level of Europe. In the European Union's 'stateless market' (Kapteyn 1996) business interest associations and trade unions cannot and do not play the constitutive role in the production and distribution of economic and social goods like they do in some versions of 'coordinated market economies' (Hall and Soskice 2001) in individual member states.

In these coordinated market economies interest associations act as governance mechanism by (1) defining and procuring public (category) goods through organizing and enforcing cooperative behaviour among their members, (2) engaging in collective contracts with other associations, and (3) securing delegations of state authority to be used to the advantage of their members (Hollingsworth *et al.* 1994). To assume such a governance role, associations must reach a certain level of organizational development. They must be capable of processing and ordering information from and to their members and, if necessary, assume responsibility on behalf of their members in relation to other organized actors and the state. That requires some autonomy and the ability of the organization's leadership to rise above the particularistic interests of its members.

The emergence of these organizational characteristics for an intermediary like an interest association depends on relations with its membership and with key actors in its environment. Schmitter and Streeck (1999 [1981]) have offered two organizing concepts to study this dual relationship; 'logic of membership' and 'logic of interest'. The former is concerned with the characteristics of, and relationship with, (potential) members, and the latter with the characteristics of, and relationship with, the organized environment with which an association interacts on behalf of its members. As intermediary organizations, associations must accommodate the often competing demands of these two logics.

More international competition may alter the logic of membership in ways unfavourable to organizational development, for example when it leads to increased concentration and centralization of production. Consequently, the number of firms eligible for membership in a national association may diminish, the geographical distribution of production sites may change and the very definition of the sector may broaden or narrow. Such changes will not only complicate the association's task to define and defend a common policy, it also tends to limit its resource base to fewer members and shift the balance of forces from the association to its larger members. A weakening of the national state impairs the influence game of the association, since 'it may render more difficult the delegation of state authority that is often central to associational governance' (Coleman 1997: 131). As a target or interlocutor, the national state and its panoply of institutions may become less useful for the association, while European and international institutions absorb more attention, but with fewer possibilities of building stable and predictable relationships.

These very broad predictions will guide our analysis of the changes in the associative order of Dutch business during the past two decades. Our two key questions are: (1) To what extent, and how, has the increased participation in the international economy, and in the process of European market making, changed the traditional 'corporatist' organization of Dutch business? (2) To what extent do we witness a process of internationalization, or more specifically Europeanization, of Dutch business associations? We define Europeanization, in this context, not as a vertical or upward transfer of authority, but as an increase in the connectedness of Dutch firms and associations, and their leaders, in the network of European firms and business associations. This understanding of Europeanization acknowledges the emergence of a more international (if mainly European) pattern of interaction and orientation among firms and business associations, together with the persistence of nationally defined interests and identities.

Our guiding hypothesis is that given the 'good fit' between the liberal bias in Dutch corporatism and in the European market-making process since the 1980s, the changes in the Dutch system of interest associations have been modest and the impact of the changes coming from Europe minor. Already used to exposure to international markets and with a strong

Atlantic or Anglo-Saxon bias in its business culture (Metze 1999), the Netherlands found itself most of the time in the pro-market coalition in Europe, for instance with regard to financial services, telecommunication, air transport, railways and road haulage, monetary integration, pension and labour market reform. The success of the Dutch economy in the 1990s, coinciding with a new version of 'supply-side corporatism' (Visser and Hemerijck 1997), contributed to institutional stability amidst economic dynamism and confidence in pushing liberal policies in Europe.

Our data on the organization and activities of business interest associations in the Netherlands come from various sources. For the purpose of this study, we conducted a postal survey of business interest associations in 2000, with questions concerning the relative importance of European and domestic activities and representation structures, both at present and in the 1980s. The sample was drawn from the lists of associations in the database on interest organizations at the Max Planck Institute in Cologne (Europeanization of Organized Interests (EOI) database). In addition, we interviewed leading officials of seven major peak and sector federations, and several smaller associations (see list in Appendix at end of chapter).

The chapter is organized in four sections. We start with a brief characterization of the Dutch economy and Dutch corporatism. Next, we discuss the major characteristics and changes in the associative order of Dutch business in recent times. In the third section, we discuss the organizational changes and representation strategies of business interest associations, with special attention to the European dimension. In the final section we draw some conclusions, returning to our leading hypothesis and research questions.

The open economy and its corporatism

Though modest in size and with a small domestic market, the Netherlands is the world's fourteenth biggest economy and eighth largest exporter. As a transit economy, with the largest port of mainland Europe and exports averaging more than 50 per cent of GDP, the Netherlands is very dependent on access to foreign markets. Unsurprisingly, Dutch governments, business representatives and trade unions, have been ardent supporters of European economic integration.

Small domestic markets encourage open economies to seek competitive advantage through product specialization and economies of scale in export markets. The Dutch economy is specialized in transportation and logistics, international finance, business services and the agro-industry. Foreign trade is a tradition that goes back to the seventeenth century colonial ventures of the Dutch East-India Trading Company. The country is home to large indigenous and Anglo-Dutch multinational firms, like Philips, Unilever, Shell, Akzo-Nobel, Heineken, Ahold and some of Europe's largest banks and insurers.[1] Philips, for example, is Europe's leading company in consumer electronics. Of the four Anglo-Dutch firms, Royal Dutch/Shell is the world's third largest oil giant, Unilever its biggest in food and consumer goods, Reed-Elsevier one of the giants in publishing, Corus (British Steel/Hoogovens) Europe's second-biggest steel producer. Until its recent financial mishap, Ahold was world leader in food retailing, with large stakes in the markets of North and South America. ABN AMRO, ING and Rabo rank among the top 30 banks in the world.

In all, multinational firms employ about one million people, one-seventh of total employment; in manufacturing this share rises to two-fifths. Many Dutch multinationals, however, have more employees and more sales abroad than at home. Although Germany is the most important trading partner and 60 per cent of Dutch imports and 80 per cent of exports are within the European Union, connections and orientations in business circles are Atlantic rather than continental. The markets in which the members of business associations operate may have become more international, but not necessarily more European. We find for instance that 60 per cent of Ahold's sales are in the United States. Forty per cent of ABN-AMRO staff work in the United States, more than in the Netherlands, and the company has seriously contemplated the possibility of moving its headquarters from Amsterdam to Chicago. Philips considers Germany as a 'no go' area for its production because of high costs and low (time) flexibility;[2] insurer Aegon sees Germany as a closed shop, according to *The Economist* (4 May 2000).

The Netherlands likes to advertise itself as the most Anglo-Saxon country in continental Europe. English is the language in the boardrooms of these firms and Dutch multinational corporations were among the first, with the Swedes and the Swiss, to appoint foreigners in their top management boards (Ruigrok and van Tulder 1995: 162). Fritz Bolkestein, parliamentary leader of the Liberal Party between 1989 and 1998 and Commissioner for the Internal Market in Brussels from 1999 to 2004, calls it the 'mid-Atlantic' position of a welfare state based on market incentives and trade openness.

In the international literature the Netherlands is characterized as a liberal-corporatist political economy (Crouch 1995; Katzenstein 1985). It figures among the 'coordinated market economies' (Hall and Soskice 2001), but it is an outlier (often with Switzerland) on variables such as 'market capitalization' (high), 'trade union power' (low) and, in recent times, 'flexibility of business practices' (high) and 'flexible working hours' (high). As a variant of the Rhineland model, intense relationships between finance and industry have been a dominant feature throughout the twentieth century (Helmers *et al.* 1975). There is some evidence that these networks, through interlocking boardroom positions, have somewhat loosened, that the position of the banks has become less central, and that there is an ongoing shift from stakeholder to shareholder capitalism (Heemskerk *et al.* 2002). Companies tend to operate more internationally and more independently from one another and vis-à-vis their associations.

With the exception of a handful of firms like Philips or steel producer Hoogovens (Corus, since its merger with British Steel) that were monopolists in their sector, the relationships between firms and the state were rarely direct but used to be channelled through the associations. From its inception in 1931, the Economics Ministry encouraged sectoral organization, market sharing and price fixing arrangements as a means to prevent cut-throat competition. It thus hoped to create larger units and a more efficient structure of production, though with little overall success (de Hen 1980). With what may have been the weakest anti-cartel law in Europe (Zahn 1984: 254), the Netherlands remained a 'cartel paradise' well into the 1990s. In its 1993 survey the Organization of Economic Cooperation and Development judged that many sectors were 'enmeshed in a web of restrictive agreements, regulations and barriers to entry' (OECD 1993: 57). The 'regained corporatism' of the 1990s was especially attuned to supply-side policies, not only in the labour market but also in trade and business organization. In the mid-1990s, in anticipation of European legislation, and sometimes under pressure, some 350 cartels were barred or unwound, takeover and merger codes were revised, business licensing and business hour laws were deregulated, and the trade unions consented to more flexibility in labour contracts and working hours.

These policy changes behind the 'Dutch miracle' did not find their origin in European pressure or examples, but were primarily based on domestic choices responding to the home-grown social and economic crisis of the early 1980s following a period of stagnation and fiscal unbalances after the international shocks of the 1970s. The choice to enter the European Exchange Rate Mechanism, in 1979, and the choice to peg the Dutch guilder to the German Deutschmark in March 1983 had a disciplinary effect on public budgets and wage behaviour. The Wassenaar agreement on wage moderation of late 1982 and the subsequent welfare and labour market reforms were domestic policy choices that set examples to Europe. The overhaul of competition policy, on the other hand, was an adjustment to European policies after the Single European Act of 1987. With some misgivings regarding the missing 'Social dimension' on the part of the trade unions, political and social support for Europe 1992 was near universal. The attendant neo-liberal drive towards privatization and bringing market-like competition in the sector of public utilities and social services has hardly met political (or intellectual) resistance in the Netherlands. The European integration process has been important in accelerating these policy changes, by shaping the environment in which the adjustment of social-economic institutions and policies became (seen as) desirable, but that cannot be construed as external pressure, since most of the time Dutch business representatives were prominent in the neo-liberal coalition in Europe that created this environment in the first place.

The neo-liberal overtures in the past two decades have not altered the foundations of the Dutch system of industrial relations or the Dutch welfare state. The mainstays of the system are: representation through unions and collective bargaining; widespread consultation and information within the company through works councils; the possibility to apply collectively agreed rules to non-organized firms; institutionalization of social dialogue and concertation of public policies through joint bodies like the bipartite Foundation of Labour (Stichting van de Arbeid) or the tripartite Social-Economic Council (Sociaal-Economische Raad). These are the two most important, though not the only organizations, that exert a centralizing and aggregating force on the organization of Dutch business (and labour). The formation of successive coalition governments with Christian-democratic, social-democratic and liberal participation, in all possible combinations, illustrates the stability of the Dutch political system.[3] Changes in the Dutch welfare state since the early 1980s have consisted of a series of concerted reforms. These reforms were often contested by the unions but not seriously disturbed by social unrest or large, disruptive labour conflicts.

Over the postwar period, through various mergers across the religious divide and by unifying trade and employers' associations, the number of overarching peak associations representing business in the two aforementioned central bodies of Dutch corporatism was reduced from ten in 1970 to three in 1995. In that year the Confederation of Dutch Businesses (VNO) federated with the Christian Confederation of Dutch Employers (NCW). VNO-NCW is the one and only peak association for large and medium-sized firms in industry and services; MKB-Nederland represents small and medium-sized enterprises; LTO-Nederland organizes agricultural interests (see list in Appendix). Each represents the employer and trade interests of their members. Between VNO-NCW and MKB-Nederland there is some domain overlap.

With few exceptions, business leaders are full of praise for the new edition of corporatism. *The Economist* (4 May 2002) cites Mr Cees van der Hoeven, the chief executive officer (CEO) of Ahold who was forced out in February 2003 following the financial embroilment of the company, praising Dutch trade unions as 'the best in the world'. Former CEO Mr Jan Timmer admits that the Philips' turnaround and rescue from bankruptcy in 1992 was due to a large extent to the support from union headquarters in Amsterdam.[4] Mr Alexander Rinnooy Kan, who was VNO's president between 1990 and 1996 and has since joined the board of ING bank, is a keen defender of the consultation economy: 'by making complex decisions only after full debate, it ensures a stronger commitment to the results'. Mr Anthony Burghmans, the Dutch CEO of Unilever, echoes this and says that 'red-blooded Anglo-American capitalism would not be popular with the consensus-minded, egalitarian Dutch'. Mr Kees Storm, outgoing CEO of insurer Aegon, objects that 'every now and then, a country needs a Thatcher' (ours was a very mild variant, Mr Ruud Lubbers, the Christian-Democratic leader who was prime minister between 1982 and 1994), but rates Dutch people and their governments as 'pro-business'.[5] This judgement applies also to the two coalition governments in the 1990s (1994–1998; 1998–2002) that were led by Mr Wim Kok, the leader of the Labour Party. (It is noted in passing that Mr Kok had been the leader of the unions and chief negotiator of the Wassenaar agreement of 1982.)

Continuity and change in the organization of Dutch business

At a first glance, the system of Dutch business interest associations is quite stable (see Table 2.1). In our database, we counted 831 business interest associations in 2001, only 83 less than in 1981.[6] Disregarding agriculture and firms 'without staff', i.e. self-employed entrepreneurs, there is now one association for every 400 firms in the Netherlands. In manufacturing we find the largest number of associations (38 per cent of all associations against less than 10 per cent of all firms) as well as those with the smallest average size (96 firms).

The high degree of differentiation, by product and market segment, in the Dutch associational system mirrors an age-effect. In emerging sectors, especially in business services, but also in education, health and community services, associations have been founded in recent times and tend to have a much larger size. Because firms in these sectors tend to be smaller, associations will have more difficulty in raising the necessary resources from membership contributions. Therefore, they will search for greater economy of scale.

Beneath the surface there is far more change. Some 350 or two-fifths of

Table 2.1 Number of associations across sectors

Sector[a]	*1981*		*2001*	
	N	*%*	*N*	*%*
Agriculture, hunting and forestry, fishing	41	4.5	41	4.9
Mining, manufacturing, utilities	324	35.4	318	38.3
Construction	49	5.4	63	7.6
Wholesale and retail trade	336	36.2	234	28.2
Transport, storage and communications	49	5.3	39	4.7
Financial and business services	47	5.1	53	6.4
Education, health, community services	40	4.4	48	5.8
Intersectoral	7	0.8	5	0.6
Not classifiable	21	2.3	30	3.6
Total	914	100.0	831	100.0

Sources: SER Almanac (Social Economic Council's Yearbook) and Pyttersen's Almanac (Organization's Yearbook). European associations based in the Netherlands, Foundations, Round tables, Chambers and regional associations not operating at the national level are not included in the table.

Note

a Sectors based on ISIC Rev. 3 (NACE).

the associations that were present in 2001 did not exist in 1991. Of those existing in 1991, some 200 do no longer exist in 2001. Taking these figures together, we learn that the associational system, measured by sheer number of associations, expanded in the 1990s, following contractions in the 1980s. This cyclical pattern corresponds with the differences in economic development – poor in a large part of the 1980s, buoyant in the 1990s. Some 70,000 new firms (+27 per cent) were established and one million new jobs (+17 per cent) were created since 1993. Half of all businesses with a turnover of €50 million or more in the Randstad (the urban western part of the country) were founded in the past 15 years, a dynamism as good as Silicon Valley and twice the rate of Paris or the Düsseldorf region. In addition to new foundations, in particular in services, most changes were the result of mergers, takeovers and branching-off. In services and utilities there was a spate of new foundations due to privatization and independent collective bargaining connected with the establishment of employer associations. In our postal survey, we found that 28 per cent of all associations were founded in the last ten years and that as many as 86 per cent had changed their by-laws in response to takeovers, domain changes, change of affiliation and new activities.

Of the four traditional fault lines dividing Dutch business associations – religion, function, market segment and size – the first two have more or less disappeared. Many of the associations that disappeared, mostly through amalgamations, had a denominational background. Until 1970 there was a general, Protestant and Catholic association in virtually all sectors of the economy, and in all domains of social, cultural and political life. This segmented or 'pillarized' system began to break down in the second half of the 1960s. During the following years, with political and ideological differences quickly eroding, Protestant and Catholic business associations amalgamated in nearly all branches and sectors of the economy. In politics this had its manifestation in the formation of a Christian Democratic party. (The trade union movement represents a deviant case in so far as the Catholic unions amalgamated, not with the Protestants, but with the general or Social Democrat unions.) Twenty years later, general and Christian business associations took the final step and federated or amalgamated into one organization. (Again, the trade unions refrained from taking this step to unity and instead opted for conglomerate unions, straddling sectoral domains, but respecting the religious dividing line.)

The major force behind these merger drives has been an economic one. In the 1970s, following nearly two decades of state-imposed wage regulation and entering a far more troublesome period of bargaining and bickering with the unions and the state, the interest associations of Dutch business rapidly professionalized, expanding the number and quality of their staff. With rapidly rising salary costs and a stagnating economy, mergers helped to obtain economy of scale and contain costs (see Streeck and Visser 1998). (With far fewer paid officials that needed to be pensioned off, this was a much cheaper operation than in the union movement, where a similar merger drive took place, leading to vastly rising costs.) Already in the early 1980s the large member firms and biggest paymasters of the main sectoral and peak associations found the time ripe for overcoming the schism between Christian and general associations and called on the leadership of VNO and NCW to join forces. However, personal ill-feelings and the threat of a breakaway in the smaller Christian federation shipwrecked merger plans at the time. Some parts of the Christian association, more open to the interests of small firms, feared domination by the large firm sector. At the time it was argued that the existence of two peak associations permitted business to play a tactical game of 'two voices, one interest', allowing the smaller organization to confront the unions with radical proposals, thus creating space for compromises with the main business federation (Nobelen 1983). Arguably, in recent times lobbying the political authorities, at home and in Europe, has become more important, requiring greater unity and more economy of resources. Although speaking with one voice in Europe was an extra impetus to overcome the century-old division in Dutch business representation, the primary influence was pressure from large firms, as well as from some sectoral affiliates, to end their 'double membership' and increase economic efficiency. According to the official VNO-NCW story, 'the continuation of two professional organizations became simply too expensive' (Bruggeman and Camijn 1999: 126).

Under the influence of its major company members, who were strongly interrelated with business across the Channel, Dutch businesses were the first on the European continent to follow their British counterparts and shed the functional division between trade and employers' association. In 1968, three years after the Confederation of British Industry (CBI), VNO (Vereniging van Nederlandse Ondernemingen) reunited the formerly separate economic (trade) and social (employers) associations, a division that had existed since 1920. The obstacle that had to be overcome in this case was that the employers associations had a constituency of personnel directors, often with personal membership, whereas the trade associations had a constituency of general managers or public affairs officials, usually with corporate membership. The merger settled the matter in favour of the latter. Personnel directors, however, have maintained relationships through informal networks, within and between sectoral associations. One current example is the 'Club of Eleven', composed of the personnel directors of the most prominent multinational firms. Such horizontal ('round table') structures, based on personal invitation and direct links between firms, are also found within sectors, and are a prominent albeit somewhat unknown and under-researched feature of Dutch business associability.

In another aspect, Dutch business associations also resemble British examples. Though sectoral association and hierarchical ordering have remained predominant features of the Dutch system of business associability, the independent role (and financial importance) of mostly larger companies has always been acknowledged. Thus, like a similar practice in the CBI, VNO-NCW allows membership of individual, mostly larger firms and has adopted a sizeable number of firm representatives in its General Council. In addition to its current number of 150 sectoral and branch affiliates, the organization has about 250 company members, nearly all the larger ones operating in the country (even those with foreign ownership). Note that these firms are also represented through sectoral or general federations affiliated to VNO-NCW. For instance, Philips is also member of the Federation of Metal and Electrotechnical Industry (FME-CWM), Shell and Unilever also of the General Employers' Association (AWVN), ABN-AMRO also of the Dutch Association of Banks (NVB). Within these sector federations or associations, the independence of the large firms manifests itself in the fact that most conduct their own negotiations and sign their own collective agreements with the trade unions.

Despite the changes in the Dutch associational system in past years, its highly differentiated structure has remained. However, the differentiation of business interest organization, by product market segment and size, is held in check through mutual cooperation within 'higher order' federations. In a range of industries we observe a concentration pattern at the level of federations – broadening their domain and overcoming old divisions within sectors. The process of integration between trade and employment associations has accelerated. Currently few associations with the sole task of representing employers' interests have remained. The typical trade associations, without representing firms as employers, have survived at the level of subsectors and branches. Less than half of the associations in our postal survey represented members' interests vis-à-vis trade unions and only 37 per cent were involved in negotiating collective agreements with the unions. Increasingly, trade associations mandate such representing and negotiating tasks to 'higher order' federations.

This is the case, for instance, in the metal and electrical engineering sector. In this industry, the 160 (sectoral) affiliates of FME-CWM have 'mandated' the federation to negotiate the two main sectoral collective agreements, one for large and one for small firms, which are defined as firms with less than 35 employees. Since the integration of the representative of small firms (CWM) in 1996, the federation now represents the socio-economic interests of large and small firms, from Philips to the bicycle repair shop. Though a prominent member of the federation, Philips has always negotiated its own agreements and maintains its own influential lobby in The Hague (and elsewhere), but that is exceptional, at least in Dutch politics. FME-CWM is probably VNO-NCW's most powerful affiliate, with 225 staff and most likely the strongest financial position of all.

Similar developments – concentration of the employer function in broad sectoral associations, charged with the responsibility to represent the sector politically and if need be to negotiate collective agreements with the unions, while the affiliates continue their activities as trade association – can be observed in sectors like printing, transport and construction. Following the 1993 'New Direction' central agreement with the unions, this development is part of a process of 'organized decentralization' in industrial relations towards sectoral collective labour agreements that can be complemented at lower (company) levels with greater participation of works councils (Visser 1998). This decentralization process requires better information services and more economy of scale – similar to developments that could be observed among the trade unions (Streeck and Visser 1998). The 'logic of membership' forces these associations to differentiate their internal organization in order to meet varying demands and expectations of the members. This can be achieved through hierarchical ordering (as appears to be the case in most sectors) and through internal differentiation, introducing new types and ties of membership (see below). Thus, continuing the tradition of its Christian component, VNO-NCW also has five regional associations and a separate structure grouping the personal membership of some 1,200 young managers. These 'club-like' structures are meant to stimulate personal involvement and balance the growing emphasis on commercial services, but also to find out what services are truly needed. The 'logic of influence', on the other hand, continues to press into the direction of organizational concentration, through affiliation with broad sectoral or intersectoral associations, which have not only established ties within the corporatist network at home but can also help create valuable connections within the more fragmented, changing and more difficult to decipher network in Europe.

VNO-NCW claims to represent 80,000 of the 330,000 firms in the Netherlands:[7] all larger firms of 500 and more employees, 90 per cent of those over 100 employees and 50 per cent of those between 20 and 100 employees. The 125 affiliates of MKB-Nederland, the peak association for small and medium-sized firms, boast the membership of some 125,000 firms, roughly 40 per cent of all firms with less than 50 staff. In total the organizational density of Dutch business, i.e. the proportion of firms which have joined business interest associations, can be estimated to lie between 55 and 60 per cent, with higher rates (70 per cent or more) in manufacturing and lower rates (40 per cent) in commercial services.[8] If measured in terms of the employment share of these organized firms, 'employer density' rises to 80 or 85 per cent, which is high by international standards. In contrast to the erosion in union representation (since the early 1980s union density dropped from 37 to 24 per cent), there are no signs of a decline in the associability of business.

Firms negotiating their own collective agreements with the unions are not alone. With a membership of 500 firms and 40 branch associations, the General Employers' Association (AWVN) organizes firms throughout the economy, in industry and services, assuming an advisory role in three out of four company agreements (AWVN negotiates only a sector agreement in the textile industry). In this capacity, the organization is the main bargaining partner of FNV-Bondgenoten (FNV-Allies), the largest trade union in the country and signatory to some 100 sectoral and 650 company agreements (out of a total of some 200 sectoral and 850 company agreements). Since AWVN, itself, does not usually sign the agreements it helps to negotiate, it is spared the difficulty of developing organizational capacities to enforce them. It presents itself rather as a 'service organization'. Historically, the organization was strongly involved in advising firms on job classification and merit pay systems, as part of the centralizing approach to Dutch wage setting. In recent times, the organization has moved towards a broader human resources' management profile, including consultancy on work organization, training and career development. However, staying within its tradition, the AWVN does not extend its activities to strictly business issues. Advising international firms on investment decisions or international labour relations, for instance, is left to private consultancy firms (Buitelaar and van den Toren 1999: 96).

Like FME-CWM, AWVN built up a central joint resistance fund in the 1970s in order to bolster internal discipline and uphold the employers' veto against union demands of wage levelling (in the 1970s) and general working time reduction (in the 1980s). The 'New Course' central agreement of 1993, with its promise of decentralization and differentiation, has led to the discontinuation of these central funds. Through a new division of labour and reshuffling of tasks with the peak association VNO-NCW, since 1996, the AWVN has acted as the 'social' or 'employers' branch of Dutch business; a further integration of activities is in preparation. AWVN already incorporates the Advisory Bureau for Labour Affairs of the former NCW, and has broadened its domain from industry to services (Buitelaar and van den Toren 1999: 90). Like FME-CWM and alongside its peak federation, AWVN is directly represented in the nation's main consultation bodies such as the Foundation of Labour and the Social Economic Council.

Dutch business association and Europe

Like they do at home, Dutch business interest groups tend to present a mixed profile in their European lobbying strategies. They tend to act, and feel at ease, in EU federations, of which they often occupy the secretariat while at the same time displaying a tendency towards self-reliance, sometimes using the practical services and connections of large firms with offices in Brussels, similar to the British approach (van Schendelen 2002: 125). Trendsetters in Europe, according to the author, have been multinational companies like Philips, and Anglo-Dutch firms like Shell and Unilever, all of them founding members of the European Round Table of Industrialists (ERT). Philips, in particular, has tried to present itself as European rather than Dutch (Middlemas 1995: 456). The ERT proposal for an 'Open Market 1992', first presented in 1984, was drafted in the Public Affairs department of Philips (Middlemas 1995: 104; Verwey 1994). Current ERT members are the CEOs of Philips, Shell, Unilever, Akzo-Nobel and Reed-Elsevier.

According to van Schendelen (2002: 124) 'the major Dutch public and private interest groups usually have a utilitarian preference for more supranational and negative integration. They believe in having more room to manoeuvre inside the Commission and the Parliament than inside the Council.' The dependence on trade pushes Dutch business interests towards negative integration, especially in such sectors as foods, chemicals, electronics and transports. Acting through the EU associations, with access to the Commission and the Parliament, and through large firms pushing for trade liberalization, would seem to have been a rational strategy as long as the Council could be ignored.

Unlike the larger multinational corporations, Dutch business associations were latecomers in Brussels. Before 1989 only three associations had an office in Brussels. According to our survey their current number has increased to at least 14. In our interviews we found confirmation of the hypothesis (Kohler-Koch 1999) that the expansion of qualified majority voting in the Council, and the expanded role of the Parliament, corresponded with a change of lobbying strategy. This necessitated the investment in contacts and expertise at both the national and European level, and more attention to horizontal coalitions and contacts. The adaptation to multilevel governance, away from older federalist leanings that had been common in Dutch politics and business, implied that the type of committed and pragmatic lobbying, using all channels, that had been common in The Hague was now also necessary in Brussels. In nearly all the interviews with representatives of business interest associations (see below), the connection between the national and European level had become a matter of utmost importance, closely followed by the question how this connection could be made to work for the membership. At the same time it became useful to increase the permanent presence in Brussels, following the example of other national federations. This reflects the importance of connections with Members of the EU Parliament, the Committee of Permanent Representatives (Coreper) and horizontal networking with business representatives from other EU member states. It is obvious that the late establishment of permanent offices by Dutch business associations is in part explained as an effect of geographical proximity. It is only two hours by train between The Hague and Brussels. In our interview with the head of the Brussels bureau of VNO-NCW this was described as 'a big advantage' since it is easy to send specialists from headquarters or from affiliates to Brussels, whereas national peak associations from other EU member states must rely on the small staff of generalists permanently based in Brussels.[9] However, in the 1990s the absence during evening meetings, dinners and informal networking came to be seen as a disadvantage (see also van Schendelen 2002: 125).

In their postal survey of business interest associations in Britain, France and Germany, Kohler-Koch and Quittkat (1999) report that more than 80 per cent of associations in the three largest member states do target European authorities and institutions on behalf of their members. One-fifth of these associations had their own office or a special branch in Brussels for the purpose of lobbying EU institutions. A majority of these associations also engaged in regular contacts with their national government administrations. The authors confirmed the national variation in patterns, reported elsewhere (Middlemas 1995; van Schendelen 2002), showing that lobbying by British firms and business groups is marked by self-reliance, that French business groups act under coordination of the state and that German business tends to present its case in a sectoral or regional capacity. According to Kohler-Koch and Quittkat (1999: 14) these national variations in the European strategies of business can be partly explained in terms of differences between the political systems and legislative traditions in EU member states. Their point is that activities in the national and European arena are closely related and cannot easily be separated from one another. Our postal survey among a large sample of trade and employers' associations in the Netherlands confirms that national contacts and affiliations remain strategically important for all organizations (Wilts 2001).[10]

As expected, Dutch business interest associations tend to be smaller, in terms of membership size, staff and resources, than their sister organizations in Germany and France. The average association in our survey had between 100 and 200 members, employed between five and ten officials, and commanded an annual budget of less than €500,000. Differences across sectors are slight if we exclude the major (higher-order) federations. In 1999, 55 per cent of all federations had a full-time staff of less than five people, compared to 49 per cent in Germany and 47 per cent in France. Only around one in five associations had a full-time staff of over 20, and almost one-third an annual budget exceeding €1 million. Of these associations, 56 per cent report that they are exclusively financed by member contributions. On average, membership dues provided 86 per cent of total associational income, other sources (interest on assets, etc.) 9 per cent and service provision to members a further 5 per cent.[11] Of the annual revenue almost half is spent on direct representation of members, almost a third on services to members, and nearly 10 per cent on the payment of contributions to other national and European federations. Many associations find themselves in financial dire straits; 47 per cent had financial reserves less than half their annual budget and no significant income outside membership contributions. They were extremely vulnerable to membership decline. In their case, European or international representation, often representation in The Hague as well, was only possible through affiliation in (Dutch) higher-order federations. Like Kohler-Koch and Quitkatt (1999) we found that a larger budget is associated with more frequent contacts with political institutions in *both* the national and European arena. This points to the more interesting finding, in their research and in ours, that a greater investment in European representation and activity does not subtract from and lead to less representation and activity in the national arena.

Although less than with national ones, Dutch business associations have

Table 2.2 Contact patterns at national and European levels

	At least once a year	*Never*
National level		
Top civil servants	68	12
MPs and parliamentary committees	61	21
Regulatory bodies	53	27
Committees/tripartite bodies	46	34
Bipartite bodies	26	48
Cabinet members	22	60
European level		
Civil servants of Directorates	58	28
Commission and top levels of DGs	39	42
MEPs and parliamentary committees	43	31
Regulatory bodies	30	47
Coreper	21	58
Council secretariat or Council members	27	53

frequent contacts with European authorities and representatives. More than two-thirds of the associations contact top civil servants in The Hague at least once a year; almost 40 per cent report contacts with the Commission and top officials in Brussels. While 61 per cent have contact with members and committees of the Dutch Parliament at least once a year, 43 per cent do so with members and committees of the European Parliament. Furthermore, 53 per cent frequently contact a regulatory body at the national level, while 30 per cent do so at the European level. As expected (Streeck and Schmitter 1991), the largest difference has to do with the strength of the overarching corporatist institutions in the national, and the weakness of these institutions in the European arena. The Labour Foundation, the Socio-Economic Council and related committees are regularly contacted by half of all Dutch business associations, while the Brussels homologues (the Economic and Social Committee and the Social Dialogue committees) by only 14 per cent. Similarly, Dutch peak and sector associations are contacted far more often, and are much more important as sources or targets of information than their European homologues. On the other hand, the executive is important at both levels. One-fifth of the Dutch business associations contact members of the Dutch Cabinet at least once a year; a similar percentage reports contacts with members of the Committee of Permanent Representatives (Coreper) and 27 per cent contact the Council Secretariat or members of the Council. These contacts will mostly involve the Dutch Minister or representative.

In conclusion, corresponding with the findings reported in the literature (Kohler-Koch 1999), our survey clearly brings out that the pattern of lobbying at home is replicated, with lower intensity, at the European level. These findings, moreover, underline that national associations generally do not replace national strategies with European ones. European and national contact patterns are highly correlated ($r = 0.72$). Dutch associations increasingly turn to Brussels, but their European strategies come in addition to national ones. Moreover, they do not replace or erode established forms in interest representation towards the national government and trade unions. (Changes in representation strategies towards the union may vary, as they did in for instance banking or printing with the break-up or differentiation of the sectoral agreement, but they are entirely unrelated to Europe and mostly caused by technological and organizational factors.)

Our interviews with representatives of Dutch associations confirm that national and European strategies cannot easily be separated in the activities of business associations. The expansion, let alone the concentration, of representational activities at the European level is hardly popular with the membership. In associations with many small firms, in particular, officials have a hard time defending the expenditure of scarce resources on representation in Brussels.[12] In associations with many large firms, there are other constraints. These firms may be able to put their European concerns on the agenda independently, bypassing the association, or they may serve instead as the ears and eyes of the national association in Brussels. This is the case, for instance, in the banking association NVB, the European activities of which are coordinated through the Brussels offices of the major commercial banks.[13] On the other hand, most associations cannot afford to abstain from European activities either, provided they want to supply adequate services to members and prevent parts of their membership leaving the organization.[14]

In sum, the composition of the membership tends to structure how business associations will try and articulate their interests at the national and the European level. Because of the resources and in-house expertise of large companies, they are often able to exert considerable influence on the strategies of their associations. Representatives of the leading Dutch association in the construction sector observed, for example, that smaller members mostly turn to their association for individual support and advice, for instance on how to interpret the consequences of EU regulations – as in the case of small subcontractors in construction.[15] Larger members, on the other hand, often stand on a more equal footing with their association and may even coordinate their European strategies with them – as we saw in the case of large commercial banks.

New ways of representing members' interests

In recent years, many Dutch business associations have adjusted their organizational structures and created special units to offer individualized service and management support to their members. Interviews suggest that this development reflects a change in the functioning of associations. Increasing the commitment and loyalty of members becomes more important as economic sectors become more heterogeneous, competition between associations intensifies, cartel arrangements are discontinued or made illegal and sectoral wage agreements are decentralized. More than ever before, business associations are becoming information intermediaries. Offering selective services to individual members becomes more important to associations as a way to enhance membership loyalty. Members are not only the target, but also the association's most important source of information. In our postal surveys, two out of three associations report that their members are the most frequently used source of knowledge.[16]

VNO-NCW, for instance, has established different channels to communicate directly with the membership. The organization directly responds to questions for support and advice from individual companies through a telephone help desk. Also, the organization provides practical support on Internet use to member associations. Through the channel of the General Employers' Association AWVN, the peak association also supports the membership with legal advice, in particular in matters of labour law and the application of central recommendations and wage agreements of the Foundation of Labour. Through an associated, but formally independent centre for management development, VNO-NCW offers training facilities to individual companies. These activities come in addition to the organization's involvement in the structures of Dutch corporatism and its activities at EU level.

VNO-NCW represents its members interests in Brussels through a number of channels. The head of its Brussels Bureau describes UNICE and Coreper as the organization's most valuable EU contacts.[17] Through those contacts, VNO-NCW hopes to be an important channel for Dutch associations and firms of all kinds, an expectation which is confirmed in a number of interviews with sectoral associations (we have not yet conducted interviews with firms on this). The General Employers' Association of the Netherlands AWVN, for instance, channels its European contacts mainly through the peak association. This applies also to the companies that are, directly or indirectly, member of the VNO-NCW or AWVN. These companies have their own contacts in Brussels, e.g. through involvement in networks like the ERT or through membership in the multitude of European sectoral federations. In their private lobbying, however, they often coordinate their activities with the VNO-NCW, thus pursuing common interests such as defending the room of manoeuvre for national regulation, avoiding stringent EU regulation and realizing national subsidiarity.[18]

Although VNO-NCW is a latecomer in setting up shop in Brussels, it preceded other Dutch peak associations like the Federation of Small and Medium-sized Businesses (MKB-Nederland) which now has a small office with two staff officials in Brussels (and a huge organization at home). This is seen as too small but, according to the organization's headquarters, the budget permits no expansion of its European bureau. The organization must, therefore, rely on some of its sector affiliates and their relationships with European federations, but it has to be conceded that MKB-Nederland, according to its European representative, 'has not yet good access in Brussels'.[19] The organization finds it difficult to demonstrate the usefulness of EU lobbying to its members. This problem is aggravated by the low involvement and passive attitude of its affiliates. Unlike VNO-NCW, AWVN or the engineering federation FME-CWM, MKB-Nederland maintains no direct contacts with firms. Its sectoral and regional affiliates represent mostly very small companies with very specific interests. Many of these member associations do not see EU legislation 'coming' and do not appreciate the weakening of such legislation through lobbying.[20]

Therefore, rather than building a stronger European profile, MKB-Nederland looks at other ways to enhance its standing among the members. The organization currently uses quarterly surveys, commissioned to the Dutch Institute for Public Opinion Research, in order to find out what its members actually want, what their expectations regarding Europe are and how they think their interests are best served at the national and European level. In its capacity as peak federation, MKB-Nederland remains a player in the national corporatist arena, representing the collective interests of the small firm sector. Direct services towards the members have become more important and individual services are now offered at a low (membership only) price. The organization expects this to be a key means of financing its activities and maintaining member loyalty.

Most sectoral peak federations in the Netherlands are experimenting with similar arrangements for responding to their members. FME-CWM has founded a separate division for management support, offering services to the companies on a 'pay for services' basis. In an interview at the organization's headquarters, founding the division for management support was described as being illustrative of a gradual change in the functioning of the organization.[21] Selling individualized service and advice is becoming more important in relation to established forms of collective interest representation financed out of regular membership fees. Each of the 160 member associations of FME-CWM has its own 'account manager' and the federation tries hard to achieve 'active customer services'. Through its division for management support, FME-CWM is able to respond directly to questions that individual member associations and companies have concerning, for instance, EU regulations. This is a precious communication channel, which comes in addition to regular ways of communicating with the members via regional offices and membership meetings. In the internal government of the organization, informal networking, *ad hoc* workgroups and committees, and information processing, tend to take the place of formal deliberation and decision making.

In its European activities, the organization tries to provide important information services, but leaves member associations free to establish their own channels. The Association of Domestic Equipment Suppliers (VLEHAN), itself a member of FME-CWM, relies on its membership in the European Committee of Manufacturers of Domestic Equipment (CEDED) when trade interests are concerned, and even keeps links with the European Federation of Engineering (ORGALIME) when broader trade or environmental issues are at stake. General and social affairs are channelled through the FME-CWM and the general national and European federations, like VNO-NCW and UNICE. Direct contacts with similar federations in other European countries rarely occur.[22] Our interviews with smaller trade associations confirm this pattern of reliance on national or European federations.[23] Even a large association like the AWVN, with its membership of multinational firms, retains a national outlook. AWVN has not invested in a horizontal European network with similar organizations in other member states and runs its European affairs mainly through the national peak association VNO-NCW.[24] This is probably the consequence of its internal diversity. FME-CWM, for instance, maintains close contacts with Gesamtmetall, its powerful German counterpart, and is very conscious of the importance of the German market for its members.

Associations like FME-CWM and VNO-NCW try and combine forms of interest representation and lobbying at both the national and the EU level with new ways to communicate directly with their members. Most sectoral federations are going down the same road trying new organizational solutions in order to meet membership demands. In the transport sector, following the example of metal engineering, Transport en Logistiek Nederland (TLN), the largest business association representing all except the largest firms, has founded TLN Consultancy, a separate division for management support. In the chemical sector, the peak association VNCI has founded Chemserve, also a separate consultancy company. Through this company, VNCI sells consultancy and advice and maintains contacts with its larger company members. While drawing on the network of contacts of VNCI, Chemserve cooperates with the knowledge centres of large chemical companies such as DSM and Akzo-Nobel.

There are numerous other examples of the founding of organizational divisions for management support. LTO, the main peak federation in agriculture, has founded a division that offers consultancy to members and to third parties. Through its division, LTO Commerce, the association offers discounts on sector specific purchases. Other associations, like KHN in the hotel and restaurant sector, offer their members direct economic benefits as well.[25] Because these associations represent most companies in their respective sectors, they have become commercially interesting for suppliers and financial organizations like credit card companies. This creates opportunities to develop ways of making membership in the associations financially interesting. Arguably, realizing selective membership incentives is a way of binding members that becomes more important as the political role of associations changes along with the decentralization of labour relations and the Europeanization of public decision making.

By establishing new information channels to reach their members and creating new ways to meet membership demands, business associations in the Netherlands attempt to integrate their European and national activities. Our survey shows that 87 per cent of the business associations in the Netherlands actively monitor political developments. An almost equal percentage stresses the importance of disseminating information to members. Dutch associations tend to rate their function as (political) information intermediary higher than their representational activities (see Table 2.3). From other research, we know that they also rely less on formal and written statements, and more on personal and informal contacts (van Schendelen 2002). In this respect, Dutch associations tend to differ from those in Germany or France. German associations are more absorbed by their involvement in the formal representation of members' interests in political institutions and committees. French associations spend more time on supporting their members with legal advice, market research and promotional activities (see Quitkatt 2002).

The monitoring of political developments necessarily includes an orientation towards European developments. Relative to the 1980s, Europe has become more important for Dutch business associations and the impact of the EU at the national level is now acutely felt. Moreover, EU regulation, in particular since the Single European Act of 1987, has changed national interest politics. Competition law and anti-trust legislation are examples of regulations that originate from the EU and have a direct impact on the way in which associations will represent their members' interests. VNO-NCW, for instance, favours the social dialogue and negotiation procedures created under the Treaties of Maastricht and Amsterdam and providing for agreements with the unions over social policy issues if it helps to prevent or improve EU legislation. However, its representatives are also conscious of

Table 2.3 Activities of business associations

	NL	*D*	*F*
Monitoring of political developments	88	64	52
Political information to members	83	81	34
Representation of members in political institutions or committees	58	80	34
Representation of member interests to other associations	84	92	95
Representation of member interests to trade unions	48	25	61
Statistical and sector information to members	79	97	86
Market research	46	60	78
Legal and economic advice	41	69	86
Access to consultancy firms	43	46	57
Publicity and promotional activities	49	82	90
Professional training	58	66	60

Source: Quitkatt (2002), Table 1 for France and Germany.

Notes
NL: Netherlands, D: Germany, F: France.

the fact that the abandonment of 'integration through law', and its replacement by regulation through voluntary agreement, increases the need for common norms that may be available nationally but tend to be absent or fragile in the European arena. Defending the integrity of Dutch regulations, for instance in the area of accounting standards or pension provision, is still seen as very important.[26]

National representation and lobbying, however, have not decreased and 'require still most of the time of the organization' even in an eminently international sector like financial services, with its host of new European and international regulation.[27] This conclusion holds even stronger for domestic sectors like construction, where European representation is still low-key and member firms do not as yet have their own European connections.[28] In both sectors, effective interest politics in Brussels means that one must have good contacts with national government and lawmakers. At this point, in an organized market economy like the Netherlands, with its corporatist institutions and representation patterns, the role of the peak associations is crucial and affiliation remains a vital resource. In this sense, the peak associations have an added value even for large and international firms. VNO-NCW clearly sees its presence and alliances in Brussels for the purpose of influencing EU policies also as a means to strengthen its leverage over national interlocutors, in particular the government and the unions. The organization is acutely aware of playing in two quite different yet interconnected arenas, and using the advantages in one arena strategically in the other.

Conclusion

We began our study with some general predictions concerning the nature of the changes in business associability due to changing patterns in production and services and current trends in concentration and internationalization. According to the literature, such changes make it harder for business interest associations to find a solid resource base and tend to relocate the centre of activities, representation and power from the association to its larger firm members. If this were not already enough as a force undermining a corporatist system of business associability based on sectoral representation and bureaucratic leadership elevated above and detached from the level of the firm, the erosion is also predicted to come from the other end. The declining capacity of the national state to guarantee and deliver the intangible (future) goods promised in exchange for difficult internal balancing acts, would seem to be another blow to the corporatist system.

We found, broadly, a confirmation of the predicted trend that the logic of membership has become more important and that the weight of companies in business interest associations and in the representation strategies of these associations has increased. This is most clearly seen with respect to the most internationalized and larger companies. But even in relation to smaller firms business interest associations had to introduce new instruments to make themselves useful to firms. In order to widen their financial resources, the larger and more successful associations are moving away from a contributions-only based affiliation to various forms of charges for direct servicing, combined with several types of direct communication with members. We observed several commercial ventures that were meant to strengthen the ties with members and broaden the resource base of the organization.

However, the expectation that the sectoral and corporatist pattern of associability of Dutch business would be weakened did not come true. In fact, what we have seen is not only a gradual modernization, with elements of decentralization (especially in the domain of labour relations) and more space for individual firms or specialized branches, but also an increase in concentration and coordination. National peak associations and the broad sectoral federations within them have not become weaker. They still occupy the dominant place in the national network of lobbying and interest intermediation and are very important in connecting with the European scene. In neither arena can they claim a monopoly on representation, however. In the supply side corporatism of the 1990s, the peak associations have been made to share their central position with some other large players on the side of business (mostly the large sector associations with the voice of multinational firms in them); in the European arena, their position was always more marginal, alongside independently operating company representatives, lobbyists and a myriad of sector interests.

The response to European integration and the impact of Europe on Dutch business organizations take a central place in our analysis, but Europe or Europeanization cannot be conceived as an independent variable explaining change. First, it is very hard, especially for an internationalized economy like the Netherlands, with many prominent global firms, to separate European from global influences and responses. Second, many of the changes apparently coming from Europe were co-authored by Dutch business lobbies. Third, the emphasis on the domestic constellation helps to weigh the impact of European and international developments against other influences. Following the strategic reorientation and reinvention of Dutch corporatism in recent times, organizational changes have been incremental and small. Europe has sometimes played a modest role in motivating or explaining these changes. European issues have surely gained a more prominent place on the agenda of these associations and more time and resources are now spent on Europe. Yet, associational development in the Netherlands does not mirror, let alone foreshadow, changes at the European level. Dutch associations remain strongly oriented towards a national arena of interest politics and follow domestic patterns and preferences in their European approach. Even where European influences did trigger the organizational and policy changes, for instance, by shaping the neo-liberal climate in which the adjustment of social-economic institutions and policies became (seen as) desirable or unavoidable, this cannot be classified as external pressure, since Dutch business was very much part of the coalition that created this climate.

Part of the explanation for the modest impact of Europe in explaining change, is the congruence, especially at the level of strategy and beliefs, between the liberal market making policies in Europe and the dominant policy orientation in liberal corporatism in the Netherlands. We see the changes in the organization of Dutch business as an example of how politics and policies are *Europeanized*, not through centralization or harmonization, but through a combination of soft multilateral constraints and pressures, increasing the awareness of national actors and institutions of their European context, but leaving them to act and operate within still highly national, and hence varying, political conditions.

This chapter has shown that changes in the associational system and in associational politics were gradual and modest. Our main explanation is that Dutch business associations were already adapted to a large extent to the more international and competitive climate that came to dominate. In other words, we find confirmation of our main hypothesis, that given the 'good fit' between the liberal bias in Dutch corporatism and in the European market-making process, the changes in the Dutch system of interest associations would be limited and the impact of the changes coming from Europe minor. However, as is shown by its ability to defend its share in world trade, in this new competitive environment the institutional basis of national corporatism and its attending associative order were renewed but not discarded. This leads directly to our final conclusion, concerning multilevel governance.

We have observed that for these business associations and for firms, European representation and activities have become more important. But we also show that these European investments in representation, although by no means futile, are still small and that they supplement and not replace or devalue national ones. Dutch business interest associations are not Europeanized in the sense that they become less interested in their national contacts and affiliations or lose their Dutch identity, for instance the cultural mix of compromise, group meetings, individualism and self-reliance. Rather than taking their members' interests to Brussels and blending in a new European compromise, Dutch business associations tend to fit in Europe for their own sake and also seek ways to support and, if need be, mobilize their members and their governments at home.

Appendix: list of abbreviations and names of business associations

European, peak level

ERT	European Round Table of Industrialists
UEAPME	European Association of Craft and Small and Medium-sized Enterprises
UNICE	Union of Industrial and Employers' Confederation of Europe

European, sectoral level

BFEU	Banking Federation of the European Union
CEDED	European Committee of Manufacturers of Domestic Equipment
CEFIC	European Chemical Industry Council
FIEC	European Construction Industry Federation
ORGALIME	European Federation of Engineering
WEM	Employers' Organization of the Metal Trades in Europe

Dutch, peak level

VNO-NCW	Vereniging van Nederlandse Ondernemingen – Nederlands Christelijke Werkgeversvereniging (General Confederation of Dutch Businesses)
MKB-Nederland	Midden- en Kleinbedrijf – Nederland (Confederation of Small and Medium-sized Businesses)
LTO-Nederland	Land- en Tuinbouworganisatie Nederland (Farmers' and Horticulture Association)

Dutch, cross-sectoral level

AWVN	Algemene Werkgeversveeniging Nederland (General Employers' Association)

Dutch, sectoral level

AVBB	Algemeen Verbond voor het Bouwbedrijf (General Federation for the Construction Industry)
Bovag	Bovag (Association of Car Repair Shops and Stations)
COV	Centrale Organisatie voor de Vleessector (Central Organization for the Meat Industry)
FENIT	Federatie van Nederlandse Ondernemingen in de Informatietechnologie (Federation of Dutch IT Businesses)
FME-CWM	Federatie Metaal- en Electrotechnische Industrie/Centrum van Werkgevers in de Metaalindustrie (Federation of Metal and Electrotechnical Industry/Centre of Metal Industry Employers)
HBS	Bond van Handelaren en Bewerkers van Slachtproducten (Association of Traders and Slaughterhouses)
KHN	Koninklijke Horeca Nederland (Royal Dutch Association of Hotels, Restaurants and Cafés)
NEFARMA	Nederlandse Vereniging voor de Research-georiënteerde Farmaceutische Industrie (Dutch Association of Research-oriented Pharmaceutical Industry)

NEVI	Nederlandse Vereniging van Inkoopmanagement (Association of Procurement and Purchasing Management)
NICT	Nederland-ICT (Dutch ICT-Platform)
NOBOL	Nederlandse Organisatie van Bureaus voor Outplacement en Loopbaanbegeleiding (Dutch Organization of Outplacement and Career Management Bureaus)
NVB	Nederlandse Vereniging van Banken (Dutch Association of Banks)
NVOB	Nederlands Verbond van Ondernemers in de Bouwnijverheid (Association of Small and Medium-size Construction Firms)
RNDT	Raad van de Nederlandse Detailhandel (Council of Dutch Retailers)
TLN	Transport en Logistiek Nederland (Transport Sector Association)
VDF	Vereniging van Drogisterij- en Filiaalbedrijven (Association of Chemists and Related Businesses)
VGB	Vereniging Grootbedrijf in de Bouw (Association of Large Construction Firms)
VLEHAN	Vereniging van Leveranciers van Huishoudelijke Artikelen in Nederland (Association of Domestic Equipment Suppliers)
VNCI	Vereniging van de Nederlandse Chemische Industrie (Association of Dutch Chemical Industry)

Notes

1 Fifteen Dutch firms made it into the FT 500 list of the world's largest companies of 2001, based on stock market valuation or market capitalization. Among European countries, the UK leads the FT 500 list with 41 firms, followed by France with 28 and Germany with 21. The Netherlands is followed by Switzerland (12), Italy (11) and Spain (6). Source: *Financial Times*, 10 May 2002.

2 Interview with the head of IR/HR Department at Philips, Eindhoven, 11 May 1999.

3 This statement would seem to have been falsified by the sudden advent of a radical anti-system and anti-immigrants party and the extraordinary success of that party in the general elections of 15 May 2002, nine days after the murder of its leader, Fortuyn. However, new elections on 22 January 2003, following the downfall of the Cabinet caused by the disintegration of the Fortuyn party, restored the usual larger parties to their former electoral fortunes. However, a strong populist sentiment has since characterized Dutch politics, causing much greater volatility and instability in the party system.

4 Interview with the author, Luxembourg, 23 September 1997.

5 Interviews reported in *The Economist*, in its Survey of The Netherlands, 4 May 2002.

6 The main source is Pyttersen's Almanac of 1981, 1991 and 2001. Van Waarden (1989) counted as many as 1,424 business interest associations, citing the same source and the Social Economic Council's Almanac of 1980. He did, however, include professional associations, foundations, study societies, Chambers of Commerce, regional and local associations and bodies under public law. It

would appear that this figure includes some 400 local or regional associations. On the basis of the register of the Chambers of Commerce it would appear that there were 1,129 business associations in 2001, including Foundations, but not counting local organizations (Schmidt *et al.* 2003: 35). It is unclear how many double counts that includes. Comparison with their results suggests that our count is rather complete except in the case of the collective sector and in business services where we may have underestimated business associability.

7 According to the Enterprise Statistic of the Netherlands Central Bureau of Statistics (CBS), counting all firms with at least one employee in 2000.

8 These estimates are confirmed by a recent study of sectoral business interest associations undertaken by the Berenschot Foundation, a private consultancy firm (Schmidt *et al.* 2003).

9 Interview at VNO-NCW headquarters, The Hague, 11 February 2000. VNO-NCW boasts some 1,300 specialists that can be counted on. Policies are prepared through some 100–150 committees and working parties in which representatives of affiliates and member firms actively participate. This is also seen as a way to demonstrate the importance of the organization to its members as a channel of information.

10 The survey was conducted in early 2000; a questionnaire was sent to 289 associations, for which the address and existence could be established, as recorded in the EOI database. The design of the questionnaire and wording of the questions followed the survey of German, French and British associations by Kohler-Koch and her team (see Kohler-Koch and Quitkatt 1999). After two recalls, 103 associations sent back a completed questionnaire, which represents a response rate of 36 per cent.

11 Since many Dutch associations have set up special 'firms' for the purpose of service provision to members (see below), the revenue from services will not show up in the association's financial statement.

12 Interview MKB-Nederland, Delft, 29 February 2001.

13 Interview NVB, Amsterdam, 19 February 2001.

14 Interview VNO-NCW, The Hague, 11 February 2000.

15 Interview General Construction Federation AVBB, The Hague, 7 March 2001.

16 Other associations (47 per cent) and government bodies (46 per cent) are in second and third place as sources of information, far ahead of research (18 per cent) and management consulting (9 per cent).

17 Interview VNO-NCW, The Hague, 11 February 2000.

18 Interview AWVN, Haarlem, 21 February 2000.

19 Interview MKB-Nederland, Delft, 29 February 2000.

20 Interview MKB-Nederland, Delft, 29 February 2000. There appears to be a problem of membership heterogeneity (orientation towards the domestic or international sector), which is also felt in national lobbying, for instance with respect to fiscal and wage policy.

21 Interview FME-CWM, Zoetermeer, 28 February 2000.

22 Interview VLEHAN, Zoetermeer, 6 February 2000.

23 Interviews COV, Rijswijk, 7 February 2001; interview NEVI, Zoetermeer, 8 February 2001; interview NOBOL, Haarlem, 19 February 2001.

24 Interviews AWVN, Haarlem, 21 February 2000.

25 Interview KHN, Woerden, 6 March 2001. KHN negotiates the main collective agreement in the hotel and restaurant sector and is a very important interlocutor for politicians and unions. The organization is internally differentiated by sector and region. It has an extensive committee structure and is supported by some 1,500 local officials.

26 Interview with the international affairs and social affairs officials at VNO-NCW, The Hague, 11 February 2000 and 19 February 2002.
27 Interview NVB, Amsterdam, 19 February 2001.
28 Interview AVBB, The Hague, 7 March 2001.

References

Bruggeman, J. and Camijn, A. (1999) *Ondernemers verbonden. 100 jaar centrale ondernemersorganizaties in Nederland*, Wormer: Immerc.

Buitelaar, W. L. and van den Toren, J. P. (1999) *Tijd in beweging. De AWVN 1919–1999*, Haarlem: AWVN.

Coleman, W. D. (1997) 'Associational Governance in a Globalizing Era: Weathering the Storm', in J. R. Hollingsworth and R. Boyer (eds) *Contemporary Capitalism. The Embeddedness of Institutions*, Cambridge MA: Cambridge University Press, pp. 127–153.

Crouch, C. J. (1995) 'Reconstructing Corporatism? Organized Decentralization and Other Paradoxes', in C. Crouch and F. Traxler (eds) *Organized Industrial Relations: What Future?* Avebury: Aldershot, pp. 311–330.

Hall, P. and Soskice, D. (2001) 'An Introduction to Varieties of Capitalism', in P. Hall and D. Soskice (eds) *Varieties of Capitalism. The Institutional Foundations of Comparative Advantage*, Oxford: Oxford University Press, pp. 1–68.

Heemskerk, E., Mokken, R. and Fennema, M. (2002) 'From Stakeholders to Shareholders: Networks of Banks and Industry in the Netherlands', University of Amsterdam, research paper (unpublished).

Helmers, H. M., Mokken, R. J., Plijter, R. C. and Stokman, F. N. (1975) *Graven naar Macht*, Amsterdam: Van Gennep.

Hen, P. E. de (1980) 'Aspecten van het Nederlandse industriebeleid sinds 1931', *Economisch-Statistische Berichten* 3271: 1001–1005.

Hollingsworth, J. R., Schmitter, P. C. and Streeck, W. (1994) 'Capitalism, Sectors, Institutions and Performance', in J. R. Hollingsworth, P. C. Schmitter and W. Streeck (eds) *Governing Capitalist Economies: Performance and Control of Economic Sectors*, New York: Oxford University Press, pp. 3–16.

Kapteyn, P. (1996) *The Stateless Market. The European Dilemma of Integration and Civilization*, London: Routledge.

Katzenstein, P. J. (1985) *Small States in World Markets*, Ithaca NY: Cornell University Press.

Kohler-Koch, B. (1999) 'The Evolution and Transformation of European Governance', in B. Kohler-Koch and R. Eising (eds) *The Transformation of Governance in the European Union*, London: Routledge, pp. 14–35.

Kohler-Koch, B. and Quittkat, C. (1999) 'Intermediation of Interests in the European Union', Working Paper 9/1999, Mannheim: Mannheimer Zentrum für Europäische Sozialforschung.

Metze, M. (1999) *Let's Talk Dutch Now: Harmonie in de polder: uitvinding of erfenis?* Amsterdam: Arbeiderspers.

Middlemas, K. (1995) *Orchestrating Europe. The Informal Politics of European Union 1973–1995*, Glasgow: Fontana.

Nobelen, P. W. M. (1983) *Ondernemersorganizaties in beweging*, Deventer: Kluwer.

OECD (1993) *The Netherlands. Economic Survey*, Paris: Organization for Economic Co-operation and Development.

Quitkatt, C. (2002) 'Les organizations professionelles françaises: Europeanization de l'intermediation des interets?' *Politique Européennes* 7: 66–95.

Ruigrok, W. and van Tulder, R. (1995) *The Logic of International Restructuring*, London: Routledge.

Schendelen, M. P. C. M. van (2002) *Machiavelli in Brussels. The Art of Lobbying the EU*, Amsterdam: Amsterdam University Press.

Schmidt, D., van den Toren, J. P. and de Wal, M. (2003) *Ondernemende brancheorganizaties. Balanceren tussen belangen*, Assen: van Gorcum en VNO-NCW.

Schmitter, P. C. and Streeck, W. (1981; 2nd edn 1999) 'The Organization of Business Interests: A Research Design to Study the Associative Action of Business in the Advanced Industrial Societies of Europe', IIM/LMP Discussion paper 81-3, Berlin: Wissenschaftszentrum; reprint as Discussion paper, no. 99-3, Cologne, Max Planck Institute for the Study of Societies.

Streeck, W. and Schmitter, P. C. (1991) 'From National Corporatism to Transnational Pluralism: Organized Interests in the Single European Market', *Politics and Society*, 19: 133–164.

Streeck, W. and Visser, J. (1998) 'An Evolutionary Dynamic of Trade Union Systems', MPIfG Discussion Papers, no. 98-4, Cologne: Max Planck Institute for the Study of Societies.

Verwey, W. (1994) 'HDTV and Philips', in R. Pedler and M. P. C. M. van Schendelen (eds) *Lobbying the EU*, Aldershot: Dartmouth, pp. 23–40.

Visser, J. (1998) 'Two Cheers for Corporatism. One for the Market', *British Journal of Industrial Relations*, 36 (2): 269–292.

Visser, J. and Hemerijck, A. (1997) *A Dutch Miracle, Job Growth, Welfare Reform and Corporatism in the Netherlands*, Amsterdam: Amsterdam University Press.

Visser, J. and Jongen, P. J. (1999) 'Institutions, Markets, Strategies and Labour Management in Dutch Banks', in J. Kitay, M. Regini and M. Baethge (eds) *From Tellers to Sellers. Industrial Relations and Human Resource Management in the Banking Industry*, Cambridge MA: MIT Press, pp. 255–286.

Waarden, F. van (1989) *Organizatiemacht van belangenverenigingen. De ondernemersorganizaties in de bouwnijverheid als voorbeeld*, Amersfoort: Acco.

Wilts, A. (2001) 'Europeanization and Means of Interest Representation by National Business Associations', *European Journal of Industrial Relations* 7 (3): 269–286.

Zahn, E. (1984) *Das unbekannte Holland*, Berlin: Siedler Verlag.

3 Institutional filters and path dependency

The impact of Europeanization on Swiss business associations

Hanspeter Kriesi

National systems of business interest associations have been undergoing a profound change in recent years.[1] This change has been explained by three main factors – globalization, liberalization of the national economies and changes in social partnership (Zervudacki 1999: 151). According to many observers, globalization has played the most important role. In its simplest sense, this widely used term refers to 'the widening, deepening and speeding up of global interconnectedness' (Held *et al.* 1999: 14). It implies, first and foremost, 'a stretching of social, political and economic activities across frontiers such that events, decisions and activities in one region of the world can come to have significance for individuals and communities in distant regions of the globe'. It can be understood as a master process of 'denationalization' (Beisheim *et al.* 1999; Zürn 1998), i.e. as an encompassing process which gives rise to the dissolution and unbundling of national borders (Ruggie 1993). In the economic realm, the term refers to a cluster of processes which include the growing intensity of international trade and the emergence of global markets, the liberalization of the international financial system and the growth of multinational firms and global production networks. In the European context, globalization primarily takes the form of Europeanization – or, more precisely, European integration. For the purposes of this chapter, I consider European integration to be part and parcel of the more encompassing phenomenon of globalization.

The processes involved in this global phenomenon have modified the identity of the business community, raised new expectations among its members, given it a new ideological impulse, changed the addressees of its interventions and called into question the nature and intensity of its involvement in social partnerships. By fundamentally modifying the role and the place of the national state, and by increasing international market competition, globalization has critically affected the business interest associations (BIAs). Globalization has introduced a new topography of power within the national political space – one which has transformed the role of interest associations in general and of BIAs in particular (Zervudacki 1999: 151–155; von Alemann 2000: 5). However, as Kohler-Koch (1997: 52) has pointed out, the specific form that this transformation takes remains 'dependent on the persistence of national institutional constellations'. The future, as she maintains, is path-dependent, in the sense that the process of globalization – or, more specifically, of Europeanization – will take different shapes and create different types of entities in different national settings. If external factors are having an increasingly important influence on internal political processes and on the options available in national politics, this does not mean that there is a direct causal link between the development of the external context and the configuration of power and the political results within a given national context. As Mach (1999: 423) has suggested, domestic factors function as filters or mediators between the external environment and internal politics. In my presentation of the current transformation of the system of Swiss BIAs, I will concentrate here on these internal filters and mediators. In the first section, I shall briefly describe the recent events of restructuring to the extent that they have become known to me. In the next two sections, I shall give an account of the domestic factors which are currently changing the BIAs' logic of membership as well as their logic of influence. Finally, I shall suggest some general conclusions.

Restructuring Swiss BIAs

By weakening the nation state and reinforcing international market competition, the process of globalization is profoundly changing the environment of the BIAs: it weakens the forces associated with the logic of influence and reinforces those associated with the logic of membership. On the one hand, as the nation state loses part of its relevance for the business community, the BIAs – major interlocutors of the nation state – are losing a substantial amount of the external support which used to reinforce them with respect to their members. On the other hand, as international market competition increases, some of the BIAs' members – especially the large multinational firms operating on the global marketplace – are increasingly unwilling to accept the constraints of the national policy networks in which their BIAs are major participants and by the rules of which their BIAs are obliged to play. In other words, globalization reduces the dependency of business – especially of large firms – on its interest associations and reinforces the position of (large) firms with regard to the BIAs representing their interests. In many countries, the business community has responded to these changes by restructuring its system of BIAs in two ways: one concerning the sectoral level, the other concerning the level of peak associations. At the level of *sectoral* or *territorial membership associations*, the key words are 're-engineering' and 'downsizing' (Zervudacki 1999: 150). The sectoral and territorial associations are being transformed under the leadership of some key personalities in the business community – personalities who mainly come from the highly dynamic, export-oriented sectors that have felt the competitive pressure of globalization most directly.

In Switzerland, efforts at sectoral restructuring began in the *chemical and pharmaceutical industry*. The chemical and pharmaceutical industry is not only a highly dynamic sector of the Swiss business community, it is also its most internationalized sector, and the one that is best organized at the international level. The decisive factor in explaining why restructuring started precisely in this sector and not in any other may, however, have been its composition – the fact that it is highly concentrated, composed of only relatively few firms and controlled by leading multinational companies (Novartis, Hoffmann-La Roche, Clariant). In autumn 1998, the board of the sectoral association of the chemical industry (a member of the Vorort – the Swiss Federation of Commerce and Industry) cut its operational budget for 1999 by 50 per cent (i.e. by SFr2.5 million) and announced the dismissal of more than half of its 28 collaborators.[2] This critical step had its origins in a certain irritation and discontent with national politics on the part of the member firms. The members perceived their association as being too close to national politics. To formulate it pointedly, they had the impression that the association had become the deputy of the state. In their view, the purpose of the association was to improve 'the dialogue between politics and society'[3] – to close what some leading personalities perceived as an increasing gap between politics and the public on the one hand, and politics and the business community on the other. More specifically, the association had (a) to focus its activities (which have always concentrated on lobbying) on issues deemed essential for the sector – i.e. on issues which have direct effects on the costs and benefits of its members – and (b) to strictly adhere to the principles of a liberal market economy. It also needed to change its mode of operation from that of a paper-producing organization to that of an Internet-based communicator. In addition to a concentration on essentials and a more pronounced reliance on new technologies (especially the Internet), the reduction of resources also implied a more intensive involvement of the members of the board in the association's operations. The board created four working groups composed of board members: one each for the areas of economic policy, environment–security–technology, pharma and public relations. In other words, the members of the board became more involved in 'issue-management'. As a consequence, the board now bases its crucial decisions on the propositions of the working groups. The communication between the working groups and the association's staff is facilitated by e-mail. The reconfigured infrastructure of the association constitutes the basis for a possible future expansion of its activities. Such an expansion will be project-specific.

Not much later, the *machine industry* – which, together with the chemical industry, is the most important sector of the Swiss economy – also got involved in restructuring. In this case, the issue was, above all, one of the concentration of the dual structure of the industry's representation. Its two associations – the employers' association (ASM) and the industrial association (VSM) – created a new organization (SWISSMEM) and merged their boards and their office staffs. The president of the new common board declared that the new structure had two advantages: it helped to reduce the number of meetings (for those who had been members of both boards before), and the industry was now speaking with a single voice.[4] The two associations did not merge completely, however. The old associations continue to exist as formal constructions.

'Concentration' and 'unification' are the key words with regard to the restructuring of the *peak associations*. Under pressure from the imperatives of international competition, and as a result of the increasing importance of regulatory policies handed down from the supranational level, internal pressure from the labour unions is diminishing, and the dual structure of the national system of BIAs has been losing much of its importance. As a result, the dualistic structure of the peak association is being replaced by a unified structure (Zervudacki 1999: 182). The British Confederation of British Industry (CBI) and the Dutch VNO adopted such a structure as early as 1965 and 1968, respectively. Other countries have followed. In Germany, however, a merger of the three existing peak associations – Bundesverband der Deutschen Industrie (BDI), Bundesvereinigung Deutscher Arbeitgeberverbände (BDA) and Deutscher Industrie – und Handelstag (DIHT) – has not yet succeeded, although the three associations have joined their headquarters under a single roof in Berlin. Belatedly, the Swiss business community has joined the movement as well.

Let me briefly recall the point of departure before restructuring began. Swiss BIAs have traditionally been grouped into four subsystems, each headed by an encompassing peak association: the Vorort, the Union of Swiss Employers' Associations (UPS), the Union of Swiss Small Businesses and Trade (USAM), and the Union of Swiss Farmers (USP).[5] The first two have typically organized the export-oriented sectors, while the latter two have represented the domestic sectors and the smaller firms. The two subsystems representing the export-oriented sectors and the larger firms (which are not quite identical, given that many smaller firms are also engaged in production for this sector, or are linked to it via subcontracting) have traditionally operated via a division of labour: the Vorort represented the economy in matters of economic and fiscal policy – especially with respect to international trade policy – while the employers' association dealt with social policy and labour market policy, including relations with the unions. In addition, the business community has created an organization specializing in public relations – one which is not itself a peak association, but which is responsible for managing its political campaigns: the Society for the Promotion of the Swiss Economy (SDES).

As in the German case, the peak associations had already been concentrated in the same building some years before, but the idea was now to merge them outright. A small group of leading personalities from the Vorort and the SDES, which had constituted itself without an official mandate, prepared the merger. It was probably no accident that at the time, both the president of the Vorort and the president of the SDES came from big chemical multinationals. This group did not include any representatives from the peak employers' association. The motives behind the restructuring plans were similar to those which were already driving the restructuring of the sectoral associations: the closer cooperation was intended to allow the business community to speak to the public and the political authorities with a single voice and to increase its organizational efficiency. The president of the Vorort argued that business needed to regain the confidence of the citizens by clearly explaining the economic realities to them: 'Today, the problems are more complex and more diverse. The majoritarian [*sic*] coalitions do no longer form automatically, the economic interests of the parliamentarians diversify more and more. We need to make a greater effort of persuasion.'[6] The problem, as he perceived it, was that the message provided by the business community was too vague and often contradictory. The plan prepared by the small group was leaked to the press before the staff and the president of the UPS had been informed about it, which got it off to a very bad start in the peak employers' association. When the members of the board of the UPS finally discussed the plan in September 1999, they rejected it almost unanimously: only two of the board's 32 members (the representatives of the machine industry and the chemical industry) voted in its favour.

The opposition in the UPS was not only motivated by the clumsy management of the process by the responsible working group, but it also reflected more substantial divergences. First of all, there are differences between the Vorort and the UPS with regard to representation: their memberships overlap, but they are by no means identical. The global vision of the Vorort is not necessarily the same as that of the smaller firms represented by some of the associations in the UPS. These smaller firms are afraid of being overpowered by the large firms which dominate the Vorort and the SDES.[7] Second, from the point of view of the UPS, it was by no means clear whether it was to the advantage of the business community to speak with only one voice. Two coordinated voices – 'marching separately but striking jointly' – might have a greater political impact than a single one, especially given the alleged current practice on the part of federal authorities of ignoring the political weight of the proposals submitted in pre-parliamentarian consultation procedures. Third, the UPS pointed out that internal consensus building would be more difficult in the merged association. The merged peak association would have no less than 170 member associations (59 associations from the UPS plus 130 associations from the Vorort, with 20 overlapping memberships). Fourth, the influence of the smaller member associations belonging to the UPS would greatly diminish in the merged association. Finally, financial considerations also played a role. The three associations had entirely incompatible contribution systems: the UPS was financed by a percentage fee on the payroll of the firms represented by the member associations; contributions to the Vorort were based on individual negotiations with each member association and did not follow any coherent criteria; and the SDES was financed exclusively through donations from its 2,500 individual member firms. Given that at present, the machine industry is by far the largest member of the UPS, this industry finances almost half of its budget. The smaller associations of the UPS were afraid that in the case of a merger, they would have to take up a larger financial burden.

Finally, in September 2000,[8] the Vorort and the SDES merged under the new name of 'economiesuisse'. Following the model of the merger between the ASM and the VSM, their staffs (20 collaborators for the Vorort and 40 for the SDES) and their boards merged, while formally, the two organizations continue to exist. The obstacle to a complete merger was the fact that no common solution could be found for the financing of the merged organizations. In other words, the separate organizations continue to exist only as instruments to collect contributions. This is a transitional solution. In time, the UPS (12 collaborators) may also join the merger, and the problem of financing the new peak association (with a current global budget of about SFr25 million) will most likely be solved as well. The outcome will depend on the sensitivity for internal associational democracy on the part of a few key personalities.

The logic of membership

If the efforts at restructuring result from the reinforcement of the logic of membership at the expense of the logic of influence, they also serve to stabilize the new relationship between the two logics. But as far as the representation of business interests is concerned, the logic of membership is not without problems of its own. As a result of the ongoing structural transformation of the Swiss economy, the membership of the BIAs has become more heterogeneous and less representative of the economy as a whole. First of all, *concentration processes* have transformed the structure of the Swiss economy to introduce a greater amount of heterogeneity among its firms. These processes have created very large enterprises such as Nestlé (in the food industry), Novartis and Roche (in the chemical and pharmaceutical industry), ABB (the Swedish–Swiss key enterprise in the machine industry) and UBS and Crédit Suisse (in banking). These enterprises have become world players with preoccupations of their own, which are very different from the traditional concerns of most Swiss firms. This problem of heterogeneity varies according to sector. It is probably more important in the machine industry and in employers' associations in general than in the chemical industry.[9] In the chemical industry, the problem is attenuated by its technical homogeneity and by the close links between smaller firms and multinationals among the 200 members of the sectoral association. Although genetic engineering and biotechnology have introduced new differentiations of interest into the sector, the different firms within the sector are still rather similar technologically. If larger firms cover larger varieties of products than smaller firms, within a given variety, their products are rather similar. Moreover, the smaller firms are linked to the larger ones through subcontracting and outsourcing. Therefore, they are all affected by the same pieces of legislation.

Changes in the international economic context have contributed to the internal heterogeneity of the Swiss business community as well. They have done so indirectly, by weakening the internal pressure on business exerted by the labour unions: given the weakness of the unions, the need to demonstrate unity has decreased considerably. But they have also contributed to heterogeneity in a more direct way: in Switzerland, the groups which had to be compensated for the country's integration into world markets have traditionally included not only the social partners represented by the labour unions, as Katzenstein (1985) maintains, but also farmers, small businesses and trades. These conservative groups, which are mainly oriented towards the domestic markets, had traditionally benefited from the 'selective protectionism' of what Mach (2000) calls Switzerland's 'national-conservative' version of 'democratic corporatism'. Under pressure brought on by the changes in the international environment in the 1990s, this kind of compensation has come under increasing attack from the neo-liberal forces which dominate the export-oriented sectors. As a result, a divide has been opening up between the domestically oriented sectors represented by the USP, the USAM – and, at least in part, the UPS – on the one hand, and the export oriented sectors represented by the restructured peak association, 'economiesuisse' on the other.[10]

One indication of the increasing heterogeneity of interests in the business community is its division on the issue of the recent liberalization of the domestic markets – and, most notably, cartel legislation (Mach 2000), where the USAM opposed a reform which was supported by the Vorort – as well as on a number of issues recently submitted to popular referenda: projects for the financing of the new railway tunnels through the Alps (1998), the introduction of an ecological tax on trucks (1998) and the promotion of housing ownership (1999). The Vorort eventually sided with the supporters of the first two projects, but important minorities within the Swiss business communities mobilized strongly against them. Thus, the UPS and the USAM opted against the tax on trucks. The USAM remained undecided with respect to the financing of the railway tunnels, torn as it was between the construction sector (in favour) and the trucking firms (against), and the UPS did not take a stance. In the case of the promotion of housing ownership, the Vorort was undecided, the UPS did not take a stance and the USAM supported the initiative of the homeowners' association. In the agriculture sector in particular, the division between the interests of different categories of farmers has led to the creation of oppositional associations – the VKMB, the Swiss German association for the defence of small and medium-sized farmers, and its French-speaking equivalent, the UPS (Union des Producteurs Suisses).

In addition to increasing heterogeneity, the processes of sectoral transformation have diminished the *representative quality* of the BIAs. Deindustrialization and tertiarization are eroding their traditional basis.

Although the Vorort and the UPS have always organized branches from both industry and services, there are some exceptions from the tertiary sector which do not yet belong to these two peak associations.[11] Moreover, the rapidly growing new economy (Internet), the recently privatized public sector (in particular, the telecommunications companies Swisscom, Sunrise and Orange) and the parastate sector (Swiss) are not organized into any subsystem. Finally, the largest Swiss employer – Migros, a retail store chain (with 80,000 employees) – is not a member of any BIA either. However, just like the BIAs in other countries (Zervudacki 1999: 247), the Swiss BIAs do not seem to be suffering from a membership crisis. Firms continue to adhere to the BIAs, mainly because they still *identify* with them to some extent, and certainly because they have a selective incentive to do so: they receive quality *services* from them. For the regional and sectoral BIAs, services to their members play a crucial and probably increasing role.

Take the example of the Chamber of Commerce in Geneva:[12] It provides general business services (promotion of members, business introductions, VAT recovery, electronic signature registration and certification, export document services and issuing of ATA carnets, arbitration), counselling (help in starting a business, legal advice, contracts, labour law, administrative and tax problems) and business information (mailing lists, general economic and legal information, statistics, information on customs procedures and tariffs, trade agreements and foreign markets) for its approximately 1,400 members. To give a concrete example of the creative development of the service function of regional BIAs: most recently, the Geneva Chamber of Commerce negotiated a contract with one of the new private telecommunications companies for the preferential treatment of its members, allowing its members to reduce their telecommunications bills by up to 40 per cent.[13] Another example is provided by the FSP – the *peak employers' association* in Geneva. The services provided to its 14,000 member firms and 102 member associations are largely complementary to those provided by the Chamber of Commerce. Most importantly, this peak association runs the secretariat of its member associations (15 employees) and the social insurance institutions (100 employees) of the Genevan economy. In addition, it offers legal advice, courses and seminars on legal and tax matters, services for the payment of salaries, an information service about Europe, a documentation centre, its own publications (including a weekly with a circulation of 20,000 copies) and conference rooms, as well as an excellent restaurant (important for its socializing function). It is important to note that cartel functions no longer seem to play any significant role for either of the two organizations.

The logic of influence

The irritation and discontent of leading figures in the Swiss business community with their peak BIAs not only led to the restructuring efforts described above, but are also at the root of a spectacular lobbying initiative taken at the beginning of the 1990s by a group composed of chief executive officers (CEOs) from key enterprises in the export-oriented sector and influential academic economists. Preoccupied with Swiss competitiveness in world markets, these key actors launched a campaign for the liberalization of the Swiss home market (see Mach 1999a: 427). Instead of passing through the Vorort, however, they published a 'White Book' formulating a programme for a neo-liberal reform of Swiss economic and social policy, which included three aspects (Leutwiler *et al.* 1991): liberalization of the domestic markets, integration into the EU and the reform of fiscal and social policies. Their neo-liberal reform programme was addressed directly to the federal government and to the general public, since the group felt that it was no longer adequately represented by the Vorort.[14] This is not to say that large firms have chosen to dispense with the lobbying efforts of their BIAs altogether. In fact, the creation of an informal pressure group was quite an exceptional step. In formal pre-parliamentarian consultation procedures, the large firms continue to operate through their BIAs, and do not write statements of their own. The central figures in the Swiss business community still consider it very important to speak with a single voice.

The informal pressure group achieved unmitigated procedural success, since the federal government subsequently created a working group composed of seven persons and directed by one of the authors of the White Book (David de Pury, ABB). The working group formulated 33 propositions for the 'revitalization of the Swiss economy', which were immediately taken up by four motions introduced by the bourgeois parties in the Federal Assembly. After the failure of the vote on the EEA (European Economic Area) in December 1992, the government launched a programme for the liberalization of the Swiss economy in January 1993, which essentially adopted the propositions formulated by the authors of the White Book. In 1995, these authors published a second White Book outlining – from their point of view – the mixed results of the implementation of their programme and formulating additional propositions to complement their original ones (de Pury *et al.* 1995). As we have already observed, this programme – most notably the liberalization of the domestic markets – clearly goes against the vested interests of some of the domestic branches of the Swiss economy.

The perception by crucial members of the Swiss business community that their voice is less heard than it used to be is, however, not only the result of some deficiency in the mode of operation and the internal structure of their interest representation. Nor does it simply reflect the structural transformation of the economy. There are other factors which contribute to this perception and which have to do with the changing logic of influence. Among these factors, I will mention at least five here; (a) some recent successes of the labour movement, (b) the increasing number of actors in the system of interest intermediation and the shifting of issue-specific alliances, (c) the transformation of the bourgeois camp in the party system, (d) the political consequences of the internal divisions and (e) the rising influence of the media on politics.

At first glance, the fact that the business community has the impression that it is losing influence in domestic politics seems rather strange, given that its political clout has been demonstrated by the success of important elements of the neo-liberal programme launched by some of its chief exponents, and given that its traditional opponent, the *labour movement* was badly hit by a decade of stagnation in the Swiss economy in the 1990s. Overall, the Swiss unions lost members throughout the nineties. In addition, the percentage of employees covered by collective wage agreements in the private sector is comparatively low (50 per cent) by international standards (Bonoli and Mach 2000: 137), and these agreements lost in substance with regard to the determination of wage levels (although not in other respects). Swiss industrial relations had always been rather decentralized, but the global tendency towards further decentralization in this domain has also made itself felt in Switzerland. With the increasing latitude of the member firms, the role of their social partners, employers' associations and unions have all diminished in Switzerland as well.[15] Moreover, as Mach (1999a) has observed, the division between employees' associations and unions for blue collar workers allowed for the emergence of the type of 'cross-class flexibility coalitions between firms producing high quality goods for fragmented and volatile international markets and groups of highly skilled workers enjoying favourable market positions' which had played such an important role in Scandinavia (see Iversen 1996). In Switzerland, there has always been a status division between employees and workers, but it acquired additional significance in the 1990s. Although they also lost members, the major employees' associations gained a pivotal position in the collective negotiations that took place in the nineties. Thus, in the machine industry, the differences between the FTMH (blue collar workers) and the VSAM (employees) with regard to the reduction of working time reached their peak during the 1998 negotiations.

Diminished in their role as social partners in industrial relations, the unions responded by increasingly turning to the legislative process in order to improve their chances of success. It is in this way that they achieved some important successes in the 1990s. Thus, the unions made their support of the bilateral treaty with the EU – a treaty which the Swiss economy badly wanted – dependent on the adoption of collateral domestic measures, i.e. they used the leverage they gained through European regulation policies to push through important pieces of labour legislation designed to strengthen their position in industrial relations. These measures were of three types:

- A law on the dispatching of foreign workers. This law guarantees that firms pay the usual regional salaries to workers who are dispatched to work in Switzerland for a limited period of time (very important for the construction sector and related branches);

- A modification of the labour law: in branches without collective agreements, the government has the authority to fix minimum salaries for certain professions, should abuses occur. In Parliament, the definition of the term 'abuse' gave rise to a major conflict between union and business representatives, which was finally decided through an intervention on the part of the minister of the economy, who pleaded for a flexible formulation favouring the unions' point of view;
- A modification of the law on the collective agreements: in branches where collective agreements already fix minimum salaries, the government obtains the right to extend the scope of these collective agreements to include the whole sector – i.e. including unorganized firms – if the density rate of both the unions and the employers' associations in the branch reaches at least 30 per cent. Again, the struggle over the percentage that the law would require was very intense in Parliament; and again, the solution that was finally adopted (30 per cent instead of the 50 per cent demanded by business) favoured the unions.

After a series of significant defeats in the early 1990s, the unions also scored two substantial victories in direct democratic procedures: by way of a referendum, they succeeded in blocking both the first version of the revised labour law in 1996 and a modification of unemployment insurance in 1997. More generally, as Bonoli (1999) argues convincingly, the institution of the referendum makes policies of welfare state retrenchment quite difficult in Switzerland. Measures of retrenchment, which the business community tries to impose, only become possible if they are combined with improvements for specific groups. Thus, the 10th revision of the Swiss pension scheme combined a measure of retrenchment (increasing the retirement age for women from 62 to 64) with a specific concession for women (introducing the educational bonus and the splitting of pensions for married couples).

The influence of the business community is further restricted by the *multiplication of relevant actors in the domain of economic policy* (Mach 1999a: 429ff.): (a) by exerting pressure for the adaptation of Swiss legislation to meet European standards, the European Union is playing an increasing role in Swiss national economic policy making, even though Switzerland is not an EU member (the famous 'autonomous implementation of EU legislation'); (b) by formulating precise recommendations on behalf of national governments, international institutions such as the OECD or the IMF play an increasing role in the definition of national economic policies; (c) through their applied research, publications and direct recommendations, certain economists at Swiss universities and private consulting firms also have an increasing influence on the public decision-making process and, last but not least, (d) thanks to their mobilizing capacity, newly institutionalized actors from the new social movements – especially from the ecology movement – are increasingly interfering with policy making in domains that are of particular interest for the business community. The ecology movement has had a considerable impact on transportation policy, research policy and energy policy – domains of great interest to the business community. With the adoption of the Initiative of the Alps in 1994, it scored a resounding success, which forced the government to adapt its transportation policy to ecological constraints. Its initiative against genetic engineering – which posed a major threat to the chemical and pharmaceutical industry – was voted down after a protracted and (for the business community) exceptionally expensive campaign in 1998.

Still, the issue was not settled, and the ecologists continue to influence legislation on the subject. In energy policy, the configuration of power is gradually shifting in favour of a 'pro-ecology coalition' and against the business-dominated 'pro-growth coalition' (see Kriesi and Jegen 2000, 2001). The adoption of the initiative imposing a moratorium on nuclear energy in 1990 demonstrated the increasing political clout of the ecologists. Since then, the 'pro-ecology coalition' has become strong enough to have passed an ecological tax on energy in Parliament.

The gradual strengthening of the 'pro-ecology coalition' in the domain of infrastructural policies is a result of shifting alliances. For a long time, the pro-ecology camp has been firmly allied to the left. More recently, however, it has benefited from a new alliance with cantonal governments from the Alpine region, some of which are fed up with the nuisance of transit traffic, and most of which (the Alpine OPEC) are discovering that the electricity they produce is a sustainable, 'clean' source of energy. In addition, the movement has also made inroads into the camp of the bourgeois parties, where it has found some 'defectors' who have played a crucial brokering role in the protracted parliamentary debates on energy policy. The business community has responded with an intensive political campaign. Thus, in spite of the increasing clout of the pro-ecology coalition, the debate on the ecological tax finally ended with a resounding success for the business community: after an intensive campaign led by the major BIAs, the proposition was voted down in a popular referendum in September 2000.

The *transformation of the bourgeois camp of the party system*: the ties between the major parties of the centre right – the liberal Free Democrats (PRD), the Christian Democrats (PDC) and the conservative People's Party (UDC) – and the Swiss business community have traditionally been very close (Kriesi 1980, 1998): The members of Parliament who belong to these parties hold large numbers of seats on the boards of the major Swiss corporations. Moreover, some staff members of important BIAs and employees of major corporations simultaneously hold seats in Parliament for these very same parties, and large firms rely on members of the national Parliament to represent their interests.[16] Although the three bourgeois parties broadly adhere to similar positions in economic and social policy, they are increasingly divided on the crucial question of the Swiss response to European integration: a 'pro-European' faction (majorities of the Christian Democrats and Free Democrats) is opposed by an 'anti-European' faction (led by the Swiss People's

Party, but joined by minorities of the other two major bourgeois parties). The Swiss People's Party, which has taken a national-populist turn since the early 1990s, has become the champion of the 'isolationists'. It campaigned against the Treaty on the European Economic Area in 1992, and ever since, it has been opposed to Swiss participation in the EU, the UN and NATO. This political programme has been paying off: the People's Party approximately doubled its share of the vote in the National Council in the 1990s (from 12 per cent to 23 per cent) and became the strongest bourgeois party in the three largest Swiss German cantons and in the country as a whole. In other words, on the crucial issue of its integration into the European economy, the business community can no longer automatically rely on support from its traditional allies in the bourgeois camp. We might add an intriguing detail: the charismatic leader of the Swiss People's Party was, at the same time, the CEO of an important chemical industry firm, which he has represented on the board of the sectoral BIA for almost 20 years. His influence on that board was important but not central; however, it is interesting to note that as a politician and member of Parliament, he was fervently opposed to Switzerland's integration into the EU in general and to the bilateral treaty with the EU in particular, while the chemical industry clearly supported the bilateral treaty with the EU.

The *political consequences of the internal divisions within the business community*: These consequences are linked to the divisions within the party system and to the recent successes of the labour movement. They spell defeats in popular votes. The export sector lost the crucial vote on the Treaty on the European Economic Area in 1992, which a tiny majority of the population – but a substantial majority of the cantons – refused to accept. In all the other instances mentioned above, where the domestic sector (represented by either the USAM, the USP or both) opposed the export sector (represented by the Vorort and/or the UPS), it was the domestic sector which lost out in the vote. Overall, the domestic sector – both agriculture and small and medium-sized artisanal and industrial firms – has lost much of its traditionally very important influence in Swiss politics. Whereas in the 1970s, the USAM was capable of mobilizing a majority of Swiss voters against major reforms – such as fiscal reform (including the introduction of the VAT), territorial planning or the introduction of macroeconomic policy instruments – it has much less political clout nowadays. The farmers' peak association, the USP, is even more weakened. Against its resistance, agricultural reform has been imposed by a coalition of the federal administration and the export sector (Sciarini 1994), and voters no longer habitually accept the policy propositions of the farmers' associations.

Finally, the *rising influence of the media* has had a profound influence on the opportunity structure of the BIAs and on their mode of operating. Increasingly, success in politics depends upon one's success in the media. This implies that politics has to adapt to the conditions of the media (Kepplinger 1998: 161). The media are no longer the ready servants of politicians. They have moved from the periphery to the centre stage of the political process and submit politicians to journalists' criteria of success. Following their own rationale, the media prefer reporting on stars and spectacular events, and they do not hesitate to stage events accordingly. Politicians and those who wish to influence them have to adapt to this rationale. Political influence is increasingly taking an indirect route, passing through the public space and the public's reactions as measured by opinion surveys. This also means that an increasing number of issues are being brought onto the public stage – issues which in the past would never have been in the limelight.

It is true that the public's interest in politics has a rather superficial character. But even so, the public is no longer as docile as it was in the 'golden age'. It has become more volatile and more likely to react to short-term influences and personalities. This is a result of both the expansion of television and of the erosion of traditional social milieux and their corresponding party identifications. Those who succeed in the media arena accumulate resources which they can then put to good use in the parliamentary and administrative arenas, where the actual political decision making takes place. Public relations and political marketing have become increasingly important for the BIAs and, to a considerable extent, public communications have replaced negotiations in smoke-filled back rooms. Top politicians and business representatives turn increasingly to the media in order to address the public directly. The capacity to present themselves convincingly on television has become a crucial asset for key business leaders.

The increasing importance of the media has transformed the operation of the BIAs, not only in Switzerland. Lobbying is no longer limited to direct interventions with public authorities, but increasingly includes attempts to influence public opinion and to instrumentalize it in order to exert pressure on public authorities (Kollman 1998; Zervudacki 1999: 162, 175ff.). Thus, the director of the UPS maintains that he now spends approximately half of his time on public relations (working for and with the media). Using the example of the recent debate on security policy, he maintains that the point of view of the employers' association was much more effectively defended by an article in the Sunday press than by his lobbying efforts in Berne. Politicians are compulsive readers of the press (Kepplinger 1998: 145): They are interested in how they themselves are presented in the press, in what the burning issues are and in how the public reacts to these issues. From the point of view of the BIA, compared to lobbying in Berne, interventions in the media have the additional advantage of being visible to the organization's own members, who will then have the impression that the association is doing something on their behalf.

The business leaders who wished to restructure the peak associations were also motivated by the perception that the Vorort in particular did not sufficiently adapt to this new situation. Thus, one of them complained about the '*Vernehmlassungs*-mentality' (the mentality of public consultation) of the Vorort:[17] in the course of the federal government's consultation procedures, the Vorort was writing solid, thorough reports on behalf of the economy, the critic said, but it was not doing enough in symbolic politics, and it was not sufficiently present in the media, where it did not have a clear profile. Significantly, the informal group that launched the White Books on Swiss economic policy addressed itself directly to the media as well. More recently, the CEO of Crédit-Suisse, one of the two large Swiss banking corporations, prominently went to the press to state his views on the relationship between politics and the business community.[18] The Swiss business community's recent creation of a think tank ('Avenir Suisse') can also be interpreted in this context: Its think tank is intended to provide a thorough intellectual basis for the business community's political communications.

Conclusion

According to this analysis, the situation facing the Swiss BIAs is one of an increasingly pluralizing field of influence. On the one hand, the business community itself is pluralizing, and the BIAs are experiencing less solidarity among their membership than in the past. The trusting relationship which traditionally existed between the members and the leading representatives of the associations is no longer as firmly established as it used to be. Neo-liberalism has left its imprint on internal relations within the business community. Individual interests are put before the common good, the short term takes precedence over the long term, members often lack identification with the associations and personal involvement is becoming scarce. On the other hand, the traditionally closed circuits between the BIAs and public administration are opening up to the public space. New actors are introducing new types of alliances, and the cosy relationship between the bourgeois parties and the BIAs is becoming more strained. Twenty or 30 years ago, the director of the Vorort was considered to be something like the eighth member of the federal government, and the BIAs' influence in Swiss politics was absolutely crucial (see Kriesi 1980). Compared to their very advantageous position in the past, the BIAs' present situation in Switzerland is, indeed, more difficult.

As we have seen, the Swiss business community is attempting to tighten its structure with the intention of becoming more coherent and efficient. Whether the measures it is taking will allow it to attain these goals is questionable. First of all, if there is a lack of coherence, it has hardly been due to a lack of cooperation between the peak associations. Rather, it stems much more from the increasing heterogeneity between and within their member associations. This heterogeneity, in turn, has in no way disappeared as a result of the merger at the top. Second, the tightening of control over the associations by their members – and their insistence on the purity of their liberal market orientation – may not be the best strategy for increasing the business community's influence in Swiss politics. The CEOs of the large member firms are not necessarily very knowledgeable about how politics function in Switzerland, and their leadership style may be less adapted to Swiss politics than it is to the hierarchical structure of a large corporation. Given that an increasing number of CEOs of large Swiss firms are of foreign origin, this may be a particularly ill-advised strategy. The restructuring of the BIAs was directed by leaders of Swiss origin, but in the future it will be ever more difficult to find members of the boards of the BIAs who simultaneously hold key positions in the member firms, speak both German and French and have an idea of the style of Swiss politics. The CEOs who no longer trust their association's officials – who feel that these officials are too close to their political opponents and make overly large concessions to them – may discover that Swiss politics are more intractable than they had imagined. The insistence on ideological purity (the 'clarity of the message') may contribute to the polarization of Swiss politics, which in turn may serve to unite the business community, but which does not guarantee its success.

At first glance, these developments seem to be largely domestically determined and independent of globalization. Globalization only comes into play at one remove: it contributes (a) to the increasing internal heterogeneity of the business community and (b) to the division between the bourgeois parties; (c) it provides the weakened labour unions with external leverage; and (d) it contributes to the increasing number of relevant actors. It does not have an effect on the increasing role of the media. More generally, globalization is putting pressure on the Swiss political system to adapt. This pressure is of a more general nature and it clashes with the rhythm of Swiss politics, which is slow and has difficulties keeping pace with transformations in the international environment. This is one of the central complaints of the internationally oriented branches of the Swiss business community. Thus, the former CEO of Crédit Suisse, Lukas Mühlemann, wished to adapt the rhythm of politics to the rhythm of the economy.[19]

We should keep in mind that integration into world markets is nothing new for the Swiss business community (see Katzenstein 1985). Globalization and Europeanization have only accentuated and reinforced a situation which the Swiss business community has been used to for a long time. This community is well represented in the European BIAs, and its multinational firms are members of BIAs in the countries of their respective activities.[20] However, even for the most globalized among the Swiss industries – the chemical and pharmaceutical industry – Switzerland still constitutes a key location for production and, accordingly, for research.[21] Therefore, the national context is still of crucial importance, even for this sector. Traditionally, the negative internal repercussions of the Swiss business community's integration into the world markets have been compensated for by political concessions negotiated by its BIAs with the organizations of the labour movement, the partners representing the sectors producing for the home market and the political authorities. What seems to have changed now is the attitude of the CEOs of the major firms in the export-oriented sectors with regard to these compensations. Under the pressure of globalization, the price which has traditionally had to be paid to maintain favourable conditions for the internationally oriented business community in Switzerland seems to have become too high for them. Moreover, throughout the 1990s, they seemed to believe that they were in a position to impose conditions more favourable to themselves without having to pay a political price for it. As the (partial) successes of the unions in popular votes and the (more substantial) successes of the national-populist right in recent elections suggest, they may have been wrong on both counts. With the benefit of hindsight, it appears that they might have been even more wrong: some recent events in the Swiss business community – such as the 'grounding' of Swissair, the widely publicized excessive compensations for some celebrated members of a select group of these CEOs, and the difficulties experienced by the insurance industry and some major banks – have severely tarnished its public image. This image is a factor which is likely to constitute one of the major determinants of its political influence in the future.

Appendix: list of abbreviations

ASM	Arbeitgeberverband der Schweizer Maschinenindustrie (employers' association of the Swiss machine industry)
BDA	Bundesvereinigung Deutscher Arbeitgeberverbände
BDI	Bundesverband der Deutschen Industrie
CBI	Confederation of British Industry
DIHT	Deutscher Industrie- und Handelstag
FTMH	Fédération des travailleurs dans la métallurgie et l'horlogerie (major union in the machine industry sector)
SDES	Société pour la promotion de l'économie suisse (society for the promotion of the Swiss economy)
UBS	Union des banques suisses (largest Swiss bank)
USAM	Union suisse des arts et métiers (union of Swiss small businesses and trade)
UPS	Union patronale suisse (union of Swiss employers' associations)
USP	Union suisse des paysans (union of Swiss farmers)
VNO	Verbond van Nederlandse Ondernemingen
VSM	Verein Schweizerischer Maschinenindustrieller (industrial association of the Swiss machine industry)

Notes

1 The author would like to thank the representatives of the Swiss business interest associations who have provided him with the information that forms the basis of this essay. He would also like to thank Jelle Visser for his thoughtful comments.
2 *Neue Zürcher Zeitung* (NZZ), No. 216, 18 September 1998, p. 25.
3 www.sgci.ch.
4 *Le Temps*, Saturday 12 September 1998, p. 23.
5 I am using the French abbreviations.

6 *Le Temps*, Saturday 12 September 1998, p. 23.
7 Ibid.
8 NZZ, No. 216, Saturday/Sunday 16/17 September 2000, p. 23.
9 Concentration processes not only increase the problem of consensus building in the Swiss economy, they also reduce the resource base of the BIAs. Thus, mergers are typically accompanied by a reduction in the number of employees, which implies a reduction in contributions to the UPS, given that these contributions are based on the payroll of its member firms.
10 For a similar argument, see also Sciarini, Pascal 1992. 'La Suisse dans la négociation sur l'Espace économique européen: de la rupture à l'apprentissage', Annuaire suisse de science politique 32: 297–322.
11 The banking sector, which has traditionally been a member of the SDES, but not of the Vorort, is now a member of the merged peak association 'economiesuisse'.
12 Membership in Chambers of Commerce is not compulsory in Switzerland, which is why services are important for them to attract and keep members.
13 www.cci.ch/genève.
14 Fritz Leutwiler expressed himself accordingly in *Die Weltwoche*, 4 June 1992.
15 For the general trend, see Zervudacki (1999: 156).
16 Thus, an employee of Novartis is currently a member of the National Council for the Radical Party of the Canton of Basle-City, and the director of USAM is a member of the Council for the Radical Party of the Canton of Berne.
17 Heini Lippuner in the NZZ, 19 October 1999.
18 *Das Magazin/Tagesanzeiger*, 31 December 1999, pp. 40–43.
19 Ibid.
20 The Swiss chemical industry employs 66,000 people in Switzerland and 70,000 in other European countries.
21 The chemical industry only sells 2–3 per cent of its production on the home market, but Switzerland still accounts for about 50 per cent of its production value.

Bibliography

Alemann, U. von (2000) 'Vom Korporatismus zum Lobbyismus? Die Zukunft der Verbände zwischen Globalisierung, Europäisierung und Berlinisierung', *Politik und Zeitgeschichte* B26–27, 23, June 2000: 3–6.

Beisheim, M., Dreher, S., Walter, G., Zangl, B. and Zürn, M. (1999) *Im Zeitalter der Globalisierung? Thesen und Daten zur gesellschaftlichen und politischen Denationalisierung*, Baden-Baden: Nomos-Verlag.

Bonoli, G. (1999) 'La réforme de l'Etat social suisse: Contraintes institutionnelles et opportunités de changement', *Revue suisse de science politique* 5 (3): 57–78.

Bonoli, G. and Mach, A. (2000) 'Switzerland. Adjustment Politics Within Institutional Constraints', in F. W. Scharpf and V. A. Schmidt (eds) *Welfare and Work in the Open Economy*, Vol. II, Oxford: Oxford University Press, pp. 130–174.

Held, D., McGrew, A., Goldblatt, D. and Perraton, J. (1999) *Global Transformations*, Cambridge: Polity Press.

Iversen, T. (1996) 'Power, Flexibility, and the Breakdown of Centralized Wage Bargaining. Denmark and Sweden in Comparative Perspective', *Comparative Politics* 26 (3): 399–436.

Katzenstein, P. (1985) *Small States in World Markets*. Ithaca NY: Cornell University Press.

Kepplinger, H. M. (1998) *Die Demontage der Politik in der Informationsgesellschaft*, Freiburg and Munich: Verlag Karl Alber.

Kohler-Koch, B. (1997) 'Organized Interests in European Integration: The Evolution of a New Type of Governance?', in H. Wallace and R. Young (eds) *Participation and Policy-Making in the European Union*, Oxford: Clarendon Press, pp. 42–68.

Kollman, N. (1998) *Outside Lobbying. Public Opinion and Interest Group Strategies*, Princeton NJ: Princeton University Press.

Kriesi, H. (1980) *Entscheidungsstrukturen und Entscheidungsprozesse in der Schweizer Politik*, Frankfurt: Campus.

Kriesi, H. (1998) *Le système politique suisse*, 2e édition, Paris: Economica.

Kriesi, H. and Jegen, M. (2000) 'Decision-making in the Swiss Energy Policy Elite', *The Journal of Public Policy* 20 (1): 21–53.

Kriesi, H. and Jegen, M. (2001) 'The Swiss Energy Policy Elite', *European Journal of Political Science* 39: 251–287.

Leutwiler, F., Moser, P., Hauser, H., Schwarz, C. and Vallender, K. A. (1991) *Schweizerische Wirtschaftspolitik im internationalen Wettbewerb. Ein ordnungspolitisches Programm*, Zurich: Orell-Füssli.

Mach, A. (1999a) 'L'articulation entre facteurs externes et internes comme clef d'analyse des réformes économiques et sociales', in A. Mach (ed.) *Globalisation, néo-libéralisme et politiques publiques dans la Suisse des années 1990*, Zurich: Seismo, pp. 419–454.

Mach, A. (1999b) *Evolution des relations industrielles en Suisse dans les années 90: une lente évolution vers le 'modèle anglo-saxon'?*, Department of Political Science, Université de Lausanne, Switzerland.

Mach, A. (2000) 'Entre internationalisation et changements politiques internes: la révision de la loi sur les cartels et l'évolution des relations industrielles en Suisse dans les années 1990', doctoral thesis, Université de Lausanne, Switzerland.

Prince, J.-C. (1994) *L'impact des conventions collectives de travail en Suisse*, Zurich: Schulthess.

Pury, D. de, Hauser, H. and Schmid, B. (1995) *Mut zum Aufbruch. Eine wirtschafts politische Agenda für die Schweiz*, Zurich: Orell Füssli.

Ruggie, J. G. (1993) 'Territoriality and Beyond: Problematizing Modernity in International Relations', *International Organization* 47 (1): 139–174.

Sciarini, P. (1992) 'La Suisse dans la négociation sur l'Espace économique européen: de la rupture à l'apprentissage,' Annuaire suisse de science politique 32: 297–322.

Sciarini, P. (1994) *Le système politique Suisse face à la Communauté européene et au GATT: le cas-test de la politique agricole*, Geneva: Georg.

Zervudacki, D. (1999) *Patronats dans le monde*, Paris: Presses universitaires de France.

Zürn, M. (1998) 'Schwarz-Rot-Grün-Braun: Reaktionsweisen auf Denationalisierung', in U. Beck (ed.) *Politik der Globalisierung*, Frankfurt: Suhrkamp, pp. 297–330.

4 Globalization and Swedish business interest associations in the twenty-first century

Victor A. Pestoff

> The owner of capital is by nature a citizen of the world and is not necessarily bound to a single country. He would probably quickly renounce a country where he was the object of a detailed investigation designed to subject him to a heavy tax, and would move his capital to another country.
>
> (Adam Smith 1776; *The Wealth of Nations*)

Sweden experienced sweeping institutional changes in the past 20 years in its system of centralized collective bargaining, the institutions of organizational representation in public policy making and the structure and composition of its business interest associations (BIAs). It will be argued here that many of these changes can be explained by the rapid internationalization of large Swedish firms. In the 1980s, Sweden ranked high among the neo-corporatist countries (Schmitter and Lehmbruch 1982) and had one of the most centralized systems of collective bargaining (Wallerstein and Golden 2001; Berger and Compston 2002), both of which were part of a distinctive, if not exceptional national model. It contained several unique features for a highly developed market economy. It was often characterized by Social Democratic minority governments; a strong trade union movement, which played a prominent role in politics; highly centralized collective bargaining covering most of the workforce and the politics of compromise based on collaboration between employers and unions; a universal welfare state where most of the personal social services were financed and provided by the public sector; an active labour market policy to fight unemployment; and a small open negotiated economy with a highly concentrated industrial structure and a number of big multinational enterprises (MNEs).

These were essential parts of the Swedish Model. However, in 1990, the Swedish Model was declared 'dead and buried' by Ulf Laurin the Chairman of SAF, Svenska Arbetsgivareföreningen (the Swedish Employers' Confederation), when he wrote:

> I am convinced that SAF's role during the 1990s will be more significant for Swedish business than until recently. After a long-term illness,

> the 'Swedish model' is dead. The historic decision made by SAF on 2 February means that there is no return. The course for our wage policy is totally clear. It is focused upon decentralization – with the intent of providing a dominant role for firm level bargaining.
>
> (*SAF-tidning*, 16 February 1990, author's translation)

The following week SAF relieved Mr L.G. Albåge, the Director of its Negotiations Division since the early 1970s, of his responsibilities and terminated the services of the entire negotiating staff.

Various explanations have been provided for the break-up of the Swedish Model and two of its most important cornerstones – centralized collective bargaining and participation in administrative corporatism. Pontusson and Swenson (1996) emphasize the microeconomic forces promoting flexible specialization among Swedish industrialists and an open conflict among the members of SAF that eventually tipped the scales in favour of greater flexibility in wage bargaining in order to meet increased international competition. However, their interpretation has been challenged (Soskice 1999; Wallerstein and Golden 1997; Golden *et al.* 1999; Wallerstein and Golden 2001; Huber and Stephens 2001; Martin 2001). While Pontusson and Swenson may be on the right track, pitting the export-oriented sector against the domestic sector of Swedish industry seems insufficient.

SAF's decision in early 1991 to withdraw its more than 6,000 representatives from various governing bodies of public authorities at the national, regional and local levels changed the Swedish political–administrative landscape overnight. This change in SAF's strategy, from collaboration with the trade unions and the state to an uncertain strategy focusing on far-reaching changes in socio-economic policy making, means that other ways of gaining influence have come into focus. In recent decades SAF has mounted numerous political campaigns, e.g. for the continued use of nuclear energy, against the wage-earner funds, for deregulation and privatization, and for membership in both the European Union and European Monetary Union. Influencing public opinion and lobbying have now replaced earlier means of gaining authority/influence, like participation in expert panels, nominating lay representatives to the governing bodies of public authorities and seeking consensus with the trade unions.

Numerous events during the 1970s and early 1980s convinced SAF to change strategy. Very little was achieved by the non-socialist coalition in office between 1976 and 1982 and SAF realized that if any fundamental changes were to take place, it would have to push them through. The return to power of the Social Democrats in 1982 and their Wage Earner Fund proposal in 1983 only served to aggravate matters from a business perspective. SAF's newly found role as a major force in influencing public opinion was made possible by repeated increases in SAF's membership dues between the mid 1970s and the mid 1980s (Pestoff 1988 and 1989), and by a significant increase in the amount of funds devoted to opinion formation. In the election year 1991, SAF spent SEK 225 million on lobbying and public opinion campaigns, which was twice the amount available to all the political parties in a *Riksdags* election (Pestoff 1995a). Thus, change was not only deemed necessary, but also within reach given the growing resources devoted to opinion formation.

Rothstein and Bergström (2000) ask why an organization like SAF would choose to withdraw its representatives from the corporative system and thereby forfeit guaranteed influence. They argue that the social democratic government emptied the corporative governing boards of the national public authorities of most of the power they held earlier. However, Johansson (2000) shows that SAF's decision was a well thought out and long-term initiative that aimed at fundamentally changing the power relations between capital and labour in central arenas of politics (ibid.: 199). This meant in part an intensive promotion of SAF's lobbying and opinion formation capacity, and in part the scuttling of institutional arrangements that were considered closely related to union influence in social policy (ibid.: 202).

Alternative explanations have been put forward for the demise of the Swedish Model. Micheletti (1994) maintains that SAF was more astute than the trade unions in adjusting and adapting to post-modern social changes. Stephens (1996) and Huber and Stephens (2001) highlight the importance of, and shift in, power resources in bringing about these changes. Blyth (2001) emphasizes the importance of changing ideological preferences among the leaders of SAF. Rothstein (2001) argues that the trade unions flaunted the rules of the game set up by the basic agreement or *Saltsjöbadsavtalet*; thereby, eroding the mutual trust between them. Martin (2001) emphasizes both macroeconomic policies, in particular the failure of the Third Way economic policy, and political variables in his analysis.

While each of these accounts contributes something new, none seems to provide an adequate understanding of these dramatic changes. Thus, I am suggesting that while several explanations of the fundamental changes in Swedish society may be relevant and contribute some important insights, none provides the entire picture. Perhaps an analysis that builds on both economic or structural forces and political resources is necessary to arrive at a more balanced understanding of these dramatic changes. Moreover, given the growing awareness of and interest in internationalization, it is surprising that so few scholars have analysed its role when studying the collective activities of capital, and in particular when studying the activities of Swedish business interest associations. It is my claim that it is here that we need to seek a more detailed explanation of the breakdown of the Swedish Model and the recent changes in Swedish business interest associations. However, part of the problem stems from a lack of a common definition of internationalization.

Visser and Wilts argue in their chapter in this volume that thanks to 'goodness of fit' between liberal corporatism in the Netherlands and the market building processes in the European Union, changes in the Dutch system of interest associations and the impact of Europe were modest. Sweden provides an illustration of the opposite response, i.e. an extensive transformation was necessary due to the lack of fit between Swedish institutions of social corporatism and market requirements in Europe and internationally. The pressure for change in the Swedish system of business interest associations and in its relation to the trade unions and the political system was fed by the growing internationalization of the Swedish economy in general and by the growth of Swedish multinational enterprises in particular.

This chapter on internationalization and business interest associations at the beginning of the twenty-first century will explore two important, but previously unexamined issues: the internationalization of the Swedish economy, firms and politics; and the restructuring of employer organizations and trade associations at both the branch and peak levels. Both these developments emphasize the continued importance of Swedish BIAs as political actors and underline the importance of internationalization and MNEs for the development of national systems of BIAs.

In particular, I want to emphasize three themes from earlier discussions of organized business interests and the impact of globalization, internationalization and Europeanization on national systems of business interest associations. First, internationalization creates 'disembedded' actors: in order to succeed internationally, they must learn to operate independently from any given national context and to survive in a fragmented and international context. Such disembeddedness goes beyond merely responding to international competition or an export orientation. Second, multinational companies or enterprises are important international, European and national actors in their own right, but they have previously been overlooked, in particular in the lively debate about recent changes in Sweden (Iversen *et al.* 2001). However, here I will not focus primarily on their international or European activities per se, but rather on the impact of increasing internationalization on their domestic networks. Sweden provides a good example since it has so many large multinationals. Third, national systems of BIAs do not wither away as sometimes suggested by the literature on Europeanization. They adapt and adjust, to a greater or lesser extent, to changes in their environment and to the demands of their most influential members, i.e. the multinational enterprises. Their adaptation and adjustment may eventually require the transformation of major social institutions in their home country.

Internationalization of Swedish firms and the Swedish economy

Export and ownership

Historically, Sweden differs from many small open economies in at least two, or perhaps three respects. First, Swedish industrial policy traditionally supported growth by favouring the formation of large firms. Given the limited size of the domestic market, large firms could only grow by expanding their foreign operations. Once a large firm has exhausted its domestic opportunities, multinational expansion has been the natural next step, often beginning with expansion in neighbouring Nordic countries. Swedish macroeconomic policy focused on productive and scale efficiency rather than antitrust issues, thus facilitating the growth of large firms and oligopolies at the expense of small and medium sized firms (Blomström and Kakka 1997). Competition has been upheld by free-trade policies. Second, the Swedish trade union movement did not and still does not oppose this strategy, including the tendency of foreign direct investments. However, many Swedish multinational enterprises, have become so international that they now may favour innovations and growth opportunities in their foreign affiliates rather than at home (Andersson *et al.* 1996).

By contrast, the attitude of Swedish trade unions and politicians traditionally has been more negative to foreign ownership at home. This was initially motivated by fears of a loss of national independence. Nearly 100 years ago several laws were passed restricting foreign ownership of Swedish assets and firms. In 1985 still only 9 per cent of domestic employment was in foreign subsidiaries operating in Sweden. Several restrictions were amended or repealed following EU membership, including the requirement of Swedish nationality in the Companies Act. A dramatic increase in foreign investment was observed during the 1990s. Its share in total employment doubled and in 1999 foreign-owned firms accounted for 19 per cent of total employment in Sweden. It should also be kept in mind that the weakness of the Swedish *krona* during most of the 1990s has made Swedish assets relatively cheap, which helped to spark a rapid increase of investment inflows (ibid.).

The debate in 2001 about changing Swedish rules governing differing votes for different categories of stockholders demonstrates a continued scepticism towards foreign ownership. Several big Swedish companies still distinguish between A and B shares, where the former are worth anywhere between ten and 1,000 times the latter. This is often seen as a technique which not only protects Swedish control of key firms, but also favours large owners. For example, the Swedish industrialist family, Wallenberg, control 4.7 per cent of A shares in Ericsson, which gives them 38.7 per cent of the votes. The sale of A shares is also strongly restricted to insiders who can gain the approval of the current owners. Needless to say, the Wallenbergs support maintaining differentiated votes for different categories of owners, as does the Social Democrat Party, in order to retain control of firms within Sweden's borders. However, some of the major institutional investors, like the Swedish pension funds, want to change these rules to get more votes for themselves (*Dagens Nyheter*, 5 June 2002).

Internationalization and export orientation

The third major difference from other small countries concerns the degree of internationalization of Swedish firms. At the micro level a firm's export orientation is important and often is used as an explanation for the collective action of business. A dichotomy commonly used for analysing the role of Swedish business is the distinction between firms producing for the export or domestic markets. The engineering industry belongs to the former, while the wholesale and retail trades and building and construction sector are part of the latter. The former supposedly face 'fierce competition' from foreign competitors, while the latter belong to a 'sheltered' domestic sector. The existence of competition exposes them to different economic forces, which in turn is expressed in different strategies of collective bargaining. Belonging to the 'sheltered domestic' sector makes it possible for firms to pass on the costs of wage increases to their customers, a luxury the export sector cannot afford given the stiff international competition. This dichotomy enforces the well-known Pontusson and Swenson 1996 thesis of growing tensions between these two groups of Swedish employers. This was expressed in the divergent demands by Sveriges Verkstadsindustrier (VI) and Sveriges Byggindustrier. The outcome of this conflict eventually led the Confederation of Swedish Employers, SAF, to scuttle centralized collective bargaining at the beginning of the 1990s and to abandon corporatism.

However, it is necessary to examine the concepts of export-oriented firms and internationalization more closely. At face value the dichotomy between production for export or domestic consumption may be misleading. Many Swedish firms operate successfully in both markets. At what point does a firm become an export-oriented firm? When 10, 40 or 60 per cent of its sales are abroad; or perhaps when 10, 40 or 60 per cent of its staff is employed abroad? In order to raise some questions concerning the export orientation of different sectors, a few well-known examples will be provided. More than 85 per cent of both ABB's and Electrolux's staff and sales were abroad in 1996, while less than 40 per cent of Volvo's staff, but 90 per cent of its sales were abroad the same year (*Svenska Dagbladet*, *Näringslivsbilaga*, 17 May 1997). However, the figures for Volvo should be compared with two other firms found in the wholesale and retail trades and the building and construction sector. Three-quarters of the multinational clothing wholesaler and retailer H&M's staff and sales were abroad, while nearly half of Skanska's staff and sales were abroad the same year (ibid.). The first three of these Swedish multinational companies belong to the engineering industry, the classical export sector in Sweden, while the latter two belong to the 'sheltered domestic sector', if branch employer organization is used as the measure. But, H&M and Skanska had a larger proportion of their employees abroad than Volvo in 1996. There are many other Swedish firms that operate both on the domestic and export markets. Thus, the concept 'export-oriented firms' needs to be examined closely and compared with other measures of internationalization. So, sectors are an inappropriate proxy for internationalization.

If the term 'export oriented' is used as shorthand for a firm that has most of its workforce at home, while most of its sales are abroad, then Volvo is the only one of the five aforementioned Swedish MNEs that fits this definition. Arguably, the importance attached to any national system of collective bargaining and the efforts needed to change stand in proportion to the benefit that can be gained from that effort. This in turn depends on the proportion of a firm's total staff employed under that system's rules. Thus, both ABB and Electrolux now only have a 15 per cent stake in bringing about a major change in the Swedish collective bargaining system compared with domestic firms, as most of their employees are hired, paid and fired or retired according to standards set in other countries according to different rules.

Foreign direct investment (FDI)

Huber and Stephens (2001) argue that outward foreign direct investment provides a significant measure of a country's internationalization. Foreign direct investment implies something both quantitatively and qualitatively different from a firm's export orientation or a country's openness. In 1990 Sweden was the OECD country with the most rapidly expanding FDI and ranked fourth in terms of outward stock of FDI as a proportion of GDP (Andersson *et al.* 1996). Sweden's FDI reached 21.9 per cent of her GDP that year. Other important actors in terms of FDI were the Netherlands (38.2 per cent), Switzerland (29.1 per cent) and the UK (23.5 per cent). Germany (10.1 per cent), France (9.2 per cent), the USA (7.9 per cent) and Japan (6.9 per cent) had considerably lower levels of outward FDI, while Norway (9.6 per cent) and Finland (8.8 per cent) reached less than half of the Swedish level and Denmark (5.6 per cent) less than one-quarter. The Swedish proportion of the OECD's total FDI tripled between 1980 and 1990, and it was three times more than her three Nordic neighbours combined in 1990 (Andersson *et al.* 1996: 4, Table 1). Here we find an important difference among the Nordic countries in terms of their degree of internationalization, in spite of similar scores in terms of trade openness, as reported by Wallerstein and Golden (2001). This may help to explain some of the differences in recent developments among the neighbouring Nordic countries.

The pattern of heavy outflows of Swedish FDI continued during the 1990s and nearly tripled from SEK 282 billion in 1990 to SEK 727 billion in 1998. The inflow of FDI to Sweden remained much lower, but also increased significantly, from SEK 71 billion in 1990 to SEK 418 billion in 1998 (Ekholm and Hesselman 2000). More than half of the outflow of Swedish FDI went to EU countries during the 1990s, while the EU's share of the inflow of FDI to Sweden increased from one-third to two-thirds during the same period. The Nordic countries' share of outward FDI from

Sweden increased from 12 to 18 per cent, while their share of the inward FDI to Sweden remained at nearly one-third during the 1990s (ibid.).

The 1990 study of Swedish MNEs showed a change in the importance of Sweden as a home base for its big Swedish MNEs (Andersson *et al.* 1996). Between 1970 and 1990 the Swedish share of the sales, production, value added and employment of Swedish MNEs all decreased dramatically. Sales decreased by nearly half, from 41 per cent to 23 per cent; the Swedish share of production decreased by more than one third, from 73 per cent to 46 per cent; the share of the value added in Sweden decreased by nearly one-third, from 62 per cent in 1978 to only 44 per cent in 1990 and the share of employment decreased by more than a third, from 64 per cent to under 40 per cent in 1990. A follow-up study shows that the trend of expanding production resources more rapidly abroad than at home continued during the 1990s (Ekholm and Hasselman 2000), thus, Swedish MNEs have become increasingly prone to locate their activities abroad. This suggests that the decreasing relative importance of Sweden as a location for production is mainly related to the decreased importance of Swedish markets for Swedish MNEs (ibid.). Most of the expansion of Swedish MNEs abroad has come in the form of acquisitions, rather than as greenfield or new operation (ibid.).

Concentration, employment abroad and inward investment

Wallerstein and Golden (2001) maintain that Sweden does not differ from her Nordic neighbours concerning the degree of internationalization or openness of the economy, expressed as the share of imports and exports in the GDP. But, the openness of an economy in terms of the proportion of imports and exports is still too imprecise a concept to understand the interests and behaviour of internationally oriented firms. In my view, both the concentration of business and its internationalization in terms of the proportion of staff employed abroad are more relevant for understanding the impact of internationalization on changing the attitude of Swedish business toward centralized collective bargaining and administrative corporatism. This is particularly notable when comparing business in Sweden with that in the neighbouring Nordic countries.

It should be kept in mind that Swedish business is, and has always been, a major actor in the trend toward greater Europeanization and internationalization. Swedish business is one of the most concentrated in Europe. For example, Sweden ranked number one in terms of firm concentration in several of the sectors selected for study in the OBI project (Pestoff and Ronit 1990: 16, Table 4). In terms of firm size and employment, Swedish firms were considerably more concentrated than their competitors in the neighbouring Nordic countries in 1987. The 30 largest firms employed nearly nine out of ten employees in Swedish manufacturing and industry, but only one of four in Danish manufacturing and industry (see Table 4.1). Data from 1982 show that the domestic operations of the ten largest manufacturing

Table 4.1 Employment share of the 10 or 30 largest manufacturing firms, as a percentage of manufacturing employment, 1974 and 1986

	10 largest		*30 largest*	
	1974	*1987*	*1974*	*1987*
Sweden	41.0	58.6[a]	59.3	85.3[a]
Finland	22.3[b]	34.3	40.1[b]	61.5
Norway	16.9	31.9	27.7	44.4
Denmark	11.6	15.8	20.8	27.2

Source: 'Firm Dynamics', as presented in ETLA *et al.* 1990: 34, Table 1.8.

Notes
a 1986.
b 1975.

companies in Denmark contributed 14 per cent to the total national value added, while the ten largest Swedish companies contributed 33 per cent (Oxelheim 1984: 184–201). If the foreign operations of these same firms are included, we notice little change for Denmark, an increase to only 17 per cent, while it nearly doubles for Sweden, reaching 62 per cent (ibid.). Furthermore, the unique economic concentration of the Swedish economy has facilitated collective action. Under the system of proportional voting practised by SAF, the number of votes attributed to member firms is directly related to the amount of dues they paid, which in turn reflect their annual wage bill. Consequently, the big MNEs dominated SAF by grace of its internal decision-making rules (Pestoff 1988 and 1989).

Another aspect of concentration is related to stock ownership. The 204 firms listed in July 1997 on the Stockholm Stock Market were valued at SEK 1,967 billion. The ten largest stock owners held 48 per cent of the total value of the stock market, the 25 largest owners had 57 per cent, while the 100 largest had 63 per cent (S-I. Sundqvist *Dagens Nyheter*, 10 July 1997). Thus, the Swedish economy demonstrates a very high degree of economic concentration. Large-scale or baron capitalism (Stephens 1996) sets Sweden apart from its neighbouring Nordic countries, regardless of similarities in the openness of their economies in terms of foreign trade.

Moreover, the biggest Swedish firms experienced a strong and continuous international shift in terms of their production, employment and investments in recent decades. In 1965 two-thirds of the staff of the 25 largest Swedish multinational companies were employed within Swedish borders, while today less than two-fifths of the staff are employed at home and the remainder are employed abroad (*Dagens Nyheter*, 22 May 1997). In addition, the number of employees abroad in all Swedish owned firms with foreign subsidiaries continued to increase throughout the 1990s. By 1998 these firms on the whole had more employees abroad than at home; 701,000 abroad compared with nearly 650,000 at home (Table 4.2). They show a high concentration in a few countries, with 112,000 employees in the USA, almost 100,000 in neighbouring Nordic countries, 76,000 in Germany and 53,000 in both the UK and France. The overall degree of internationalization of Swedish firms operating abroad grew in terms of employment from 39 per cent in 1987 to 52 per cent in 1998. However, this varies with the sector or industry. In 1998 it averaged 60 per cent for manufacturing, but reached 70 per cent in textiles, 72 per cent in the chemical industry, 78 per cent in machine tools and 86 per cent in precision instruments. By contrast, in the service sector the average was only 37 per cent in 1998. Size of firm is also an important factor for explaining the internationalization of Swedish firms, as seen on Table 4.2. Only firms with 5,000 or more employees had a majority of their staff employed abroad.

While investment and production abroad is dominated by a few large manufacturing firms, there are also notable differences between the investment patterns of Swedish and foreign business. Three-quarters of Swedish investments abroad are concentrated in manufacturing, while foreign investors in Sweden have more employees in the service sector. Foreign ownership in Sweden also increased dramatically in recent decades, but in 1998 Swedish firms still had more than twice as many employees abroad as foreign concerns had in Sweden, i.e. 701,000 Swedish employees abroad as opposed to 334,000 foreign employees in Sweden (ITPS 2001a–c).

Both the number of foreign firms and the number of their employees in Sweden have more than doubled in the past ten years. In 1990 there were 2,563 foreign firms with 204,000 employees. By the end of 2000 there were 5,519 foreign owned enterprises operating in Sweden, with nearly 450,000 employees. Today foreign firms account for 19 per cent of the total employment in the Swedish business sector. The USA is the largest country of origin with over 100,000 employees, followed by the UK with nearly

Table 4.2 Employment at home and abroad in Swedish firms with subsidiaries abroad, by firm size, 1998

Firm size	*Number of firms*	*Employees in Sweden*	*Employees abroad*	*Average size*
1–49	349	4,791	2,632	22
50–249	308	24,826	12,109	120
250–499	92	21,856	10,335	350
500–999	64	32,517	14,513	511
1,000–4,999	72	87,641	64,078	2,107
5,000+	58	476,655	597,011	18,516
Total	943	648,286	700,678	1,431

Source: ITPS (2001c); Table 3 in Swedish owned enterprise groups with subsidiaries abroad 1998.

50,000, the Netherlands with 46,000 and both Finland and Denmark with just over 40,000 employees in Sweden (ibid.).

Foreign ownership surpassed 50 per cent in six of the 25 largest companies on the Stockholm Stock Exchange in 1996 (*Svenska Dagbladet*, 17 May 1997). However, there have been some dramatic foreign acquisitions in recent years. In the mid-1990s General Motors (GM) bought a 50 per cent share of the second largest Swedish automaker Saab and GM announced that it would execute its option to buy the remaining 50 per cent in 1999. Recently, the flagship of Swedish industry, Volvo Cars, was sold to Ford Motor Company, while the remaining Swedish part of Volvo, Volvo Trucks, proceeded to make an unsuccessful takeover bid on its only national competitor Scania. This was blocked by the European Commissioner in the spring of 2000. Volvo Trucks then went on to bid for Renault Trucks, which included Renault's joint ownership with Mitsubishi and Mack Trucks. Volkswagen bought a 35 per cent share of Scania when Volvo decided to divest itself of Scania in order to finance its bid on Renault.

The massive outflow of FDI and the modest size of the economy have made Sweden one of the most internationalized economies in the world. By 1998 Sweden was perhaps the first OECD country with more employees in the foreign operations of its MNEs than in their home operations. Thus, Swedish MNEs can afford to ignore Sweden, but Sweden cannot afford to ignore them. Nor can Swedish business interest associations afford to ignore them, as members' votes are distributed in relation to dues they pay, which in turn are related to a member firm's annual wage bill.

Resource dependency

The usual sequence in developing international business activities is success at home first, then sales abroad and finally production abroad. The importance attributed to the home market will obviously vary with its size. If closeness to the market is paramount for success, firms must not only develop their sales and marketing abroad, but also locate their manufacturing capacity outside Sweden's borders. A Nordic expansion is often the first step, soon followed by moves closer to the more densely populated markets of Europe, North America and Asia.

The basic argument put forward here is that it does in fact make a difference if firms are home-market oriented, export oriented or truly multinational in their operations: first, for their policies in the area of wage setting and collective bargaining, and second, for their willingness to collaborate with domestic political forces. On the basis of resource dependency theory (Pfeffer 1982), we may expect that the weight and diversity of its foreign operations reduces the dependency upon, and the allegiance to, the domestic situation.

Institutions of collective bargaining, industrial relations and patterns of collaboration with governments and public agencies vary from country to country. Successful international firms will have to adapt to these variations. The greater the number of different national institutions and patterns of external relations a MNE faces in its operations, the greater the demands on its management to accept cultural diversity as a natural part of doing business. This implies that the attachment of owners and managers to their home country's institutions and patterns of relations cannot be permitted to dominate their overall approach.

Moreover, firms operating in different countries or sectors with production regimes will pursue different strategies vis-à-vis their employees (Soskice 1999). Internationalization implies the need to balance the strategies of various production regimes. Kitschelt *et al.* (1999) argue against the idea of general convergence of production regimes in advanced capitalist democracies. Yet they suggest that Sweden may be moving from a National Coordinated Market Economy toward a Sector Coordinated Market Economy more like the German economy. Iversen and Pontusson (2001) express a similar belief that Sweden is gradually progressing toward a sectorally coordinated economy. However, the activities and intentions of SAF and the Confederation of Swedish Enterprise (SN) in the past decades rather indicate a desire to move Sweden in the direction of an Uncoordinated or Liberal Market Economy (Hooghe and Marks 1999) and to adhere to the Neo-Liberal project for Europe. The 2002 general election results showed, however, that these attempts are not supported by the voters in Sweden.

Conclusion

This discussion of internationalization demonstrates two things: first, various indicators of internationalization (sales, FDI, production sites, ownership etc.) are needed to understand the full impact on domestic politics. Second, long before becoming a member of the European Union, Swedish firms were on the cutting edge of European integration and were pushing to internationalize the Swedish economy. As the European and international activities grow in importance, both economically and politically, Swedish firms have become more interested in finding flexible, internationally applicable solutions that fit conditions in a number of nations where they operate. To the extent that the centralized Swedish model of collective bargaining is a specifically Swedish or Nordic phenomenon, it can therefore be expected to lose importance for and support among Swedish multinational enterprises that will continue to opt for more general market-oriented solutions to the problems they face in several countries.

Amalgamations among Swedish business interest associations

Swedish BIAs demonstrated several distinctive features when compared to BIAs in the other eight countries of the Organized Business Interest (OBI) project. First, Sweden was one country to have a clear division of jurisdiction and responsibilities between branch trade associations (TA) and branch employer organizations (EO) in each and every of four of the sectors included in the OBI project, as well as at the peak or central level. Second, several Swedish BIAs were significantly better financed than their counterparts in other OECD countries. Third, the nearly 1,000 BIAs that existed in the 1980s demonstrated a very high capacity of coordination through their peak associations and through meta-organizations not found elsewhere in Europe (Pestoff 1988 and 1989). However, many of these distinctive features began to change, most notably in the 1990s.

Three waves of amalgamations

In recent decades, SAF experienced three waves of reorganization. The first was when many service sector employer organizations, like the Hotel and Restaurant Employers, the Commercial Employers (HAO), the Forest and Agricultural Employers (SLA and other independent employer organizations) joined SAF in the 1960s and 1970s (Kjellberg 2000). Firms that remained outside SAF were found in the retail cooperatives, the public and cooperative housing authorities, the newspapers and mass media, and the banks (ibid.: 186–187). By and large they are still outside SAF today. This first wave of reorganization resulted in a transformation of SAF from mainly an industrial body to one for all private employers, in recent years even including some public employers. Thus, SAF's membership has become more heterogeneous, complicating both wage negotiations and SAF's reorganization. Parallel with the growing heterogeneity of SAF's membership, we notice a growing internationalization and growing dominance of the engineering industry within the export sector. The engineering industry's contribution to Swedish exports increased from 27 per cent in 1950 to 56 per cent in 1998, while the export contribution of the pulp and paper industry decreased to only 14 per cent in 1998 (ibid.). This went together with a shift in favour of big multinational companies and to the engineering industry's branch employer organization, VF/VI inside SAF.

The second wave of reorganization was a process of mergers starting in the mid-1980s that blurred the previous division between trade associations (TA) and employer organizations (EO). Several of the branch organizations of Industriförbundet (SI), the Swedish Federation of Industry, and SAF amalgamated to form new joint branch organizations and combine the functions and responsibilities of both TAs and EOs. Two of the more significant examples of this merger process involved organizations in the building and construction sector to form Sveriges Byggindustrier (BI) in the late 1980s and organizations in the engineering industry to form Sveriges Verkstadsindustrier (VI) in the early 1990s. Most of the newly amalgamated branch organizations have retained their affiliation with SAF, but they have not always remained members of SI. At the end of the 1990s, 60 per cent of the employees covered by the affiliates of SAF were represented through BIAs that combined the trade and employer functions (ibid.: 203).

At the central level the integration of trade and employer associations took place ten years earlier in the neighbouring Nordic countries than in Sweden. In Norway the peak organizations for employers, commerce and industry, NAF, NHF and NI, formed NHO in 1989, after a failed lockout by employers. An amalgamation between the central employer and trade associations took place in Finland in 1993, while in Denmark the central employers' federation DIA simply joined the Federation of Industry, DI, as a branch organization in 1989. In Sweden the central peak organizations, SI and SAF, had intermittently discussed joining hands to form a new central organization for Swedish business for several decades. The first serious proposal came in the mid-1960s, but nothing substantial resulted from these discussions, and as recently as 1995 SAF and SI had failed to join hands. However, one SAF branch employer organization, Handelns Arbetsgivareorganization, HAO, proceeded in 1995 to merge with Grossistförbundet and Köpmannaförbundet to form Svensk Handel. Approximately one-third of the new organization's members were also members of HAO, and thereby of SAF, now SN.

Then, in the spring of 2000 both SI and SAF took a decisive step toward merging their respective organizations and creating Svenskt Näringsliv, SN (the Confederation of Swedish Enterprise). *Dagens Nyheter*, the major morning newspaper, lists several reasons for this decision. SAF lost, or rather shed, its role as a negotiation partner. The borderline between industry and service became less rigid. Membership in the EU favoured that Swedish enterprise be represented by a single organization or voice. Apparently, the division between employer and trade issues became less relevant, as exemplified by the amalgamation between many branch EOs and TAs in recent years. *Dagens Nyheter* went on to argue that there was no room for a separate employer federation now that collective bargaining was firmly located at the branch level, nor for a trade association representing industry now that the industrial sector was decreasing in size (*Dagens Nyheter*, 3 December 2000). The merger of SAF and SI was completed in March 2001, and the new central organization, Svenskt Näringsliv, combines the resources of both of its predecessors and their branch organizations. SN represents all of Swedish industry and services, except firms and sectors with a clear domestic orientation in transportation, news media, retail cooperatives, public and cooperative housing, and banking. In addition, most of the public sector employers of personal social services are represented through the *Kommunförbundet* and *Landstingsförbundet*.

Changing resources: staff, dues, the insurance fund, etc.

After signing the basic agreement of 1938, the *Saltsjöbadsavtal*, new responsibilities and a growing demand for negotiators meant new tasks for

SAF as an organization. SAF's staff increased more than tenfold, from some 30 people in 1930 to 360 in 1970 (De Geer 1986: 32). SAF employed 500 people in 1990, while another 500 were employed by its affiliates (Myrdal 1991, as quoted in Visser 1996). This rapid expansion meant a professionalization of SAF's staff, with many lawyers joining the organization during the first period. SAF's culture includes several groups of professionals that at times may come in conflict with each other, as illustrated by SAF's decision to abandon neo-corporatism in 1991 (Johansson 2000). We can distinguish a negotiation culture, an expert culture and a firm or member culture. SAF's new chairman in 1976, Curt Nicolin, brought with him a new culture of public relations, proactive opinion formation and ideological offensive that corresponded with the expectations of many individual firms that were frustrated by the radicalization of politics in the late 1960s. SAF's staff set the tone in the struggle against the Wage Earner Funds and its section for 'Societal Contacts' grew rapidly. Then in 1990, when SAF terminated its 'Negotiations' section, its staff diminished from nearly 500 to approximately 300 in 2000, of whom 80 are now found in the regional offices (Kjellberg 2000: 181–182). The reduction in staff was accompanied by a reduction in dues starting in 1991 (see Table 4.3).

Table 4.3 SAF's membership dues and insurance fund, 1965 to 2000

Year	*Membership dues*[a]	*Membership dues in per cent of total income*	*Insurance fund**[c]	*Conflict remuneration**
1965	0.28/0.18*	77.0	269	0
1970	–	73.5	446	8
1971	–	70.3	489	2
1972	–	67.7	552	1
1973	–	67.4	627	6
1974	–	64.1	663	17
1975	–	63.1	693	21
1976	–	66.1	735	11
1977	–	67.4	649	134[d]
1978	0.30/0.22	70.2	764	9
1979	–	68.7	852	24
1980	0.38/0.32	71.0	874	129[d]
1981	–	68.6	941	115[d]
1982	0.40/0.35	65.9	1,156	9
1983	–	59.2	1,429	3
1984	0.42/0.40	63.4	1,720	9
1985	–	61.7	2,002	21
1986	–	58.5	2,273	65
1987	–	59.1	2,609	36
1988	–	45.7	2,543	634[d]
1989	–	44.1	3,069	50
1990	–	52.6	3,527	59

Table 4.3 continued

Year	*Membership dues*[a]	*Membership dues in per cent of total income*	*Insurance fund**[c]	*Conflict remuneration**
1991	0.38	54.7	4,011	17
1992	0.25	59.9	4,816	35
1993	0.10 + 0.12[b]	36.6	4,708	47
1994	0.10 + 0.10	38.4	4,758	12
1995	0.04 + 0.10	37.7	4,610	82
1996	–	28.7	4,890	38
1997	0.03 + 0.09	20.3	5,653	44
1998	0.036 + 0.084	22.4	6,221	31
1999	0.044 + 0.076	19.9	5,477	25
2000	0.054 + 0.066	16.6	5,896	22

Source: SAF's annual General Reports, 1965 to 2000.

Notes

* in SEK per employee and year.

a As a proportion (0/00) of a member firm's total annual wage bill; between 1965 and 1990 to the left of the line (/) the member's dues in per mill of the total annual wage bill per 'collectively employed' or blue-collar worker, and to the right the dues per white-collar worker.

b Starting in 1993 member's dues are to the left and to the right their service fees as a proportion of the total annual wage bill.

c SAF's conflict fund expressed as SEK per employee in all SAF member firms and year, based on the declared value of the Insurance Fund, which is substantially lower than the market value. In 2000 the total came to SEK 8.2 billion (see Table 4.4).

d In 1977 3,000 white-collar workers in PTK went on strike and 220,000 were 'locked out', in 1980 there was a major labour market conflict with 100,000 LO blue-collar workers on strike and 700,000 'locked out', in 1981 17,000 white-collar PTK workers went on strike and 250,000 were 'locked out', and in 1988 there were 40,000 SIF white-collar workers on strike and 40,000 more were 'locked out'. Conflict remuneration for companies participating in these lockouts represents a proportion of SAF's annual income of 78% in 1977, 41% in 1980, 32% in 1981 and 58% in 1988 in these years respectively. During the postwar period the amount available at the end of the year for transfer to the Insurance Fund was only negative once in 1988 (see Table 4.4).

SAF's dues represent a fraction or per mill (0/00) of the annual wage bill of a member firm's total annual wages (see the first column of Table 4.3 for details). Given wage increases throughout the post-Second World War period SAF received more revenue each year. Nevertheless, starting in 1977, SAF raised membership dues every second year, doubling them by 1990. However, in 1991, SAF decided to decrease its dues, and by 2000 membership dues and service fees were less than a third of what they were ten years previously (see Table 4.3). As a result, the proportion of the income stemming from membership dues and service fees decreased sharply from nearly two-thirds of SAF's total annual income in the 1970s and 1980s to just one-third in the 1990s; and today it is less than one-fifth (see column 2 of Table 4.3). The income stemming from interest on the assets in the Insurance Fund has grown proportionally. Thus, SAF has grown less dependent on its members' dues as a source of income (Tables 4.3 and 4.4). In the future

Table 4.4 SAF's revenue and expenditure, 1970 to 2000 (in million SEK)

	1970	*1980*	*1988*	*1990*	*1995*	*2000*
Revenue						
Dues	75.8	292.1	631.9	781.5	340.4	409.7
Interest	28.4	119.5	716.2	704.2	622.3	1,987.6
Total	103.1	411.6	1348.0	1.485.7	1.008.5	2,286.1
Expenses[a]						
Salaries	17.7	77.7	134.8	161.9	–	283.2
Other admin.	16.5	89.3	272.0	360.2	457.2	389.2
Taxes	9.5	51.9	191.1	229.9	147.5	427.7
Total	50.2	218.9	597.9	751.9	604.7	923.5
Conflict remuneration	10.0	170.4[b]	787.0[b]	77.0	101.3	31.2
Assets and funds						
Assets	569.7	1,329.6	4,168.0	5,129.5	6,869.9	12,177.3
Insurance fund	553.2	1,147.6	3,207.4	4,598.6	5,712.9	8,203.7
Annual increase	42.9	2.2	−35.9	656.8	246.8	747.7
Contingency fund[c]	603.3	1,663.4	4,627.9	5,704.4	–	–

Source: Annual Reports, 1970 to 2000.

Notes

a These expenses were combined into 'operating costs' during the period 1994–1998.

b These unusually high figures for conflict remuneration are due to the General Conflict in 1980 and the conflict regarding 19 MNEs and SIF in 1988.

c The 'contingency fund' was set at 3% of members' annual wage bill, but it was discontinued in 1994.

there is a risk that SAF's/SN's leaders may pay less attention to members' wishes since four-fifths of their income comes from interest rather than dues.

SAF's Insurance Fund is a conflict or lockout fund. Normally the amount remaining in SAF's annual budget at the end of each year, after all expenses and taxes have been paid, is transferred to the Insurance Fund. The 'annual increase' entry on Table 4.4 shows the amount transferred from the previous year to the Insurance Fund. This fund contained a declared value of SEK 8.2 billion at the end of 2000, but its market value was worth considerably more. The value of the assets in SAF's Insurance Fund can be divided by the total number of employees in member firms in order to follow the development of the Insurance fund over time. This is expressed in column three of Table 4.3. In 2000 there were nearly 6,000 SEK per employee in SAF's Insurance Fund.

Conflict remuneration to SAF members (found in column four of Table 4.3) for labour market conflicts has remained low in most years. Normally it is less than 1 or 2 per cent of the value of SAF's Insurance Fund per employee in all member firms. Also it is usually confined to a single digit figure expressed as a proportion of SAF's annual income. However, four years are exceptions and, therefore, stand out: 1977, 1980, 1981 and 1988. Here conflict remuneration to member firms, expressed as SEK per employee in all member firms, reached double digit figures. For example, in 1980, during the largest labour market conflict in the postwar period, SEK 170 million were paid out as conflict remuneration. The total conflict remuneration per worker employed by all SAF members reached 14.8 per cent of the declared value of the Insurance Fund that year. This large conflict involved 100,000 workers on strike and 700,000 workers locked out by SAF's members. A much smaller conflict in 1988 involved 40,000 workers on strike and 40,000 locked out, but the conflict remuneration paid to the 19 MNEs involved reached almost five times as much, or SEK 787 million. The total conflict remuneration per worker employed by all SAF members reached 24.9 per cent of the declared value of the Insurance Fund that year. Expressed as a proportion of its annual income, conflict remuneration during these two years represent 41 and 58 per cent respectively of SAF's annual income. Only in 1988 do we notice a negative transfer to the Insurance Fund at the end of the year. Thus only once in the postwar period did SAF have to dig into its Insurance Fund to cover conflict remuneration during any given year.

In addition SAF's statutes and budget included a unique feature not found in employer organizations in most other OECD countries, namely a 'Contingency Fund'. The Contingency Fund represented a mandatory agreement between SAF, its members and their bank, whereby each member agreed to let SAF withdraw up to 3 per cent of its total annual wage bill directly from their bank upon certain contingencies. The main contingencies were in case of emergency, like a strike or lockout, or if members failed to follow SAF's instructions during a labour market conflict. The Contingency Fund and its obligations were discontinued in 1994. The amount of the Contingency Fund was regularly included in SAF's annual financial statement and it was always greater than the Insurance Fund (see Table 4.4 for details). It permitted SAF quick access to liquid assets in case of a labour market conflict or to directly fine members if they failed to conform to SAF's directives during a labour market conflict. Although this rarely happened, it gave SAF a powerful veto point on members' actions during labour market conflicts and helped to maintain discipline during the period of centralized wage bargaining. It apparently outlived itself when centralized bargaining was finally scuttled in 1990.

By international standards, Swedish employer organizations and SAF were very well endowed in terms of staff and finances. Data from 1992 permit us to compare the budgets of the central employers organization in seven OECD countries, including Austria, France, Germany, Italy, Japan and the United Kingdom, in terms of 1992 average annual exchange rates in US dollars (Pestoff 1995b; see also Table 4.5). We notice that the income of the peak organization in one country far exceeds that of all others, namely Austria. This is primarily explained by the special nature and functions of

Table 4.5 Income of employer organizations, total annual budget per member firm and per employee in selected countries, 1992

Country	*Annual budget (in 1,000 US dollars)*	*Per firm (in US dollars)*	*Per employee (in US dollars)*
Austria	459,098	na	222
Sweden	171,196	3,717	140
Italy	44,628	406	11
United Kingdom	29,643	1,976	na
West Germany	25,641	na	na
France	22,642	13	na
Japan	10,947	365	1

Source: Pestoff, 1995b: 10, Table 5.

the Austria chamber system (Traxler 1982). However, if Austria is excluded, SAF, which was at the time a 'pure' employer organization, had considerably greater income than employer organizations in all other countries, both in relative and absolute terms.

Understanding the changes

Why did changes in Swedish BIAs take so long? Five partial answers seem evident. First, the statutes of employers' organizations strongly discouraged independent action by individual members, since dissenting members could be heavily fined directly by their EOs. Second, Swedish trade unions were strong enough until the 1980s to dissuade dissenting members, and discourage them from going it alone. Third, dues and votes within Swedish BIAs are proportional and related to firm size. The larger the staff of a firm the more dues it pays and the more votes it has. Thus, a small number of large firms can easily control the decisions in most major Swedish BIAs. Fourth, as long as these firms accepted increasing dues, SAF and its member associations could continue business as usual, but as most big Swedish firms expanded abroad during the 1980s and 1990s, their commitment to Sweden and Swedish BIAs diminished. Thus, their willingness to financially support the complex and expensive system of business interest associations decreased with expanding operations outside Sweden. In addition, their experience from other national settings showed them that elaborate BIAs are not always a necessity, and perhaps even an expensive luxury. Fifth, until changes in Swedish laws in the early 1990s made it possible, foreign ownership in major Swedish companies was exceptional. As more Swedish companies came under foreign ownership in the 1990s, new traditions concerning the collective action of organized business interests were introduced. These factors brought about a gradual change in attitudes towards the need of duplicating membership in TAs and EOs serving the same sector or industry, and pressure on financial resources.

The changing logic of influence contributed to bring about changes in the organizational structure of Swedish BIAs in at least three respects. First, as national level political decision making began to lose importance, national BIAs also lost some of their previous relevance to their members. The significance of the European level sharply gained weight with Sweden's adhesion to the European Union in 1994. More resources had to go to European-level representation adding to the pressure on the resources of national BIAs. Second, the expansion of Swedish firms abroad also contributed to shifts in the importance attributed to Swedish BIAs by their multinational members. Through foreign daughter companies, joint ventures, alliances, etc. Swedish firms have access to BIAs in other countries. They not only can compare their activities with BIAs back home, they can also avail themselves of the services of BIAs in other countries to achieve their economic and political goals.

Third, many Swedish firms expanded so far beyond their original domestic markets that they now consider Europe as their home base. They must now operate and compete in several European states and join European BIAs; therefore, they need to develop a strategy to cope with such complexity, both for economic and political reasons. Operations in a new country not only open up new opportunities, but also imply new expenses and contacts. Membership in each new host country's BIAs may be desirable, but it comes with costs. Swedish multinationals must divide their attention, funding and loyalty between BIAs in several countries and the European level BIAs. This too contributes to their reluctance to continue to fund an expensive system of interest associations, with duplications of staff and functions, as well as growing dues at home. In addition, by operating in multiple environments, Swedish multinationals often obtain a level of sophistication in analysing complex political problems and developing relevant responses at multiple levels and in multiple political environments that far surpass that of national BIAs in any single country. Thus, not putting all the eggs into one basket becomes a realistic motto for multinational companies.

The constraints of the logic of membership and the logic of influence need to be considered in light of the growing number of multinational enterprises and the Europeanization and globalization of business. A MNE from a country where there are only a few or weak BIAs may find great difficulty adapting to a new host business community with many or strong BIAs. Similarly, a MNE from a country with few or weak trade unions may find difficulty adapting to a business climate where there are many or strong trade unions. For example, the American company 'Toys Я Us' refused to negotiate a collective agreement with its workers when it first established itself in Sweden. But after a long union-led consumer boycott it gave in, joined SAF and negotiated a collective agreement with the Swedish trade unions. The point is that MNE's appreciation of the benefits of BIAs probably varies from country to country. The inclination to join the BIAs in a new host country is not equal for all MNEs, regardless of their origin.

The dependency of a MNE on its home country's economy, business community and BIAs diminishes as it grows out of its home base and becomes disembedded. Similarly a MNEs dependency on its new host country's economy, business community and BIAs grows as more and more of its sales and/or production is located inside that country. If a MNE has most or all of its sales and/or production in a single country outside its home base, it will be more dependent on that host country and its BIAs than if it has them spread in several new host countries.

Similarly, the resources a MNE can devote to financing the activities of the host country's BIAs will depend to some extent on what other BIAs it must help finance. As European representation – direct or through European federations and round tables – grows in importance, more scarce resources must be devoted to financing their activities. This may be perceived as a zero-sum situation, where MNEs are only willing to devote more funds to Euro-BIAs if they devote fewer funds to national BIAs. However, operating in several countries may result in a situation where a MNE acquires more skills in analysing and promoting its multiple interests and complex environments than most national BIAs or even many under-financed Euro-BIAs. Such a development could result in a declining tendency of MNEs to join BIAs in several national settings or even in Europe. This complexity posed by a growing number of MNEs and international mergers deserves greater attention in the future by researchers interested in the impact of Europeanization and globalization on national and international forms of business associability.

Conclusion

Sweden lacks the goodness of fit between its social institutions and market requirements found in the Netherlands, in particular as understood by many of its MNEs and BIAs. Thus, major changes were necessary in the national institutions comprising the Swedish Model. These changes required sacrificing some of the better-known features of the Swedish Model, in particular centralized collective bargaining and administrative corporatism. The CEO of Svenskt Näringsliv, Mr. Göran Tunhammar, stated in a recent debate article in *Dagens Nyheter* (17 March 2002) that:

> Corporatism was an effective way to bridge the interest conflicts when building a homogeneous society. But it is no longer feasible and has long since been abandoned by business organizations as a method for building a society characterized by pluralism and competition.

He went on to say that:

> It is time to choose. We must definitely leave the corporatist negotiation economy behind us and embrace a market economy, in which competition and openness limit the room for concessions and sweet deals. Do our politicians dare? And does business dare?

The process of transforming Swedish social institutions and adjusting to the requirements of the market has not yet been completed and different views and positions are voiced. Sweden will hold a referendum on the European Monetary Union and adoption of the euro as its currency in September 2003. Here, too, major changes in Swedish social institutions may be in store. There is no reason to believe that Svenskt Näringsliv will be any less ambitious in promoting such changes than its predecessor, SAF. Swedish BIAs played an active role in Swedish politics for several decades and will continue to do so for the foreseeable future. Today they are as interested in promoting structural changes and changing the Swedish political landscape, as they were in the past. Their strategy may shift with changing conditions, but they are intent on maintaining their influence in the future.

Appendix: frequently used acronyms

BI	Byggindustrier – the Association of the Swedish Building Industry.
BIAs	Business interest associations.
DN	*Dagens Nyheter*, the major morning daily newspaper in Sweden.
EO	Employer organization.
EU	European Union.
FDI	Foreign direct investments.
HAO	Sveriges Handelns Arbetsgivareorganization – the Swedish Commercial Employers Association.
IUI	Industrins Utredningsinstitutet – The Industry's Investigation Institute.
LO	Landsorganizationen i Sverige – the Confederation of Swedish Trade Unions.
MNE	Multinational enterprise.
OBI	Organized Business Interest.
OECD	Organization for Economic Cooperation and Development.
PTK	Privattjänstemannakartellen – (Negotiation) Cartel of Salaried Employees.
SAF	Svenska Arbetsgivareföreningen – Swedish Employers' Confederation.
SAP	Socialdemokratiska Arbetarepartiet – Social Democratic (Worker) Party.
SEK	Swedish crowns (krona).
SI	Sveriges Industriförbund – the Federation of Swedish Industry.
SN	Svenskt Näringsliv – Confederation of Swedish Enterprise.

TA	Trade association.
TCO	Tjänstemännens Centralorganization – the Central Organization of Salaried Employees.
VF	Verkstadsföreningen – the Engineering Employers' Association.
VI	Verkstadsindustrier – the Association of the Swedish Engineering Industry.

Bibliography

Andersson, T., Fredriksson, F. and Svensson, R. (1996) *Multinational Restructuring, Internationalization and Small Economies. The Swedish Case*, London and New York: Routledge.

Berger, S. and Compston, H. (eds) (2002) *Policy Concertation in Western Europe. Lessons for the 21st Century*, New York and Oxford: Berghahn Books.

Blomström, M. and Kakka, A. (1997) 'Sweden', in J. D. Dunning (ed.) *Government, Globalization and International Business*, Oxford and New York: Oxford University Press.

Blyth, M. (2001) 'The Transformation of the Swedish Model: Economic Ideas, Distributional Conflicts, and Institutional Change', *World Politics* 53 (3).

Dagens Nyheter, 25 May and 10 July 1997; 3 December 2000 and 17 March and 5 June 2002.

Ekholm, K. and Hesselman, M. (2000) 'The Foreign Operations of Swedish Manufacturing Firms: Evidence from a Survey of Swedish Multinationals in 1998', Stockholm: IUI, WP 540/200.

ETLA *et al.* (1990) *Firm Dynamics*, Stockholm: IUI, Institute of Industrial Investigation.

Geer, H. de (1986) *SAF i förhandlingar 1930–1970*, Stockholm: SAF.

Golden, M., Wallerstein, M. and Lange, P. (1999) 'Postwar Trade-Union Organization and Industrial Relations in Twelve Countries', in H. Kitschelt, P. Lange, G. Marks and J. D. Stephens (eds) *Continuity and Change in Contemporary Capitalism*, Cambridge, New York and Melbourne: Cambridge University Press.

Hooghe, L. and Marks, G. (1999) 'The Making of a Policy: the Struggle over European Integration', in H. Kitschelt, P. Lange, G. Marks and J. D. Stephens (eds) *Continuity and Change in Contemporary Capitalism*, Cambridge, New York and Melbourne: Cambridge University Press.

Huber, E. and Stephens, J. D. (2001) *Development and Crisis of the Welfare State. Parties and Politics in Global Markets*, Chicago and London: Chicago University Press.

Iversen, T. and Pontusson, J. (2001) 'Comparative Political Economy: a Northern European Perspective', Ch. 1 in T. Iversen, J. Pontusson and D. Soskice (eds) *Unions, Employers and Central Banks: Macroeconomic Coordination and Institutional Change in Social Market Economies*, Cambridge and New York: Cambridge University Press.

Iversen, T., Pontusson, J. and Soskice, D. (eds) (2001) *Unions, Employers and Central Banks: Macroeconomic Coordination and Institutional Change in Social Market Economies*, Cambridge and New York: Cambridge University Press.

ITPS, Institutet för tillväxtpolitiska studier (2001a) *International business. Foreign Owned Enterprise, 1998*, Östersund: ITPS, report no. 2001:002.

ITPS, Institutet för tillväxtpolitiska studier (2001b) *Utlandsägda företag 2000*, Östersund: ITPS, report no. 2001:007.

ITPS, Institutet för tillväxtpolitiska studier (2001c) *Svenskägda företag med verksamhet i utlandet 1998*, Östersund: ITPS, report no. 2001:010.

Johansson, J. (2000) *SAF och den svenska modellen. En studie av uppbrott från förvaltningskorporatism 1982–91*, Uppsala: Acta Universitatis Upsalensis, No. 142.

Kitschelt, H., Lange P., Marks, G. and Stevens, J. D. (1999) 'Convergence and Divergence in Advanced Capitalist Democracies', in H. Kitschelt, P. Lange, G. Marks and J. D. Stevens (eds) *Continuity and Change in Contemporary Capitalism*, Cambridge, New York and Melbourne: Cambridge University Press.

Kjellberg, A. (2000) 'Arbetsgivarstrategier i Sverige under 100 år', *Arbejdsgivare i Norden. En sociologisk analyse af arbejdsgivareorganizering i Norge, Sverige, Finland og Danmark*, Copenhagen: Nordic Council of Ministers.

Martin, A. (2001) 'The Politics of Macroeconomic Policy and Wage Negotiations in Sweden', Ch. 8 in T. Iversen, J. Pontusson and D. Soskice (eds) *Unions, Employers and Central Banks: Macroeconomic Coordination and Institutional Change in Social Market Economies*, Cambridge: Cambridge University Press.

Micheletti, M. (1994) *Den civila samhället och staten. Medborgarsammanslutningarnas roll i svensk politik*, Stockholm: Publica.

Oxelheim, L. (1984) 'The Largest Nordic Manufacturing Companies', special study in *Economic Growth in a Nordic Perspective*, Copenhagen and Stockholm: DÖR secretartiat and IUI.

Pestoff, V. (1988 and 1989) *Näringslivsorganizationerna och politiken i Sverige*, Stockholm: TCO.

Pestoff, V. (1995a) 'Towards a New Swedish Model of Collective Bargaining and Politics', in C. Crouch and F. Traxler (eds) *Organized Industrial Relations in Europe: What Future?*, Aldershot: Avebury.

Pestoff, V. (1995b) 'Employer Organizations and Collective Bargaining in Nine OECD Countries – an Overview', Paris: OECD; also in the proceedings of the 4th Regional Congress of the International Industrial Relations Association, Helsinki, Finland, 23–26 August 1994.

Pestoff, V. and Ronit, K. (1990) 'Changing Environments and European Integration: Accommodation by Organized Business in Denmark and Sweden', Reykjavik: conference paper.

Pfeffer, J. (1982) 'Resource Dependency', in *Organizations and Organization Theory*, Marshfield MA: Pitman.

Pontusson, J. and Swenson, P. (1996) 'Labour Markets, Production Strategies and Wage Bargaining Institutions. The Swedish Employers Offensive in Comparative Perspective', *Comparative Political Studies*, 29 (2): 223–250.

Rothstein, B. (2001) 'Socialt kaptial i den socialdemokratiska staten. Den svenska modellen och det civila samhället', *Arkiv* 79: 1–55.

Rothstein, B. and Bergström, J. (2000) *Korporatismens fall och den svenska modellens kris*, Stockholm: SNS förlag.

SAF's Annual General Reports, 1965 to 2000, Stockholm: SAF.

SAF-tidningen, 16 February 2000, *Ett nytt SAF håller på ta form – Ett öppet brev*, 16 May 1990; 1 February 1991; 5 November 1993.

Schmitter, P. and Lehmbruch, G. (eds) (1982) *Patterns of Corporatist Policy-Making*, London and Thousand Oaks CA: Sage.

Smith, A. (1776) *The Wealth of Nations*, London: Stratton and Cadell.

Soskice, D. (1999) 'Divergent Production Regimes: Coordinated and Uncoordinated Market Economies in the 1980s and 1990s', in H. Kitschelt, P. Lange, G. Marks and J. D. Stevens (eds) *Continuity and Change in Contemporary Capitalism*, Cambridge, New York and Melbourne: Cambridge University Press.

Stephens, J. D. (1996) 'The Scandinavian Welfare States: Achievements, Crisis and Prospects', in G. Esping-Andersen (ed.) *Welfare States in Transition. National Adaptations in Global Economies*, London and Thousand Oaks CA: Sage.

Svenska Dagbladet, 17 May 1997, Business section, p. 1.

Traxler, F. (1982) *Evolution gewerkschaftlicher Intressenvertretung*; Frankfurt and Vienna: Bramüller and Campus.

Visser, J. (1996) 'Corporatism Beyond Repair? Industrial Relations in Sweden', in J. van Ruysseveldt and J. Visser (eds) *Industrial Relations in Europe. Traditions and Transitions*, London: Sage.

Wallerstein, M. and Golden, M. (1997) 'The Fragmentation of the Bargaining Society: Wage Setting in the Nordic Countries, 1950–1992', *Comparative Political Studies* 30 (6): 699–731.

Wallerstein, M. and Golden, M. (2001) 'Postwar Wage Setting in the Nordic Countries', Ch. 4 in T. Iversen, J. Pontusson and D. Soskice (eds) *Unions, Employers and Central Banks: Macroeconomic Coordination and Institutional Change in Social Market Economies*, Cambridge and New York: Cambridge University Press.

5 Economic internationalization and the organizational dilemma of employer associations

A comparison of 20 OECD countries

Franz Traxler

The dynamics of economic internationalization stem from the ever-growing spread of market relations, which are in turn driven by processes of globalization and/or Europeanization. While these processes challenge any type of interest association, business associations are especially hard hit. The more general challenge affecting any association results from the fact that market competition is at odds with the solidaristic principle of collective action. Market competition stimulates individualistic strategies, oriented towards the self-interest of the actors. By contrast, the effectiveness of associations depends upon their ability to organize collective action, which implies overcoming self-interested behaviour.

As economic internationalization both expands and intensifies market competition on a global/European scale, it threatens to erode the individual actors' propensity to associate. In addition, there is a special threat to business associations, in that business is empowered much more than any other actor in society to respond to globalization and Europeanization by means of mobility. Cross-border mobility and transnational presence in markets threaten to devaluate the benefits of associations, whose scope of activities is always confined in territorial terms. For obvious reasons, large firms have a higher capacity for transnational mobility than small firms. At the same time, large firms have been significantly more willing to associate than their small counterparts, as evidence from cross-national studies shows (Traxler 1993, 1995). As a consequence, economic internationalization may increase the associations' difficulties in recruiting precisely that group which has been their stronghold so far.

One might object to this scenario by arguing that globalization and Europeanization differ in their impact on associations. Europeanization – far more than globalization – has paved the way not only for increased market integration but also for political integration. The latter should provide fresh impetus for associational action aimed at influencing EU decision making, including protectionist activities in response to enhanced market competition.[1] The emerging Euro-polity has indeed been accompanied by the corresponding growth of Euro-associations, especially as far as business is concerned. However, this does not necessarily counteract the destructive forces outlined above. The reason for this is that the two arguments refer to distinct dimensions of associational action. On the one hand, Europeanization as a process of *political* integration creates a *need* for Europe-wide interest representation. Needless to say, the existence of a certain need is not a guaranteed precondition for its fulfilment. Since Europe-wide interest representation is a collective good (like any other representational activity), it is also burdened with the well-known problems of collective action. On the other hand, Europeanization as a process of *economic* internationalization tends to *aggravate* the *problems of collective action*. This difference between the need for and the prospect of collective action reflects the differing logics of influence and of membership that associations have to face (Streeck and Schmitter 1991; Traxler and Schmitter 1995). The logic of influence relates to the associations' interlocutors, whose actions they wish to influence. The logic of membership refers to the associations' need to attract members. Put another way, associations have to be simultaneously *effective* and *legitimate*. As we will outline in greater detail below, this creates an organizational dilemma due to the fact that effectiveness and legitimacy impose conflicting imperatives on the organizational structure of associations. This dilemma exacerbates the contradictory consequences that Europeanization has for associations. While the political integration of Europe requires the associations to strengthen their capacity for effective action, economic integration may erode their legitimacy among their (potential) members.

Since the demand for Europe-wide interest representation resulting from political integration does not offset the disorganizing potential of economic internationalization, one cannot rule out the possibility that the rise of Euro-associations in the wake of political integration will coincide with a progressive decline in member support caused by the global/pan-European internationalization of the markets. Although Europeanization as a political process confronts associations with pressures to adapt their tasks and structures, this does not really threaten their viability. Such a threat does emerge from globalization and Europeanization driven by processes of market internationalization. Hence, Europeanization is likely to have a fairly ambivalent impact on associations: on the one hand, the shift of political governance from the national to the supranational level stimulates the expansion of the associations' structures and responsibilities to the European level; on the other hand, market-led integration threatens to hollow out these structures and responsibilities through its detrimental effect on member support.

One can infer from this that the viability of associations depends on whether they are able to cope with the challenge that economic internationalization poses to their membership base. Therefore, this chapter shall empirically analyse the effect of market internationalization on business associations with regard to member support. Methodologically, this analysis is based on a crossnational comparison that includes 20 Organization for Economic Cooperation and Development (OECD) countries (see Table 5.2).

Table 5.1 Hypothesized determinants of employer density

	Impact on density
Economic determinants	
Internationalization (OPEN1, FDI)	Negative
Change in sectoral composition (i.e. decline of manufacturing) (MAN1)	Negative
Country size (large country effect) (DEP1)	Negative
Institutional determinants	
Associational centralization of decision making (ECENF)	Negative
Comprehensive membership domain (ESYS)	Negative
Comprehensive range of representational activities (EAP)	Positive
Pervasiveness of extension practices (EXTP)	Positive
Union strength (UD1)	Positive

Note
For OPEN1, FDI, MAN1, DEP1, ECENF, ESYS, EAP, EXTP and UD1, see Appendix at end of chapter.

There are different dimensions of member support which are all necessary for effective and legitimate associational action (Traxler 1993). We will concentrate here on the constituent dimension of member support: membership measured as density (i.e. the ratio of actual to potential members).

In accordance with the argument outlined above, we can expect economic internationalization to undermine member support. This means that quantitative analysis should show a statistically negative impact of internationalization on density. It should be noted, however, that there is an alternative hypothesis pointing to the strength of (non-market) institutions that embed associational action. Accordingly, institutions can defy competitive pressures due to market imperfections (North 1990). With regard to the problem in question, this implies that associations may be able to maintain member support despite growing market internationalization, provided that they are backed by strong institutions that help them overcome their collective action problems (Traxler *et al.* 2001). We will thus test a convergence thesis (predicting a general and inevitable decline in member support as a consequence of internationalization) against a path-dependency thesis (expecting continued diversity of density due to differences between embedding institutions).

The focus of this empirical study will be on a special category of business associations: that is, national *employer* organizations. Employer organizations concentrate on representing labour market interests – in contrast to *trade* associations, which organize the interests business has in other markets. This category includes pure employer associations (specializing exclusively in labour market interests) and mixed associations (organizing both labour market interests and other business interests).

For two main reasons, one can assume that national employer organizations are especially vulnerable to the disorganizing forces of market internationalization. First of all, economic internationalization most strongly challenges associations whose activities are limited to the nation state. Second, economic internationalization should fuel the worldwide attempts on the part of employers to decentralize and/or deregulate industrial relations and to reintegrate them into the realm of the firm. Since these tendencies significantly curtail the role of employer organizations in industrial relations, their relevance for business may become increasingly dubious.

All this makes the analysis of national employer associations a very strong test case for the path-dependency thesis. If market internationalization does not significantly harm employer density, it will hardly affect member support for other types of business associations.

The remaining sections of this chapter are organized as follows: first, the convergence thesis and the path-dependency thesis will be specified and operationalized. The next section will then present the data and empirical findings. The chapter will conclude by discussing the theoretical implications of these findings.

Hypotheses and measures

While there is a huge body of existing studies on union density, comparable analysis of employer density is rare. The following hypotheses are thus drawn from general collective action theory (Olson 1965), from findings on union density (as far as they are applicable to employers) and, in particular, from recent comparative research on employer associations (Traxler 2000; Traxler *et al.* 2001).

When reviewing this literature, one finds two clusters of possible determinants of employer density. The first cluster refers to the economic context of the employers' actions. Economic internationalization is included in this cluster. As argued above, our guiding hypothesis is that economic internationalization significantly damages employer density. The key arenas of internationalization are product markets and financial markets. The standard indicator of a country's internationalization of product markets is foreign trade dependence (OPEN1).[2] To measure financial internationalization, we use foreign direct investment (FDI).

In addition to internationalization, there are two other properties of the economic context which presumably affect the tendency to associate. One factor is the sectoral composition of the economy. Analogous to the situation of the unions (Visser 1991), manufacturing may be the stronghold of employer associations, whereas employer density may be rather low in the service sector. Hence, there should be a positive relationship between density and the size of the manufacturing sector (MAN1).[3] Aside from the sectoral composition of an economy, its sheer size (DEP1)[4] is likely to influence density. Generally, growing group size has a negative effect on collective action (Olson 1965). Moreover, seen from the associations' perspective, the strategy of maximizing membership may be less rational in large countries than in small ones (Wallerstein 1989). This is because a reasonably high absolute number of members is sufficient for resourcing an association. In large countries, this absolute number of members can be reached at lower density levels compared to small countries. Since associations are normally forced to economize on resources, they will hardly invest in increasingly expensive member recruitment beyond that absolute number of members required for effective action.

The employers' institutional context represents the second cluster of factors. These factors are at the centre of the path-dependency thesis. The related question, then, is to identify those institutions which can contribute to solving the recruitment problems of employer associations. In this respect, two categories of institutions are of utmost importance: the organizational structure of employer associations and selective incentives for their members.

As far as the organizational structures are concerned, employer associations can attract potential members by tailoring their structures as closely to their members' immediate interests as possible. This involves an association's demarcation of its domain and its decision-making procedures. The demarcation of domain defines the range of interests covered by an association. Encompassing domains cause associations to internalize highly heterogeneous interests. Under these conditions, the interests of a certain member group will often be neglected and filtered out in the course of internal interest aggregation and goal formation. Hence, encompassing domains create more problems for member recruitment than narrow domains do. Our measure of the scope of domains (i.e. the concentration/fragmentation of the associational system) is the number of national, cross-sectoral employer associations (ESYS): the larger the number of associations, the narrower their interest domain tends to be, because under these circumstances, associations are forced to specialize in certain interests. Internal decision-making procedures are also important to member recruitment. The influence of an individual employer on the decision-making process decreases with growing centralization. This probably deters potential members from joining an association. When measuring centralization, we thus focus on the employers' rights and obligations in relation to higher hierarchical levels of goal formation (ECENF). The hypothesis regarding organizational structures is that employer density increases with inter-associational fragmentation (i.e. narrow interests indicated by a large number of associations) and with intra-associational decentralization.

Regardless of this, employer associations cannot simply narrow down their domains and decentralize for the sake of member recruitment, since such logic of membership conflicts with the logic of influence. In the labour market, an association's capacity for strategic action depends on how many labour-market segments it controls compared to its counterpart. Controlling fewer segments creates the risk of being played off against one another by the strategically superior counterpart. Furthermore, an encompassing domain tends to strengthen an association's position with regard to public policy making. This is because the authorities may consider narrow associations less important when seeking to consult the most 'representative' voice of business. In contrast to the logic of membership, these strategic imperatives reward the building of encompassing and centralized structures. When balancing these contradictory requirements, employers associations may well arrive at distinct solutions that are contingent on circumstances (e.g. union structures) (Traxler *et al.* 2001).

Selective incentives reward members and/or punish non-members. In principle, any associational service offered exclusively to members can work as a selective incentive for membership. In practice, however, services may also be collective goods (from which non-members also benefit) or a mixture of selective and collective goods. A case in point is the associational representation of members in labour court proceedings. The representation of the particular member involved is certainly a selective good. However, a favourable court decision on this particular case that is of general importance and thus predetermines the outcome of similar labour disputes is a collective good. Therefore, an empirical study of selective incentives would require the in-depth analysis of each single activity – something which extends beyond a comparison of 20 countries. Instead, we will take the range of an association's representational activities vis-à-vis the state (EAP) as a yardstick for its service potential. The rationale of this procedure is that an association can derive selective incentives from the provision of collective goods. For instance, an association's participation in industrial policy may serve as the basis for providing faster and better information to its members about related issues. Accordingly, we assume that density increases with the range of state-related representational activities performed by the association.

Employer associations can also derive selective incentives from bargaining with the unions. Strong unions presumably foster the employers' propensity to associate, because protection against labour's collective action is one *raison d'être* of employer associations. Another selective incentive is based on statutory provisions for extending collective agreements to those employers not affiliated with the signatory employer association (Gladstone 1984; Traxler 1998). Given such practices, employers have good reason to believe that a collective agreement will bind them even if they remain outside of the association. Hence, it is rational for them to associate in order to be entitled to participate in the bargaining process, the outcome of which may be binding on them in any case. We thus hypothesize that employer density increases with the pervasiveness of extension (EXTP). Table 5.1 summarizes the above hypotheses concerning the determinants of employer density.

Finally, we need to operationalize the dependent variable: employer density. This can be done in two ways, referring either to the firms themselves or to the firms' employees (Traxler *et al.* 2001). The power of an employer association as compared to its union counterparts depends less on the number of firms than on the number of employees covered. Hence, measuring employer density in terms of employees is preferable.

Data on employer density are sparse. Here, we are confining our considerations to a country's principal (i.e. largest) employer peak organization. Peak organizations are independent in that they are not subordinate to any other employer association. Employer density (LED) is defined as the proportion of employees organized by the largest employer peak within its own domain – understood as formal eligibility for membership laid down in the peak's constitution. This domain is always cross-sectoral and, in most cases, covers the entire private sector. In line with this operationalization, all of the above associational measures – except for inter-associational fragmentation (ESYS) – refer to the principal employer peak.

Data and findings

Due to the limited availability of comparable time series data on employer density, it is impossible to employ a pooled time-series design. Instead, this analysis adopts a cross-sectional and a simple longitudinal approach focusing on two periods (i.e. 1986–1990 and 1994–1996). For the sake of brevity, descriptive statistics are presented here only for the dependent variable – that is, density (Table 5.2).

Employers are particularly well organized in Austria, where density is 100 per cent. This is because all firms in the Wirtschaftskammer Österreich's (WKÖ) domain are legally required to be members. Although the WKÖ is the only principal employer peak relying on obligatory membership, informal mechanisms of compulsory member recruitment combine with formally voluntary membership in several other countries as well. For instance, compulsory payment of dues – which most closely approaches compulsory membership – is institutionalized at the sectoral level in Belgium and the Netherlands. In Belgium's textile industry, all employers are obliged to pay 1 per cent of gross wages to a central fund primarily designed to finance the payment of additional unemployment benefits to union members. This fund also sponsors the sector's employer association, which keeps 5 per cent of all contributions for the running of its own organization (Blanpain 1998: 282). A similar arrangement exists in the Dutch construction industry. About 95 per cent of the staff working on behalf of the sector's employer organization is financed out of a fund created under a clause in the collective agreement which requires that every firm in the sector pay a certain sum per worker (van Waarden 1995). In both cases, the employer associations – in cooperation with their union counterparts – are able to impose levies on non-members via a legally-based extension of collective agreements to unaffiliated firms. Given the obligatory payment of dues, employers have every reason to join their associations.

Following behind Austria, the principal peaks of Australia, New Zealand,

Table 5.2 Largest employer peak organization, and change in density (LED)

Country	*Name*	*LED** 1986–1990	*LED** 1994–1996	*Change*
Austria	WKÖ	100.0	100.0	0
Australia	CAI (1986–1995), ACCI	62.0	75.0[g]	+13
Belgium	VBO/FEB	–	72.0	–
Canada	–	0.0	0.0	0
Switzerland	ZSAO, SAV[c]	39.0	37.0	−2
Germany	BDA	73.0[h]	72.0[h]	−1
Denmark	DA	38.0	39.0	+1
Spain[a]	CEOE	75.0	72.0	−3
France	CNPF[d]	75.0	74.0	−1
Finland	STK (1986–1993), TT	42.0	44.0	+2
UK	CBI	–	54.0	–
Italy	C	81.0	39.0	−42
Ireland	FUE, FIE[e] (1986–1993), IBEC	36.0	39.0	+3
Japan	Nikkeiren	39.0	40.0[g]	+1
Norway	NAF, NHO[f]	32.0	31.0	−1
Netherlands	VNO (1986–1994), VNO-NCW	–	79.0	–
New Zealand	NZEF	90.0	90.0	0
Portugal[b]	CIP	–	34.0	–
Sweden	SAF	54.0	55.0	+1
USA	–	0.0	0.0	0
Mean		52.3	52.3	
Standard deviation		28.4	26.3	

Source: Traxler *et al.* (2001).

Notes
* Period means or most recent data.
a Since 1977.
b Since 1975.
c ZSAO renamed as SAV in 1996.
d CNPF renamed as MEDEF in 1998.
e FUE renamed as FIE in 1989.
f NAF renamed as NHO in 1990.
g 1997.
h West Germany.
For the definition of LED and abbreviations, see Appendix.

(West) Germany, France, Belgium, the Netherlands and Spain record high density levels of more than 70 per cent. Until the 1990s, Confindustria also belonged to this group. The subsequent decline in density does not indicate an absolute loss of membership (which grew continuously, from 2.8 million in 1970 to 4.12 million in 1996) but ensues from an extension of its domain from manufacturing to services since 1991. While this has broadened Confindustria's potential membership, the level of actual membership in the new domain still lags behind that of manufacturing. In contrast to what one might expect, employer density is below average in the Nordic countries. Two factors (that will prove essential to density in the statistical analysis below) mainly account for this situation: extension practices do not exist in any of these countries except Finland. Furthermore, all the Nordic peaks are characterized by extremely high centralization, which makes them strong in terms of strategic capacity but negatively affects their membership strength.

In Australia, the strong increase in density from the early to the mid-1990s has to do with the merger of the Confederation of Australian Industry (CAI) and the Australian Chamber of Commerce to form the Australian Chamber of Commerce and Industry (ACCI). Finally, the USA and Canada lack any form of employer peak associations. In the USA, employer organizations are also absent below peak level. In Canada, employer associations have been established in a few sectors, and differ considerably in their roles across the distinct provincial jurisdictions.

As far as the development of density is concerned, there have been only slight changes. The notable exceptions are Confindustria and the ACCI, both of which underwent major changes due to substantial processes of organizational restructuring, as outlined above. Furthermore, the direction of the changes shows no particular trend. Of the 16 countries for which data for both periods are available, density increased in six cases and decreased in six others, whereas no change occurred in four countries.

The very small scale of observable changes may be attributed to the rather short time period under examination. However, it is nevertheless an interesting and remarkable finding, since the development of union density for the same 16 countries during the same time period shows a comparatively higher decline. While the average change is a decline of 1.9 percentage points in the case of the employer associations, the comparable figure for union density is a decline of 3.1 percentage points.[5]

Turning now to the empirical examination of our hypotheses, we will leave out the case of Austria, since its principal peak relies on obligatory membership. In line with the above reasoning, we will differentiate between the economic cluster and the institutional cluster of independent variables, and start by testing the impact of the economic variables. We will adopt a longitudinal design for this multivariate analysis by using the change in the independent variables from 1986 to 1996 as a predictor for the change in density during this period.

The results of this analysis (Table 5.3) show that none of the economic variables exerts a significantly negative impact on density. While the effect of the changes in FDI – as well as the size of manufacturing – remain insignificant, employer density actually tends to increase significantly with growing foreign trade dependence, in stark contrast to the hypothesis. Since OPEN1 correlates strongly with DEP1, one may doubt that there actually is a causal relationship between foreign trade dependence and employer density. It is more reasonable to assume that the observed relationship

Table 5.3 Economic determinants of change in employer density (DLED)

	Change from 1980–1990 to 1994–1996	
DMAN1	0.57	[1.27]
DFDI	−2.25	[−1.39]
DOPEN1	0.20*	[1.72]
Constant	3.41	[1.62]
R^2	0.09	
N	14	

Notes
* $p \leq 0.10$; ** $p \leq 0.05$; *** $p \leq 0.01$; R^2 = adjusted coefficient of determination.
Entries are OLS-coefficients; t-statistics in square brackets are based on White's heteroskedasticity-robust standard errors.
D indicates the difference in the score of variables between the two periods.
Austria omitted.
For variable definitions, see Appendix.

between these two variables represents the positive effect of small country size on density, in accordance with the logic outlined above (see also Table 5.1). In this respect, however, it is important to note that this positive effect cannot generally be traced to the corporatist profile of small countries, which – it has been argued – can cushion the repercussions of strong exposure to world market competition (Katzenstein 1985). This is because EAP – which can be taken as an indicator of corporatism – has a detrimental rather than a favourable impact on density, as the negative correlation between EAP and LED reveals (i.e. $r = -0.21$ and -0.26 for 1986–1990, $n = 13$, and 1994–1996, $n = 17$, respectively). The positive relationship between small country size and employer density thus results from the difference between small and large countries in terms of economizing on the costs of member recruitment.

At any rate, the above findings all suggest that economic change does not seriously challenge the capacity of employer associations to attract members. This capacity is much more contingent on institutional factors. As their bivariate correlations with LED (which are not reported here for reasons of space) indicate, all but two institutional factors correlate with density in the expected way. The two exceptions are associational participation in public policy and union density. As its negative relationship with density (see above) reveals, associational participation (EAP) works primarily as a collective good from which selective incentives cannot be extracted systematically. The irrelevance of union density is amazing.[6]

This is due to such intervening variables as external, state-provided membership incentives. Such incentives are essential to both employees and employers. However, the two sides of industry differ with regard to which external selective incentives are significant: in the case of employees, the decisive incentives are union-led, state-sponsored unemployment schemes (Ebbinghaus and Visser 1997; Traxler *et al.* 2001); for employers, the extension of collective agreements is what matters. The reason that the density of employers and employees tend to be independent of one another is the fact that any establishment of these two types of incentives does not co-vary across countries. For instance, in most of the Scandinavian countries, union-led unemployment schemes exist, but an extension practice is completely lacking. This is an important factor contributing to the employees' clearly higher density there as compared to the employers. A diametrically opposed pattern characterizes such countries as France, Portugal and Spain, where extension is pervasive, and union-led unemployment schemes do not exist at all. In all these cases, employer density surpasses union density. Another intervening factor is product market interests. When employer associations are mixed, businesses may join for the mere reason of product market interests, implying that the unions have no effect on association. One example of this is the CBI. It has lost most of its profile as an employer association but has largely retained its density over time. In contrast, Britain's lower-level employer associations lost approximately half their density (in terms of establishments) during the 1980s (Millward *et al.* 1992), when multi-employer bargaining withered away. Hence, the CBI's ability to attract members stems primarily from its activities as a trade association dealing with product market interests.

As a consequence, one can expect union density to affect employer density most strongly in those countries where pure employer associations are established and where *neither* union-led unemployment schemes *nor* extension practices exist as the two key selective incentives for employees and employers. However, in testing this hypothesis, we encounter serious problems. Above all, any differentiation between mixed and pure employer peaks is insufficient in this context, because many affiliates – even of pure employer peaks – are mixed. This explains why mixed and pure employer peaks hardly differ in their level of membership, with an average density of 54.1 per cent and 57.7 per cent, respectively (most recent data).

There is evidence that the product market is more important than the labour market as a reason to associate. Cross-national comparison at the sectoral level shows that the domains of pure employer associations are significantly broader than those of pure sectoral trade associations (Traxler 1993). As we will show in greater detail below, employer density decreases significantly with associational concentration. This, in turn, suggests that the density of pure sectoral employer associations is notably lower than that of their trade counterparts. However, since it is impossible to disentangle the impact of labour market and product market interests on membership in mixed associations, we must disregard the functional differentiation of employer associations. We can control only for selective incentives: there are seven countries where neither union-led unemployment schemes nor extension provisions are in operation (Ireland, Italy, Norway, the UK, Japan,

Canada and the USA). Comparison of the density of employers and unions corroborates a positive correlation (r LED/UD = 0.34 [n = 7, 1994–1996]).

To capture this finding for the multivariate analysis, we will construct a dummy variable (NGNE) that discriminates between those countries having neither a union-led unemployment scheme nor extension practices and all other countries. Table 5.4 presents the most powerful multivariate model for both reference periods. We can limit this analysis to a cross-sectional model computed for each of the two periods under examination, because the institutional variables which enter the model remained almost completely stable over time. Taking into account that centralization does not matter in the case of the USA and Canada, the mean for ECENF was assigned to these countries, and a dummy variable (USCDN) was introduced to control for the distinction between these two countries and the others.

With the exception of manufacturing, none of the economic variables enter the model, since their inclusion would deteriorate the model's explanatory power. Although manufacturing contributes to the explanatory power of the model, this variable does not have a consistent effect. In combination with the differing number of countries entering the models for the two

Table 5.4 Determinants of employer density (LED)

	1986–1990	*1994–1996*
MAN1	0.70 [0.93]	−1.24 [−1.42]
ECENF	−8.32** [−2.52]	−10.75*** [−5.12]
ESYS	5.60*** [5.23]	3.53*** [3.33]
USCDN	−20.78** [−2.32]	−33.44*** [−7.25]
NGNE	−25.07*** [−3.21]	−28.46*** [−6.09]
Constant	14.36 [0.83]	56.41*** [3.58]
R^2	0.78	0.82
N	15	19

Notes

* $p \leq 0.10$; ** $p \leq 0.05$; *** $p \leq 0.01$; R^2 = adjusted coefficient of determination.

Entries are OLS-coefficients in period-specific cross-section models; t-statistics in square brackets are based on White's heteroskedasticity-robust standard errors.

USA and Canada: Values for ECENF are set to the overall mean and controlled for by a dummy variable (USCDN); Austria omitted.

For variable definitions, see Table 5.1 and Appendix.

periods, this lack of consistency probably emanates from the ways in which the principal peak organizations themselves and other, smaller associations relate their domain to manufacturing.

Employer density is thus predominantly shaped by its institutional context, implying a strong path-dependent effect in dynamic respects. Furthermore, the dampening effect on density of both inter-associational concentration and centralization reveals that employer organizations do face the dilemma of a conflict between the logic of influence and the logic of membership: while the capacity for strategically exerted influence increases with concentration and centralization, the members tend to prefer narrow, decentralized associations. The fact that the associations' participation in public policy (EAP) negatively correlates with their density (see above) also indicates the presence of this dilemma. Public policy functions which correspond with the strategic imperative to exert influence conflict with the possibility of accommodating the immediate interests of the members.

The impact of union density and extension practices, as captured by NGNE, indicates the relevance of engagement by employer organizations in labour relations in general and collective bargaining in particular. The multivariate analysis also expands upon the bivariate analysis by stressing the importance of differentiating the USA and Canada from the other countries. In fact, this variable (USCDN) is a very powerful predictor. Since USCDN represents the fact that employer peaks are absent in the USA and Canada – in contrast to the other countries – it refers to a crucial analytical distinction: between the *need* to associate and the *ability* to do so. American employers obviously feel no need to associate, implying that the ability to overcome the collective action problem recedes into the background.

Conclusions

The above analysis has provided strong evidence that employers' propensity to associate is still shaped almost exclusively by their institutional context. This context, in turn, is determined by the properties of the nation state: extension practices, union density, the associational system of employers and the degree of centralization of the principal employer peak all vary considerably from country to country. This implies that the density of employer associations is not *directly* affected by the pressures of market internationalization. However, we must consider the fact that this analysis covers only one decade. In the long run, internationalization may have an *indirect* effect that is processed by the given institutions. Since these institutions all vary considerably across countries, density may diverge more strongly in the long run. Employer associations embedded in strong and supportive institutions are likely to sustain or even increase their membership strength, whereas, in unfavourable institutional contexts, other national associations may undergo decay.

Furthermore, since density is just one dimension of the organization of employer interests, one cannot rule out the possibility of stronger effects of economic internationalization on employer associations in other organizational respects. Indeed, case-study analysis suggests that – especially from the early 1990s onwards – employers have put strong pressures on their associations to restructure for the sake of economizing on resources. Membership dues have been a key issue in this respect. For instance, Dansk Arbejdsgiveforening's (DA) resources have been cut by half in the wake of dues reductions (Due *et al.* 1997: 117). SAF's annual budget has been reduced by more than 20 per cent in connection with an almost 50 per cent lowering of subscriptions (EIRR 1993: 12). In 2000, the WKÖ decided to reduce its dues by 30 per cent. In all three countries, the cuts in dues were enforced by the group of large firms. These member-driven pressures for lower dues are part of a set of more general employer efforts to curb costs against a background of intensified competition which is certainly being fuelled by economic internationalization. Hence, the employers' primary response to the challenge of internationalization is not recourse to exit, but rather to voice – in the sense of attempts to 'modernize' their associations.

In addition to these changes, there have also been adjustments in terms of functions. The most remarkable component of these functional adaptations has been a gradual reorientation from labour market interests towards product market interests. There are two important manifestations of this reorientation. On the one hand, a series of mergers between pure employer associations and trade associations has occurred, resulting in the formation of mixed associations. As far as the principal employer peak associations are concerned, mergers with their trade association counterparts happened in Norway in 1989, in Ireland in 1993, in Sweden in 2001 and in Japan in 2002. The employer peaks of Portugal and New Zealand moved to a mixed status by incorporating regional trade associations in the 1980s and late 1990s, respectively. Such mergers make sense in terms of the logic of influence as well as that of membership. As far as the logic of influence is concerned, economic internationalization and European integration have strongly increased the mutual externalities and functional interdependencies of policy fields, such that it has become extremely difficult for associations to disentangle issues of labour market interests from those of product market interests. The building of mixed associations also helps cope with the logic of membership. This is because mixed associations can attract members not only for reasons of labour market interests but also for those of product market interests. The latter have gained in importance as an incentive to associate, since collective labour market interests have become less important – not least as a consequence of alterations in bargaining. This brings us to the second manifestation of functional adjustments: in the course of tendencies towards the decentralization of collective bargaining, the employer associations of almost all countries have handed over bargaining tasks to their member firms (Traxler *et al.* 2001).

While cuts in dues – as well as a more limited role in bargaining –

conform to member demands, they restrain the associations' capacity for strategic action. Economic internationalization thus exacerbates the organizational dilemma between the conflicting logics of membership and influence, and prompts the associations to adjust themselves in a way that prioritizes the requirements for membership at the cost of strategic imperatives. In stark contrast to the employees (Traxler 1995; Traxler *et al.* 2001), the individual employers are so powerful vis-à-vis their own associations that they can enforce structures tailored to their immediate interests, even when doing so threatens to harm their associations' capacity for strategic action. This especially applies to large companies. In formal terms, the superior power position of large companies in relation to smaller businesses is institutionalized within employer associations by the fact that voting rights are normally weighted according to the amount of dues paid – which, in turn, is linked to firm size (in particular, employment and the wage sum). It is thus no mere coincidence that it has been the group of large companies which has pressed for the 'modernization' of employer associations. Large companies can be content with 'lean' associations, since they are less dependent on their support. For instance, cuts in dues necessarily imply a reduction of services. Large companies can easily accept this trade-off, since they have far less need for the services, and at the same time pay much higher dues than their smaller counterparts. Likewise, large companies will enforce reforms inside the associations rather than leaving them, since their extraordinary power makes 'voice' the better option than 'exit' when it comes to advancing their interests. This means that the direction of associational modernization tends to favour the interests of the large companies. As a result, they are also more willing to maintain their membership – something which helps employer associations sustain a high level of density in terms of employment, even under difficult circumstances. Put another way, numerous small companies are needed to match the level of employment and dues covered by one single large company. Hence, appeasing their large member companies must be the top priority of employer associations.

There are two theoretical conclusions that can be derived from these findings – one concerning collective action theory and the other concerning organization theory. These conclusions, in turn, have important implications for the practice of interest representation.

The first point is that the collective action problems of employers tends to transcend the conventional analytical framework as put forward by Olson (1965). His premise – and that of other related reasoning – is that self-interested behaviour makes it difficult for the actors involved to produce the desired collective good. This presupposes the existence of a basic interest in the collective good. This does not fully match the situation of employers, who may clearly prefer individual exchange relations with labour over collective ones. Hence, the interest in associational action as such is dubious.

When it comes to associating, employers enjoy the advantage of a 'small' group because a relatively small number of large employers suffice to set up a powerful association. Hence, the lack of employer peak associations in the USA and Canada results not from insurmountable difficulties in associational action but from a lack of interest in it. This brings us back to the distinction between the need to associate and the ability to do so. Although the dummy variable (USCDN) that distinguishes the USA and Canada takes up this point, it does not capture the full effect of variations in the need to associate on density. This is because the lack of such need affects density in *all* countries; in America, it has taken on an extreme form, with employer peaks being completely absent. In the other countries, employer disinterest in association is most visible in a smaller or larger number of huge, unaffiliated companies. In Britain, for instance, none of the large car manufacturers are members of their sector's employer organization (Edwards *et al.* 1998). The upshot is that the employers' need to associate tends to fall short of their capacity to do so. This contrasts with the standard assumption of collective action theory, which proceeds from the polar opposite situation: that is, a certain interest group has a need to associate but faces serious problems of collective action.

With regard to organization theory, it is commonly assumed that organizations are collective entities which enjoy 'relative' autonomy from their members. Above all, relative autonomy relates to an organization's capacity to determine its own goals and select the means of advancing them. This includes processes of goal displacement, in so far as organizations are presumed to develop an interest in themselves that intermediates the members' interests for the sake of which the organization was originally set up. Following Robert Michels' 'Iron Law of Oligarchy' (2001), the literature widely agrees that this kind of relative autonomy also characterizes voluntary interest associations. In contrast to this, the above findings on the strong conflict between the logics of membership and of influence suggest that the dependency of employer associations on their members is extremely high, and that conversely, their autonomy is particularly restricted. This dependency emanates from the fact that large firms – which are the backbone of employer associations – control more resources and thus wield more power than their associations do. Hence, associational power is borrowed from the member firms rather than constituting an emergent property of the association as such. As a consequence, associational policies have to echo the interests of the (large) member firms, even when doing so conflicts with the associations' interest in themselves. This is exemplified by New Zealand and Sweden, whose employer associations struggled fiercely to dismantle multi-employer bargaining, even though this goal obviously curtails their role in a key arena of labour relations.

For employer associations, there are only two possibilities for acquiring some degree of autonomy from their members. The first is commercialization (i.e. selling products and services on the market). New Zealand's employer associations have taken this route following their success in doing away with multi-employer bargaining (Carrol and Tremewan 1993).

However, converting into a commercial organization implies losing the genuine profile of an employer association. The second path to relative autonomy from members is state sponsorship. Extension practices are most important to employer associations in this respect. Moreover, the strong correlation between extension practices and employer density indicates that membership by employers is not purely voluntary. If state-guaranteed extension is absent, many employers – in particular those running small and medium-sized enterprises – prefer staying outside of their associations. This is because individual contracting offers a more attractive alternative, since it enables the companies to escape from collective bargaining. In addition, large companies are powerful enough to resort to single-employer collective bargaining as another alternative, even when employer associations are backed by extension practices. This qualifies the effectiveness of such practices as a means of ensuring the associations' relative autonomy vis-à-vis their core member group. The options of both individual contracting and single-employer bargaining magnify the divergence between the ability and the need to associate to an extent that makes employer associations a very special case for both collective action theory and organization theory.

These alternatives to association-based, multi-employer bargaining work as a vehicle for preventing employer associations from moving away from their members' immediate interests. Up to now, these immediate interests have centred on reintegrating as many industrial relations issues as possible into the realm of the company. Given the divergence between the ability and the need to associate, employer associations have to take this interest into account, even though it diminishes their relevance as agents of business.

Economic internationalization exacerbates this divergence still further, and makes the logic of membership clearly prevail over the logic of influence. This is because economic internationalization increases the companies' capacity for transnational action, whereas organized labour still acts primarily within the confines of the nation state. An analogous effect emanates from Europeanization as a market-led economic process which counters the association-building effect of Europeanization as a political process. However, the above empirical findings document that this happens in a way other than that which we assumed in the introductory section. The internationalization of markets does not hollow out the rise of European employer associations through a decline in density; rather, it does so by shrinking the governance capacities of their national affiliates. It goes without saying that European associations cannot wield more power than that which is aggregated at lower levels. This, in turn, explains why such elaborate Euro-corporatist institutions as those first endorsed in the Social Protocol have proved so limited in terms of actual governance (e.g. Keller and Sörries 1998; Keller and Bansbach 2000).

It is important to note that this decline in associational capacity does not translate into a corresponding weakness on the part of employers in relation to their labour counterparts. This is because the structural (i.e. pre-associational) power asymmetry that works in favour of employers in the labour market (Offe 1985) more than offsets this associational weakness. Paradoxically, this weakness tends to be converted into a strategic advantage in negotiations by employers' associations with the unions, since the bargaining party less interested in an agreement and less capable of binding its members obtains the stronger bargaining position. In other words, employers can force their associations to focus on the logic of membership at the risk of harming their strategic capacities, since the increase in strategic capacity that accrues to the companies themselves in the wake of internationalization overcompensates for the inverse effect on their employer associations.

Appendix

Operationalization of variables

DEP1 Dependent employment, except for Germany (West Germany only).

EAP Associational (employer) participation in state regulation (non-wage issues): aggregate index of activities listed below. Each generalized activity counts as 11; each specialized activity counts as 1. The scale is standardized to the interval 0–1.

General activities

- Influences national government or parliamentary bodies with regard to labour-market issues
- Represents members' labour-market interests on national corporatist institutions

Specialized activities

Participation in the formulation of:

- Industrial policy programmes
- Regional development programmes
- Public occupational programmes (including apprenticeship) and active labour-market policy
- Research and development programmes
- Quality control programmes and/or standardization of products

Implements or participates in the implementation of:

- Industrial policy programmes
- Regional development programmes
- Public occupational programmes (including apprenticeship) and active labour-market policy
- Research and development programmes
- Quality control programs and/or standardization of products

ECENF Associational centralization: control of employer organizations over member firms under the umbrella of the largest peak. Formal control over member firms decreases when they are entitled to (1) obtain the status of a 'non-conforming' member generally not subject to collective agreements signed by the association; (2) conduct separate negotiations on their own when a collective agreement by the association is not in line with the firm's interest; (3) autonomously organize industrial action; (4) pay their employees more than the amount fixed by the collective agreement signed by the association. Aggregate index of items 1–4 each coded yes = −1, no = 0. Reference is to the most common pattern or the most influential affiliate in the case of intra-confederal variation.

ESYS Inter-associational fragmentation/concentration: number of national, cross-sectoral employer peak organizations covering at least two complete one-digit ISIC sectors.

EXTP Practice of extending multi-employer agreements to employers unaffiliated to the bargaining units, measured as the percentage of private-sector employees exclusively covered by extension. 1 = no notable extension practice, 2 = moderate practice (i.e. 5–25% of all private-sector employees covered), 3 = pervasive practice.

FDI Foreign direct investment (inward and outward) as a percentage of nominal GDP in US dollars.

LED Density of the largest employer peak: percentage of employees organized by the peak within its domain, except for Germany (West Germany only).

MAN1 Share of employees in manufacturing in the total number of employees, except for Germany (West Germany only).

NGNE 1 = countries where neither union-led unemployment schemes nor extension practices exist; 0 = other countries.

OPEN1 Foreign trade dependence (sum of exports and imports) as a percentage of GDP, except for Germany (West Germany only).

UD1 Union density: gross or net density as defined and listed in Traxler *et al.* (2001) (gross density for Ireland, Japan and Switzerland; net density for all other countries).

USCDN 1 = USA, Canada
0 = other countries

Data sources: DEP1: OECD, *Economic Outlook*; FDI: IMF, *Balance of Payment Statistics Yearbook*; MAN1: OECD, *Labour Force Statistics*; OPEN1: OECD, *National Accounts*; all other variables: Traxler *et al.* (2001).

Abbreviations: associations

ACCI	Australian Chamber of Commerce and Industry
BDA	Bundesvereinigung der Deutschen Arbeitgeberverbände
C	Confindustria
CAI	Confederation of Australian Industry
CBI	Confederation of British Industry
CEOE	Confederación Española de Organizaciones Empresariales
CIP	Confederação da Indústria Portuguesa
CNPF	Conseil National du Patronat Français
DA	Dansk Arbejdsgiverforening
FIE	Federation of Irish Employers
FUE	Federated Union of Employers
IBEC	Irish Business and Employers' Confederation
NAF	Norges Arbeidsgiverforening
NHO	Næringslivets Hovedorganisasjon
NZEF	New Zealand Employers' Federation
SAF	Svenska Arbetsgivareföreningen
SAV	Schweizerischer Arbeitgeberverband
STK	Suomen Työnantajain Keskusliitto
TT	Teollisuus ja Työnantajat
VBO/FEB	Verband van Belgische Ondernemingen – Fédération des Entreprises Belgique
VNO	Verbond van Nederlandse Ondernemingen
VNO-NCW	Vereniging van Nederlandse Ondernemers – Nederlands Christelijke Werksgeversverbond
WKÖ	Wirtschaftskammer Österreich
ZSAO	Zentralverband Schweizerischer Arbeitgeber-Organisationen

Notes

1 There are also tendencies towards building global non-market institutions (like the WTO) which may stimulate associational action on a global scale in a way analogous to but less pronounced than in the case of Europeanization.

2 For the detailed operationalization of all variables, see the Appendix.

3 This variable is closely related to economic internationalization, since market-driven changes in the international division of labour tend to reduce the size of the manufacturing sector in all developed countries.

4 Notably, this variable strongly correlates with OPEN1 (i.e. $r = -0.55$ for both 1986–1990 and 1994–1996; all countries listed in Table 5.2), since small countries are much more exposed to international competition than their larger counterparts.

5 The figure for union density is computed on the basis of data from Traxler *et al.* (2001).

6 The bivariate correlations between UD1 and LED are $r = -0.01$, $n = 15$ and $r = -0.10$, $n = 19$, for 1986–1990 and 1994–1996, respectively.

References

Blanpain, R. (1998) 'Belgium', in R. Blanpain (ed.) *International Encyclopaedia for Labour Law and Industrial Relations*, Vol. 2, Deventer: Kluwer.

Carrol, P. and Tremewan, P. (1993) 'Organising Employers: The Effect of the Act on Employers and the Auckland Employer Association', in R. Harbridge (ed.) *Employment Contracts: New Zealand Experiences*, Wellington: Victory University Press.

Due, J., Madsen, J. S., Jensen, C. S. and Hansen, L. L. (1997) 'Denmark', in G. Fajertag (ed.) *Collective Bargaining in Western Europe 1996–1997*, Brussels: ETUI.

Ebbinghaus, B. and Visser, J. (1997) 'When Labour Institutions Matter: Union Growth and Decline in Western Europe, 1950–90', paper presented at the European Sociological Association Conference, University of Essex, Colchester, 27–30 August 1997.

Edwards, P., Hall, M., Hyman, R., Marginson, P., Sisson, K., Waddington, J. and Winchester, D. (1998) 'Great Britain: From Partial Collectivism to Neo-Liberalism to Where?', in A. Ferner and R. Hyman (eds) *Changing Industrial Relations in Europe*, Oxford: Blackwell.

EIRR (European Industrial Relations Review) (1993) No. 237.

Gladstone, A. (1984) 'Employers Associations in Comparative Perspective: Functions and Activities', in J. P. Windmuller and A. Gladstone (eds) *Employers Associations and Industrial Relations*, Oxford: Clarendon Press.

Katzenstein, P. J. (1985) *Small States in World Markets: Industrial Policy in Europe*, Ithaca NY: Cornell University Press.

Keller, B. and Bansbach, M. (2000) 'Social Dialogues: An Interim Report on Recent Results and Prospects', *Industrial Relations Journal* 31: 291–307.

Keller, B. and Sörries B. (1998) 'The New Social Dialogue: Procedural Structuring, First Results and Perspectives', *Industrial Relations Journal, European Annual Review 1997*: 77–98.

Michels, R. (2001/1915) *Political Parties*, Kitchener, Ontario: Batoche Books.

Millward, N., Stevens, M., Smart D. and Hawes, W. R. (1992) *Workplace Industrial Relations in Transition*, Aldershot: Dartmouth.

North, D. C. (1990) *Institutions, Institutional Change and Economic Performance*, Cambridge: Cambridge University Press.

Offe, C. (1985) *Disorganized Capitalism: Contemporary Transformations of Work and Politics*, Oxford: Polity.

Olson, M. (1965) *The Logic of Collective Action: Public Goods and the Theory of Groups*, Cambridge MA, London: Harvard University Press.

Streeck, W. and Schmitter, P. C. (1991) 'The Organization of Business Interests. A Research Design to Study the Associative Action of Business in the Advanced Industrial Societies of Western Europe', Discussion paper IIM/LMP 81-13, Wissenschaftszentrum Berlin.

Traxler, F. (1993) 'Business Associations and Labour Unions in Comparison: Theoretical Perspectives and Empirical Findings on Social Class, Collective Action and Associational Organizability', *British Journal of Sociology* 44: 673–691.

Traxler, F. (1995) 'Two Logics of Collective Action in Industrial Relations?', in C. Crouch and F. Traxler (eds) *Organized Industrial Relations in Europe: What Future?*, Aldershot: Avebury.

Traxler, F. (1998) 'Collective Bargaining in the OECD', *European Journal of Industrial Relations*, 4: 207–226.

Traxler, F. (2000) 'Employers and Employer Organisations in Europe: Membership Strength, Density and Representativeness', *Industrial Relations Journal* 31: 308–316.

Traxler, F. and Schmitter, P. C. (1995) 'The Emerging Euro-Polity and Organized Interests', *European Journal of International Relations* 1: 191–218.

Traxler, F., Blaschke, S. and Kittel, B. (2001) *National Labour Relations in Internationalized Markets. A Comparative Study of Institutions, Change and Performance*, Oxford: Oxford University Press.

Visser, J. (1991) 'Trends in Trade Union Membership', *OECD Employment Outlook 1991*, Paris: OECD.

Waarden, F. van (1995) 'The Organizational Power of Employers' Associations: Cohesion, Comprehensiveness and Organizational Development', in C. Crouch and F. Traxler (eds) *Organized Industrial Relations in Europe: What Future?*, Aldershot: Avebury.

Wallerstein, M. (1989) 'Union Organization in Advanced Industrial Democracies', *American Political Science Review* 83: 480–501.

Part II

Sectors

6 Organizations and networks in a globalizing economy

British and German chemical interest associations

Jürgen R. Grote and Volker Schneider

Introduction

Economic internationalization and regional political integration in Europe have altered the environment for organized collective action in a fundamental way. In this chapter, we study the impact of these processes by comparing two national associational systems in the chemical industry.[1] Chemicals are an interesting analytical case because the sector has always been highly international and its associational structures have a long tradition, sometimes going as far back as the nineteenth century. Germany and the UK were chosen because of their pronounced differences in politics and policy making and their specific national forms of associability.

Business associations are intermediary actors: they respond to and mediate between developments in their internal and external environments. Internationalization and European integration have impacts on both dimensions: on relations with their members – individual firms – and on relations with political interlocutors – authorities and regulatory agencies at the domestic, European and international levels. Most interest group research, in particular the literature dealing with interest intermediation at the level of the EU, tends to be influence-biased. It focuses on questions of access while membership-related matters are treated insufficiently. In our view, the most significant challenge for domestic associations is currently not a potential loss of resources supplied by public authorities (withdrawal of support and legitimacy 'from above') but, rather, the risk of losing members.

Moreover, business associations form relatively autonomous, complex and adaptive subsystems of society. When such subsystems are hit by profound upheavals in their external or internal environment, the relative autonomy of parts implies that these do not necessarily change at the same speed and to the same degree. The concrete mechanism of change hinges on the properties of the subsystems and on their functional and territorial interdependencies.

With respect to territory, business associations and their members are subject to domestic, European and international forms of pressure. Perhaps with decreasing clout and intensity, they act at each of these levels. Concerning the functional dimension, business increasingly operates both as individual enterprises and through associations. Since it is desirable to treat these levels and forms of action in an analytically integrated manner, we embed our arguments in the language of organizational ecology.[2] As emphasized by Galuncic and Weeks (2002: 75), this is not a theory but merely a platform for the reinterpretation of existing theories. As a framework for analysis, it may enhance the compatibility between accounts of business associability and recent political science concepts such as multilevel governance. The approach also allows hooking up with organizational sociology, from which the study of business associability has drawn many of its insights.

> Organizations, populations, and communities of organizations constitute the basic elements of an ecological analysis of organizations. A set of organizations engaged in similar activities and with similar patterns of resource utilization constitutes a population. [. . .] Populations themselves develop relationships with other populations engaged in other activities that bind them into organizational communities. Organizational communities are functionally integrated systems of interacting populations.
>
> (Baum 1996: 78)

While research will always focus on any one of these elements, it is necessary to consider developments at higher and lower levels as well.

In this chapter, we concentrate on the focal associations representing the interests of chemical enterprises in Britain and Germany, i.e. on the population level. Yet, we also describe recent developments of the associations' wider environment that affect their structures, attitudes and strategies. Since organizational ecology postulates processes of upward and downward causation across different levels in the explanation of change, we also consider the level of the organizational community and that of individual associations. *Influence* and competition for scarce resources among national and supranational interest associations, individual firms and multinational corporations play a crucial role at the community level: how do national associations respond to shifts in regulatory policy making; how do they act vis-à-vis activities of supranational associations; and what, finally, is their attitude towards attempts by single firms to act on their own and co-determine political decisions at home and in Brussels? At the population level, we are concerned with the configuration of organized interest domains: how do associations structure their relations to cope with the internationalization of markets and the Europeanization of politics? Finally, at the organization level, we are interested in changes of associational tasks and, in particular, of influence *versus* membership related activities.[3]

We shall draw on interviews with leading representations of 35 German and 26 British chemical associations. They were identified through Internet research, handbooks and the EOI databank on the Europeanization of

Organized Interests (Max Planck Institute for the Study of Societies, Cologne). Later in the chapter, we reduce the sample to 14 German and 14 British organizations. These represent our focal organization sets and consist of particularly important associations. They were selected with the help of reputation analysis through expert panels. The first section concentrates on potential triggers of change in the environments of the two target groups. We then turn to the leaders of our *organizations* and focus on the extent to which they actually felt challenged by these developments and how their associations reacted. In a third step, we turn to a comparative description of a core set of the two *organizational populations*, i.e. the sectors' focal associations, and add some information on individual groups. Finally, we consider the relevance of our populations' *organizational communities* which reach beyond domestic boundaries, including European and international actors. We conclude by arguing that even in the case of a highly internationalized sector such as chemicals, business interests continue to be nationally embedded. Patterns of adaptation both reflect and lend force to the persistence of varieties of capitalism in modern societies.

The organizational environment: triggers and levels of change

Business associations have to incorporate the heterogeneous demands of different environments into their organizational structures and strategies in order to arrive at a stable supply of resources and decision-making autonomy (Streeck 1987). These are demands posed by the two conflicting logics of influence and membership, i.e. the need to respond to membership expectations on the one hand and to governmental interests on the other. Internationalization impacts on both these logics, affecting public authorities as well as enterprises. Moreover, individual firms are today well-accepted actors in the influence dimension. They can, therefore, be conceptualized as a distinct population acting side by side with the more established population of business associations.

The economy

Economic developments belong to the core concerns of business. Before discussing potential implications of internationalization, we present some basic properties of the two countries' chemical sectors. The sector can be broken down into seven branches, including pharmaceuticals (Table 6.1).

Over the past two decades, the share of basic chemicals in Germany (industrial gases, dyes and pigments, basic organics and inorganics, fertilizers, plastic and synthetic rubber, etc.) has remained almost unaltered. It was at about 51 per cent in 1979 and still is at 50 per cent today. Pharmaceuticals grew from 14 per cent in 1979 at the expense of the remaining branches (agrochemicals, toiletry, paints, etc.). In the UK, basic chemicals declined

Table 6.1 Composition of the chemical sector by gross value added

	Germany (1999)	*Britain (1998)*
Basic chemicals	50.2	31.0
Agrochemicals	0.8	3.0
Paints, varnishes, inks	7.3	8.0
Pharmaceuticals	18.9	31.5
Soaps, toiletry, cosmetics	10.8	11.5
Other specialities	8.8	13.0
Man-made fibres	3.2	2.0
Total chemicals	100.0	100.0

Sources: VCI 2000; CIA 2000 (www.cia.org.uk/industry/2).

while pharmaceutical products improved their position significantly.[4] Due to restructuring, UK pharmaceuticals are today stronger than basic chemicals. Most of Britain's larger chemical companies 'have been taken over by foreign competitors' (Brophy 2000)[5] so that traditional chemicals are squeezed to an extent that 'in 2010 as many as half of today's leading ... companies may no longer be around' (Arthur D. Little 1999; quoted from Brophy 2000: 4). David Bricknell of the European Chemical Industry Council goes as far as saying that 'it looks as though the UK's chemical industry might go the way of the car industry' (ibid.).

While buy-outs and takeovers seem to be the main factors responsible for the sector's recomposition, internationalization as such is not a problem in either country. Chemical companies not only belong to the internationally most exposed sectors, but have themselves been active promoters of internationalization since the eighteenth century. Employment apart, which has significantly decreased in both countries, all other indicators show clear upward trends (Table 6.2). Germany is in third place worldwide behind the United States and Japan while holding first place in Europe ahead of France, the UK and Italy. Together, these four countries produce about 65 per cent of chemical output in Europe. Export, import, production, gross fixed capital formation and value added continuously increased between 1980 and 2000. Production has roughly doubled in both Germany and the UK and exports and imports have more than tripled. The same is probably true for foreign direct investment (FDI), though complete and reliable data for the entire period under consideration are difficult to obtain.

Internationalization is both a result of and a condition for the sectors' outstanding performance. International integration continuously increased and there were no dramatic downturns or losses in market share. Figures for Germany are roughly double those of Britain except for research and development (R&D) expenditure which is not reported here due to data shortage. While R&D spent by traditional chemical companies in Britain declined by over 16 per cent in the period between 1993 and 1997, total R&D expendi-

Table 6.2 German and British chemical industries, main economic indicators, 1980–1999[a]

		1980	*1985*	*1990*	*1995*	*1999*
Employees	D	623	620	642	585	522
	UK	405	325	306	255	249
Gross fixed capital formation	D	3,804	2,557	7,886	9,062	8,747
	UK	2,268	1,902	4,537	3,614	na
Exports	D	25,505	25,142	50,007	67,943	68,586
	UK	12,503	12,206	23,136	32,334	36,531
Imports	D	13,190	14,001	31,867	43,084	47,455
	UK	7,664	9,374	19,901	28,480	30,958
Production	D	68,096	57,635	118,838	142,773	115,427
	UK	35,531	30,702	55,396	64,112	na
Value added	D	22,170	19,211	43,101	55,016	40,944
	UK	11,448	10,255	20,776	24,116	25,305

Source: OECD STAN Database for Industrial Analysis (2003). German data for the period 1980–1989 is only available in ISIC Rev. 2 format (i.e. excluding drugs and medicines).

Notes
a Employees in thousands, all others in million US Dollars.
D: Germany.
UK: United Kingdom.

ture in pharmaceuticals 'increased by 21% in real terms, outsourced R&D by 43% in the UK and by 83% outside the UK' (Brophy 2000: 13). Basic in-house research in pharmaceuticals was £102 million, more than twice that of traditional chemicals (ibid.).

Merger activities are not only responsible for the transformation of the chemical industry. They are also of concern to the sector's interest associations. Traditional chemicals in Britain are now worth considerably less than any of the big three German chemical companies BASF, Bayer and Hoechst.[6] Mergers and takeovers lead to shrinking associational membership.[7] *Exit by extinction* invariably occurs when an acquired firm is absorbed by its buyer. Managers of reorganized companies may also decide to leave an association or to seek representation elsewhere. That this *exit by choice* is at least as relevant as the former mode of exit is confirmed by interviews with leading representatives of chemical associations in both countries. There is a decreasing propensity among the chief executive officers (CEOs) of large firms to join or stay in an association just because in the past one had to 'belong to the club'.

> More and more companies are managed by the 'country manager' of a multi-national on a three-year stint . . . as part of an international career.

> Indigenous chief executives are increasingly subject to the 'Four Years and You're Out' syndrome common in the United States. There is a danger that participation in trade association activity will become a second-order issue.
>
> (Macdonald 2001: 9)

Technology

Concerning technological change, chemical business associations are affected by at least two relevant processes. Chemical production is strongly research based. With more than €7.5 billion (VCI 2001: 97; Chemiewirtschaft in Zahlen), the German chemical industry is rated second behind the automobile industry (*c.*€16 billion) in terms of R&D expenditure. The importance of research has further increased in areas such as biotechnology or genetic engineering, often described as 'life science business'. The European market for this research-intensive branch is expected to quadruple in the next ten years (DIB 2000: 4). While Germany initially performed poorly by international standards, its biotechnology sector, with its 280 young companies, has meanwhile become Europe's front runner, ahead of the UK (VCI 2000: 10; DIB 2000: 6).

The biotech revolution has slowly started to affect the sector as a whole. From the perspective of organized interests, it is increasingly difficult to keep the branch within the boundaries of the chemical industry. The interest domain is in a state of flux. If, as suggested by our interviews and by the data on traditional chemicals and pharmaceuticals, sector identity is in decline, this is particularly pronounced among the new and dynamic entrepreneurs of the hundreds of research laboratories active in both countries. *Exit by choice* or, for that matter, non-entry into an association may not only be an effect of takeovers by multinationals but, equally, of the sector's technological recomposition. Where there are no powerful peak associations able to cross-subsidize free membership with money from other sources,[8] owners of smaller biotech companies may think twice before joining an association.

Another effect of technological innovation is of a more general nature. Many associations have come under pressure to rely on new communication facilities (Kriesi, this volume; Grant 2000). This relates to information exchange by intranet as well as to self-representation and political marketing through web pages. Competition in that area is strong and associations are forced to update their sites regularly lest their members turn to other sources. We found a number of multinationals operating in the sector whose web presentation and facilities clearly outdo the ones of their associations.

Politics

Politics appears to be the main factor imposing change on business associations. The EU is very present in the chemical sector where supranational competencies are comprehensive and have a long tradition. The significance of political challenges should not be overestimated, however. Procedural or policy change induced by the EU mainly becomes manifest in how members of chemical policy networks structure their relations and learn from each other. Change of this type concerns the influence dimension of organized collective action, that is, the organizational community rather than of individual organizations. Formal organizations are less flexible and more resistant to change than the informal relations characterizing policy networks. Moreover, even if interest associations were to restructure significantly, it would still remain difficult to disentangle the effects of legislation issued at national and European level. Within the first wave of chemicals regulation in the late 1970s, international activities by the OECD strongly interacted with legislation at the European and the national level (Brickman *et al.* 1985; Schneider 1988). Domestic politics and regulations are likely to remain of crucial importance to national business associations which, of course, have also to react to international and European challenges since these are steadily increasing in relevance (Ronit, this volume; Coleman, this volume, Ronit and Schneider 2000).

As far as the EU is concerned, environmental policy is the most important policy domain for chemical associations. Here regulatory activities have continuously increased over the past two decades. Between 1980 and 1996, 31 laws (Regulations, Recommendations, Decisions or Directives) were passed by the Council. In addition, there were 23 changes to Directives directly affecting the industry. Regulatory density has greatly increased (Munz 2001: 44–48). The EU Commission's White Paper on a 'Strategy for a Future Policy on Chemicals' of February 2001 (Commission 2001)[9] provides for 2,700 new and about 100,000 old substances to be subjected to a comparable control procedure within the framework of a unified system by 2012. Proposals for a new Directive – the so-called REACH Regulation (Registration, Evaluation and Authorization of Chemicals) – have recently been forwarded to the European Parliament and the EU's Council of Ministers for adoption under the co-decision procedure (COM 2003).

Still, the national realm of policy making cannot be neglected, nor can it be assumed that national politics would be absorbed by European politics. Some have argued (Beyers 2002; Bouwen, this volume) that the less developed the opportunities are for political influence and access at the national level, the harder it is for associations to link up to EU institutions. In our interviews with German leaders of chemical associations, we did not encounter growing difficulties regarding the number and quality of access points at the national level. In the UK, the Thatcher government's dismantling of the power, not only of unions but also of organized business, has had more drastic consequences.[10] Despite the more moderate approach under Major and the return to power of Labour, business associations are still viewed as being 'part of the problem rather than part of the solution' (Grant 2000: 59). Although these internal challenges have stirred up the associational landscape, they have also had some positive effects. As argued by one of our British interview partners, there is a lively debate underway among Britain's chemical interest groups about the most appropriate organizational forms to cope with multilayered pressures of all sorts. The main issues here are more flexible responses at the organization level and new forms of alliance-building at the population level. Inter-associational coordination in the chemical sector is today more stable than in the past. Internal political pressure may have enhanced the capacity of British associations to respond to the exigencies of multilevel politics.

The Europeanization of politics not only concerns the sheer number of regulations produced by the EU. It is equally present in the emergence and the spread of entirely new organizational forms, like European-level associations, individual firms and alliances of firms used to influence public authorities, thereby altering traditional patterns of access. The growth of EU associations has received ample attention, although with decreasing enthusiasm in more recent years.[11] Euro-associations do not seem to be a major challenge to domestic groups and this also holds for the European Chemical Industry Council (CEFIC), the European chemical industry's peak association (Wonka 2003). Although German associations have more voice in CEFIC than any other national group, tasks are generally divided between domestic and supranational associations and both seem to benefit from that complementary practice. More of a problem is direct lobbying, the rise of round tables, and the activities of law firms and consultancies all of which are quite unfamiliar to corporatist countries. Compared to economic challenges which may deprive associations of their most important source of income (exit by extinction or by choice as a result of M&A (mergers and acquisitions) activities), political challenges may be less of a problem as lobbying, at least for more powerful associations, has become a kind of standard operating procedure.

Society

Increasing consumer awareness, value change and social alertness with respect to the negative externalities of chemical production and consumption represent important societal challenges to the chemical industry and its associations. Long-term and generalized 'public' strategies are needed to cope with these. Brent Spar[12] and other events, as well as the activities of internationally organized and coordinated environmental groups, demonstrate that societal challenges have assumed an international character although, most of the time, they continue to be felt and expressed in the realm of domestic politics.

Some environmentalist activities represent a veritable physical threat especially to companies active in crop and plant protection research. Interviews with associations representing this branch revealed that these often function as security advisers if they are not directly involved in the policing of production sites. For the UK, Grant reports that 'it is animal scientists who have most frequently been the targets of violence, including bombing' (2000: 143). Moreover, the destruction of property by opponents of genetically engineered crops may inflict considerable commercial damage. These groups have 'destroyed plant and test sites, terminating the experiment which then cannot be repeated in the growing season. By midsummer 1998 at least 27 of the 163 test sites in the UK have been vandalized' (ibid.: 142). Direct action of this type is likely to increase. Appropriate countermeasures have become a new task for relevant sector associations.

Effects of societal pressure also relate to the industry's public image. Lobbying the public by public relations campaigns and media presence belongs to the tasks of chemical associations ever since the sector came to be seen as the largest polluter of all industries (Schneider 1988: 117). Today there are considerably more products that are perceived to be both socially indispensable and environmentally sustainable than 20 years ago. This is also a result of considerable investment in product marketing undertaken by some branch associations.[13] On the other hand, according to opinion polls carried out by the VCI, pesticides and fertilizers used in agriculture are still regarded as environmentally hazardous and socially dispensable. It is not clear yet whether progress in plant manipulation may make this industry more socially acceptable. In any case, 'public attitudes and opinions are an important feature of the external operating environment of groups' (Grant 2000: 206). Concerning the main goals of associations in this respect, Grant distinguishes between changes in attitudes, i.e. deeply held perceptions structuring the response of individuals to specific events, and changes in opinions which reflect these attitudes but may also be more spontaneous and superficial. The annual reports of the major chemical associations we have studied provide evidence for the high amount of investment undertaken in these areas. Both public relations and protection against the attacks of environmentalists are services that associations offer to their members.

The organization level: risk perceptions and associational outputs

Four main dimensions of challenges were identified – the economy, technology, politics and society. The combined effect of changes in these dimensions is expected to have repercussions on the way in which associations in the two national systems perceive their environment (*inputs*), how they rearrange their organizational structures in response (*outputs*), and how they structure their relations with each other to develop inter-organizational forms providing for the required flexibility without endangering identity or renouncing past organizational achievements (*networks*). If there is strong variation at the input side, one should expect that different strategies are selected. We discuss both differences in the perception of threats and in the selection of strategies. The data rests on responses of those of our 61 German and British chemical interest associations who effectively answered the respective part of the questionnaire (n = 48). Interviews were carried out exclusively at the level of director, president or secretary general.

The first question ('How important are the different dimensions of pressure to your association?') addressed all four of the challenges set out above. Respondents were asked to rate different challenges on a scale from one (very important) to four (least important). The first and the second columns of Table 6.3 combine the answers 'important' and 'very important' and 'less' and 'least important' respectively. Political threats are ranked first in both samples (89 and 92 per cent). This does not come as a surprise. Regulatory intensity and, in particular, environmental regulation have steadily increased over the past 20 years and EU activities in that area are significant. Economic challenges are ranked second by UK associations (71 per cent) while German respondents report societal challenges to be of more concern (52 per cent). Regarding the former, this reflects the salience of restructuring currently underway in Britain. Indeed, when asked for their main preoccupation, mergers were ranked first by 77 per cent of the German and 85 per cent of the British respondents. The fact that societal challenges come second in the German case reflects the industry's perception that rigid environmental regulation has a base in popular attitudes and opinions that are shaped by environmentalism. Technologically induced challenges are ranked third and fourth by both groups.

Highly significant are the judgements concerning the territorial level from which challenges originate ('Are domestic, European or global processes playing the most important role with respect to the four types of

Table 6.3 Significance and origin of different challenges, by per cent of associations[a]

Type of challenge		*Significance*		*Origin*		
		(Very) important	*Less/least important*	*National*	*European*	*Global*
Economic	D	45	55	41	33	26
	UK	71	29	50	17	33
Technological	D	30	70	28	20	52
	UK	44	56	0	22	78
Political	D	89	11	26	74	0
	UK	92	8	13	87	0
Societal	D	52	48	78	19	3
	UK	40	60	48	44	8

Source: Own data.

Notes

a 25 German and 23 British Associations.

D: Germany.

UK: United Kingdom.

challenges?'). German and British associations believe the national level to be most important for economic (50 and 41 per cent) and societal issues (78 and 48 per cent). The European level is said to be a problem primarily with respect to politics (74 and 87 per cent) while most technological challenges are believed to result from global developments (52 and 78 per cent).

The significance of the high values obtained by EU induced political challenges is cushioned by the fact that indirect and membership-related developments are given more salience than direct and influence-related ones. Some 50 per cent of respondents reported most pressure resulting from factors concerning their members, while influence-related factors were mentioned only by about a quarter. The same trend was also evident in the personal interviews we carried out with leaders of 28 particularly relevant associations in both countries.

To explore this further, respondents were asked to allocate 100 points of resources to nine different tasks. Three of these concerned lobbying activities and six direct services to the members. Only 37 per cent of the resources of both the British and the German associations are spent on the provision of public goods, such as lobbying at the domestic and the supranational levels (influence investments; Table 6.4). Interestingly, the same question submitted to 19 leaders of US chemical interest associations produced almost identical results (see Schmedes 2003: 100): 38 per cent of the US associations' resources were invested in influence-related activities and 62 per cent in tasks concerning the provision of selective goods such as consultancy, information and conferences. Albeit further removed from membership concerns and more engaged in political business than any of their individual

Table 6.4 Estimated allocation of resources to tasks, in per cent of associations*

Type of task	*Germany*	*Rank*	*Britain*	*Rank*
Influencing national institutions	16	4	20	1
Influencing EU institutions	10	6	11	5
Influencing the public	11	5	6	8
Investments in influence (lobbying)	*37*	–	*37*	–
Consultancy of members	16	3	15	3
Information for members	17	2	18	2
Conferences	21	1	13	4
Side benefits	2	9	3	9
Training	4	7	8	6
Other	3	8	6	7
Investments in membership (services)	*63*	–	*63*	–

Source: own data.

Note

a 35 German and 26 British associations.

branch associations, the same applied to Britain's and Germany's peak associations. Their values are consistent with those in Table 6.4.

Does this mean that representation, i.e. the traditional core activity of interest associations, has become secondary? We do not think so. Associations of sectors as consolidated as chemicals have had a long time for building up stable relations to public authorities. Once established, these networks tend to become self-reinforcing and require less effort to be kept in place than at the time of their initial composition. As argued in the previous section, representing interests and servicing public authorities may have become a standard operating procedure, which seems to hold even under conditions of growing legislation by international and European authorities. With the US associations sharing that trend, this possibly has to do with the internationalization of markets and less with the Europeanization of politics.

Low associational investment in lobbying may be related to increasing activities by individual enterprises at the level of the organizational community. Where such activities are not perceived to threaten associational stability, or are even endorsed by associations, lobbying by individual firms may alleviate the costs of influencing public decisions. This definitely seems to be the case in Britain. We asked our 61 respondents whether they would support their members engaging in individual lobbying independently from what their associations were doing, or try to limit such activities. Only about a quarter of the British respondents were hostile to individual lobbying, while this attitude was shared by about half of the respondents in Germany. In a study on patterns of interest of representation among German and British chemical associations at the European level, Wonka (2003) asked interest group leaders from both countries whether large multinationals or domestic interest groups played a more important role in Brussels. Consistent with the above results, almost 91 per cent of the German respondents named associations. In Britain, this figure dropped to 58 per cent.

As we know from Schmitter and Streeck (1981, 1999), the *raison d'être* of interest groups is to act as mediators between different environments. Focusing exclusively on services to members may turn associations into firms and give them a predominantly private character. The high salience of member-related efforts that we found need not have this effect. Yet, it is interesting that the chemical associations studied are active in a sphere that is increasingly populated by other types of actors such as consultancies and marketing agencies (see Lahusen 2002). Individual enterprises, on the other hand, now also occupy an increasing portion of the influence dimension once reserved to organized groups. The simultaneous occurrence of the two developments may blur the dividing line between individual and collective action.

The population level: networks of focal associations

Our next question concerns the configuration of relations that connect associations by ties used for the exchange of strategically important information. The aim is to detect evolving patterns of integration or disintegration resulting from the challenges discussed above. In this relational part of the analysis, we work with those 14 focal associations within each national interest population that are particularly prominent with respect to their organizational resources and their capacity of influencing policy making.[14]

Germany

In earlier work on Germany (Grant 1986; Grant *et al.* 1988; Grant 1991; Martinelli 1991; Grant and Martinelli 1991; Groser 1983; Platzer 1984), the country's system of chemical interest associations was characterized as typically corporatist. Little seems to have changed since then. Like 20 years ago, the associational system is dominated by one all-encompassing peak association, the Verband der Chemischen Industrie (VCI). The VCI represents more than 90 per cent of the roughly 1,750 enterprises operating in the chemical industry. There is no significant branch or sector association outside the peak association. Over the past 20 years, only few new groups have been added. Among our focal associations, there are the association for surface protection liquids in industrial applications, IHO, in 1992; the association of research-intensive pharmaceutical manufacturers, VFA, in 1993; and the sector group for biotechnology companies, DIB, in 1998.

The VCI is internally divided into ten territorial associations while its organizational core are its 20 sector associations (*Fachverbände*) and ten sector groups (*Fachvereinigungen*). Most of these operate from the association's headquarters in Frankfurt while the others have their offices close to the production sites of their major member companies. The Frankfurt centre provides member groups with a comprehensive infrastructure (information, consultancy on all sorts of issues, etc.) and hosts some 150 staff. Sector associations have between five and 20 employees. There are a total of eight Departments as well as 39 committees and permanent task forces (*Fachausschüsse*). Most of them are chaired by leading managers of the larger member companies. Two of the eight departments are offices outside of Frankfurt, one of which serves as a liaison with government departments in Berlin, and another one which coordinates the sector's European activities in Brussels. With few exceptions, this structure has been in place at least since Grant's *et al.* (1988) earlier studies on the sector. The same applies to the number of more relevant sectoral associations. The relationship between the VCI and its branch associations still is 'that of a father and his grown-up children' (Grant *et al.* 1988: 70; citing the director of one of the sector associations). Today, 14 focal associations form the core of the organizational population.

The only major event ultimately indicating a decline in the VCI's control capacity occurred about ten years ago and concerned one of the VCI's most influential and best-resourced branch associations, the Bundesverband der Pharmazeutischen Industrie (BPI), representing pharmaceutical producers. In 1993, unexpectedly even for insiders, the BPI split into an association for research-based and mostly multinational companies, the Verband Forschender Arzneimittelhersteller (VFA), and one for smaller generic producers (under the old name of the BPI). Strong disagreements about the registration of pharmaceuticals and political measures for cost control triggered this split. Both issues were indirectly linked to the internationalization of markets (Broscheid 2002). Today, the VFA is Germany's most important pharmaceutical association.[15] While affiliated to the VCI, its relationship to the peak association is comparatively weak. One expression of this is that, from its foundation, the VFA operates from Berlin where it is closer to government agencies and removed from the control of the peak association's Frankfurt headquarters.[16]

A network organization

An important insight of earlier research on organized interests has been that 'intra-organizational differentiation into specialized sub-units and inter-organizational integration through institutionalized linkages between separate organizations are functional alternatives that can be used for the same purpose' (Schmitter and Streeck 1999 [1981]: 48). While the former produces complexity, the latter orders that complexity and binds different units together in coordinated patterns of interaction. Of course, variation and selection in the patterns of organizational interaction are constrained by a number of institutional factors and cannot always be freely chosen. Although different systems may have the same purpose, the prospects for achieving the desired goals may not be quite the same. In addition, even if things have worked out quite well in the past, internal and external challenges may significantly alter existing practices.

Let us demonstrate this by examining the structure of the focal association set in Germany. Figure 6.1 represents two-way flows of information exchange among 14 focal associations. Ties among units indicate a regular exchange of strategically important information. Actors are connected only if x reports sending information to y, y certifies receipt of this information, in turn provides information to x which, finally, certifies its receipt.[17]

The structure of inter-organizational exchange corroborates what has been said above: the interest population exhibits features typical of corporatist associational systems (see also: Ronge and Körber 1994: 321). The VCI dominates the entire flow of information and acts as information broker for most other sector associations. The width of knots indicates degree centrality. That is, the normalized degree centrality obtained by the VCI is 84.6 per cent, while the mean obtained by all other members of the network is 11.2 per cent – a very large difference indeed. Accordingly, overall network centralization is 75.6 per cent which is quite high in comparative terms. Only few sector associations maintain exchange relations with others. Interestingly, the VFA as one of the VCI's most powerful members turns out to be an isolate. This is due to the fact that both the sending and receiving of information are

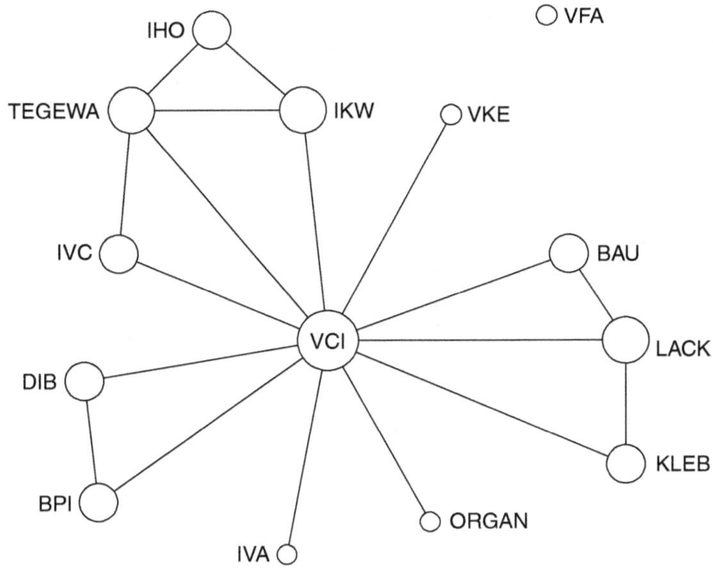

Figure 6.1 Information exchange among German focal associations.

Notes
The figures are directed graphs. Arrows have been omitted since the relations are reciprocal. The different width of knots represents indegree centrality. Actors not fulfilling the requirements of the select criterion appear as isolates. For definitions, see Appendix at end of chapter.

not reciprocated as required by the selection criterion. It also points to the VFA's more autonomous position among the other associations. The few clusters that emerge are due to product affinities (biotech and pharmaceuticals; textiles, soaps and surface protection; construction, coatings and adhesives). The overall result is an extremely pronounced hierarchy of relations with network density being comparatively low (0.19 per cent).

All this, of course, does not imply that individual sector associations do not communicate with each other. Most communication, however, is organized and mediated by the VCI's central infrastructure. Information relevant to the sector associations is 'stored' within the VCI's committees and task forces from where it can easily be retrieved. Hence, individual members are to some extent relieved from approaching each other for important information. They acquire additional (relational) resources for pursuing contacts to other actors in their organizational ecology and are free to make investments in their wider contact portfolio to an extent that would otherwise not be possible.

Compared to the findings of earlier studies, the interest system exhibits a high degree of organizational inertia. This is hardly astonishing. Not least as a result of German unification, the 50 per cent share of basic chemicals in the country's overall sectoral output (see Table 6.1) has remained almost unaltered over the past 20 years. The structures developed in this relatively labour-intensive branch have provided the basis for all sorts of corporatist arrangements. These have become frozen to such an extent that the biotechnical revolution, with the mushrooming of a myriad of small companies, did not alter established associational hierarchies. The breakaway and foundation of a new pharmaceutical association suggest that most challenges to stability result from membership-related developments. The VCI has not responded by introducing a more flexible structure or by decentralization. As a network organization in its own right, representing one of the world's most powerful chemical industries, it seems to have few incentives to modify its established organizational form. It is open for discussion whether hierarchical leadership of this sort will remain viable in the future and the VCI would not be better advised by organizing in a more flexible manner to protect itself from the risks associated with what has been called the 'weakness of strong ties', i.e. encapsulation and lock-in (Grabher 1993; see also Granovetter 1973).

The United Kingdom

Compared to Germany the associational landscape in the British chemical sector appears much more fragmented. This was the case in the mid-1980s and continues to be so today. Yet, unlike Germany, many things have changed since Grant (1986: 48) counted 15 first-order associations. At that time, three-quarters of these were affiliated to the Chemicals Industry Association (CIA). Although not quite as influential and powerful as the VCI, the CIA occupied a central position within the British chemical interest domain. Today, this is no longer the case.

As in Germany, the overall number of focal associations has remained stable and includes 14 organizations. Many of these continue to be affiliated to the CIA but do not have the strong ties found in Germany. Since its foundation in 1966, resulting from a merger of the Association of British Chemical Manufacturers (ABCM) and the Association of Chemical and Allied Employers (AC&AE), the CIA has been organizing Britain's leading chemical manufacturing companies. The Imperial Chemical Industries (ICI), a conglomerate founded in 1926 as a counterpart to Germany's IG Farben, was by far the most important of these. At least until the late 1980s, ICI was the fourth largest company by turnover in Britain and was often considered 'the flagship of the country's industrial economy' (Grant and Martinelli 1991: 62). The company accounted for roughly 35 per cent of the country's chemical output (ibid.: 81), its bulk being in industrial chemicals. Largely modelled on ICI's production structure, the CIA was initially dominated by the interests of large industrial chemical producers. With its headquarters still in a building that belongs to ICI, or what is left of it, it was highly dependent on this conglomerate.[18]

Despite significant differences in its resource endowment, in the early

1980s the CIA still exhibited features similar to Germany's VCI. Many of the smaller sectoral associations representing chemical users and speciality producers (rubber, paints, coatings, toiletry, cosmetics, fertilizers, etc.) originated from or were in some way affiliated to it. The CIA served as a peak association of older groups such as the Fertilizers Manufacturing Association (FMA), Britain's 'trade association with the longest uninterrupted history in the chemical and allied industries' (Culpin 2000: 36), and the British Chemical Distributors and Traders Association (BCDTA). More recently created groups such as the British Aerosol Manufacturers Association (BAMA), the Crop Protection Association (CPA) and the British Association for Chemical Specialities (BACS) also had strong links to the CIA and operated from its premises. The Association of the British Pharmaceutical Industry (ABPI), another large and influential sector group, has always been one of CIA's affiliate members. Nearly outdoing its peak association in staff and financial resources, it continues to be affiliated to it.

Change began in the early 1980s, when ICI started to diversify, retreated from loss-making operations and increased its presence in more profitable speciality chemicals. By 1987, ICI was divided 'into two distinct arms, the traditional bulk commodity sectors and the speciality growth sectors' (Kennedy 1986: 178). As a result the associations organizing smaller speciality producers felt uneasy with the company's dominant position within the CIA. By the end of the decade, although most of them had moved out of the CIA's headquarters and became more autonomous, they maintained some form of affiliation.

Britain's population of chemical associations is today far less centred on one single organization. With the demerger of ICI into a new ICI and Zeneca in the 1990s, the CIA lost substantial resources. At the same time, pharmaceuticals emerged as the largest subsector, accounting for more than 30 per cent of gross value added. Branches characterized as peripheral subsectors (Grant 1991: 50) only a decade ago and represented by independent associations such as BCDTA, BAMA, BACS and the British Coatings Federation (BCF), significantly increased their share in sectoral output. Accordingly, the country's organized interest population is today divided between three types of actors: the CIA, the ABPI and a so-called Alliance of Industry Associations (AIA). The CIA is still the most important, not least because it is the only group trying to cover the entire sector. It has a staff of about 56 (CIA Annual Report 2000), but probably employs close to 70 people including external experts. Among its members are 173 subscription paying companies,[19] each paying an average annual fee of about £26,000.[20] The ABPI continues to be formally affiliated to the CIA but, essentially, is an autonomous association that operates in a field having little to do with chemicals in the traditional sense. Its staff is almost as large as that of the CIA. Yet, facing a less diverse membership, it may well be more powerful than its own peak association. Finally, the third central group is AIA – an alliance of chemical speciality associations many of which had formally been associated to the CIA and some of which continue to do so albeit in a comparatively loose manner.

One of the most characteristic features of the UK's associational landscape is the building of alliances among interest groups. Many of these stop short of more formalized structures such as federations or mergers. Public initiatives to reduce associational fragmentation date from the 1970s, as witnessed by the Report of the Devlin Commission. More recent attempts also started 'in the shadow of hierarchy' as leaders of associations were told by the government that support would be withdrawn unless they adopted more encompassing organizational structures (MacDonald 2001: 6).[21] Especially smaller associations understood that diminishing resources, as the result of declining membership and company mergers made fragmentation less and less sustainable. Company mergers, ultimately called for associational mergers (interview). When this is not possible in the short term, other and less demanding organizational reforms need to be considered.

AIA is the most visible manifestation of the above developments in the chemical sector. It brings together almost all of the more relevant smaller associations outside the CIA and the ABPI.[22] In our interviews, many of AIA's leaders underlined that they do not have feelings of belonging to what the chemical sector might have been in the past. Sectoral identity, instead, is based on product groups such as plastics, coatings or cosmetics. AIA collects downstream user associations operating in these branches. Its members meet several times a year to discuss matters of common concern and often take stances on regulatory matters in contradiction to the position of the CIA. The Alliance is also trying to prevent what its members perceive to be a hostile takeover, i.e. a reintegration into the CIA.[23] Although there are no permanent offices, AIA has a number of standing committees and *ad hoc* working groups on issues such as the EU's White Paper on chemical policy. Meetings are currently at the premises of the Cosmetic, Toiletry and Perfumery Association (CTPA) while the alliance is chaired by the director of BCF. One of its most powerful members is the British Plastics Federation (BPF), an association that was never affiliated to the CIA.[24] Meanwhile, AIA is so firmly consolidated that the prospect for the CIA to reassume its leadership is quite unlikely.

In general, a structure comparable to Germany has never been, and is still not, a viable option for the British associations. During our interviews, respondents often pointed with some envy to German associations' capacity to speak with one voice. Yet, cross-national organizational learning that would result in convergence along common lines is clearly ruled out. Available documents published by the Trade Association Forum (TAF) and other organizations suggest that a potential blueprint for Britain's interest system is the US where chemical alliances have a long-established record (Boleat 2000; Schmedes 2003).

A network of organizations

Turning to the pattern of information exchange within and between the three groups mentioned, the differences from the German system are evident (Figure 6.2). There is no central actor like in the German system. Relative centrality represented by the width of the knots is almost identical for the five best positioned associations (CIA, BCF, CTPA, BACS and UKCPI). While the CIA obtains a normalized degree centrality of 76.9 per cent, the mean obtained by all other associations lies at 31.3 per cent and is much higher than in the German case (11.2 per cent). Overall network centralization is 44.9 per cent, considerably less than in Germany (75.6 per cent). In other words, Britain's chemical interest population is far less dominated by any one of its more powerful organizations. At the same time, network density is much higher (0.38 per cent). Consequently, a significant amount of time and resources tends to be absorbed by inter-organizational coordination. This may have negative implications for the relations to public authorities at the domestic and supranational levels. Interestingly, the centre of the plot, basically made up of members of AIA (grey shaded), is a network

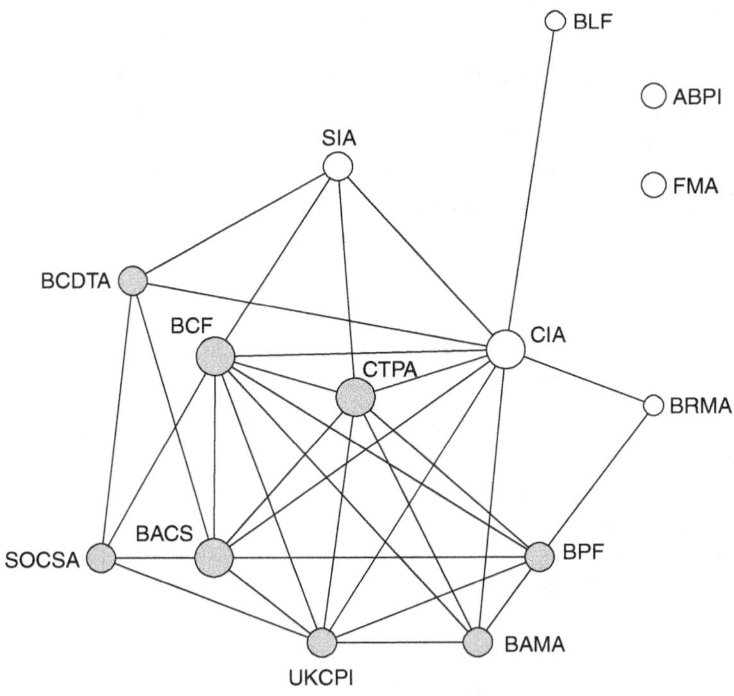

Figure 6.2 Information exchange among British focal associations.

Notes

The figures are directed graphs. Arrows have been omitted since the relations are reciprocal. The different width of knots represents indegree centrality. Actors not fulfilling the requirements of the select criterion appear as isolates. For definitions, see Appendix at end of chapter.

in its own right. The British chemical interest population is a *network of organizations*, while the German one resembles a *network organization*. Similar to Germany, one of the more important and powerful British associations, ABPI, turns out to be an isolate. This is indicative of the autonomous position pharmaceuticals have obtained in both countries.

It is unlikely that the alliance network will transform into a properly merged structure in a foreseeable future.[25] Considering the development over the past two decades, it is interesting to see how the groups that today form part of the AIA initially depended on the CIA. While assuming more autonomy, they soon recognized the need for a more robust infrastructure and have pooled their resources in a less formalized network. The picture is one of successive disintegration and reintegration. Integrative forces were particularly strong during the heydays of CIA until about the early 1980s. Disintegration set in with the departure of smaller groups from the CIA and is most evident today in the increasingly autonomous position of the ABPI, as well as in further moves away from what had once been the core of the industry both in economic and in associational terms. Reintegration, finally, takes place around AIA and yet other alliances of more peripheral actors. With respect to information exchange among the focal associations, it is important to note that none of these ties are redundant. The AIA's matrix structure, in particular, upon which most of its operations are based and according to which tasks are shared and responsibilities divided makes these ties mandatory. The task of diffusing information cannot be delegated to any one particularly authoritative association. Albeit weaker and less hierarchical than the links connecting the German interest population, the maintenance of these ties then absorbs quite substantial resources precisely in a period where associations face increasing financial constraints.

The community level: relations to other actors domestically and in the EU

Organizational communities, organizational populations, organizations in populations, routines within organizations and attitudes of professional leaders vis-à-vis developments of the organizational environment comprise a nested ecological hierarchy (Baum and Singh 1994). Interactions within each level bind entities together at the next-higher level of complexity (Rao 2002: 552). Although these levels may operate quasi-independently with some degree of autonomy, there is downward and upward causation within the hierarchy. In downward causation, processes of variation, selection and retention at higher levels limit the very same processes at lower levels. Upward causation means that features at one level constrain what emerges at the next. Following the logic of this chapter, it is the latter process whose effects shall now be discussed with respect to the way in which the two countries' associations are linked to important external actors.

The organization lists of our questionnaires included not only the names of focal associations but also some two dozen other relevant actors, like government departments and regulatory agencies and their equivalents at the EU level. Moreover, the names of European and international interest groups were also added. Table 6.5 contains information about the frequency with which four EU-level and international sector associations, nine domestic authorities and ten European Union institutions are approached by the 28 focal associations of the two countries. It also shows the extent to which these institutions and organizations provide strategically important information to focal associations and the degree to which there is similarity in opinion across types of actors with respect to important policy events.

In terms of contact, 58 per cent of the German and 41 per cent of the British associations maintain ties to EU-level and international associations.[26] Joint activity of national associations with EU institutions is reported by 28 per cent of the German but only 13 per cent of the British cases. Mean values for ties to a total of nine government institutions are 48 per cent in Germany and 55 per cent in Britain.

Do the observed patterns have implications for the way German and British chemical associations behave vis-à-vis external actors? Differences are

Table 6.5 Percentage of focal associations maintaining relations of different types with three categories of actors[a]

External actors	*Type of relation*				
	Contact	*Send information*	*Receive information*	*Joint activity*	*Mean*
EU and international associations					
German associations	58	55	58	49	55
British associations	41	37	41	41	40
Domestic institutions					
German associations	66	50	49	28	48
British associations	59	60	58	42	55
EU institutions					
German associations	60	46	37	28	43
British associations	34	32	32	13	28

Source: Own data.

Notes

a 14 German and 14 British associations.

Cells contain mean values of normalized indegrees obtained by each of the three external actor categories (univariate statistics, UCINET). International associations include CEFIC, ICCA, the respective EU branch association and the Brussels office of one's own or one's allied association (altogether 4 associations and/or offices with headquarters abroad). Domestic institutions include the main ministries, Bundeskanzleramt/Prime Minister's Office, Parliament and the respective Environmental Agency (altogether 9 domestic institutions). European institutions include the main Directorates of the EU Commission plus European Parliament and Council of Ministers (altogether 10 EU institutions).

particularly pronounced with respect to the contacts to (60 and 34 per cent) and joint activities with (28 and 13 per cent) EU institutions. Although a very large number of British associations report EU-induced political challenges to be of great concern (Table 6.3), their domestic fragmentation provides for few resources to invest in European ties. Attitudes, ideas and discourses about EU membership may also be relevant. Studying state–society relations, Vivian Schmidt argued that the British government 'had to contend with greater challenges to traditional conceptions of democratic and participatory governance . . . than Germany' (Schmidt 2002: 142). Britain has more long-term problems of adaptation to European structures and processes than Germany. Although there are conflicting views on this,[27] British associations may to some extent share the attitudes that prevail in their society. British associations are also more strongly connected to domestic institutions than their German counterparts. In some cases, government departments even functioned as 'sponsoring agencies' (e.g. DTI and TAF).

Beyers (2002) has recently argued that associations with privileged access to institutions at the domestic level have more opportunities to invest in Euro-level networking. He identifies a positive 'correlation between interest associations' domestic embeddedness . . . and their Euro-level strategies' (ibid.: 587). Our data suggest that further factors need to be considered. German associations, for instance, are less involved in joint activities with domestic government agencies and also send and receive less strategically important information than their British counterparts. Their most distinguishing feature is the equal distribution of ties across types of actors and relations. For them, international associations and EU institutions are as reachable as domestic government. Compared to UK associations, German chemical trade associations simply are stronger in both resources and relations.

Conclusions

Europeanization and internationalization have real effects and are recognized by associations as major challenges to their stability. At the *organization level*, political regulation is reported to be most relevant by the majority of our respondents. The majority also underlines the importance of Europe in this context. In terms of political risks, the EU is actually seen as more important than the national government. This is a significant change compared to the early 1980s.

The picture with respect to the internationalization of markets is different. British associations feel more affected by the economic implications than their German respondents. In both groups there is agreement that economic challenges, even if emerging from internationalization, become manifest mostly at the domestic level.

At the level of the *organizational population*, change is much less pronounced at least in Germany where the structure and hierarchical ordering of inter-organizational relations have remained unaltered. In the UK the position of the sector's peak association (CIA) has so much deteriorated that the ordering of relations is today far less hierarchical than at the time of earlier studies. Specific associations apart (biotech), few new groupings were added to the structure in either country. Interestingly, the strongest branch associations (VFA and ABPI) are isolates in the two countries' networks. German pharmaceuticals may soon become a sector in its own right as is already the case in the UK. In terms of organizational evolution, the German pattern is characterized by retention while the British one exhibits some variation and selection of new forms (alliances). Incidence and pace of inter-organizational change cannot be mono-causally explained by internationalization. It is the restructuring of the sector as a whole, the rising relevance of pharmaceuticals, the growing dominance of large multinationals and the resulting cleavages between larger and smaller companies (Coen 1997, 1998; Coen and Dannreuther 2003) which make the representation of encompassing sector interests ever more difficult. Although in some way linked to internationalization, most of this, again, is membership related.

Finally, we have also identified interesting developments in the pattern of relations to public authorities (*organizational community*). We have found that UK associations, although particularly stressed by European regulation tend to leave the business of representation either to their counterparts at the EU level or to government departments. Their comparatively modest presence in Brussels is the combined effect of a general shortage of resources, which in part results from their being tied up with domestic relationships. A general Euro-critical attitude may also play a role. German associations, on the other hand, have grown accustomed to the EU. Ties in their contact portfolios are evenly distributed across all types of actors.

While changes in perceptions may lead to the adoption of different strategies, they do not directly translate into changes at the population level. At the same time, structures at the population level may to some extent determine the configuration at the level of the organizational community. Our findings also suggest that changes at the level of the organizational community – such as, for instance, the emergence of firms and alliances of firms competing for influence and access – have significant implications at the organizational level. Less familiar with these type of activities, German interest associations try to block their growth by raising membership investments and modernizing their presentation. For British associations, competition at the community level induced by direct lobbying of firms seems less of a problem. As a consequence of organizational learning, German associations also 'may find it increasingly expedient to ally with previous interest competitors in joint attempts to defend distinctive national policies' (Grote and Schmitter 2003: 297).

Unlike firms, business associations are buffered against direct selective pressure by a ring of private firms and public institutions at different levels of an ecological hierarchy. Developments at one level may be supportive of change while developments at other levels may be constraining. The relative stability of the chemical organizational population in Germany most likely reflects an acquired position of power and a degree of organizational stability that has proved viable in a period of turbulence. The reintegration currently under way in Britain's associational landscape is a response to prior disintegrative developments. In terms of processes of variation, selection and retention, it is the organizational population which is most resistant to change. Once established, the structure of a country's or a sector's interest domain is hard to change. At least in chemicals, associational orders are far from being destabilized. The embeddedness in either corporatist or pluralist national politics still accounts for the relative strength and stability of interest systems. At the same time, it is the upper and the lower levels of the organizational hierarchy that are most affected by change. With respect to the former, this has to do with competition and with the emergence of entirely new categories of actors (individual firms and networks). Chemical policy networks are much more flexible than the focal networks of the two national populations. In addition, entry barriers for new members are low and public authorities even encourage new entrants. With respect to the latter, the causal factor is increasing interest heterogeneity (small versus large, domestic versus multinational, traditional versus research-intensive, etc.), taxing the associations' capacities. This is the most important reason for the salience of membership-related investments.

Moreover, we could demonstrate that the internationalization of markets and political developments at the level of the EU do not exert a general uniform pressure on organized interests in different countries to undertake the same modifications, aimed at the same objectives, with the same pace of adaptation. We observe cross-national variation at most of the levels studied. In addition, goodness of fit between structures, strategies and ideas of national and supranational actors is but one possible explanation of change. Interest associations 'are unlikely to "supranationalize" themselves and shift their attention and allegiance exclusively to Brussels' (Grote and Schmitter 2003: 297). Instead we observe local processes of adaptation embedded in specific institutional contexts and reflecting specific evolutionary trajectories. Varieties of capitalism, hence, remain pronounced and, 'there is more than a single optimal institutional arrangement for organizing modern societies' (Boyer and Hollingsworth 1997: 51).

Appendix

List of focal associations

Germany

BAU	Deutsche Bauchemie.
BPI	Bundesverband der Pharmazeutischen Industrie
DIB	Deutsche Industrievereinigung Biotechnologie
IHO	Industrieverbandverband Hygiene und Oberfächenschutz für Industrielle Anwendung
IKW	Industrieverband Körperpflege- und Waschmittel
IVA	Industrieverband Agrar
IVC	Industrievereinigung Chemiefaser
KLEB	Industrieverband Klebstoffe
LACK	Verband der Lackindustrie
ORGAN	Fachvereinigung Organische Chemie
TEGEWA	Verband Textil- u. Lederhilfsmittel u. Gerbstoffe
VCI	Verband der Chemischen Industrie
VFA	Verband Forschender Arzneimittelhersteller
VKE	Verband Kunststofferzeugende Industrie

Britain

ABPI	Association of the British Pharmaceutical Industry
BACS	British Association for Chemical Specialities
BAMA	British Aerosol Manufacturers Association
BCDTA	British Chemical Distributors & Traders Association
BCF	British Coatings Federation
BLF	British Lubricants Federation
BPF	British Plastics Federation
BRMA	British Rubber Manufacturers Association
CIA	Chemical Industries Association
CTPA	Cosmetic, Toiletry & Perfumery Association
FMA	Fertilizer Manufacturers Association
SIA	Solvent Industries Association
SOCSA	Specialized Organic Chemicals Sectors Association
UKCPI	Cleaning Products Industry Association

Other abbreviations

ABCM	Association of British Chemical Manufacturers
AC&AE	Association of Chemical and Allied Employers
AIA	Alliance of Industry Associations
AIC	Agricultural Industries Association

BASA	British Adhesives and Sealants Association
BCMA	British Complementary Medicine Association
CEFIC	European Chemical Industry Council
CEO	Chief Executive Officer
CPA	Crop Protection Association
ICI	Imperial Chemical Industries p.l.c.
M&A	Mergers and acquisitions
SME	Small and medium-sized enterprise
TAF	Trade Association Forum
UKASTA	UK Agricultural Supply Trade Association. Together with FMA (see list of focal associations), UKASTA is now part of the Agricultural Industries Association (AIC).

Notes

1 This paper is part of a larger project in which eight countries (Germany, the UK and the US and, in part, Japan, Spain, Italy, Switzerland and Austria) and three sectors (chemicals, information and communication technologies, the dairy sector) are included. The project is funded by the German Research Council (DFG) which has granted financial assistance since 2000 (see Schneider *et al.* 2000). While complete results are expected to appear later in 2006, some papers are available (Grote and Lang 2003; Schmedes 2003; Wonka 2003; Schaumayer 2003; Lang and Grote 2005). Thanks for critical readership and assistance go to Wyn Grant, Wolfgang Streeck, Jelle Visser, to our collaborator Achim Lang, to our student assistants (Dorothea Dürr, Hans-Jörg Schmedes, Arndt Wonka, Frank Häge, Nina Beck, Lilli Bialluch), to the participants of the various Florence, Mannheim and Amsterdam conferences on interest intermediation and, not least, to the directors of dozens of British and German chemical interest associations who have kindly accepted to be interviewed and have completed our questionnaires.

2 Having employed this terminology in earlier work (see Ronit and Schneider 1997; Grote 1998), we here turn to a more systematic body of literature best represented by the volume edited by Joel A. C. Baum (2002). Note that organizational ecology should not be confounded with population ecology, which is but one of the approaches on which the former is resting.

3 For a complete list of associational properties, see Schmitter and Streeck (1999 [1981]).

4 Concerning the worldwide output of pharmaceuticals, Germany (€17.691 million) is at fourth and the UK (€16.552 million) at fifth place behind the US, Japan and France. In terms of exports, Germany is world leader followed by the US and Britain (VFA 2000: 18); in terms of R&D expenditure, the UK is first and Germany second in Europe, behind the US and Japan (ibid.: 28).

5 Of the 153 companies on the membership list of Britain's sector organization, the Chemicals Industry Association (CIA), only 53 were UK owned in 2000 while 32 per cent (49) were US and 7 per cent (11) German owned (see Brophy 2000: 10). Interestingly, 39 of these 53 companies are effectively small- and medium-sized enterprises (SMEs) which leaves Britain with no more than five pure chemical companies valued at over £500 million: ICI, Johnson Matthey, Burmah Castrol, Laporte and BTB (ibid.: 8).

6 Total market capitalization taken from the *Financial Times* Stock Exchange listings for 4 December 1999 ranked the UK sector with £19 billion and was

expected to drop to £12.6 billion (Brophy 2000: 8). BASF arrives at £19 billion, Bayer at £19.5 billion and Hoechst at £17 billion (ibid.).

7 For data on worldwide M&A activity in chemicals, pharmaceuticals and biotechnology see: Young and Partners 2003.

8 DIB, the German peak association's (VCI) sector group for biotechnology, exempts members from subscription fees for the first three years after joining.

9 The White Paper is a review of four legal instruments governing chemicals in the EU. These mainly concerned matters of classification, packaging and labelling of dangerous substances, or the latter's evaluation and risk control.

10 For example, turning to the Confederation of British Industry, Grant (2000: 4) mentions that the CBI 'once occupied fifteen floors of Centre Point in Tottenham Court Road, but its smaller staff can now be accommodated on just two floors'.

11 Decreasing enthusiasm among scholars somehow reflects the decreasing attraction of this organizational form among the associations themselves. Rather than the benefits of membership inducing national groups to join EU associations, it is the 'costs of non-membership' (Greenwood and Webster 2000), i.e. the risk of foregoing strategically relevant information, which is a more decisive factor.

12 Shell is a large oil company based in the United Kingdom. In 1995 they needed to decide how to get rid of a disused oil storage platform called the Brent Spar in the North Sea. Shell wanted to sink the Brent Spar. The environmental group Greenpeace campaigned to stop them.

13 For example, the German plastics industry association, VKE, spends a large part of its annual budget on the promotion and marketing of plastic products on behalf of its members.

14 Focal association sets were identified with the help of expert panels in both countries. At least 20 per cent of the experts on a panel had to agree on the prominence of an association for it to be included.

15 The VFA organizes some 36 leading pharmaceutical manufacturers that account for 86 per cent (76,000) of subsector employment (113,000). On average, each member employs 2,100 people. Among these, there are many foreign-owned corporations often with CEOs from abroad.

16 The BPI has recently (2002) followed the VFA's example and moved its offices to Berlin. In coming years, it is expected that the VCI will also move to the capital.

17 For processing the data, we used UCINET, the most widely diffused software programme for this type of analysis. Results were then exported to VISONE, a new programme for the visualization of social networks (see Brandes *et al.* 1999).

18 Grant and Martinelli (1991: 84) underline that ICI was careful not to control the association and that its role tended to be hegemonic rather than dominant. It tried

> to ensure that [it did] not exert such an influence that the viewpoints of other firms are inadvertently downgraded in importance. . . . Such a stance could discourage smaller firms from joining the association, hence undermining its representative character, and counteracting the beneficial effects of the selective incentives cross-subsidized by the larger firms.

This notwithstanding, many of our British respondents characterized the CIA as still being 'imperious'.

19 Many are large multinationals. German companies like Bayer, BASF, Degussa, Merck, Aventis and others are also well represented.

20 Income from subscriptions amounted to £4,591,199 in 2000 (CIA Annual

Report 2000). British Petroleum alone paid some £400,000. It does not come as a surprise that other members withdrew due to high subscriptions.

21 In 1995 the process was initiated by the Department for Trade and Industry (DTI), which set up a Trade Association Initiative and published a widely diffused document on the 'Model Trade Association' (DTI 1996). A year later, the Trade Association Forum (TAF) was established and a first benchmarking exercise carried out (TAF 1999; see also TAF 2002). TAF was initially financed by its sponsoring agency, the DTI, which reimbursed subscription fees to participating associations. Since 1999, the organization operates on a self-financing basis and has since delivered three benchmarking reports (MacDonald 2001; Boleat 2000). It also outlines procedures that may help associations to form loose alliances, joint ventures, federations or properly merged organizations. Quite a few TAF members belong to our chemicals association set and, accordingly, have reshaped their inter-organizational relations.

22 AIA member associations are: CTPA, BPF, BRMA, BACS, BCMA, BCF, BASA, BCDTA, BAMA, SOCSA and UKCPI.

23 As mentioned by one of the CIA's directors in the late 1980s, 'However hard it tried, the CIA was unable to shake off entirely the feelings amongst some of the others that it was a club for big fish, dominating the smaller fry' (Culpin 2000: 41).

24 Apart from the CIA and the ABPI which both employ a staff of some 60 each, BPF and BCF have some 20 employees each, while the other focal associations have no more than ten.

25 This may be different for some of AIA's members. For example, BCDTA and BACS have formed a limited company and a merger is envisaged. FMA, CPA, UKASTA and the British Seed and Plant Association have formed a fertilizer's alliance.

26 Since we are interested in contact with associations outside the domestic system, we have included the VCI's Brussels office although it is only the prolonged arm of the national association. The fact that British associations cannot rely on such a structure is interesting in its own right and partly explains the inferior values obtained by the UK in Table 6.5.

27 Maria Green Cowles, for instance, has argued that 'there is a misfit between the German and the European business-government relationship, and one can expect there to be some difficulty' (Cowles 2001: 166). British associations by comparison are said to be less in need of changing their behaviour when entering Europe. In our view, the issue is not one of 'goodness of fit' (see also Börzel and Risse 2002; Featherstone and Radaelli 2003) but, rather, one of power.

Bibliography

Baum, J. A. C. (ed.) (2002) *The Blackwell Companion to Organizations*, Oxford: Blackwell Business.

Baum, J. A. C. and Singh, J. V. (1994) 'Organizational Hierarchies and Evolutionary Processes: Some Reflections on a Theory of Organizational Evolution', in J. A. C. Baum and J. V. Singh (eds) *Evolutionary Dynamics of Organizations*, New York and Oxford: Oxford University Press, pp. 3–20.

Baum, J. A. C. (1996) 'Organizational Ecology', in S. R. Clegg, C. Hardy, W. Nord (eds) *Handbook of Organization Studies*, London, Thousand Oaks CA, New Delhi: Sage, pp. 77–114.

Beyers, J. (2002) 'Gaining and Seeking Access. The European Adaptation of Domestic Interest Associations', *European Journal of Political Research* 41 (5): 585–612.

Boleat, M. (2000) *Models of Trade Association Co-operation*, London: Trade Association Forum.

Börzel, T. and Risse, T. (2002) 'Europäisierung und die Transformation der Nationalstaaten', in V. Schneider (ed.) *Entgrenzte Märkte – grenzenlose Bürokratie*, Frankfurt am Main: Campus.

Boyer, R. and Hollingsworth, J. R. (1997) 'The Variety of Institutional Arrangements and their Complementarity in Modern Economies', in J. R. Hollingsworth and R. Boyer (eds) *Contemporary Capitalism. The Embeddedness of Institutions*. New York and Cambridge: Cambridge University Press, pp. 49–55.

Brandes, U., Kenis, P., Raab, J., Schneider, V. and Wagner, D. (1999) 'Explorations into the Visualization of Policy Networks', *Journal of Theoretical Politics* 11: 75–106.

Brickman, R., Jasanoff, S. and Ilgen, T. (1985) *Controlling Chemicals: The Politics of Regulation in Europe and the United States*, Ithaca NY: Cornell University Press.

Brophy, J. (2000) 'The Impact of Chemicals Industry Mergers, Acquisitions and Restructuring on the UK Chemistry Infrastructure'. Online, available at: www.rsc.org/pdf/general/mergers.pdf.

Broscheid, A. (2002) 'When Groups Break Up: a Formal Model of Organizational Change in German Pharmaceutical Interest Representation', *MPI* Working Paper, version of 23 July 2002, Cologne: Max Planck Institute for the Studies of Societies. Online, available at: www.mpi-fg-koeln.mpg.de/people/bs/Broscheid_BPI.pdf.

CIA (2000) *Annual Report and Accounts 2000*, London: Chemical Industries Association.

Coen, D. (1997) 'The Evolution of the Large Firm as a Political Actor in the European Union', *Journal of European Public Policy* 4 (1), 91–108.

Coen, D. (1998) 'The European Business Interest and the Nation State: Large Firm Lobbying in the European Union and Member States', *Journal of Public Policy* 18 (1): 75–100.

Coen, D. and Dannreuther, W. (2003) 'Differentiated Europeanization: Large and Small Firms in the EU Policy Process', in K. Featherstone and C. M. Radaelli (eds) *The Politics of Europeanization*, op. cit.: 255–278.

Cowles, M. G. (2001) 'The Transatlantic Business Dialogue and Domestic Business-Government Relations', in M. Green Cowles, J. Caporaso and T. Risse (eds) *Transforming Europe*, Ithaca NY, London: Cornell University Press, pp. 159–179.

Culpin, D. (2000) *Development of the UK Chemical Industry. A Historical Review of the UK Chemical Industry, including Reference to External Policy Issues and the Role of the Chemical Industries Association and its Forerunners*, London: CIA.

DIB (2000) *BioTech 2000. Die wirtschaftliche Bedeutung von Biotechnologie und Gentechnik in Deutschland*, Frankfurt am Main: Deutsche Industrievereinigung Biotechnologie.

DTI (1996) *A Best Practice Guide for the Model Trade Association*, London: Department of Trade and Industry.

European Commission (2001) *White Paper on the Strategy for a Future Chemicals Policy, COM (2001) 88 final, 27.2.2001*, Brussels: EU Commission.

European Commission (2003) 'Proposal for a Regulation of the European Parliament and of the Council concerning the Registration, Evaluation, Authorization and Restriction of Chemicals (REACH), establishing a European Chemicals Agency', *COM (2003) 644 final*, Brussels: EU Commission.

Featherstone, K. and Radaelli, C. (eds) (2003) *The Politics of Europeanization: Theory and Analysis*, Oxford: Oxford University Press.

Galunic, D. C. and Weeks, J. R. (2002) 'Intraorganizational Ecology', in J. A. C. Baum (ed.) *The Blackwell Companion to Organizations*, Oxford: Blackwell Business, pp. 75–97.

Grabher, G. (1993) 'The Weakness of Strong Ties: The Lock-In of Regional Development in the Ruhr Area', in G. Grabher (ed.) *The Embedded Firm. On the Socio-Economics of Industrial Networks*, London and New York: Routledge, pp. 255–277.

Granovetter, M. (1973) 'The Strength of Weak Ties', *American Journal of Sociology* 78 (6): 1360–1380.

Grant, W. (1986) 'Associational Systems in the Chemical Industry', in A. Martinelli (ed.) *International Markets and Global Firms. A Comparative Study of Organized Business in the Chemical Industry*, London, New Delhi: Sage, pp. 47–60.

Grant, W. (1991) 'Associational Systems in the Chemical Industry', in A. Martinelli (ed.) *International Markets and Global Firms*, London: Sage, pp. 47–61.

Grant, W. (2000) *Pressure Groups and British Politics*, London: Macmillan Press Ltd.

Grant, W. and Martinelli, A. (1991) 'Political Turbulence, Enterprise Crisis and Industrial Recovery: ICI and Montedison', in A. Martinelli (ed.) *International Markets and Global Firms*, London: Sage, pp. 61–91.

Grant, W., Paterson, W. and Whitston, C. (1988) *Government and the Chemical Industry. A Comparative Study of Britain and West Germany*, Oxford: Oxford University Press.

Greenwood, J. and Webster, R. (2000) 'Are EU Business Associations Governable?', *European Integration online Papers* 4,3. Online, available at: www.eiop.or.at/eiop/texte/2000-003.htm.

Greenwood, J., Grote, J. R. and Ronit, K. (eds) (1992) *Organized Interests and the European Community*, London, New Delhi: Sage.

Groser, M. (1983) 'Die Organisation von Wirtschaftsinteressen in der Chemischen Industrie der Bundesrepublik Deutschland', unpublished paper.

Grote, J. R. (1998) 'The Political Ecology of Regionalism. State-Society Relations in Nine European Regions', PhD dissertation, Florence: European University Institute.

Grote, J. R. and Lang, A. (2003) 'Europeanization and Organizational Change in National Trade Associations – An Organizational Ecology Perspective' in K. Featherstone and C. Radaelli (eds) *The Politics of Europeanization*, Oxford: Oxford University Press.

Grote, J. R. and Schmitter, P. C. (2003) 'The Renaissance of National Corporatism: Unintended Side-effects of European Economic and Monetary Union, or Calculated Response to the Absence of European Social Policy?', in F. van Waarden and G. Lehmbruch (eds) *Renegotiating the Welfare State. Flexible Adjustment Through Corporatist Concertation*, London: Routledge, pp. 279–302.

Kennedy, C. (1986) *ICI: the Company That Changed Our Lives*, London: Hutchinson.

Lahusen, C. (2002) 'Commercial Consultancies in the European Union: The Shape and Structure of Professional Interest Intermediation', *Journal of European Public Policy*, 9 (5), October 2002: 695–714.

Lang, A. and Grote, J. R. (2005) 'Facetten des Wandels – Anpassungsstrategien von Wirtschaftsverbänden an ihre Umwelt', in R. Eising and B. Kohler-Koch (eds) *Intevessenpolitik n Europa, Regieven in Europa Bd.* 7, Baden-Baden: Nomos, 363–389.

Macdonald. A. (2001) *The Business of Representation. The Modern Trade Association – A Report to the Trade Association Forum*, London: Department of Trade and Industry and Trade Association Forum.

Martinelli, A. (ed.) (1991) *International Markets and Global Firms. A Comparative Study of Organized Business in the Chemical Industry*, London, New Delhi: Sage.

Munz, C. M. (2001) 'Europäisierung und verbandliche Orientierungen: Eine Inhaltsanalyse der Wahrnehmung von Umweltveränderungen durch den Verband der Chemischen Industrie', University of Konstanz, MA Thesis.

OECD (Organization for Economic Cooperation and Development) (2003). STAN Industry Structural Analysis Database, 2003 edition.

Platzer, H. (1984) 'Industrieverbände im Prozess der Internationalisierung von Wirtschaft und Politik. Die Verbände der chemischen und pharmazeutischen Industrie', Sektorstudie im Rahmen eines DFG-Forschungsprojektes, Tübingen/Darmstadt 1984.

Rao, H. (2002) 'Interorganizational Ecology', in J. A. C. Baum (ed.) *The Oxford Companion to Organizations*, Oxford: Blackwell Business, pp. 541–556.

Ronge, V. and Körber, S. (1994) 'Die Europäisierung der Chemikalienkontrolle und ihre Folgen für Verbandspolitik – aus deutscher Sicht', in V. Eichener and H. Voelzkow (eds) *Europäische Integration und verbandliche Interessenvermittlung*, Marburg: Metropolis, pp. 321–348.

Ronit, K. and Schneider, V. (1997) 'Organisierte Interessen in nationalen und supranationalen Politökologien: Ein Vergleich der G7-Länder mit der Europäischen Union', in U. von Alemann and B. Weßels (eds) *Verbände in vergleichender Perspektive*, Berlin: Edition Sigma, pp. 29–62.

Ronit, K. and Schneider, V. (2000) *Private Organizations in Global Politics*, London, Routledge.

Schaumayer, A. (2003) 'Japanische Wirtschaftsverbände im ICT Sektor zwischen organisatorischer Persistenz und Wandel – Eine empirische Analyse verbandlicher Organisationsstrukturen', University of Konstanz, MA Thesis.

Schmedes, H. J. (2003) 'Trade Associations in the US Chemical Industry: An Empirical Assessment of Organizational Change', University of Konstanz, MA Thesis.

Schmidt, V. A. (2002) 'The Effects of European Integration on National Forms of Governance. Reconstructing Practices and Reconceptualizing Democracy', in J. R. Grote and B. Gbikpi (eds) *Participatory Governance. Political and Societal Implications*, Opladen: Leske und Budrich, pp. 141–177.

Schmitter, P. C. and Streeck, W. (1981; 2nd edn 1999) 'The Organization of Business Interests. Studying the Associative Action of Business in Advanced Industrial Societies', MPIfG Discussion paper 99/1, Cologne: Max Planck Institute for the Study of Societies.

Schneider, V. (1988) *Politiknetzwerke in der Chemikalienkontrolle*, Berlin, New York: Walter de Gruyter.

Schneider, V., Schmitter, P. C. and Grote, J. (2000) 'Die Veränderung von Einfluss- und Mitgliedschaftslogiken sektoraler Dachverbände im Kontext von Europäisierung und Internationalisierung', Projektantrag and die Deutsche Forschungsgemeinschaft, March 2000.

Streeck, W. (1987) 'Vielfalt und Interdependenz. Überlegungen zur Rolle von intermediären Organisationen in sich ändernden Umwelten', *Kölner Zeitschrift für Soziologie und Sozialpsychologie* 3 (39), 471–495.

Trade Association Forum (1999) *Trade Association Performance. Report of the 1999 Benchmarking Study of Trade Associations*, London: Trade Association Forum.

Trade Association Forum (2002) *Trade Association Performance – A Five-year View*, London: Trade Association Forum.

VCI (2000) *Facts, Analyses, Perspectives: The Chemical Industry 2000, Annual Report*, Frankfurt am Main: Verband der Chemischen Industrie.

VCI (2001) *Chemiewirtschaft in Zahlen*, Frankfurt am Main: Verband der Chemischen Industrie.

VFA (2000) *Die Arzneimittelindustrie in Deutschland*, Berlin: Verband Forschender Arzneimittelhersteller.

Wonka, A. (2003) 'Nationale Interessengruppen in der EU-Interessenvermittlung. Eine empirische Fallstudie zum Vergleich der europäischen Lobbyingstrategien deutscher und britischer Unternehmensverbände', University of Konstanz, MA Thesis.

Young and Partners, Chemical and Life Science Investment Banking, New York (2003) 'Mergers and Acquisitions in the Chemical, the Pharmaceutical and the Biotechnology Industries – Summaries'. Online, available at: www.chemicalindustry.com/mat.html; www.pharmaindustry.com/pmat.html and www.pharmaindustry.com/bmat.html.

7 Against all odds

Adaptation and survival of national associations[1]

Dirk Lehmkuhl

Since the mid-1990s, an increasing number of studies have departed from the well-trodden path in European integration research that analyses the processes of institution building and policy making at the European level. Instead they have focused on the impact and repercussions of the EU on the institutions and regulations of the member states or on the adaptation and adjustment of these same institutions and regulations to the EU. Inspired both by what scholars of International Relations used to call the 'second image reversed perspective', that is, the impact of international influences on domestic structures (Gourevitch 1978), and by comparativists' interest in developments of convergence and divergence in the policies and politics of EU member states, this branch of research has flourished such that it is very difficult to keep track of.[2] What aggravates the situation is that there is little consensus among scholars concerning definitions, criteria and concepts employed in examining and explaining the impact of European integration on domestic political and socio-economic structures. With respect to the consequences of European integration on domestic associations and on patterns of private–public interaction, one is left with little more than educated yet speculative guesses that lead one to predict either a withering away of the various forms of national corporatism or their reinforcement (Olson 1995; Schmitter and Grote 1997).[3]

Given this unsatisfactory premise, the intention of this chapter is twofold. First, it provides a detailed empirical study on changes in two national associational systems, specifically among the business associations in the transport sector in Germany and the Netherlands. The central message here is that the established frameworks of transport regulation have changed profoundly with the advent of a Common European Transport Policy. This, however, did not do away with national interest associations. Rather, these remained important for both the implementation of national policies and for the firms in the sector, although it meant that the associations had to adjust to the new conditions by restructuring their policies, activities and organizations.

Second, the chapter provides a framework to help explain how the actual translation of external influences into patterns of change or adjustment at the domestic level takes place. The concept of associations as intermediate organizations that operate at the interface between private and public actors and incorporate the dynamics of their political and economic environments in both structural and strategic terms lies at the core of this analysis. This focus on the complex patterns of interaction between the associations and their environments makes it possible to discard the assumption that societal structures at the domestic level functionally adapt to external pressures. Instead, it is proposed here that the way in which the configuration of associations within the European transport sector changes when a supranational regime of governance emerges is dependent, for one, on the degree to which the balance established by associations between the demands of their constituencies and of their public interlocutors has relied on the pre-existing regulatory framework and, for another, on the capacity of public actors to offer compensation to associations for participating in policies of competitive deregulation.

Being in line with European policies of deregulation, the Dutch government's carrot and stick policy paved the way for both an early regulatory reform and a reorganization of transport associations. In contrast, strong reliance on the established protectionist regulation spurred significant resistance against regulatory reform and considerably hindered a reorganization of the associational landscape in Germany. While in both countries state–society relations in the transport sector were and still are corporatist in nature, the impact of Europeanization was different. In the Netherlands, Europeanization added economic thrust to a societal process of depillarization and contributed to a strengthening rather than a weakening of corporatist patterns of interaction. In Germany, the major pattern underlying the associational organization changed from being legally defined to being economically focused. At the same time, the influence of Europeanization 'purified' the patterns of state–society interactions as client-based elements in government intervention disappeared.

In the following chapter, the conceptual framework will be presented first, then two empirical sections will provide vital information concerning changes in the economic and political environment of the associations, on the one hand, and their organizational and strategic adjustment, on the other. The final section will summarize the major findings and draw the ensuing conclusions.

Associational adjustment

Europeanization refers to the process of political, legal and economic integration in Europe. As such, it also comprises processes of economic internationalization. Accordingly, the Europeanization of business associations is interpreted as a process in which individual and corporate actors structurally and strategically adapt to changes in their political, legal and economic environment. Underlying this understanding is the assumption that economic and political integration in Europe significantly influences the organizational development of associations. Numerous questions arise in reference to this: which patterns of reaction can be observed and how can they be explained? Is it true that 'jurisdictional integration in Europe undercuts the guilds and other special-interest groups of the day' (Olson 1995: 13) or 'will the corporatist Sisyphus be on his way uphill again as associations manage to successfully adapt to their members' strategies within the internal market and to politics within a multilevel polity' (Schmitter and Grote 1997)?

Why focus on the national level?

Generally speaking, European integration can be conceived as generating integrative forces that lead both to closer interactions among the formerly separated political units and to the economic enmeshing of markets. Based on *neo-functionalist arguments*,[4] the vertical dynamics of supranational policy-making are about to prompt a shift in decision-making competencies and actors' loyalties from the national to the European level and thus contribute to a gradual erosion of the importance of the nation state as a point of reference for associations. In so doing, European integration is supposed to generate organizational adaptations by improving organizational representation at the European level, even though this will occur at the expense of national associations.

Empirical evidence, however, undermines these neo-functional assumptions and instead strongly supports the conclusion that, despite the high degree of transnational interaction, associational attention has not been diverted from the national theatre (Kohler-Koch 2000a: 5). Rather, the findings show that associations and firms have established contacts with both levels of decision making (Eising 2003; Grote and Lang 2003), and in some cases, interest groups address national targets even more often than before (Sidenius 1999).

There are further reasons that merit focusing on the national level. Especially in light of policy areas where there is greater interest in *not* making decisions than in making them, the first and foremost reason for associations to maintain a strong national base is to exert pressure at the national level (Schmitter and Streeck 1991: 143). Second, the large majority of organized action and sectoral forms of public–private intermingling take place at the national level. It is here that one would expect the changes caused by the integration process to leave their most visible marks. According to the proponents of 'private governance dumping'[5] (van Waarden 1994: 220), the most dramatic consequence of negative integration is that it can restrict the existent patterns of discriminatory treatment between public interlocutors and associations. Third, recent studies have suggested that national arrangements of concertation and dispute at both the macro- and the mesolevel can survive *if* the participants manage to shift the functional content from demand to supply issues (Heinisch 2000; Traxler 1995; Traxler and Unger 1994; Visser and Hemerijck 1997). In their attempt to meet their increasing European obligations, governments also 'will have to rely more-and-more on the negotiated consent of their respective social partners in order to obtain the "voluntary and active assent" that is so important for competitive success' (Schmitter and Grote 1997: 36).

This shows that it is necessary to account for the political and socio-economic context in individual member states in order to realistically assess how Europeanization impacts on the organization of interests at a national level (Eising and Kohler-Koch 1994: 178). Assuming that associational landscapes within the members states are equipped with a certain robustness against corrosive influences, one might expect that 'while European integration may induce some regulatory convergence, nevertheless national specificities regarding self-regulation persist and maintain regulatory diversity across Europe' (van Waarden 1994: 257).

How to analyse change and adjustment

The effects of the integration process can be expected to manifest themselves in three dimensions: the socio-economic environment in which interest associations act, the formal organization of associations and the institutional target structure of associations (Streeck 1987: 492). Taking the economic and the political–institutional environment as independent variables, this study investigates how changes in these variables caused by Europe impact on the associational configuration within the transport sector in Germany and the Netherlands. Generally, it is assumed that factors deriving from the economic environment exert different pressures on the associational landscape from those deriving from the political–institutional environment. While the former primarily lead to differentiation and fragmentation, the latter foster a concentration of the representation of interests in the system.

This assumption is based on the idea that business associations – like other organizations – strive for a stable and (relatively) autonomous supply of resources and independence in making strategic decisions. To do so, associations have to incorporate the heterogeneous demands of different environments in their organizational structures and strategies. The *logic of membership* requires organizational structures that are capable of adapting to fragmented and segmented interests. In this context, uncertainties about financial and political support pose a risk to the associations' objective of autonomy. To reduce this risk and to increase their organizational security, associations may address their external environment, within which public actors are of utmost importance. When targeting public interlocutors, however, it is expected that associations contribute in one way or another to the performance of public policies. Thus, the *logic of influence* requires certain organizational prerequisites: for example, the most encompassing membership structures possible and/or the capacity to get their members to act in the interest of some wider collectivity (Schmitter and Streeck 1981).[6]

In line with the results of current research on Europeanization, we assume that Europe's differentiated impact not only relates to how firms in different countries have responded to the external pressure of European integration or to how they and their governments have dealt with the internal problems related to industrial competitiveness (Schmidt 1999: 243), but also relates to changes in associational systems. To describe the changes in the economic and political environment of associations, the next section summarizes the major features of embedded European integration in the field of road haulage, a sector that has only relatively recently been subject to substantive European policy decisions.

Economic and political integration and European transport policy

The Europeanization of the transport industry

The specific character of the transport sector, derived both from industrial production (on the demand side of transport services) and from being an industry in its own right (on the supply side of transport services), implies that the economic integration process has had a twofold impact on the sector. Both the changing status of transport in the industrial production process and sector specific developments must be taken into account if one wants to assess the impact that economic integration in the European Union has had on the associational systems in the German and Dutch road haulage sectors. The overall impression is that, on the demand side as well as on the supply side, transport has manifested itself as an extremely dynamic sector in the past two decades.

In response to increased international competition, European industry has been generally restructured. The reorganization of the production system has affected all three stages of business activity: namely, the *acquisition* of resources, the *production* of goods or services and *distribution and sales* (O'Donnell 1994: 47). The general growth of trade and restructuring of the entire production and retailing system has had a significant impact on the transport industry. The increase in the exchange of interregional and international goods went hand in hand with an even greater demand for transport services. Given the differentiation between product and production concepts, the transport industry faced demands for high-quality services, specifically in terms of flexibility, reliability and more generally, comprehensiveness and logistical content. As a consequence, transport markets became internationalized, diversified and specialized (Coopers & Lybrand 1997).

Faced with new developments, the road haulage industry has been undergoing radical changes, and the transport supply industry reflects the specialization and segmentation that has developed on the demand and product side. In general, 'value-adding' has become the catchword, while the role of physical transport has been declining. Larger enterprises are developing into logistics organizers that offer comprehensive control of the logistics chain. Medium-sized firms face more difficulties in adjusting. To achieve an efficient size, networks that allow them to expand geographically and to use 'shared-utilities' are being increasingly set up. However, the majority of firms are small enterprises that compete for physical distribution in highly contested markets (NEA 1997).

The Common European Transport Policy

'Agriculture is a story of action and success; transport is a story of inaction and failure' (Lindberg and Scheingold 1970: 141). In contrast to the Common Agriculture Policy, a Common Transport Policy in Europe did not come to be, although it was envisaged by the Treaty of Rome. Rather, a deadlock existed until the mid-1980s, between proponents of a straightforward liberalization (the United Kingdom and the Netherlands) and countries that linked their support for liberalization to the concomitant harmonization of technical, social and fiscal measures (France, Germany and Italy). Since international transport was governed by a complex patchwork of bilateral agreements between member states, customs and border controls constituted significant obstacles to cross-border transactions and trade among member states. Since 1985, however, transport policies have made significant progress. The most important policy changes consisted of abolishing all the restrictions to cross-border transport and opening domestic markets to foreign hauliers (Kerwer and Teutsch 2001; Lehmkuhl 1999: 36–54).[7]

The most significant effect caused by the development of a Common European Transport Policy and by the contemporaneous economic developments was that the established regulatory framework at the national level began to erode. As such, European provisions that were to be translated into national legislation had a less significant impact than those concerned with liberalizing international transport. To put it more bluntly, indirect pressure was more important in bringing about changes of regulatory regimes at the national level than was the requirement of implementing binding European legislation. While the provisions on technical, social and fiscal issues could mostly be translated into national legislation without any great difficulty, the pressure exerted by the liberalization of international transport played a larger role, especially for those regimes that were highly regulated. In particular, the right of non-resident hauliers to operate in other members' states (cabotage) was of utmost importance. The significance of cabotage derives from the fact that it confronts liberalized international transport markets directly with national regulatory regimes. Thus, cabotage has become a symbol for the need to liberalize those domestic markets that were previously relatively closed. Consequently, the questions to be addressed are how these changes were processed at the national level and how they have affected the systems of interest representation in Germany and the Netherlands.

European integration and national associational systems

To analyse the dynamics in the relationship between the organization of interests and the changes in their major task environments, we proceed in six steps: steps one and two analyse changes in the logic of membership and influence, respectively. In a comparative way, it will be analysed how changes in these two dimensions affected the transport sector in the two countries under study. Step three describes how the changes in the economic and political environment have impacted on the resource influx of associations, before step four looks at how associations have adapted to these changes. Based on the descriptive part of steps two to four, the final two steps address the actual transformation of the associational landscapes (step six) and provide explanation for the observations (step six). As will be shown, attention to the micropolitics of associations helps to explain why associations in the two countries acted differently.

Logic of membership: sector structure

As has been described, the economic transformation from Fordist mass production to post-Fordist, flexible specialization has brought about new production patterns and a differentiation within the transport industry defined by size, product and territory; all three are frequently linked to each other.

The road haulage industry in both countries is characterized by a huge number of small and very small firms and a relatively small number of big companies that, despite their limited number, have a large share of the total turnover within the industry. Compared with a country like Italy, in which about 95 per cent of all haulage firms are one-man businesses (Sleuwaegen *et al.* 1993: 228), the average firm size in Germany and the Netherlands is quite large.[8] Nevertheless, over time the two countries have shared common trends as well as exhibited distinct differences. Both countries have experienced a growth in average firm size since the 1970s, particularly from the 1980s onwards. Yet, this increase has been significantly greater in the Netherlands than it has been in Germany. Today, despite the numerical dominance of very small, small and medium-sized enterprises, about 5–7 per cent of the big and very big companies in both countries have a market share of about 40 per cent.

By focusing on the type of performance, we can differentiate between various degrees of competition in the different market areas. In general, it can be said that competitive pressure decreases relative to an increase in specialization. This aspect can be illustrated by extreme cases of mere physical transport, on the one hand, and the very technologically advanced provision of logistics services on the other. The first describes a market segment in which international and national policies of deregulation and liberalization have lowered entry barriers, thus further contributing to a tendency for overcapacity. In this segment, it is primarily small hauliers who compete fiercely among themselves with transport prices being the central arena of this competition. In contrast, competition in highly sophisticated services is relatively weak. Suppliers of logistics services have generally managed to establish close relationships with their clients and both technical and organizational skills make their services difficult to substitute.

Both countries under study in this chapter are characterized by a significant heterogeneity in the sector: different markets are characterized by different degrees of competition, and firms differ with respect to their size, their performance and the degree to which they cooperate with other companies. This last point hints at a final aspect of the heterogeneity of transport markets. The more manufacturers and the general industry expand their resourcing and delivery activities in territorial terms, the more the markets for transport services grow to cover local, regional, national and international distances. In the transport industry, this significant regional market segmentation is reflected by the fact that smaller hauliers dominate in short-distance markets, while medium-sized firms frequently offer interregional transport and larger companies concentrate on international transport.

Taking into account the difference in size between Germany and the Netherlands, it is no surprise that the relative share of hauliers active in international transport is larger in the Netherlands than in Germany. In addition, the relatively large domestic market in Germany generates a huge demand for national transport, whereas the combination of Rotterdam as one of the biggest ports in the world and a relatively small Dutch domestic market favours a greater international orientation in the transport industry. The different size of the German and the Dutch domestic markets has established a further significant difference with respect to the function and importance of forwarding agencies. In contrast to the Netherlands, where a relatively small number of forwarding agents operate mainly with international maritime shipping or aviation, forwarding agents play a much more prominent role in Germany. In addition to functions such as storage and consolidation of cargo, their activities substantially overlap with those of transport firms in terms of regional differentiation and types of activity. In the next section, we look at what changes have been observed in the legal–institutional environment of road transport associations in both countries.

Logic of influence: the legal-institutional environment

The regulatory changes in both countries have been characterized by a transformation toward more deregulated and liberal provisions that aim less at restricting market access than at regulating market functioning.

In Germany, legal provisions governing the transport industry have revolved around the nationalized railways. Regulations affected other modes of transport especially where they endangered the quasi-monopoly of the railways; that is, road haulage over middle and long distances. In addition to differentiating between short-, medium- and long-distance transport, the Road Freight Haulage Act of 1952 contained a licence requirement, a limitation on the total number of licences and tariff structures resembling the railway tariffs. A federal agency (Bundesanstalt für den Güterfernverkehr) was assigned to monitor compliance to the regulations.

Since 1998, three important elements have significantly transformed German transport regulation. First, the translation of the European cabotage provisions into national legislation led to an abolition of the distinction between short- and long-distance haulage so as not to discriminate against German hauliers. Second, the quantitative restriction of licensing was replaced by a licensing policy that harmonized with the Community provision on qualitative licensing. Third, the taxation system has gradually been transformed by lowering the taxation on fixed costs (vehicle tax) and by increasing variable costs (fuel), including the introduction of road pricing elements. Why this shift from market substitution to market regulation (Teutsch 2001) was strongly opposed by the hauliers associations will be discussed below.

In contrast to Germany, the regulation of the Dutch transport sector has never been driven by the motivation to restrict one sector in favour of another.[9] Rooted in its tradition of regional planning, public intervention was legitimized by the objective of public actors to coordinate the development of the transport sector as such by regulating the demand for and supply of transport services. Nevertheless, the instruments used to achieve this objective were the same: the control of market entry, the use of tariffs and the application of fiscal instruments. The recession in the 1970s highlighted the failure of these measures to balance market supply and demand; the sector suffered from overcapacity and cut-throat competition. The ineffective system of compulsory tariffs was abolished and the government tightened restrictions to cope with oversupply by fixing a maximum loading capacity for single firms in 1975 ('tonnage stop'). However, the new system used to regulate capacity proved insufficient, impractical and a hindrance to economic activity and innovation. Moreover, the implementation and control of the entire regulatory system was cost intensive. Thus, from the early 1980s onwards, the government, the regulatory agencies, the industrial representatives and the carriers and forwarders – in other words, all transport-related actors in the Netherlands – were clearly dissatisfied with the existing regulatory arrangements.

In this situation, the Dutch government set the agenda for a shift toward liberalized transport markets from 1984 onwards (Lehmkuhl 1999: 136ff). The preparation for new legislation was based on 'Community ideas, [. . .] liberal ideas and driven by the market oriented thinking of the government' (interview Ministerie Verkeer en Waterstaat, November 1995). Until 1992, amendments gradually abolished fixed tariffs and replaced quantitative restrictions on market access with qualitative ones, such as those regulating occupational qualification, solvency and reliability.

Despite certain similarities between Germany and the Netherlands in the area of regulatory change, there were also a number of *significant differences*. The transformation in the Netherlands occurred in anticipation of the advent of a Common European Transport Policy that was to be based on a liberalization of market access. In contrast, the European liberalization policies made the changes in Germany less voluntary and more compulsory because they took place only after the major European decisions had been made. The nature of each of these processes of national de-regulation, be it voluntary or involuntary, was mirrored in the respective politics of regulatory changes. While in Germany, the shift from market substitution to market regulation (Teutsch 2001) was not, a broad consensus supported the transformation of the regulatory framework in the Netherlands. To a large extent, these different patterns of transformation can be explained by their differing impact on the resource influx of the associations.

Changes in resource influx

In Germany, as in the Netherlands, changes in the economic and political environment of associations in the transport industry have significantly impacted on the influx of resources, such as financial support and legitimacy. Associations in both countries experienced similar developments regarding the financial aspect of their relationship to their constituencies. The internationalization and differentiation of markets contributed to a general lack of transparency, which – in conjunction with a permanent oversupply – fostered the trend toward cut-throat competition. As a consequence, the financial resources of many associations were diminished by company bankruptcies resulting from increased competition and the sale of firms as part of a growth process on an international scale.

With respect to the legitimacy conferred to them by their members, the associations in Germany were much more challenged by the European policies of liberalization and the subsequent national policies of deregulation than were their counterparts in the Netherlands. To a large extent, this was because deregulation rendered unnecessary the political *raison d'être* of German transport associations, namely the preservation of the existing regulatory framework to guarantee protection against domestic and foreign competition. After liberalisation, protection no longer provided an incentive to become or remain a member of an association in Germany. Since protection against competition was never quite so important in the Netherlands, European and national policies of deregulation were not perceived as a threat. On the contrary, the link between Dutch associations and their constituency was strengthened because, in addition to the help the associations offered companies in opening doors to international expansion, smaller firms in particular relied on their association as a vital source of information concerning market developments.

With respect to the relationship between associations and their public interlocutors, significant differences between Germany and the Netherlands have been observed. For reasons of clarity, these changes are described separately for each country.

Germany

In light of the various ways in which private interests are involved in the implementation of policy in the German road haulage sector, the interaction between the public and private realms can be justifiably classified as corporatist in nature. Within this corporatist structure, however, the particular patterns of participation have tended to benefit the input of road haulier interests in policy making and implementation over the interests of the demand side of transport. This holds true both for the price-fixing committees and the regulatory agency. The dominance of the road transport associations in price-fixing committees was evidenced by their numerical dominance and their privileged legal status as compared to the associations on the transport demand side. A look at the Bundesanstalt für Güterfernverkehr (BAG) reveals similar evidence. For one thing, the associations of the controlled parties were able to exercise a certain influence on the BAG because the agency was financed by the fees and fines of the road hauliers and shippers – in other words, by those it was obliged to control. For another, the associations of hauliers and forwarders were not only represented in the administrative council of the BAG, but dominated the side of the transport users by a ratio of ten to four. What is more, this fraternization between the controlled and the controller went even further, as the BAG bestowed on the haulier cooperatives (*Straßenverkehrsgenossenschaften*) – the economic arm of haulier associations – the right to check waybills and tariff compliancy. The obligatory fee represented not only an important part of the cooperatives' budget but also allowed the associations to maintain certain services.

The agreements at the European level to liberalize international transport and cabotage and the subsequent deregulation of transport markets in Germany rendered invalid the forms of institutionalized public–private coordination described above. First, the tariff commissions were dissolved following the abolition of the mandatory tariff system. Second, the BAG was reorganized and rate controlling lapsed as one of its important duties. A change in legal status was also part of the reorganization. Since 1994, the agency has been called the *Bundesamt für den Güterverkehr. It reports directly to the Ministry of Transp*ort and is no longer financed by fees and fines from the industry but entirely from the state budget. Part of the change in legal status has consisted of removing the executive board and thus the possibility of the industry to exercise control through it.

To summarize, the most remarkable change in the patterns of interest intermediation in the German road haulage sector has been the 'purification' of sectoral corporatism in the sense that the client based nature of government intervention has disappeared. Parallel to this transformation, associations lost a number of political privileges that had been available in the past to increase the willingness of their constituency to participate in the implementation of public policies. However, strong reliance of most associations on the pre-existing regulatory framework gave the process of regulatory reform quite a controversial character. What is more, not only was the timing of the reform relatively late, but also the adaptation on the part of the associations occurred significantly later than in the Netherlands.

The Netherlands

The Netherlands is known as a country in which neo-corporatist structures of policy making and implementation prevail, and in general, the road freight sector is no exception. Branch associations are involved in the preparation and implementation of legislation, and participation takes place either through direct contacts between the Ministry and one of several organizations or within the several forums of consultation and bargaining that exist. What is striking about the Dutch case is not so much that the changes affected the basic form of institutionalized interactions between public and private actors, but that neo-corporatist structures successfully adapted to the neo-liberal context and allowed for a substantive policy change. European integration in general, and the reform of transport regulation in particular, actually reinforced characteristic features of the Dutch institutional context and led to a strengthening of corporatist patterns of concertation and consultation. One way in which the new developments differed considerably from the former situation is that the functional content of concertation shifted from the regulation of market access to the stimulation of market forces and industrial competition.

One characteristic of the developments in Dutch road haulage is that the self-regulation of the industry has been strengthened by upgrading privatized or delegated public responsibilities, such as registration (carried out by the Rijksdienst voor het Wegvervoer) or licensing. For hire-and-reward transport, licensing is carried out by the National and International Road Transport Organization (Stichting Nationale en Internationale Wegvervoer Organisatie, NIWO).[10] The NIWO was founded in 1946 as a non-profit based association, the main objective of which was to promote Dutch international road transport. Its activities have always been public and private, covering licensing, administration and analysis of data and participation in bilateral negotiations between the Dutch government and governments of other countries in the field of road haulage.[11] In the early 1990s, as stipulated by the new domestic transport legislation, the public body formerly responsible for national transport licensing (Commissie Vergunningen

Wegvervoer) became part of the NIWO. This left the granting of licences for international and national transport to the industry, so that licensing was in effect privatized, while inspection remained a public competence carried out by the Rijksverkeersinspectie. In this way, the shift from strict market regulation to a liberal regime led to a reduction of government intervention and simultaneously increased the responsibility the transport industry had. Parts of NIWO's upgraded portfolio – for example the responsibility for market analysis, public relations activities and information on developments in foreign markets – were further delegated to the new association Transport en Logistiek Nederland (TLN).

The creation of 'win-win strategies' constituted a key mechanism for achieving integrated political leadership. The resistance of the smaller hauliers and their associations to deregulation and liberalization diminished as the government agreed to provide the industry with enough time to prepare for a deregulated market and to accompany its competitive deregulation with a significant degree of state guidance. A whole host of supportive measures were developed that aimed at upgrading the production side of enterprises, i.e. the quality of transport services, the skills and capacities of the individual firm. By accompanying competitive deregulation with a host of compensatory policies, policy makers were able to unite public and private forces in a coalition to strengthen the competitiveness of the industry.

Thus, an important prerequisite for the smooth and relatively early shift toward 'supply-side economics' and a parallelization between Dutch and European transport policy making was the government's acceptance of its triple function as the guardian of liberal regulation, the stimulator of quality improvements and the advocate of domestic industry interests at the European level. A second important factor was that the government's credibility to compensate for potential losses was not restricted to the restructuring of the transport industry, but also included the industry's collective representation and self-regulation. Indeed, by delegating public authority to the sector's interest representation, the government achieved a twofold objective: it provided an incentive for a concentration process in the associational landscape and compensated the associations for transmitting public policy objectives regarding, for instance, environmental concerns to the industry. This leads us to now look at the way in which associations in both countries coped with the changes in their resource influx.

Associational adaptation

Taking the characteristics of the sector into account, we would have expected fragmented associational systems in both countries. The existence of a large number of small and very small firms, fierce competition, market differentiation and regional segmentation are all indicators favouring poorly developed associational systems. What was observed, however, in the German case was a highly concentrated associational system that faced significant challenges from the mid-1990s onwards, while in the Dutch case a process toward concentration only began in the late 1980s. Based on the theoretical model guiding this article, these developments are interpreted as the outcome of the tension between centrifugal economic push factors and centripetal political pull factors. In what follows, we will delineate how associations in both countries coped with these forces.

Embedded in economic internationalization, European integration has induced significant changes in the business and political environment of firms and thereby also altered the demands that enterprises in the road haulage sector impose upon their interest organizations. The way in which associations in the road haulage sector in both countries have been adapting to these changing demands has been very similar. The general trend has been characterized by internal differentiation.

Just a few examples will illustrate these patterns of adaptation. The first set of examples refers to the provision of collective or, more precisely, *categoric goods*, meaning goods affecting the sector as such. An important change in this dimension has occurred in the representational function because associations are attaching more and more importance to European institutions in the policy-making process. Establishing offices in Brussels is only the most visible expression of the increased importance placed on European institutions by the association. Other examples for categoric goods are the activities of associations in providing tariff guidelines, their participation in vocational training and involvement in fields of research, such as technical studies to increase road safety or strategic studies on expected market developments.

A second set of examples refers to the provision of *selective goods*. Selective incentives make it possible to discriminate between members and non-members. The dynamics of restructuring industrial patterns of resourcing, production, delivery and the differentiation of transport markets have increased the demands on firms in the transport sector for information, for instance, on changes in national and foreign legislation and on developments in regional, national and international markets. Faced with this heterogeneity of demands, associations had to create structures that guaranteed the provision and the delivery of such information. As a consequence, technical, legal and economic consulting services have become increasingly important for all associations. To provide these services, associations have either created in-house specialized units or have established associated external consultancy services.

Generally, one can say that in both countries, European integration has tended to have a negative impact on the willingness of firms to remain or to become a member of a business association. Faced with this drop in support, associations in both countries have made great efforts to play up their importance by expanding their activities, increasing their internal differentiation and providing specialized services for their members. However, associations have been unevenly affected by the demand for specific services. For example, the demand of smaller hauliers for advice on legal, technical and economic matters is much greater than that of bigger companies, which are equipped with sufficient internal knowledge. Hence, the activities of those associations organizing larger companies lie much more in the field of strategic consulting on future market developments, whereas the major activities of those associations that have a high percentage of smaller hauliers are more related to the daily business of the industry.

Why no strong transport association exists at the EU level

The fact that substantial policy making did not take place for a long time at the European level is still reflected in the ways interests are represented in Brussels. Even now, transport sector interests are not integrated at the European level by centralized efforts within existing organizations, but are integrated in the following four ways.

The International Road Union (IRU), a Geneva-based association organizing a variety of modes of transport on a worldwide scale, never played a significant role in transport policy making at the European level prior to the mid-1980s, although it was an established interest organization with an office in Brussels. Since the advent of the Common Transport Policy, the IRU's role has further declined. For a long time the lack of progress in European policy making overshadowed the disadvantages of the vast heterogeneity of its membership and of the time-consuming and inflexible decision-making procedures. As the Common Transport Policy in Europe took shape, the conflicts amongst national associations at the European level increased and the willingness of national associations to compromise within the IRU declined. The fact that the IRU is a pan-European (more precisely: worldwide) association nourished another conflict within Europe. Since its creation in 1973, the Brussels office of the Geneva-based organization has been seen as a representation of Western European hauliers. The more the Brussels office is pushed by its headquarters to take into account the interests of Eastern European hauliers – which are perceived by Western European hauliers as unwelcome competition – the more the national headquarters of Western European hauliers' associations is critical of the IRU position in general. In addition, national associations were faced with the fact that policy competencies had shifted from the national to the European level and that it was becoming increasingly insufficient to attempt to influence policy making merely via national public actors. Consequently, German and Dutch hauliers' associations – being those with the most at stake in European policy making in both a negative and positive sense – established offices in Brussels in the late 1980s, just as the most important decisions concerning the future of European transport policies were being discussed. Since then, the Brussels offices of national associations have steadily gained importance. Given the deepening and broadening of EU policies, national experts have become increasingly involved in the analysis of information collected by the Brussels offices and in the preparation of and participation in decision-making processes at the European level.

A third form of associational adaptation to European integration is the extension of *horizontal* contacts between national associations. In this respect, an increase in the number of associations and an intensification of the degree of normalization between them has been observed since the early 1990s. For instance, the presidents of the German Bundesverband Güterverkehr und Logistik (BGL) and the Dutch Transport en Logistiek Nederlands (TLN), who until the late 1980s had permanently been at loggerheads with each other, now meet twice a year. These formal contacts are supplemented by numerous informal contacts between experts at the associations. In a similar vein, the German and Dutch associations representing larger firms, the Vereinigung Deutscher Kraftwagenspediteure (VDK) and the Koninklijk Nederlands Vervoer (KNV), cooperate regularly.

A final means of participation in policy-making processes at the European level can be gleaned from the following statement made by a representative from the European Council of Transport Users: 'Persons and organizations find their natural partners' (interview Brussels, June 1997). Because they have a similar approach to addressing problems, organizations, associations and actors of different provenance come together to develop solutions. The plethora of committees revolving around the European Commission seems particularly fertile for the emergence of such forums, which increase the exchange of information and prepare policy proposals. Frustrated by the lack of organizational aggregation of different interests at the European level, the European Commission frequently initiates such an exchange by hand-picking representatives of firms and different interest groups to join the search for solutions to a specific problem. An example is the 'wise men committee on best practice', which investigated the possibilities of reconciling economic and environmental concerns in the field of road haulage between 1998 and 2000. This committee nicely illustrated that interest representation in the transport sector did not have to take place by upgrading existing European associations. Two aspects were of particular interest. In addition to representatives from large firms, some national associations, including the Dutch TLN and KNV, were represented in the committee either as an organization or by members of their association, while others, including the German BGL, were only indirectly represented via the IRU. Furthermore, the committee was not only composed of representatives from the transport industry, but also included people representing transport users and their associations, such as the Union of Industrial and Employers' Confederation Europe.

The composition of this committee may illustrate an important aspect of European transport policy making and its implication for strategies of associations at the European level. The increasingly inclusive approach to transport policy making at the European level, which acknowledges the interdependence of various modes of transport, limits the potential for a dominance of patterns of public–private interactions involving strictly subsectoral firms, associations and administrative units. Now that this spell of administrative fragmentation and policy preparation via subsectoral structures has been broken (Lehmbruch 1992: 172), associations cannot restrict their activities at the European level to short-term influence seeking. On the contrary, to be accepted as important actors in the policy-making process, they must establish a broader view that extends beyond the short-term interests of their members and must develop a medium-term perspective that, in addition to their members' interests, takes into account the general developments of the sector (Lehmkuhl 1998: 230).

Whereas German associations had great difficulty in understanding these requirements as they defended the established protectionist regulation, Dutch associations were much more accustomed to negotiating with the associations of the industry or with public actors whose ambition it was not only to guarantee a balance between the demand and supply of transport services, but also to reconcile economic and environmental objectives in the transport sector. This leads us, finally, to take a closer look at the organizational landscape and its changes in both countries.

The transformation of associational systems

Germany

In Germany, the combination of sector-specific traditions and the regulatory framework stimulated the emergence of an associational system composed of four associations active in the field of road haulage over short and long distances and of forwarding. For short distances the Bundesverband Wirtschaftsverkehr und Entsorgung (BWE) was responsible and, for long distances, the Bundesverband des Güterkraftverkehr und Logistik (BGL). However, many firms were members both of one of these transport associations and of the forwarding association, the Bundesverband Spedition und Logistic (BSL). While this was partly due to the economic link between transport and forwarding activities (such as storage and cargo consolidation), the existence of a fixed tariff structure with high prices made many forwarding firms enter transport markets themselves. In contrast to the federal structure of these associations, the Vereinigung Deutscher Kraftwagenspediteure (VKS) had firms as its direct members, thereby representing about 500 of the 600–700 economically important enterprises. Certain particularities of the German transport market, such as its geographical size and the traditional importance of freight forwarding, created a functional distinction between local, regional and interregional transport, on the one hand, and between transport and forwarding, on the other. The legal framework strengthened this functional distinction by legally differentiating between short- and long-distance transport and, in addition, by creating certain overlaps in the domains of transport and forwarding associations. These overlaps between associational domains were governed by agreements either of cooperation or of demarcation.

The Common European Transport Policy, with its liberalization policies for international transport and the introduction of cabotage, rendered obsolete the main pillars of the existing regulations in the German road haulage sector. By eliminating rent seeking possibilities and the option of protection against domestic and foreign hauliers, European integration called into question what could have been labelled a redistribution coalition between the associations. Thus, one important consequence of European integration has been to bring out in the open conflicts that had previously merely been pacified bilaterally between associations. This impact has been amplified by the second consequence of European integration. European economic integration has induced enormous dynamics in the transport industry that have led to a fragmentation and differentiation of transport markets. Such powerful dynamics have given new momentum to the demarcation of associational domains. In particular, associations have started to compete for members in areas in which associational domains overlap, that is, between short- and long-distance transports and between transport and value-added services.

As shown in Figure 7.1, a first and very obvious pattern of adaptation was to rename the association. On the one hand, both the association of long-distance hauliers and the forwarding association changed their name to include the term 'logistics' in a bid to indicate modernity. On the other hand, to distinguish itself from both the former long-distance and the forwarding associations, the former short-distance association changed its name

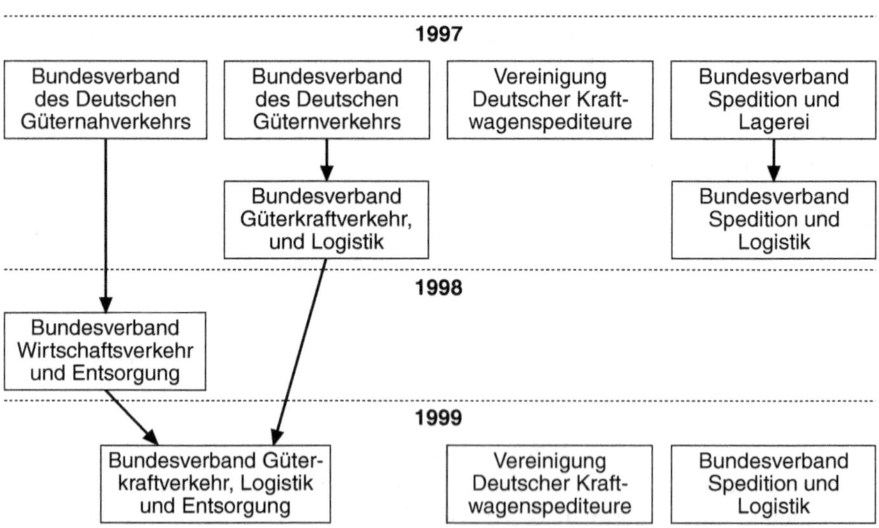

Figure 7.1 Changes in the German associational configuration.

to include the term 'disposal' – a specialization of local and regional economic activities. However, renaming associations was only the first step in the now open struggle between short- and long-distance transports. Under pressure from their member firms and because the majority of the *Landesverbände* decided to remain or to become members of the larger association, namely that former long-distance transport association, the restructuring contributed to a further centralization in the representation of interests. In 1999, the former rivals merged to become the Bundesverband des Güterkraftverkehr, Logistik und Entsorgung.

In contrast to this strategy of inclusion, other associations aimed at sharpening their profile by being more exclusive. For instance, the VKS an association that organizes the majority of economically important transport enterprises aims to represent the economic clout of its membership and therefore wants to avoid compromising its aims by commitments evolving from membership in any other association.

Hence, the overall impact of European integration on the associational system in the German road haulage sector can be described as follows: economic and political integration induced a *shift from a legally generated segmentation of associational patterns to patterns of organization that correspond with economic and functional interests of enterprises* in the transport industry. The overall impact of this shift on the associational system was ambiguous as it prompted both an inclusive trend and an exclusive strategy simultaneously. Given both the strong reliance on the pre-existing framework and organizational as well as personal obstacles, the process of associational adaptation occurred significantly later than in the Netherlands.

The Netherlands

The associational landscape in Dutch road freight transport is similar in a number of ways to the German case. Despite a fragmented market structure, the organizational representation is highly concentrated. The pre-existing fragmentation was not caused by the legal framework, as in Germany; it was instead the expression of a Dutch phenomenon, namely, the highly institutionalized, vertical fragmentation of subsocietal structures along the lines of denominational and social differences. Since the mid-1980s, the process of depillarization has affected the road transport sector and has contributed to the concentration of interest representation. In this respect, three factors – market driven impacts, regulatory reform and the active involvement of government – reinforced one another and led to a process of organizational restructuring.

Traditionally, the field of road freight haulage reflected the pillared organization of Dutch society; that is, numerous small and medium-sized enterprises were organized dependent on their denominational or societal frame of reference. With the onset of the mid-1980s, several attempts were made to overcome the organizational fragmentation, all of which failed due to heterogeneous interests between small and large enterprises or due to personal rivalries between the major actors involved. The pressure to unify the interests of the road freight sector increased with the ongoing changes in the economic and institutional environment. By pursuing a carrot and stick policy, the government in particular was actively involved in pushing ahead the restructuring of associations.

In an initial response to this pressure, two denominational organizations – the Catholic Transporter Organization (Katholieke Vervoerders Organisatie) and the Protestant-Christian Professional Freight Transporters (Protestants-Christelijke Beroepsgoerderenvervoer) – merged to form the Christian Transporter Organization (Christelijke Vervoerders Organisatie, CVO) in 1991, then representing about one third of all small enterprises (see Figure 7.2). To further concentrate resources – and again prompted to no small extent by the Ministry for Transport – the CVO and the National Organization of Professional Freight Transport (Nationale Organisatie voor het Beroepsgoederenvervoer, NOB) then merged to form Dutch Transport and Logistics (Transport en Logistiek Nederland, TLN) in 1993. Thus, at the end of a process of associational mergers, the TLN became the encompassing association representing about 70 per cent of hauliers, and Koninklijk Nederlands Vervoer remained the smaller, more exclusive association organizing the most economically powerful enterprises. Despite cooperation between these two associations in many fields and on many issues, the continued associational overlap in the upper segment of economically important firms still causes competition between them.

In summary, European integration has primarily impacted on associational systems in the Dutch road haulage sector by *adding economic impetus to a societal process of depillarization*, resulting in a decline of cohesion within subsocietal units. While the cohesion deriving from denominational sources has been in general decline since the 1970s, the common interest in strengthening the sector's competitiveness has been increasing since the

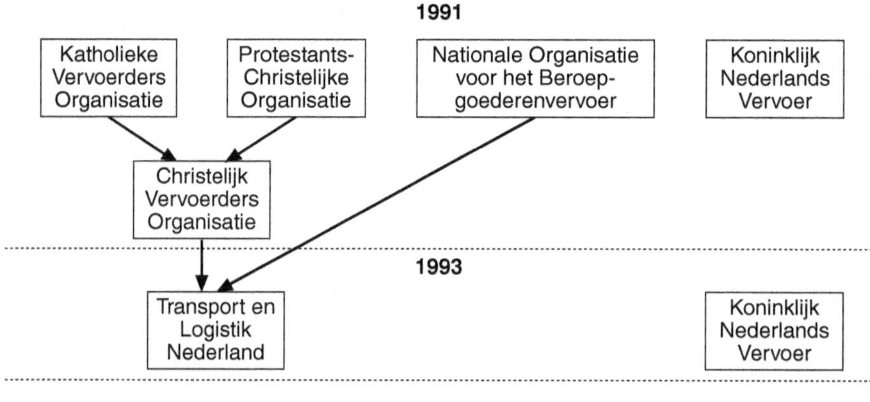

Figure 7.2 Changes in the Dutch associational configuration.

1980s and has led to a bundling of associational forces. In general, this can be interpreted as an indicator that the logic of influence variables proved more forceful than the logic of membership variables.

The micropolitics of associations

What we have observed up to now were, on the one hand, similarities in the way in which associations in both countries have adapted to the changing demands of their constituencies and, on the other hand, *significant differences* with respect to the *timing of restructuring* the associational system and the *way in which the transformation of this regulatory framework* occurred. The assumption is that these differences can be explained by the relative dependence of the associational resource influx on pre-existing regulations.

In Germany, the involvement of associations in implementing pre-existing provisions had guaranteed them an income that financed an expansion of their internal structure and their services, which in turn increased their importance for their constituencies. European integration has led to abolishing the tariff system and has thereby closed off this source of revenue. In addition, the revision of the transport regulations in Germany that occurred concurrently with European integration removed some avenues of preferential treatment for the transport associations. Thus, European integration has not only affected the associations materially, it has also challenged a central aspect of their representational function, since this was based on protecting firms established in the market against competition from domestic and foreign hauliers.

Associations tried to cope with both challenges in various ways. In light of the changing demands of their members, they expanded their representational activities to the European level and generally expanded services offered to their members. In an effort to increase its legitimacy to its members, the association representing a relatively small number of larger and economically important firms also pursued a strategy of exclusiveness. In contrast, strategies of inclusiveness used by other associations were supposed to enhance the representation level and, consequently, the legitimacy of associations to their public interlocutors.

An additional feature of the situation in Germany was that established patterns of public–private interactions were not equipped with built-in incentives for structural change. Both the associations and their membership found it in their interest to lobby for preservation of the protectionist regulatory framework. This structurally conservative character of transport policy making in Germany was strengthened by the fact that public actors did not have the strength to initiate a reorganization of the regulatory framework for the transport sector in general. Rather, the government was a prisoner of its own legislation, which had been built primarily around the state-run railways.[12] European policies both in road haulage and the railway sector have significantly contributed to undoing this knot of intended and unintended structural conservatism and have allowed public actors to pull themselves away from the tentacles of the transport industry.

The *most interesting difference* between the German and Dutch cases is that, in the latter case, the patterns of public–private interactions have been strengthened and the associational system has been further centralized. These two aspects have been both the conditions for and the effects of the changes that have taken place in the Netherlands in the context of European integration. Several factors explain these findings. First, the inflow of resources to the hauliers associations in the Netherlands did not depend on a specific, that is, protectionist regulatory framework, as was the case in Germany. Thus, taking into account a reduction of their resources, the associations were affected by European integration not through changes in the regulatory framework, but through their members. Faced with an increase in competition, transport firms were less willing to pay their membership fees, while at the same time they pleaded for a better representation of their interests in the ever-increasing complexity of multilevel policy making.

The fact that hauliers associations were not in a position to realistically ask for protectionist measures was caused by a second factor, one which also constitutes a difference from the German case. In contrast to the preferential treatment and to the client-based relationship between hauliers and the Ministry for Transport in Germany, the interactions between public and private actors in the Dutch transport sector were always tripartite in nature. Whereas the sectoral corporatism in Germany had a strong client bias, the Dutch constellation was better characterized as corporatist concertation involving an equal treatment of users and suppliers of transport services. Moreover, despite all the economic differences deriving from confrontation in the market place, the maintenance of international competitiveness of Dutch industry in general and that of the transport industry in particular constituted a common interest.

The restructuring of the associational system has been the *effect* of the transformation process because both the demands placed on associations by their constituencies and their interlocutors have advanced concentration and centralization. For the members, overcoming traditional fragmentation has been important for enhancing the representation of their interests with respect to both national and European policy makers. In contrast, public actors have preferred to deal with a more encompassing association because they can 'place a lot of the burden of reconciling divergent interests upon the associations' internal decision-making process' (Traxler 1987: 19). Government compensated the associations for taking on the burdensome role of convincing reluctant groups in their constituencies to participate in the restructuring process by increasing the degree of authoritative power delegated to the associations. At the same time, the centralization of the associational system has been a necessary *condition* for the realization of the Dutch government's proactive policy-making approach. Only in cooperation with well-developed interest associations the government has been capable both 'of developing a longer term view of the sector's development and of convincing members to abide by that view' (Coleman 1997: 135).

Conclusion

For the present purpose, Europeanization has been interpreted as internationalization in Europe, comprising of processes of political, legal and economic integration. The question of how various individual and corporate actors structurally adapt to changes in their economic and political environment has been at the heart of the analysis. The most important finding of this study is that these changes in the economic and political environment in Europe do not necessarily have a negative impact on the capacity of associations either to aggregate and represent their constituency's interests or to participate in the making and implementation of public policies. Generally speaking, this conclusion indicates that there is a future for national associations in a world of internationalized markets.

Nevertheless, Europeanization-cum-internationalization affected associations in both countries by influencing the established balance between the demands of their constituencies and those of their public interlocutors. In answering the question how the increase in cross-border transactions and the emergence of supranational political institutions have had an impact on associations at the national level, four aspects need to be emphasized.

First, there were changes in the economic environment of associations. In general, an increase in market integration on an international scale occurred concurrently with an intensification of international competition, which contributed to internationally changing patterns of production including the entire production and retailing system. In turn, these changes on the users' part of transport services led to changes in the road haulage industry; transport markets became internationalized, diversified and segmented. Second and in addition to these economic factors, the liberalization of European transport markets drove change not only by extending the market for economic activities, but also by challenging pre-existing national regulations and by opening up formerly protected domestic markets.

Third, although economic and political changes left their marks in both Germany and the Netherlands, sector associations in the two countries displayed differences in their ability to adapt to the changes. In the German case, most associations relied a great deal on protectionist regulations, which not only supplied them with material income and helped maintain their legitimacy, but also pacified domains in which there were overlapping interests. The liberal bias of European policies led to a dramatic decrease in the influx of resources to the associations. Since this dramatic break could not be compensated for by their public interlocutors, it was critical that the associations adapt to the changing demands immediately in order to regain organizational stability. In the Netherlands, by contrast, it was argued that adapting domestic regulation to economic and political changes in Europe would result in more efficiency indicating that at the end of the process both the transport industry and their associations would be better off. After a process of mergers, the newly emerged association, the TLN, managed to incorporate the sector's very heterogeneous interests and to play its role in the sector's transformation; it was then granted additional public authority. Thus, it became even more autonomous from its constituency. Despite the differences in both the timing of the restructuring of the associational system and the way in which the transformation of this regulatory framework occurred, competitive deregulation in both countries displayed corporatist patterns.

A final difference between the associations of the countries has been identified with respect to the capacity of associations to adapt strategically to the rules of the policy-making game at the European level. Given these peculiarities, e.g. a more encompassing approach to transport policy making in terms of both a participation of heterogeneous interests and a greater awareness of intermodal interdependencies, the structural-conservative approach of the major German transport association was much less appropriate than the proactive and pragmatic approach of their Dutch counterparts. This, finally, is yet another dimension in which national patterns of governance came under siege by European integration (Schmidt 1999) and thus required the strategic adaptation of national associations.

Notes

1 My special thanks go to the editors of this volume for their very helpful comments.

2 See, for instance, Adshead 2002; Börzel 1999, 2001; Börzel and Risse 2000; Bulmer and Burch 1998; Checkel 2001; Dimitrova and Steunenberg 2000; Falkner 2000, 2001; Falkner *et al.* 2002; Featherstone and Radaelli 2003; Fischer *et al.* 2002; Goetz 2001; Goetz and Hix 2000; Green Cowles *et al.* 2001; Hanf and Soetendorp 1998; Harmsen 1999; Haverland 2000; Héritier and Knill 2001; Kerwer 2001; Kerwer and Teutsch 2001; Kohler-Koch 1998, 1999, 2000a, b, forthcoming; Knill 1998; 2001; Knill and Lehmkuhl 1999, 2000, 2002; Knill and Lenschow 2000; Knodt and Kohler-Koch 2000; Ladrech 1994; Lavenex 2001a, b; Lehmkuhl 1999; Mach *et al.* 2003; Mény *et al.* 1996; Olson 2001; Radaelli 2000; Vink 2001; Sciarini *et al.* 2002; Special Issues: *West European Politics* 2002, 23 (4); and *Journal of European Public Policy* 2001, 8 (6).

3 For exceptions, see Eising 2003; Kohler-Koch and Quittkat 1999; Lehmkuhl 1999.

4 See Corbey 1995; Haas 1968.

5 The idea of 'private governance dumping' refers to the threat of sectoral self-regulation by business that may either be directly outlawed by European provisions or indirectly undercut by mechanisms of political integration, such as mutual recognition, or the economic opening of markets and increased factor mobility.

6 In addition to these 'political' imperatives, there are two 'organizational' imperatives – the logic of goal formation and the logic of efficient implementation – which are part of the micropolitics within any association.

7 Council Regulation 1841/88; Council Regulation 881/92; Council Regulation 3118/93.

8 Firm size not only relates to employee figures but also refers to the number of vehicles and licences owned by a company. In addition to the description of the overall development of firm size, it should be mentioned that a contributing factor to the increase of firm growth after deregulation in both countries was the fact that many larger firms sold their vehicles to the drivers and entered into close contractual relationships with these owner-drivers. This 'vehicle sell-out' and the concomitant sharp increase of competition between self-exploiting owner-drivers brought the trade unions into the scene. Trade unions pressed, first, for a concentration and rationalization of the sector to drive out firms with 'bad' labour standards and second, for an improvement of social regulation at the European level.

9 In the Netherlands, the role of the railways in transport has not been as important as in larger European countries such as France or Germany. This can be explained by the historical role of the waterways, on the one hand, and by the fact that after the Second World War passenger and freight transport developed along different lines, on the other. While passenger transport became the main product and developed into a kind of subsidized nationwide operating public transport undertaking, freight transport by rail was regarded as a by-product that had to operate on a strictly commercial basis. Since the mid-1990s, however, there have been efforts to foster the neglected child and to revitalize freight transport by rail (Lehmkuhl 2001: 234ff).

10 The National Registration for Own Account Transport (Stichting Inschrijving Eigen Vervoer, SIEV) is responsible for own-account transport licensing.

11 The board of the NIWO consists of representatives from two employers' organizations, two trade unions, and the transport users' organization; in addition, two representatives of the government are entitled to attend the board meeting as observers.

12 Given the poor competitiveness of the railways, any deregulation of road transport would have implied a further increase of competition in transport markets that, in turn, would have led to a further decrease of the share of the railways, thus implying an additional increase in the subsidies required for the railways.

Bibliography

Adshead, M. (2002) 'Europeanization, Changing Patterns of Governance and the Welfare State in Ireland', paper presented to the ECPR Joint Session Workshop on 'Europeanization and National Political Institutions', University of Turin, 22–22 March 2002.

Börzel, T. A. (1999) 'Towards Convergence in Europe? Institutional Adaptation to Europeanization in Germany and Spain', *Journal of Common Market Studies*, 39: 573–596.

Börzel, T. A. (2001) *States and Regions in the European Union. Institutional Adaptation in Germany and Spain*, Cambridge: Cambridge University Press.

Börzel, T. A. and Risse, T. (2000) 'When Europe Hits Home: Europeanization and Domestic Change', European Integration online Papers (EIoP) 4 (2000) No. 15. Online, available at: eiop.or.at/eiop/texte/2000-015a.htm.

Bulmer, S. and Burch, M. (1998) 'Organizing for Europe: Whitehall, the British State and the European Union', *Public Administration*, 76 (3): 601–628.

Checkel, J. T. (2001) 'The Europeanization of Citizenship?', in J. A. Caporaso,

M. Green Cowles and T. Risse (eds) *Transforming Europe. Europeanization and Domestic Change*, Ithaca NY: Cornell University Press, pp. 180–197.

Coleman, W. D. (1997) 'Associational Governance in a Globalizing Era: Weathering in the Storm', in J. R. Hollingsworth and R. Boyer (eds) *Contemporary Capitalism: The Embeddedness of Institutions*, Cambridge MA: Cambridge University Press, pp. 127–153.

Coopers & Lybrand (European Commission) (1997) 'Distribution', *The Single Market Review*, Subseries II, Vol. 4, London: Earthscan (Kogan Page).

Corbey, D. (1995) 'Dialectical functionalism: Stagnation as a Booster of European Integration', *International Organization* 2: 253–284.

Dimitrova, A. and Steunenberg, B. (2000) 'The Search for Convergence of National Policies in the European Union. An Impossible Quest?', *European Union Politics* 1 (2): 201–226.

Douillet, A.-C. and Lehmkuhl, D. (2001) 'Pushing Reform and Opposition Alike: The European Impact on the French Transport Sector', in A. Héritier *et al.* (eds) op. cit., pp. 99–132.

Eising, R. (2003) 'Die Europäisierung der deutschen Interessenvermittlung', in R. Eising and B. Kohler-Koch (eds) *Interessendurchsetzung im Mehrebenensystem* (working title), Baden-Baden: Nomos.

Eising, R. and Kohler-Koch, B. (1994) 'Inflation und Zerfaserung: Trends der Interessenvermittlung', in W. Streeck *Europäischen Gemeinschaft. Staat una Verbüande*, Opladen: Westdeutscher Verlag, pp. 175–206.

Falkner, G. (2000) 'How Pervasive are Euro-Politics? Effects of EU Membership on a New Member State', *Journal of Common Market Studies*, 38: 223–250.

Falkner, G. (2001) 'The Europeanization of Austria: Misfit, Adaptation and Controversies', European Integration online Papers, 5, 13. Online, available at: eiop.or.at/eiop/texte/2001-013a.Htm.

Falkner, G., Hartlapp, M., Leiber, S. and Treib, O. (2002) 'Transforming Social Policy in Europe? The EC's Parental Leave Directive and Misfit in the 15 Member States', MPIfG Working Paper, October 2002, No. 02/11.

Featherstone, K. and Radaelli, C. (2003) *The Politics of Europeanization*, Oxford: Oxford University Press.

Fischer, A., Nicolet, S. and Sciarini, P. (2002) 'Europeanization of a Non-EU Country: The Case of Swiss Immigration Policy', *West European Politics* 25 (4): 143–170.

Goetz, K. H. (2001) 'European Integration and National Executives: A Cause in Search for an Effect?', *West European Politics* 23 (4): 211–231.

Goetz, K. H. and Hix, S. (eds) (2000) 'Europeanized Politics? European Integration and National Political Systems', *West European Politics* (Special Issue), 23 (4).

Gourevitch, P. (1978) 'The Second Image Reversed: The International Sources of Domestic Politics', *International Organization*, 32: 881–911.

Green Cowles, M., Caporaso, J. and Risse, T. (eds) (2001) *Transforming Europe: Europeanization and Domestic Change*, Ithaca NY: Cornell University Press.

Grote, J. R. and Lang, A. (2003) 'Europeanization and the Organizational Change in National Trade Associations – An Organizational Ecology Perspective', in K. Featherstone and C. Radaelli (eds) *The Politics of Europeanization*, Oxford: Oxford University Press.

Haas, E. B. (1968) *The Uniting of Europe. Political, Economic and Social Forces 1950–1957*, London: Stevens.

Hanf, K. and Soetendorp, B. (eds) (1998) *Adapting to European Integration. Small States and the European Union*, London and New York: Longman.

Harmsen, R. (1999) 'The Europeanization of National Administrations: A Comparative Study of France and the Netherlands', *Governance* 12 (1): 81–113.

Haverland, M. (2000) 'National Adaptation to European Integration: The Importance of National Veto Points', *Journal of Public Policy* 20 (1): 83–103.

Heinisch, R. (2000) 'Coping With Economic Integration: Corporatist Strategies in Germany and Austria in the 1990s', *West European Politics* 23 (3): 67–98.

Héritier, A. and Knill, C. (2001) 'Differential Responses to European Policies: A Comparison', in A. Héritier *et al.* op. cit., pp. 257–294.

Héritier, A., Knill, C. and Mingers, S. (1996) *Ringing the Changes in Europe. Regulatory Competition and the Transformation of the State*, Berlin: de Gruyter.

Héritier, A., Kerwer, D., Knill, C., Lehmkuhl, D., Teutsch, M. and Douillet, A.-C. (eds) (2001) *Differential Europe. European Union Impact on National Policymaking*, Boulder CO: Rowman & Littlefield Publishers.

Kerwer, D. (2001) *Regulatory Reforms in Italy. A Case Study in Europeanization*, Aldershot: Ashgate.

Kerwer, D. and Teutsch, M. (2001) 'Elusive Europeanization. Liberalizing Road Haulage in the European Union', *Journal of European Public Policy* 8: 124–143.

Knill, C. (1998) 'European Policies: The Impact of National Administrative Traditions', *Journal of Public Policy* 18: 1–28.

Knill, C. (1999) 'Explaining Cross-National Variance in Administrative Reform: Autonomous versus Instrumental Bureaucracies', *Journal of Public Policy* 19 (2): 113–139.

Knill, C. (2001) *The Europeanization of National Administrations. Patterns of Institutional Change*, Cambridge: Cambridge University Press.

Knill, C. and Lehmkuhl, D. (1999) 'How Europeanization Matters: Different Mechanisms of Europeanization', in European Integration online Papers (EIoP) 3 (1999) N 7 (http://eiop.or.at/texte/1999-007a.htm).

Knill, C. and Lehmkuhl, D. (2000) 'An Alternative Route of European Integration: The Community's Railway Policies', *West European Politics* 23 (1): 65–88.

Knill, C. and Lehmkuhl, D. (2002) 'The National Impact of EU Regulatory Policy: Three Europeanization Mechanisms', *European Journal of Political Research* 41 (2): 255–280.

Knill, C. and Lenschow, A. (eds) (2000) *Implementing European Environmental Policies: New Regulations, Old Problems*, Manchester: Manchester University Press.

Knodt, M. and Kohler-Koch, B. (eds) (2000) *Deutschland zwischen Europäisierung und Selbstbehauptung*, Frankfurt am Main: Campus.

Kohler-Koch, B. (1998) 'Europäisierung der Regionen: Institutioneller Wandel als sozialer Prozeß', in B. Kohler-Koch, B. Jouvre and E. Negrier (eds) *Interaktive Politik in Europa. Regionen im Netzwerk der Integration*, Opladen: Leske und Budrich, pp. 13–30.

Kohler-Koch, B. (1999). 'The Evolution and Transformation of European Governance', in B. Kohler-Koch and R. Eising (eds) *The Transformation of Governance in the European Union*, London: Routledge, pp. 14–35.

Kohler-Koch, B. (2000a) 'Europäisierung: Plädoyer für eine Horizonterweiterung', in M. Knodt and B. Kohler-Koch (eds) *Deutschland zwischen Europäisierung und Selbstbehauptung*, Frankfurt am Main: Campus, pp. 11–31.

Kohler-Koch, B. (2000b) 'Network Governance Within and Beyond an Enlarging

EU', Paper presented to ECSA-Canada Conference European Odyssey: The EU in the New Millennium, Québec, 30 July–1 August 2000.

Kohler-Koch, B. (ed.) (forthcoming) *Linking EU and National Governance*, Oxford: Oxford University Press.

Kohler-Koch, B. and Quittkat, C. (1999) 'Intermediation of Interests in the European Union', Mannheimer Zentrum für Europäische Sozialforschung, Arbeitspapiere- Mannheimer Zentrum für Europäische Sozialforschung, 9, 9.

Kohler-Koch, B., Brümmer, R., Myrzik, B. and Platzelt, H. W. (1988) 'Wirtschaftsverbände als transnationale Akteure: Der Beitrag deutscher Verbände zum Management von internationaler Interdependenz', DFG-Abschlußbericht, Darmstadt.

Ladrech, R. (1994) 'Europeanization of Domestic Politics and Institutions: The Case of France', *Journal of the Common Market Studies*, 32: 69–88.

Lavenex, S. (2001a) *The Europeanization of Refugee Policies: Between Human Rights and Internal Security*, Aldershot: Ashgate.

Lavenex, S. (2001b) 'The Europeanization of Refugee Policies: Normative Challenges and Institutional Legacies', *Journal of Common Market Studies*, 39 (5): 851–874.

Lehmbruch, G. (1992) 'Bedingungen und Grenzen politischer Steuerung im Verkehrssektor', in Verband Deutscher Elektroingenieure (VDE) (ed.) Politik und Technik in der Verantwortung, Frankfurt am Main: VDE, 168–193.

Lehmkuhl, D. (1998) 'The Importance of Small Differences. The Impact of European Integration on Road Haulage Associations in Germany and the Netherlands', PhD Thesis, Florence: European University Institute.

Lehmkuhl, D. (1999) 'The Importance of Small Differences. The Impact of European Integration on Road Haulage Associations in Germany and the Netherlands', The Hague: Thela Thesis.

Lehmkuhl, D. (2001) 'From Regulation to Stimulation. Dutch Transport Policy in Europe', in Héritier, A. *et al.* op. cit., pp. 217–256.

Lindberg, L. N. and Scheingold, S. A. (1970) *Europe's Would-Be Polity*, Englewoods Cliffs NJ: Prentice Hall.

Mach, A., Häusermann, S. and Papadopoulos, Y. (2003) 'Economic Regulatory Reforms in Switzerland: Adjustment without European Integration or how Rigidities become flexible', *Journal of European Public Policy* 10 (2): 302–319.

Mény, Y., Muller, P. and Quermonne, J.-L. (eds) (1996) *Adjusting to Europe: the Impact of European Integration on National Institutions and Policies*, London: Routledge.

Milner, H. V. and Keohane, R. O. (1996) 'Internationalization and Domestic Politics: A Conclusion', in R. O. Keohane and H. V. Milner (eds) *Internationalization and Domestic Politics*, Cambridge: Cambridge University Press, pp. 243–258.

NEA (European Commission) (1997) 'Road Freight Transport', *The Single Market Review*, Subseries II, Vol. 5, London: Earthscan (Kogan Page).

O'Donnell, R. (1994) 'The Economic Environment', in N. Nugent and R. O'Donnell (eds) *The European Business Environment*, Basingstoke: Macmillan, pp. 47–90.

Olson, J. P. (2001) 'The Many Faces of Europeanization', Arena Working Papers, 2001, 2.

Olson, M. Jr (1995) 'The Varieties of Eurosclerosis: The Rise and Decline of Nations since 1982', *Jean Monnet Chair Papers* 32, Florence: The Robert Schuman Centre at the European University Institute.

Radaelli, C. (2000) 'Whither Europeanization? Concept Stretching and Substantive

Change', European Integration online Papers, 4, 8. Online, available at: eiop.or.at/eiop/texte/2000-008.html.

Schmidt, V. (1999) 'National Patterns of Government under Siege. The Impact of European Integration', in B. Kohler-Koch and R. Eising (eds) *The Transformation of Governance in the European Union*, London: Routledge, pp. 155–172.

Schmitter, P. C. (1997) 'The Emerging Europolity and its Impact Upon National Systems of Production', in J. R. Hollingsworth and R. Boyer (eds) *Contemporary Capitalism. The Embeddedness of Institutions*, New York: Cambridge University Press, pp. 395–430.

Schmitter, P. C. and Grote, J. R. (1997) 'The Corporatist Sisyphus: Past, Present and Future', EUI Working Papers; *SPS* No. 97/4.

Schmitter, P. C. and Streeck, W. (1981) 'The Organization of Business Interests. A Research Design to Study the Associative Action of Business in the Advanced Industrial Societies of Western Europe', Berlin: Wissenschaftszentrum Berlin.

Sciarini, P., Nicolet, S. and Fischer, A. (2002) 'L'impact de l'internatinalisation sur les processus de décision en Suisse', *Schweizerische Zeitschrift für Politikwissenschaft* 8 (3/4): 1–34.

Sidenius, N. C. (1999) 'Business, Governance Structures and the EU: The Case of Denmark', in B. Kohler-Koch and R. Eising (eds) *The Transformation of Governance in the European Union*, London: Routledge, pp. 173–188.

Sleuwaegen, L., Pot, F. and Lashtek, S. (1993) 'Road haulage', in P. Buigues, F. Ilzkovitz, J. F. Lebrun and A. Sapir (eds) *Market Services and European Integration. The Challenges for the 1990s*, European Economy: Social Europe. Reports and Studies, Brussels: Commission of the European Communities, pp. 211–258.

Streeck, W. (1987) 'Vielfalt und Interdependenz. Überlegungen zur Rolle von intermediären Organizationen in sich ändernden Umwelten', *Kölner Zeitschrift für Soziologie und Sozialpsychologie* 39: 471–495.

Streeck, W. and Schmitter, P. C. (1991) 'From National Corporatism to Transnational Pluralism: Organized Interests in the Single European Market', *Politics and Society* 19: 133–164.

Sverdrup, U. (2000) 'Ambiguity and Adaptation – Europeanization of Administrative Institutions as Loosely Coupled Processes', Arena Report 8/2000.

Teutsch, M. (2001) 'Regulatory Reforms in the German Transport Sector: How to Overcome Multiple Veto Points', in A. Héritier *et al.* op. cit., 133–172.

Traxler, F. (1987) 'Patterns of Associative Action', in W. Grant (ed.) *Business Interests, Organizational Development and Private Interest Government*, Berlin and New York: Walter de Gruyter, pp. 18–33.

Traxler, F. (1995) 'From Demand-side to Supply-side Corporatism? Austria's Labour Relations and Public Policy', in C. Crouch and F. Traxler (eds) *Organized Industrial Relations in Europe: What Future?*, Aldershot: Avebury, pp. 271–286.

Traxler, F. and Unger, B. (1994) 'Governance, Economic Restructuring, and International Competitiveness', *Journal of Economic Issues* 27 (1): 1–23.

Vink, M. (2001) 'The Limited Europeanization of Domestic Citizenship Policy: Evidence from the Netherlands', *Journal of Common Market Studies*, 39 (5): 875–896.

Visser, J. and Hemerijck, A. (1997) *The Dutch Miracle*, Amsterdam: Amsterdam University Press.

Waarden, F. van (1994) 'Is European Law a Threat to Associational Governance', in V. Eichener and H. Voelzkow (eds) *Europäische Integration und verbandliche Interessenvermittlung*, Marburg: Metropolis, pp. 217–262.

8 National business associations and European integration

The case of the financial sector[1]

Pieter Bouwen

In this chapter, I study the behaviour of national business associations in the European integration process. When internationalization is defined as an increase in cross-border transactions, social relations and structures, the European integration process can be considered as a special case of internationalization. It is special to the extent that the upward transfer of state authority to a state-like international organization in the course of internationalization has proceeded further in Europe than in other parts of the world. In this chapter, however, the concept of Europeanization goes beyond the exclusive vertical transfer of state authority to include the development of European orientations and relations among public and private actors in the European political societies and economies.[2] While Europeanizing in this way, these increasingly cosmopolitan actors remain national in their character and constitution. The aim of this chapter is to investigate the fate of national business associations in the EU as a specific category of private actors confronted with the current trend of internationalization of markets and regulation.

Whereas other studies have dealt with the impact of European integration on national associational systems or on the organizational structures of national associations (Lehmkuhl 2000; Grote and Lang 2002), I want to focus on a different research question. In this chapter, I undertake an inquiry into the lobbying strategies of national business associations against the background of increasing internationalization, i.e. Europeanization. Have national associations withered away in this process? Has the systematic increase of cross-border transactions and social relations among the different EU Member States reduced the role of national associations at home and/or increased the role of these national actors at the EU level? These questions are related to previous empirical research on the lobbying and network strategies of domestic interest associations in the European Union (Bennett 1997; Kohler-Koch and Quitkatt 1999; Beyers 2002). This chapter aims to further explore this interesting part of the European interest politics literature.

Multilevel governance and the Europeanization of lobbying strategies

As a starting point, this section investigates what different theories of integration say about the role of national associations. The neo-functionalist integration theory made clear predictions regarding the fate of national business associations. While assigning national interest groups the role of catalyst for the vertical transfer of competencies from the national to the European level, this tendency was anticipated to fuel a devaluation of nationally oriented interest organizations (Haas 1958; Lindberg 1968). European integration was supposed to generate organizational adaptations of the national business associations that would lead to an upgrading of associations at the European level, at the expense of national associations. Neo-functionalists predicted an increasing centralization of European interest-level organizations and the declining autonomy of their national affiliates. In fact, neo-functionalism predicted the withering away of the national associations. Even though the neo-functionalist integration theory was severely criticized and declined in the 1970s (Haas 1975), it remains interesting today to check the hypotheses generated by this body of literature.

In addition to the study of this traditional theory of integration, it is important to investigate in depth the more recent multilevel governance perspective on European integration. This approach also allows generating relevant hypotheses about the fate of national associations in the European integration process. According to multilevel governance, the European system of collective decision making is composed of distinct levels of negotiations (Marks *et al.* 1996; Hooghe and Marks 2001). In this multilevel structure, European politics takes place in differentiated and co-existing arenas. The national and supranational arenas are closely interlocked and form an integrated system of joint decision making (Scharpf 1988). For interest politics, multilevel governance implies an important fragmentation of the institutional target structure, which creates incentives for national associations to undertake political activities beyond their familiar domestic institutional context. Because of the increasing autonomy of supranational government arrangements vis-à-vis the national governments, the traditional national route through the Council of Ministers does not suffice anymore for national associations to influence the EU policy-making process. To the extent that national associations seek to have direct access to EU policy making, they will increasingly compete with European associations by developing direct lobbying activities at the European level. As I have argued elsewhere, private actors often prefer to have direct access to policy-making processes because it allows them to exercise greater influence. When national associations have no direct access, it means concretely that there is no direct contact between the national associations and the institutional target. National associations have, for example, indirect access to the EU decision-making process through participation in European associations. As intermediary or 'go-between actor', the European association can filter and interpret the information before transmitting it to the targeted public institution. This becomes particularly problematic when the position of the European association does not coincide with that of the national association.

The so-called paradox of weakness is an additional insight of the multilevel governance literature that allows to further specify the behaviour of national associations in the increasingly complex multilevel decision-making structure of the EU (Grande 1996). The paradox of weakness points at substantial changes in the bargaining power of public and private actors caused by multilevel decision making. Rather than being weakened by the pooling of sovereignty at the EU level, it might actually increase the independence of the national executives and administrations from organized interests at the national level. National authorities are involved in negotiations at different policy-making levels and can, therefore, operate with tactical self-commitment (Schelling 1960). In their interaction with national associations at home, they can claim to be bound by a bargaining position at the EU level hoping that the associations will make more concessions. A situation of asymmetric information whereby national associations are badly informed about policy making at the EU level is at the basis of the national authorities' tactical behaviour. In order to remedy this situation, national associations will develop political activities at the European level. By increasing their information and monitoring capacity of EU affairs, national associations improve their capacity to check the claims made by the national authorities. Direct political action of the national associations at the EU level will be more efficient for the implementation of this information and monitoring strategy than indirect action through a European association. Finally, it can be expected that national associations remain the most important players at the national level to the extent that no pooling of sovereignty takes place and national authorities remain responsible for the policy area concerned. An additional argument for the continuing importance of national associations at home is their key role in the implementation process even when the policy is actually designed and decided at the supranational level.

It can be concluded that the multilevel governance perspective on EU interest politics allows generating hypotheses about the likely lobbying strategies of national associations at the European level. Because of the interlocked role of the EU Member States both as expression of the national sovereign states at home and as participants at the EU level in the Council of Ministers decision-making process, the national associations' traditional national route is likely to remain an important lobbying strategy. With the strengthening of the supranational arena in the EU multilevel system, national associations are increasingly developing political activities vis-à-vis the European Commission and/or the European Parliament either directly or indirectly through the participation in European associations. While in some cases indirect political action might be envisaged, in other cases national associations prefer to compete with Euro-level associations by developing direct action at the EU level. Taking the definitions at the beginning of this chapter into account, it can be expected, on the basis of insights from multilevel governance, that national associations 'Europeanize' to the extent that they develop non-parochial and transnational orientations and relations while remaining national in their character and constitution.

The process of European and global financial integration

The behavioural adaptation of national business associations due to Europeanization is studied in the EU financial services sector. This sector can be divided into three subsectors: credit institutions, investment services and insurance.[3] The borders between different market segments and subsectors are, however, becoming more and more blurred. Commercial banking is increasingly combined with investment banking (Lewis 1996). Furthermore, it is worth mentioning that there is a movement towards bancassurance (Nicholson 1992). During the last decade, banks started to distribute insurance products through their branch networks. The traditional segmentation of banking and insurance remains in the case of the production of insurance (i.e. underwriting).[4] In this section, I discuss the main changes that have taken place in the EU financial regulatory framework and EU institutional setting. The changes in EU financial services regulation have had significant distributive effects for the financial services providers and have, consequently, generated intense interaction between these private interests and the EU institutions through lobbying and public consultation. This lobbying activity occurred while important institutional transformations were taking place in the EU multilevel system. Frequently changing regulations and institutional transformation in a time of internationalization and Europeanization of markets have been the background against which national business associations have had to develop lobbying strategies in the EU multilevel system.

The issue of financial integration received little attention from politicians in the Member States during the 1960s and 1970s. Far more progress was made in removing barriers to trade than was made in removing barriers to provision of services (Pool 1990). Progress in the financial sector towards an integrated financial market was particularly low. The result of this lack of cross-border trading of financial services was that the financial services industry, particularly with regard to retail services, remained very much a national business (Dixon 1991). From the mid-1980s, true progress was made. At the same time that individual governments began to liberalize, the European Commission started to promote financial deregulation and liberalization. This is reflected in a substantial increase of legislation from the 1980s and the 1990s onwards (Figure 8.1).

A programme to complete the internal financial European market was

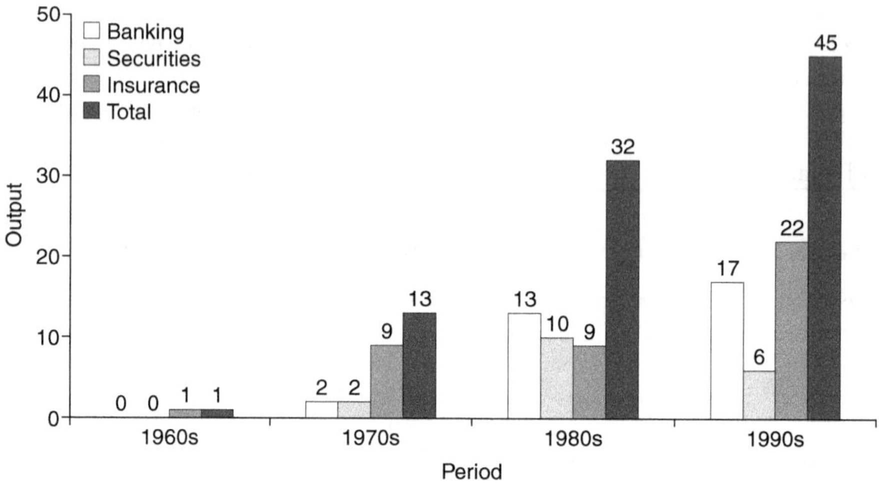

Figure 8.1 Output of legislation (source: Celex database, June 2001).

outlined in the Commission's White Paper of 1985 drafted by Lord Cockfield, Commissioner responsible for the internal market (Bakker 1996). The recommendations of the White Paper were adopted into primary law as the Single European Act (SEA) of 1 July 1986. The Member States agreed that three major principles would govern trade in financial services: minimum harmonization of national rules, mutual recognition and home country control.[5] The traditional approach to financial integration saw it as a process involving a detailed harmonization of all laws and regulations applicable to the financial sector. The White Paper, by contrast, based the completion of the internal market on the principle of mutual recognition (Llewellyn 1993).

From the mid-1980s, an increasing number of legislative measures were adopted in the financial sector. The three major principles in the EU financial services legislation were introduced by four key directives: the Second Banking Directive (89/646/EEC), the Investment Services Directive (93/22/EEC), and the Third Life (92/96/EEC) and Non-Life Insurance Directive (92/49/EEC) (Lannoo 1992). In order to be successful, the four directives were accompanied by the crucial Directive on Capital Liberalization (89/361/EEC). It was widely expected that their phased implementation during the 1990s would have allowed the completion of the internal market for financial services. While from a strictly legal point of view many observers argued that the single market was actually in place, there was a consensus among academics and practitioners that important barriers still remained to be eliminated (Dixon 1991; Fèvre 1993; Kespohl-Willemer 1993; Llewellyn 1993; Vipond 1993; Zavvos 1994; Schliesser 1996; McGee 1998). The implementation of the project on Economic and Monetary

Union made policy makers realize that without well-functioning financial markets, the success of the single currency would not be guaranteed. Therefore, in 1998, they called upon the European Commission to devise a new plan, i.e. the so-called Financial Services Action Plan (FSAP) in order to inject new momentum into the task of building a single financial market (Mogg 1999).[6] The FSAP has led to a renewed increase of Commission proposals for the financial services sector (Figure 8.2).

In order to understand the strategies developed by national business associations to influence the EU decision-making process, a careful analysis of the multilevel institutional setting and the inter-institutional balance of power in the EU financial services policy area is indispensable. After all, national associations are likely to approach those EU institutions that can substantially shape the outcomes of the EU collective decision-making process. In 1986, the Single European Act facilitated the decision-making process by replacing unanimous voting requirements with qualified majority voting for the Council's adoption of most of the legislative measures to achieve the Internal Market, including the single financial services market (Pearson and Smits 1995). Previously, unanimity allowed any one Member State to block legislation, which made the national route an efficient channel for national associations to influence the EU decision-making process. The Single European Act also changed the balance of power between the EU institutions by strengthening the role of the European Parliament in the legislative process (Neunreither 1999). The Act introduced the cooperation procedure (Article 149(2) EEC Treaty) that added a second reading to the existing consultation procedure and allowed the Parliament to make amendments to proposed legislation. As a result, the Council became more sensitive to the Parliament's concerns. Even though the new procedure initially

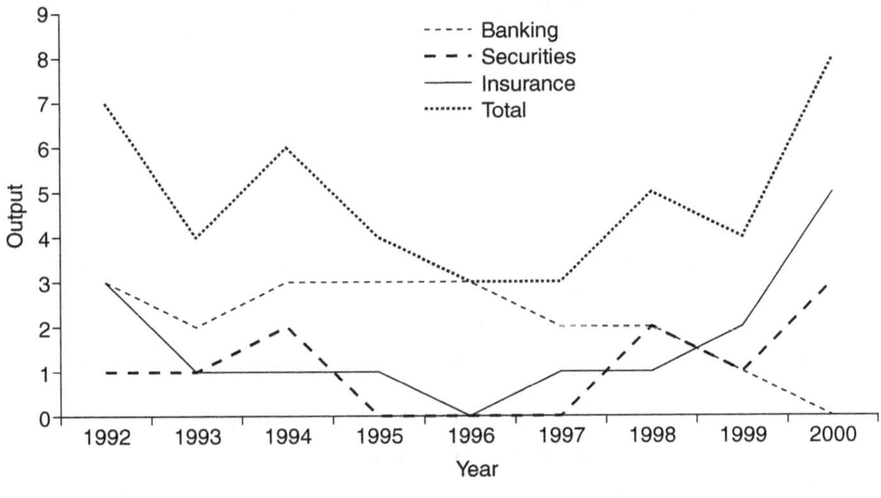

Figure 8.2 Output of Commission proposals (source: Celex database, June 2001).

applied to only ten Treaty articles, these articles covered most of the legislation necessary for the completion of the internal market (Moreiro 1993). The Maastricht Treaty on European Union (TEU) introduced a further extension of the powers of the European Parliament in internal market legislation (Pearson and Smits 1995). Furthermore, the Treaty on the European Union introduced the co-decision procedure (Article 189B TEU) which, for the first time, provided the supranational assembly with an effective legislative veto. It applied to most legislation, which the SEA had subjected to the cooperation procedure (Corbett *et al.* 1995). The consecutive amendments of the Treaties expanded the Parliament's role from mere consultation, through cooperation, to co-decision. Whereas the Commission succeeded in preserving its original agenda-setting powers, the institutional balance between the Council of Ministers and the European Parliament changed dramatically. This strengthened the supranational arena vis-à-vis the national arena in the EU multilevel system and is thereby likely to influence the lobbying strategies of business interest representatives.

Finally, it is important to point out that European financial integration is embedded in a similar process at the international level. Technological innovation, increasing deregulation of financial markets and the liberalization of capital flows are identified as major forces of the international financial integration process (Vipond 1993). Since the European financial markets are part of an international financial market, the EU regulatory and supervisory infrastructure has to be compatible with international regulatory and institutional structures (Coleman and Underhill 1995). Over the last two decades, two fora for international cooperation on financial services regulation and supervision have been important: the Basle Committee of the Bank for International Settlements (BIS), and the International Organization of Securities Commissions (IOSCO).[7] They organize and structure international cooperation and have, therefore, become focal points for business lobbying at the global level. While recognizing the importance of international regulation, this chapter's focus is limited to the EU multilevel system.

The access of national business associations to the EU institutions

On the basis of an extensive empirical study in the EU financial services sector, the hypothesized lobbying strategies were checked. As a result, this section undertakes a systematic analysis of the access of national business associations in the European Parliament, the European Commission and the Council of Ministers.[8] In order to investigate the extent to which national associations develop direct versus indirect lobbying strategies at the EU level, the access of national and European business associations is compared in the three EU institutions. Both public and private actors potentially have interesting information about access. Since I am interested in the relative access of national and European associations to the EU institutions, the focus of the data collection has to be on the public actors. Because the latter are approached by national and European associations in order to gain access, they are in the best position to evaluate the relative access granted to the private actors. Private actors are mostly unaware of the access enjoyed by other private interests; therefore, it is extremely difficult for them to correctly assess the relative access they have to the EU institutions. Rather than directly studying business associations, the entire empirical investigation is based on 63 semi-structured interviews with EU officials and politicians belonging to the three previously mentioned EU institutions.[9]

A set of structured questions was developed in order to obtain comparable and quantifiable data about the access of four different organizational forms of business interest representation: individual companies, consultants, national and European associations. Even though data was collected and processed with regard to the access of these four organizational forms, this chapter focuses mainly on the access of national and European associations (Bouwen, 2004). Whereas structured questions were inserted in the semi-structured interviews to obtain comparable and quantifiable data, open questions allowed generating more qualitative in-depth knowledge (King 1995). Both the quantitative and the qualitative data from the semi-structured interviews are used to check the hypotheses and gain insights into the lobbying strategies of national associations. The interval scale measurement of the degree of access of the national and European associations was calculated on the basis of the method of paired comparison (Guilford 1954; Swanborn 1993). This is a one-dimensional scaling method that allows converting ordinal scale values into interval scale values. The ordinal scale values were collected in the semi-structured interviews in which all interviewees had to establish a ranking of their contacts with the previously mentioned four different organizational forms of business interest representation. The interviewees, i.e. officials and politicians, had to indicate with which of the four organizational forms they had had contacts, taking the usefulness and the regularity of the contacts into account. The resultant rankings indicate which organizational forms the interviewees selected as their first, second, third and fourth choice. Once the ordinal scale values were converted into interval scale values, these were used to calculate the relative access values of the national and European associations as well as the other organizational forms across the three EU institutions. The resulting percentages are reported in Figure 8.3 below.[10]

The figure puts the relative access of national and European associations in relation to the relative access of individual firms and political consultants. Even though the focus of this chapter is on collective forms of business interest representation, it is important to realize that individual company representation and third party representation through political consultants are important forms of business interest representation at the EU level. Traditional interest group studies, however, tend to focus on collective action in isolation from other organizational forms (Olson 1965). Also the

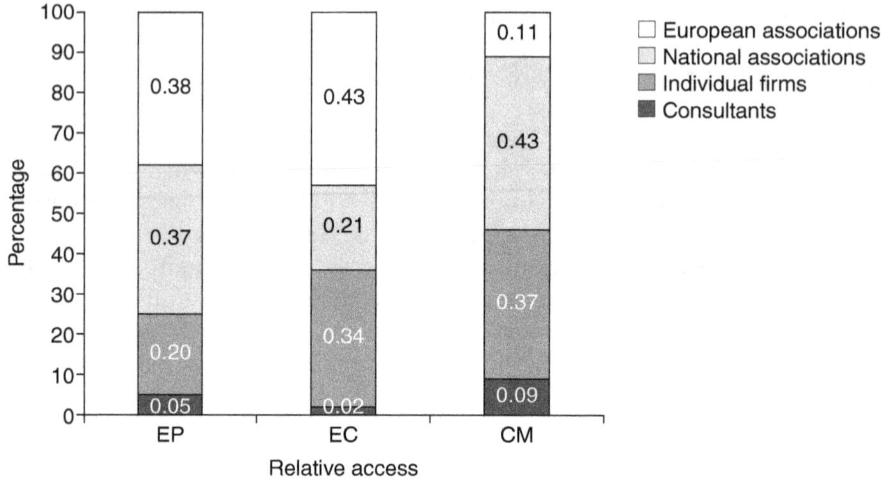

Figure 8.3 Relative access: EP, EC and CM compared (source: Bouwen 2004 (n = 63).

literature on European interest intermediation has mainly focused on collective action (Greenwood *et al.* 1992; Aspinwall and Greenwood 1998).

Numerous national business associations are active in the financial services sector of the 15 Member States. The data presented in the figure show that these national associations are not only politically active at the purely national level but that they also gain access to the three EU institutions. Moreover, the relative access values show that national associations no longer rely exclusively on the traditional national route through the Council of Ministers to participate in the EU decision-making process. National business associations also gain direct access to the European Parliament and the European Commission. The data clearly confirm the multilevel governance hypothesis that national associations undertake direct lobbying strategies at the different levels of the EU multilevel system. European financial integration seems not to have caused the withering away of national business associations as predicted by the neo-functionalist integration theory.

Furthermore, the data in Figure 8.3 also show that European business associations in the EU financial services sector have an important degree of access to the EU institutions. Until March 2001, the European associations in the financial services sector were traditional European federations consisting only of national associations. A number of the most important European associations are summarized in Table 8.1.

Direct membership associations of large firms or mixed membership associations that include both associations and firms as member were nonexistent in the financial services sector (Greenwood and Ronit 1994; Cowles 1996; Cram and Greenwood 1996).[11] In contrast with large companies in

Table 8.1 European associations in the EU financial services sector

Banking	*Investment services*	*Insurance*
European Association of Co-operative Banks	Fédération Européenne des Fonds et Sociétés d'Investissment	Association des Assureurs Coopératifs et Mutualistes Européens
European Banking Federation	Federation of European Securities Exchanges	Comité Européen des Assurances
European Savings Banks Group		
European Mortgage Federation	European Federation for Retirement Provision	

Notes
Even though the table gives a number of important European associations in the EU financial services sector, many more European associations exist. An important number of associations can be found in the CONECCS database of the Commission at http://europa.eu.int/comm/civil_society/coneccs/listedomaine2.cfm?CL=en. Also, the table does not include the important number of international associations that are lobbying in Brussels. Examples are the International Federation of Insurance Intermediaries (BIPAR) in the insurance sector, the International Swaps and Derivatives Association (ISDA) and the International Securities Market Association (ISMA) in the securities sector, and the World Savings Banks Institute in the banking sector.

other sectors, financial institutions have followed conservative political strategies and have been afraid to cooperate more closely with each other through new organizational forms of business interest representation. Only in March 2001 was the European Round Table for Financial Services (ERF) founded (Bieling 2002). It is a European direct membership association consisting of a limited number of very large financial institutions. Members of the ERF are the chairmen and chief executives of leading European financial institutions including Axa, Deutsche Bank AG, BNP Paribas, Royal Bank of Scotland and UniCredito Italiano SPA among others. In contrast, when European associations have national associations as members, they constitute an important additional channel for national associations to influence the EU legislative process. While it has already been established that national associations have developed direct lobbying strategies, they also seem to rely on their membership of European associations in order to participate indirectly in the EU decision-making process. These empirical findings confirm the multilevel governance hypothesis that national associations undertake both direct and indirect lobbying strategies to participate in the European system of collective decision making. The fact that national and European business associations enjoy a different degree of access to the EU policy-making process provides a reason for the use of these different lobbying strategies by national associations.[12] Figure 8.3 shows that while the direct lobbying strategy allows national associations to obtain a high degree of access to the Council of Ministers (43 per cent) and the European Parliament

(37 per cent), the indirect strategy provides a high degree of access to the European Commission (43 per cent). The high overall degree of access to the EU decision-making system that results from this dual strategy provides a rationale that explains why national associations are not likely to dissolve in supranational associations.

The empirical findings in this chapter corroborate the behavioural predictions that can be made on the basis of the logic of influence (Schmitter and Streeck 1981; 1999). With respect to the interaction between associations and the state, the logic of influence captures the idea that organized interests have to be organized in such a way to enable them to gain access and exercise adequate influence over the public authorities. Therefore, organized interests have to take the institutional structure of the public authorities into account. With the locus of political decision making moving up from the nation state to the EU level, important decision-making powers are now located at both the national and EU level. Consequently, lobbying strategies of national business associations have adapted to the changing institutional target structure. While remaining active in their domestic context, direct and indirect lobbying strategies have allowed national associations to develop successful political action in the EU multilevel system.

Lobbying the EU in Brussels or at home

Recent empirical research has shown that national associations increasingly establish permanent offices in Brussels in order to develop direct lobbying strategies at the EU level (Kohler-Koch and Quitkatt 1999). Notwithstanding the costs related to such an office, different German banking associations have established a permanent presence in Brussels. They represent the different niches in the German credit market. Not only the Verband Deutscher Hypotheken Banken (VDH) and the Deutsche Bausparkassen are present in Brussels, also the Bundesverband der Deutschen Volksbanken and Raffeisenbanken (BVR), the Bundesverband Öffentlicher Banken Deutschlands (VÖB) and the Deutscher Sparkassen- und Giroverband (DSGV) have a permanent office in Brussels. Moreover, it needs to be emphasized that the direct presence of these national associations constitutes a very sensitive issue for the respective European associations to which they belong. In order to avoid harmful competition between the respective national and European associations in Brussels, the representatives of the national associations invest a lot of time developing a good working relationship with their respective European association. In contrast with the other German banking associations, the Bundesverband Deutscher Banken (BDB) has consciously chosen not to establish a liaison office in Brussels. In that way, the association wants to avoid harmful competition with its respective European association, i.e. the European Banking Federation (FBE). Even though the physical presence in Brussels through the establishment of a permanent office constitutes a clear advantage for interest representatives, it is not indispensable to develop a so-called Brussels strategy. Numerous national business interest representatives travel regularly between Brussels and their national capital to implement a direct lobbying strategy.

Nevertheless, it is very important to emphasize that the national associations' EU focused political activities can take place in the national capitals as well as in Brussels. In the following paragraphs, I show that a substantial part of national associations' interest representation related to EU-specific issues actually takes place in their home country. Based on the data collected in the semi-structured interviews, it can be derived that national associations employ two different strategies to lobby the EU at home.

First, the so-called traditional national lobbying route allows national associations to influence decisions in the Council of Ministers by approaching their national government or administration at home. On the basis of the semi-structured interviews it has been possible to identify the administrative and governmental structures in the national capitals as the most important locus for lobbying the EU Member States and the presidency within the Council framework. They are much more important than the Member States' permanent representations in Brussels. Whereas 57 per cent of the interviewees answered that the national capital is lobbied more with regard to EU matters than the permanent representation, only 14 per cent indicated the opposite (Table 8.2).

However, national business associations cannot only approach their national government or administration at home. As a second strategy, they can also interact at home with their nationally elected Members of the European Parliament (MEPs). Figure 8.4 below shows how many days per week Members of the European Parliament stay on average in Brussels.[13] Under the plausible supposition that MEPs mostly reside either at home or in

Table 8.2 Who do you think is more lobbied with regard to EU matters, the permanent representation in Brussels or the national capital?

Permanent representation	14%	
National capital	57%	
Both equally	29%	
Total	100%	n = 14

Source: Own data.

Notes

The administrative and governmental structures at home were identified as the most important locus for lobbying the EU Member States within the Council framework. Nevertheless, a group of 22 financial attachés working for the 15 permanent representations of the Member States in Brussels were, for practical reasons, identified as the relevant population of officials to study the access of business interests to the Council. The very close link between the financial attachés and their counterparts in the national administrations at home justifies the choice of this alternative population. In addition to the fact that the financial attachés have daily contacts with the national officials at home, most financial attachés have previously worked for the national administration in the capital city. With the aim of obtaining data on each Member State, a sample of 15 attachés was taken from the population of 22.

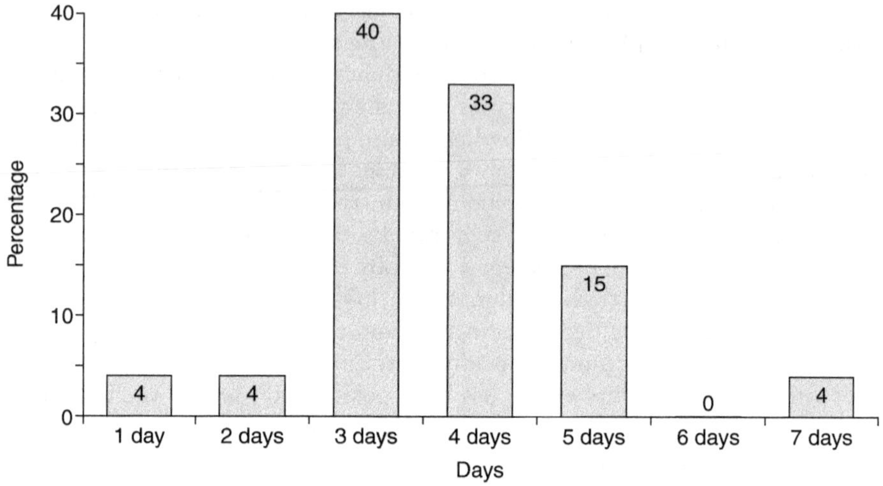

Figure 8.4 Days per week in Brussels, in per cent of MEPs (source: own data (n = 27)).

Note
The 45 full members of the Economic and Monetary Affairs Committee are identified as the relevant population to be investigated in the European Parliament. All the full Members were included in the sample of people that were invited to participate in the semi-structured interviews.

Brussels, it can be derived that more than 80 per cent of the MEPs spend on average at least three days per week in their home country. Even though the weekend is mostly included in these three days, it gives national business interests a substantial amount of time to interact with their national MEPs.

The Members of the European Parliament gave different reasons for the amount of time they spend in their home country. In my interviews, they repeatedly told me that they are active in their national political party and their country's social life. Some Members hold important positions on the board of their national party. They also need to maintain good contacts with the party officials who are responsible for ordering the candidates on the party list. In addition, MEPs want to cultivate a good relationship with the citizens and interest organizations that constitute their electorate at home.

Finally, it can be concluded that both the traditional lobbying route and the interactions with nationally elected MEPs are important strategies for national business associations to lobby the EU at home. Besides, these lobbying strategies at home are particularly important because the required resources to implement them are much less resource intensive than those needed for execution of the Brussels strategy, with or without a permanent office in Brussels. Thereby, these two strategies render European level interest representation accessible to a higher number of national business associations.

Conclusion

The creation of the single financial market does not seem to have caused the withering away of national business associations as predicted by the neo-functionalist integration theory. The Europeanization of national interest representation does not entail the absorption of national associations in European-level associations. On the contrary, the empirical study of EU financial services sector confirms the hypotheses generated on the basis of the multilevel governance perspective. The empirical analysis has established that national business associations continue to exist and undertake direct lobbying strategies at the EU level. Whereas the traditional route through the Council of Ministers remains the most successful lobbying strategy for national associations, they also increasingly develop direct political action in the European Parliament and the European Commission. In addition, the results of the empirical investigation show that national associations also undertake indirect lobbying strategies through their participation in European associations. The different degree of institutional access of national and European associations to the EU is an important reason for the multiple lobbying strategies of national associations. While their direct lobbying strategy allows them to obtain a high degree of access to the Council of Ministers and the European Parliament, the empirical data showed that their indirect strategy through the European associations provides a high degree of access to the European Commission. The fundamental regulatory and institutional changes that have accompanied the European financial integration process have substantially changed the target structure for national business associations. In line with the logic of influence, the strategies of the national associations have adapted to the changing institutional target structure (Schmitter and Streeck 1981, 1999).

An extensive empirical investigation conducted by Beyers (2002) confirms the findings of this chapter. While his study mainly focused on the extent to which the European networks of national associations have to be considered as embroidering upon domestic networks or as compensating for the lack of domestic access, it also provides systematic information about the access of national associations to the European level.[14] His investigation does not only confirm the importance of the direct lobbying strategy of national associations, it also emphasizes the importance for national associations to participate in European associations in order to indirectly influence the EU decision-making process. Moreover, it is highly interesting that his empirical findings confirm the results of this chapter regarding the different degree of access of national associations to the three EU institutions. Beyers also reports that national associations have a higher degree of access to the Council of Ministers and the European Parliament than to the European Commission. In another empirical study, Bennett (1997) also concludes that national associations employ multiple routes to influence the EU policy-making level.[15] The author points out that the most important route for national business associations remains the traditional national route, using meetings with national ministers and officials as an attempt to get them to influence the EU. However, he goes on to say that both the direct and the indirect lobbying route through European associations are valuable alternatives.

Finally, it is important to make two brief remarks regarding the sectoral focus of this study. First, it should be pointed out that the impact of Europeanization on the lobbying strategies of national business associations might differ according to the sector (Lehmkuhl 1998). The extent to which legal competencies in the sector concerned have been transferred to the EU policy-making level is a crucial variable that strongly influences the strategic behaviour of national associations. Second, it needs to be emphasized that I have only focused on sectoral associations in this investigation. However, there seem to be no reasons to assume that so-called inter-sectoral associations are likely to behave according to a different logic. Even though sectoral specificities might play a role, the existing literature seems to suggest that my findings have a rather general character.

Notes

1 I would like to thank Wolfgang Streeck, Jelle Visser, Volker Schneider and Jürgen Grote for their useful comments on earlier versions of this chapter. I am also grateful to my colleagues at the Max Planck Project Group in Bonn for their interesting comments on an earlier draft. In particular, I would like to thank Dirk De Bièvre and Dieter Kerwer.

2 A diverse literature has developed on the issue of Europeanization. For different definitions and research agendas see Schmidt 1997, Knill and Lehmkuhl 1999, Börzel and Risse 2000, Cole and Drake 2000, Lehmkuhl 1998, 2000, Montpetit 2000, Verdier and Breen 2001 and Börzel 2002. However, most of these publications do not have interest politics as their main focus.

3 The European Commission also uses this subdivision. The Commission has provided lists to indicate which institutions are covered by the secondary legislation for a particular subsector (Lannoo 1992; Verheugd 1995).

4 The process of desegmentation in the financial services sector is hardly mirrored in the legislation. The large majority of the secondary legislation has a subsectoral focus.

5 The principle of home country control implies that the community-wide activities of a financial institution come under the control of the authorities of its country of origin (Servais 1995; McGee 1998). In practice, home country control requires no transfer of national supervisory authority to the supranational level.

6 Financial Services: Building a Framework for Action. Commission Communication of 28/10/98. COM (1998): 625.

7 While the Basle Committee formulates broad supervisory standards and guidelines and recommends statements of best practice, IOSCO tries to encourage international cooperation between member agencies to establish common standards and effective surveillance of international securities transactions.

8 For the discussion of a theoretical framework to explain the access of business interests to the different EU institutions, see the 'logic of access' in Bouwen 2002.

9 Between June 2000 and May 2002 the author conducted 63 semi-structured interviews.
10 For a more detailed description of the methodology and the calculations, see Bouwen 2004.
11 De facto, a certain kind of mixed membership associations already exists in the EU financial services sector. The European Mortgage Federation and the European Savings Banks Association have, for example, both national associations and individual firms as members. The reason for their mixed membership structure is, however, fundamentally different from the 'real' mixed membership associations. Individual companies were only included in these traditional European federations because there were no national associations available in certain Member States.
12 For an explanation of the different degree of access of national and European associations to the EU policy-making process, see Bouwen 2002.
13 The MEPs were asked not to take the plenary sessions in Strasbourg into account.
14 Beyers makes a distinction between specific and diffuse interests. The distinction relates to the constituencies associations represent and upon which they rely for political mobilization. Diffuse interests are the non-producer interests or public interest groups, which lack a well-delineated constituency. Specific interests are the producer interests that represent the interests of a well-circumscribed or more concentrated constituency. Since the focus in this chapter is on business associations, only his results regarding specific interests are relevant.
15 In his survey, Bennett includes different kinds of business associations. For my purposes his category of corporate trade associations is most relevant.

Bibliography

Aspinwall, M. and Greenwood, J. (1998) *Collective Action in the European Union, Interests and the New Politics of Associability*, London: Routledge.

Bakker, A. F. P. (1996) *The Liberalization of Capital Movements in Europe. The Monetary Committee and Financial Integration, 1958–1994*, Dordrecht: Kluwer.

Bennett, R. J. (1997) 'The Impact of European Economic Integration on Business Associations: The UK Case', *West European Politics* 20 (3): 61–90.

Beyers, J. (2002) 'Gaining and Seeking Access: The European Adaptation of Domestic Interest Associations', *European Journal of Political Research* 41 (5): 585–612.

Bieling, H.-J. (2002) 'Social Forces in the Making of the New European Economy', *New Political Economy* 8 (2): 203–204.

Börzel, T. A. (2002) *States and Regions in the European Union. Institutional Adaptation in Germany and Spain*, Cambridge: Cambridge University Press.

Börzel, T. A. and Risse. T. (2000) 'When Europe Hits Home: Europeanization and Domestic Change', *European Integration Online Papers* 4 (15): 13.

Bouwen, P. (2002) 'Corporate Lobbying in the European Union: The Logic of Access', *Journal of European Public Policy* 9 (3): 365–390.

Bouwen, P. (2004) 'Exchanging Access Goods for Access. A Comparative Study of Business Lobbying in the EU Institutions', *European Journal of Political Research* 43 (3): 337–369.

Cole, A. and Drake. H. (2000) 'The Europeanization of the French Polity: Continuity, Change and Adaptation', *Journal of European Public Policy* 7 (1): 26–43.

Coleman, W. D. and Underhill, G. R. D. (1995) 'Globalization, Regionalism and the Regulation of Securities Markets', *Journal of European Public Policy* 2 (3): 488–513.

Corbett, R., Jacobs, F. and Shackleton, M. (1995) *The European Parliament*, London: Cartermill Publishing.

Cowles, M. G. (1996) 'The EU Committee of Amcham: The Powerful Voice of American Firms in Brussels', *Journal of European Public Policy* 3 (3): 339–358.

Cram, L. and Greenwood, J. (1996) 'European Level Business Collective Action: The Study Agenda Ahead', *Journal of Common Market Studies* 34 (3): 449–463.

Dixon, R. (1991) *Banking in Europe, The Single Market*, London: Routledge.

Fèvre, J.-P. (1993) 'EC Regulation in the Financial Services Sector', in Z. Mikdashi (ed.) *Financial Strategies and Public Policies. Banking, Insurance and Industry*, New York: St. Martin's Press.

Grande, E. (1996) 'The State and Interest Groups in a Framework of Multi-Level Decision-Making: The Case of the European Union', *Journal of European Public Policy* 3 (3): 318–338.

Greenwood, J. and Ronit, K. (1994) 'Interest Groups in the European Community: Newly Emerging Dynamics and Forms', *West European Politics* 17 (1): 31–52.

Greenwood, J., Grote, J. R. and Ronit, K. (1992) *Organized Interest and the European Community*, London: Sage.

Grote, J. R. and Lang, A. (2002) 'Europeanization and Organizational Change in National Trade Associations – An Organizational Ecology Perspective', in K. Featherstone and C. M. Radaelli (eds) *The Politics of Europeanization: Theory and Analysis*, Oxford: Oxford University Press.

Guilford, J. P. (1954) *Psychometric Methods*, New York, Toronto, London: McGraw-Hill.

Haas, E. (1958) *The Uniting of Europe: Political, Social and Economic Forces*, London: Stevens & Sons.

Haas, E. (1975) *The Obsolescence of Regional Integration Theory*, Berkeley CA: Institute for International Studies.

Hooghe, L. and Marks, G. (2001) *Multi-Level Governance and European Integration*, Lanham MD: Rowman & Littlefield.

Kespohl-Willemer, A. (1993) 'Harmonization of Insurance Law in the European Community', in D. Campbell and C. Flint (eds) *1993: The European Market, Myth or Reality?*, Deventer and Boston: Kluwer Law and Taxation Publishers.

King, N. (1995) 'The Qualitative Research Interview', in C. Cassell and S. Gillian (eds) *Qualitative Methods in Organizational Research*, London: Sage.

Knill, C. and Lehmkuhl, D. (1999) 'How Europe Matters: Different Mechanisms of Europeanization', European Integration Online Papers 3 (7).

Kohler-Koch, B. and Quittkat, C. (1999) 'Intermediation of Interests in the European Union', Arbeitspapiere – Mannheimer Zentrum Für Europäische Sozialforschung, 9: 1–15.

Lannoo, K. (1992) 'The Internal Market for Financial Services. What Has Been Achieved and What Remains to be Done', Centre for European Policy Studies Research Report, 10.

Lehmkuhl, D. (1998) 'The Importance of Small Differences. The Impact of European Integration on the Associations in the German and Dutch Road Haulage Industries', Dissertation, European University Institute.

Lehmkuhl, D. (2000) 'Under Stress: Europeanization and Trade Associations in the Member States', *European Integration Online Papers* 4 (14): 14.

Lewis, M. K. (1996) 'Universal Banking. Development in Financial Structure and Regulation', Seventh Melbourne Money and Finance Conference 29 and 30 November 1996.

Lindberg, L. (1968) *The Political Dynamic of European Economic Integration*, Stanford CA: Stanford University Press.

Llewellyn, D. (1993) 'Banking and Financial Services', in D. Swann (ed.) *The Single European Market and Beyond; A Study of the Wider Implications of the Single European Act*, London and New York: Routledge, pp. 106–145.

McGee, A. (1998) *The Single Market in Insurance. Breaking Down the Barriers*, Aldershot and Brookfield, USA: Ashgate and Dartmouth.

Marks, G., Hooghe, L. and Blanck, K. (1996) 'European Integration from the 1980s: State-Centric vs. Multi-Level Governance', *Journal of Common Market Studies* 34 (3): 341–378.

Mogg, J. (1999) 'Looking Ahead to the Next Century: EU Priorities for Financial Services', *Euredia, European Banking and Financial Law Journal* 1: 9–20.

Montpetit, E. (2000) 'Europeanization and Domestic Politics: Europe and the Development of a French Environmental Policy for the Agricultural Sector', *Journal of European Public Policy* 7 (4): 576–592.

Moreiro G. and Javier, C. (1993) *Banking in Europe After 1992*, Aldershot and Brookfield, USA: Dartmouth.

Neunreither, K. (1999) 'The European Parliament', in L. Cram, D. Dinan, and N. Nugent (eds) *Developments in the European Union*, New York: St. Martin's Press, pp. 62–83.

Nicholson, G. (1992) 'Competition between Banks and Insurance Companies – The Challenge of Bancassurance/Allfinanz', in A. Steinherr (ed.) *The New European Financial Market Place*, London: Longman Group UK Limited.

Olson, M. (1965) *The Logic of Collective Action; Public Goods and the Theory of Groups*, Cambridge MA: Harvard University Press.

Pearson, P. and Smits, R. (1995) 'EC Treaty Provisions Relevant to the Banking Sector', in M. van Empel and R. Smits (eds) *Banking and EC Law*, Deventer: Kluwer Law and Taxation Publishers.

Pool, B. (1990) *The Creation of the Internal Market in Insurance*, Luxembourg: Office for Official Publications of the European Communities.

Scharpf, F. (1988) 'The Joint Decision Trap: Lessons from German Federalism and European Integration', *Public Administration* 66: 229–278.

Schelling, T. (1960) *The Strategy of Conflict*, Cambridge MA: Harvard University Press.

Schliesser, W. (1996) 'Consolidation and Expansion of the European Single Insurance Market', in S. Urban (ed.) *Europe's Challenges*, Wiesbaden: Gabler, pp. 363–394.

Schmidt, V. A. (1997) 'European Integration and Democracy: The Differences among Member States', *Journal of European Public Policy* 4 (1): 128–145.

Schmitter, P. C. and Streeck. W. (1981) 'The Organization of Business Interests. A Research Design to Study the Associative Action of Business in the Advanced Industrial Societies of Western Europe', IIM Discussion Paper IIM/LPM 81-13, Wissenschaftszentrum Berlin.

Schmitter, P. C. and Streeck. W. (1999) 'The Organization of Business Interests: Studying the Associative Action of Business in Advanced Industrial Societies', MPIfG Discussion paper, 99/1, Cologne: Max Planck Institute for the Study of Societies.

Servais, D. (1995) 'A Single Financial Market', European Commission.

Swanborn, P. G. (1993) *Schaaltechnieken, Theorie en praktijk van acht eenvoudige procedures*, Amsterdam: Boom.

Verdier, D. and Breen, R. (2001) 'Europeanization and Globalization: Politics against Market in the European Union', *Comparative Political Studies* 34 (3): 227–262.

Verheugd, P. (1995) 'Definition of "Credit Institution" and List of Banking Activities', in M. van Empel and R. Smits (eds) *Banking and EC Law*, Deventer: Kluwer Law and Taxation Publishers.

Vipond, P. A. (1993) 'The European Financial Area in the 1990s: Europe and the Transnationalization of Finance', in P. G. Cerny (ed.) *Finance and World Politics, Markets, Regimes and States in the Post-Hegemonic Era*, Cheltenham: Edward Elgar Publishing Limited.

Zavvos, G. S. (1994) 'EC Financial Markets: Regulation for Stability and Openness', in E. Wymeersch (ed.) *Further Perspectives in Financial Integration in Europe*, Berlin and New York: Walter de Gruyter, pp. 27–42.

Part III

International systems

9 Global public policy, associative orders and business interest associations

William D. Coleman

In the summers of 1998, 1999 and 2000, the first and third of these being election years, the US Congress approved billions of dollars in 'disaster assistance' for American farmers. The combination of falling commodity prices and unfavourable weather conditions pushed farmers' associations to demand financial aid. For their part, politicians were happy to respond; monies were available in state coffers thanks to the economic boom of the time and votes were at stake. These decisions took place against a changed international policy environment for agriculture. In 1995, the US Congress had ratified the global trade agreement negotiated between 1986 and 1994, including its Agreement on Agriculture. Ratification meant that the US government would comply with stipulations that required World Trade Organization (WTO) members to report any new farm subsidy programmes and to indicate whether they were 'trade distorting' or not. If they were designated as 'trade distorting', they counted against a cap on subsidies specified in the trade agreement.

The issue was a complex one, so the US government had delayed. On the one side, US farmers were pressing either to ignore the WTO rules or to have the government argue that the payments were non-trade distorting. Such a response would preserve additional room for subsidy payments during 2002. On the other side, domestic agribusiness associations fighting against EU subsidies to agriculture worried that if such an argument were successful, the EU would follow suit and add to its existing arsenal of subsidy tools. Moreover, WTO member states had already begun to negotiate a new agriculture agreement; a protectionist approach by the US would undermine its broader negotiating strategy in favour of further liberalization of trade in agricultural commodities, not to speak of desires for liberalization in other areas of trade, particularly services. In the end, the US chose to inform the new Committee on Agriculture of the WTO that the disaster payments were trade distorting.

In 2002, the US began preparing a new agricultural policy or 'farm bill'. Here again, Congress, wary of forthcoming elections, proposed a significant increase in subsidies, payments that would flow principally to wealthier farmers with larger operations who tended to vote Republican. Agribusiness countered with its fears that continuing protection of US agriculture would frustrate its ambition for opening foreign markets to US processed foods. The debate that followed was framed once again, therefore, in terms of balancing domestic politics with international ambitions in a context of constraints imposed by international law.

The entanglement of domestic and global policy making in agriculture described in this example is not unusual by any means. Traditionally one of the sectors most protected by sovereign states, the production of food, has joined others, ranging from banking and finance to standards for harvesting trees in the forestry sector, that feature increasingly in global policy making. In this chapter, I argue that such global policy making is changing the structures, roles and inter-relationships among associations at the domestic level. It is also contributing to the creation of new associations with international domains and to an increase in the importance of already existing associations with international membership domains.

In having an impact on relationships between associations at the domestic level, these changes also have the potential to destabilize long-standing *associative orders* (Streeck and Schmitter 1985: 10). Such orders involve relations between associations where:

> the central principle is that of concertation, or negotiation within and among a limited and fixed set of interest organizations that mutually recognize each other's status and entitlements and are capable of reaching and implementing relatively stable compromise (*pacts*) in the pursuit of their interests.

Streeck and Schmitter (1985: 11) add that in such orders, the associations are 'contingently and strategically interdependent', a relationship which creates the basis for such pacts. Such orders have typically been built slowly over time and involve complex relationships between associational systems and state authorities. They also form and stabilize because the given nation state has the principal authority over the policy instruments and policy processes needed to enter into resource and information exchange relationships with the associations involved. It also follows, therefore, that globalizing processes that undermine such state authority might also come to destabilize existing associative orders.

This argument is developed in three steps. First, I introduce briefly the concept of a policy network, in order to review the varying relationships between states and interest associations. Second, given that policy networks have normally been studied in the context of nation states or even subnational governments, I inquire about the likely impact on policy network structures of the growing internationalization of policy environments. For this discussion, I distinguish four different types of internationalized policy environments and then examine the implications for policy networks of three of these. I then speculate whether these different types are likely to have variable impacts on associative orders. Third, with these effects of the internationalization of policy environments sketched out, I ask what are the implications of these effects on the likely roles and structural properties of individual business interest associations (BIAs). Drawing on several case studies, I trace out some initial hypotheses about the relationship between the internationalization of policy making and changes in associational structures, associative orders and roles in the policy process.

Studying BIAs in the context of policy networks

A policy network refers to a set of informal and formal interactions between a variety of usually collective public (state) and private actors, who have different, but interdependent interests. Operating in a more or less institutionalized setting, these actors are engaged in horizontal, relatively non-hierarchical discussions and negotiations to define policy alternatives, or formulate policies, or implement them (Coleman 2002a). This definition suggests that policy networks vary along two core dimensions: the structural pattern according to which public power is shared among the members and the degree and patterns of integration among the members. For this analysis, I am primarily interested in the first of these two dimensions.

As summarized in Table 9.1, scholars have distinguished different types of policy networks depending on the degree to which state actors share political power with private actors, and on the relative resource balance between private and public actors. This list is by no means exhaustive of policy network types, nor is it exclusive. Nonetheless, these ideal types of state–society relations are the principal ones used in the public policy literature. As van Waarden (1992) notes, the term policy network thus understood has permitted political scientists to move beyond considering state–society relations through the prism of pluralism or corporatism alone. And despite what has been argued by Dowding (1995), these theoretical differences among types of policy networks have been shown to explain important variations in policy processes and in policy outcomes. Nonetheless, fashioning explanations about why policy networks take particular forms in the first place remains at an elementary stage.

We also should be open to the fact that the continuing adequacy of these categories may require further refinement as studies of policy making in

Table 9.1 Types of policy networks

State–civil society relations	*Policy advocate*	*Policy participant*
Balanced	Pressure pluralism	Corporatism
Favours state actors	State-directed	State corporatism
Favours civil society actors	Issue network	Clientelism

Source: Coleman and Perl (1999).

internationalized policy domains unfold. The categorization is anchored on the long-standing distinction between public and private actors. Some transnational policy communities are built around the distinction between public actors operating at the national level and those working at supranational levels, a distinction that may take priority over the public–private one. In addition, given the lower level of development of international institutions in terms of satisfying usual criteria of democratic accountability, the very meaning of 'public' actor differs at this level, thereby blurring somewhat the traditional public–private distinction. All these things said, however, these ideal types of private–public relationships in policy making, which emerged out of the neo-corporatism debate, have stood the test of time. They capture important differences in state–civil society relations that have proven useful for the analysis of public policy.

Internationalized policy environments, policy networks and associative orders

Internationalized policy environments refer to those where at least some part of policy making takes place at a more encompassing level than the nation state. Thus defined, internationalized policy environments may be further distinguished using two criteria (Coleman and Perl 1999). First, some will feature more public sector activism than others. Public sector activism refers to the degree of direct involvement of politicians and senior public officials in coordinating activity. Thus private actors will take the lead in environments where activism is low, while politicians and civil servants will dominate in highly activist ones. The second criterion is based on the degree of development of distinct international institutions. In some environments, international institutions will possess a mandate defined in supranational law and a capacity to act that gives them an important role in governance. In others, the nation state will retain control of international interaction and decision making in the absence of autonomous international institutions. Using these two criteria, I distinguish the four ideal-typical internationalized policy environments identified in Table 9.2. For the purposes of this paper, I focus on three of these: multilevel governance (MLG), intergovernmental negotiations (IGN) and private regimes.

Multilevel governance

Scholars use the term 'multilevel governance' (MLG) to characterize the complex patterns of relationships between supranational and national institutions in the European Union, an environment quite different from classic international relations settings involving negotiations between heads of state. Equally distinct from other possible governance environments such as supranational federalism or dominance by an international bureaucracy, multilevel governance is an arrangement where there is significant institu-

Table 9.2 Variations in supranational governance arrangements

Institutionalization of supranational governing arrangements	*Public sector activism in governing arrangements*	
	High	*Low*
High	Multilevel governance	Self-regulatory and private regimes
Low	Intergovernmental negotiations	Loose couplings

Source: Coleman and Perl (1999).

tional development at *both* national and supranational levels. In addition, politicians, bureaucrats and civil society actors engage in a multitude of cooperative working arrangements that cross levels.

There is no reason to assume that MLG will emerge only in the European Union. As distinct international institutions become more common, while nation states remain strong, multilevel governance arrangements are likely to spread. Furthermore, there are likely to be some similarities between their character and what is now characteristic of MLG in the EU. Consider the following three aspects of the EU system. First, EU institutions have a remarkably small budgetary base, one that is dwarfed by the total budgets of the member states. Second, the EU bureaucracy is prominent in the agenda setting and policy formulation stages of the policy process only. Lacking its own administrative substructure, the EU must rely on member states to implement its policy decisions. Third, given its Treaty-based responsibility for market integration, the European Commission tends to favour the use of regulatory policy instruments. Compared to distributive or redistributive policy instruments, regulatory policy is less expensive, with the principal costs being borne by administrative agencies of the member states and by those whose activities are concerned. What regulatory policy does require, however, is a detailed and expert knowledge of the regulated activity. Here the Commission has gradually built up a basis of expertise on the workings and effects of different regulatory instruments.

Arrangements marking a nascent MLG arrangement have come to characterize agricultural policy making at the WTO. Article 17 of the Agreement on Agriculture made provision for the establishment of a Committee on Agriculture at the WTO, while Article 18 laid out its responsibilities. The Committee was to review the progress of member states in the implementation of commitments negotiated under the Uruguay Round reform programme. In addition as the earlier discussion of US policy indicated, members were also enjoined to notify the Committee of any new domestic support policy, or of a modification of an existing policy, for which an exemption from the Agreement was to be claimed. Finally, members were to be provided an opportunity to raise any matter relevant to implementation of commitments under the reform programme, or to bring to the attention of members any policy of another member that it thought required Committee notification. Sanitary and phytosanitary measures related to agriculture are covered by a separate Agreement on the Application of Sanitary and Phytosanitary (SPS) Measures that sets out a series of core norms and principles for their development. Parallel to the Agriculture Agreement, there is also an SPS Committee, which has similar responsibilities for monitoring the implementation of policy.

Like the EU, the WTO has a remarkably small budgetary base and the Committee on Agriculture is most prominent as a site for agenda setting and policy formulation than for policy implementation. The tiny WTO Secretariat does not have its own administrative infrastructure, so must rely on member states for the implementation of policy. The WTO agreement on agriculture is also typical of regulatory policy; the detailed and expert knowledge required for these policies is found both at the WTO Secretariat and in domestic departments of agriculture.

Multilevel governance under conditions of limited budgets, subsidiarity-like principles for policy implementation and a bias toward regulatory policy making will have a definite impact on arrangements of policy communities and policy networks as the EU has shown. First, *national-level* policy communities certainly do not disappear. To the contrary, they remain involved in each aspect of the policy process, but are particularly important when it comes to implementation (see Table 9.3). Second, we can expect the formation of *transnational* policy communities, composed of actors from both the national and international levels that serve to link national policy communities both to one another and to international institutions. These transnational policy communities may be composed primarily of governmental actors (intergovernmental), or of policy specialists (transnational expert) because of the specialized knowledge required by regulatory policy instruments, or they may include both types of actors.

As international institutions become stronger and more autonomous, we can also expect them to influence the building of these policy communities. For example, the European Commission has sought to develop its own autonomous information base by encouraging the formation of European-level interest associations and by soliciting direct contacts with corporations that operate on a Community-wide basis. Recently, the WTO has begun to formalize its relationships with non-governmental actors. Other international institutions have gone even further. In banking, the Basle Committee on Banking Supervision consults regularly with the International Institute on Finance, an association representing global banks. The Codex Alimentarius Commission, a subsidiary organization of the Food and Agriculture Organization and an organization mentioned under the WTO Agreement as preparing recognized international standards for foods, permits domestic-level associations to participate in member state delegations to its meetings. In short, transnational intergovernmental

Table 9.3 International policy environments, policy community types, and the policy process: rank order of importance

Type of internationalized policy environment	*Stages of policy development*		
	Definition, discussion and selection of policy options	*Formulation of policies*	*Implementation of policies*
Multilevel governance	TN and national policy communities all involved	1. TN intergovernmental equally involved 2. TN expert 3. National	1. National and TN expert 2. TN intergovernmental
Intergovernmental negotiations	1. National 2. TN expert	1. National 2. TN expert	1. National 2. TN expert
Private regimes	Transnational	1. Transnational 2. National	1. Transnational 2. National
Loose couplings	Transnational	Temporal participants in a transnational issue network	Loosely linked local issue niches

Source: Coleman and Perl (1999).

Note
TN = transnational.

communities will play a crucial role in the formulation of policies, and transnational-expert communities will work closely with national policy communities in the implementation of policy (see Table 9.3).

A multilevel governance environment will likely foster particular structural properties in policy communities and policy networks. Transnational policy communities will be *less integrated* than national ones, because of larger numbers of actors, more instability in members, lower institutionalization of interactions and less agreement on basic ideas and values. The lower fiscal capacity of international governance institutions and reliance on nation states for policy implementation suggests that the development of state-directed or state corporatist policy networks at the transnational level is highly unlikely (see Table 9.1). Although the analysis by Streeck and Schmitter (1991) of the EU would imply that *pluralist* networks will be the dominant form at the international level, other studies suggest additional possibilities. The involvement of multiple policy communities in the definition of policy options indicates that *issue networks* may be more common than at the national level. In addition, the reliance of international institutions on private actors for information, the likely policy interest in regulatory issues of market integration and the preference for working in committee structures may lead to transnational *clientelist* policy networks at the formulation and implementation stages (Eising and Kohler-Koch 1994: 193). Where supranational institutions are stronger, such as in agricultural policy in the EU, *corporatist* networks remain a distinct possibility (Pappi and Schnorpfeil 1995). Conversely, the presence of transnational intergovernmental policy communities may strengthen the autonomy of state officials vis-à-vis national interests (Grande 1996), perhaps enough to change *national* networks from pressure-pluralist to *state-directed.*

Accordingly, MLG environments are also likely to destabilize domestic associative orders. The institutionalization of supranational authority is likely to benefit some domestic associations, while disadvantaging others. These differential impacts may undermine domestic 'pacts' among associations. Those favoured by the supranational arrangements may begin working with similarly advantaged associations in other states in order to preserve and consolidate their position. Similarly, those disadvantaged by the changes may seek alliances with other associations in order to challenge supranational authority and to change its operating principles.

Intergovernmental negotiations

International relations scholars have devoted considerable attention to intergovernmental negotiations. Perhaps the most interesting characterization of the relationship between intergovernmental relations and domestic policy making is that provided by Robert Putnam (1988) with his two-level game metaphor. In this model, heads of state or chief negotiators seek to find an agreement at the supranational level that they can be certain will be ratified domestically within their respective polities. The likely ease or difficulty of ratification creates smaller or larger win-sets (possible ratifiable agreements) for the negotiators. The linkages between supranational and domestic levels can be complex. Negotiators can link issues to create 'synergies' in order to widen or narrow the win-sets of key constituents at the domestic level. Negotiators can also make moves that might affect win-sets in polities outside their own ('reverberations'). What does distinguish intergovernmental negotiations from multilevel governance is the almost complete absence of autonomous supranational institutions.

In this type of internationalized policy environment, consistent with Putnam's formulation of a two-level game, national policy communities will remain dominant in the definition, discussion and selection of policy options as well as in policy implementation (see Table 9.3). This point can be illustrated by recent efforts to establish minimum prudential rules in international banking. These efforts gathered steam in the 1980s, after the international debt crisis and several bank failures that had immediate international spillover effects. Discussions on minimal standards took place at the Basle Committee on Banking Supervision, an intergovernmental body composed of banking regulators and central bankers from the Group of ten countries (plus Luxembourg). The initial policy proposal came out of the British policy community, which then negotiated on a bilateral basis with US authorities. Once they agreed, the question returned to the Basle Committee where a final agreement emerged.

Consistent then with Table 9.3, national policy communities were critical for defining the policy options. Policy proposals were then refined further at the national level before coming to Basle. The Basle Committee did provide, however, the basis for a transnational expert policy community drawn from national financial regulators, which was able to amend the proposal in ways that facilitated implementation in diverse banking systems. This process involved interchanges between this transnational policy community and respective national policy communities. The principal responsibility for implementation rested with the respective national policy communities, which drew on the Basle Committee for various clarifications during that process. In the absence then of autonomous supranational organizations as occur in MLG, national policy communities retain the initiative in all stages of policy making, drawing on advice and support from transnational policy communities when necessary.

Research on the impact of intergovernmental negotiations on the types of national policy networks is still somewhat limited. Studies of banking regulation focusing on the intergovernmental forums of the Basle Committee on Banking Supervision noted above suggest that corporatist policy networks found at the national level might become more formalized and juridified, and do not necessarily evolve toward pluralist forms (Coleman 1996; Moran 1991). Preliminary interviewing also suggests the possibility that state actors may become sufficiently strengthened through access to information at the supranational level that domestic policy networks might evolve from pressure pluralism to state-directed forms.

The strong place of national policy networks in intergovernmental negotiations (IGN) environments suggests that they are less likely to destabilize domestic associative orders. National authorities retain considerable flexibility to offer side payments to key players if they wish such orders to continue. Moreover, the political power that can be mobilized in such orders may be very useful in explaining to other states why certain policy options are possible and why others will compromise any ratification of an agreement.

Self-regulatory and private regimes

Over the past century as the nation state developed, certain areas of economic and social activity engendered private systems of authority. Common examples are stock exchanges, advertising, the certification and licensing of physicians, and insurance. These private systems emerged for several reasons. The specialized, technical knowledge needed for governance often lay completely within private organizations. Private actors were interested in forestalling state intervention, while recognizing that the expansion of business activity often required a broader organization of markets. As time passed, seldom did these self-regulating systems remain purely private. The state granted them official status indirectly by incorporating their decisions into other parts of the law, or directly by giving them a legal mandate to carry out self-regulation in the 'public interest'. The core organizations of these systems tended to be interest associations, and as state supervision over these private arrangements increased, they evolved into 'private interest governments' (Streeck and Schmitter 1985).

Similar private systems of authority are associated with the phenomenon of globalization. In order to organize global economic exchange while trying to minimize intervention by nation states, societal actors on the international level are setting up 'private regimes': integrated complexes of formal and informal institutions that serve as a source of governance for an area of economic, social or cultural activity (Cutler *et al.* 1999). Financial services provide clear examples of this trend: primary and secondary markets for international and Euro-bonds (Porter 1993), private arbitration services (Cutler 1995) and insurance underwriting (Haufler 1996). Similar to earlier experience within nation states, these private regimes gain a measure of legitimacy through their control over specialized knowledge.

Distinct from MLG and intergovernmental negotiations, transnational policy communities will dominate each aspect of the policy process for private regimes (see Table 9.3). Given the potentially direct governance responsibilities assumed by such policy communities and the legitimacy coming from their control of specialized knowledge, these transnational policy communities will likely be much more *tightly integrated* than those observed in the multilevel governance environment. Furthermore, the lead role played by private actors in policy formulation and implementation suggests that *clientelist policy networks* will be the dominant form. As Streeck and Schmitter (1985: 27) caution in their analysis of private interest governments, corporatist policy networks require a balance of resources, including knowledge, between state and private actors. Such a balance is more likely to be lacking in international private regimes, particularly given the absence of autonomous state-like structures at the global level.

It is less clear what impact the development of a private regime policy environment will have on domestic associative orders. In effect, such an environment is often itself likely to be anchored on a transnational associative order. Many private regimes are organized by transnational BIAs, who enter into agreements among themselves on rules for decision making. These pacts then serve as the basis for negotiating useful complementary policies implemented at the nation state level by domestic governments.

Case studies of changing policy environments and associative action

In this section, I reflect on these relationships between policy environments and associative action by focusing on two different paths of internationalization of policy environments. The first is a trajectory that goes from national autarky to an intergovernmental negotiations environment and thence to a multilevel governance one. The second follows a path from national autarky to self-regulatory and private regimes.

Case study 1: the movement from national policy environments to intergovernmental negotiations to multilevel governance

Agriculture provides a useful case for study, because the sector enjoyed a rather exceptional place in the postwar economic order, a place that sheltered agricultural production from many of the economic and political pressures emanating from the international trade regime found in other sectors. Accordingly, policy making was almost exclusively the responsibility of nation states acting in isolation from one another. For various reasons, this autarkic position came under severe strain in the late 1970s and early 1980s, bringing on a situation of 'thin' globalization by the mid-1980s (Held *et al.* 1999). We describe this change as 'thin' globalization because it includes an increase in the extensiveness of global relations in the policy realm, without much autonomous institutional development at the international level. Furthermore, the international fora were dominated for the most part by the most economically advanced states. With policy making remaining firmly in the hands of nation states, who, in turn, were meeting and engaging in policy discussions with one another, the policy environment shifts from one of national autarky to IGN. Two distinct, but clearly linked, intergovernmental organizations provided the environment for this change in policy making: the Organization for Economic Cooperation and Development (OECD) and the General Agreement on Tariffs and Trade (GATT) (Coleman 2001).

After 1986, the level of political globalization then thickens considerably. The intensification of political globalization encourages the further institutionalization of transnational policy networks. These networks depart from their long-standing domestic antecedents in being less open to the participation of non-state actors in policy making. As noted above, I describe this change as a move towards more of a MLG policy environment which is centred at the WTO, and particularly at its new Committees on Agriculture and on Sanitary and Phytosanitary Measures.

Faced with changes of these kinds, national associations will need to adapt to a situation where they participate in both national and transnational policy communities and where they need to attain some influence on transnational communities. We can think of three ways that they might adapt:

1 They can pool their resources and strengthen the organizational development of a transnational peak association.
2 They can reorganize their internal functions so as to allocate increased resources to transnational policy issues, and thereby develop a policy advocacy capacity of their own at the transnational level.
3 They can reorganize their internal functions so as to allocate increased resources to transnational policy issues so as to better influence domestic state actors participating in global policy negotiations.

Of these three possibilities, both within the EU and more broadly in the global sphere, associations have typically chosen the first and third of these approaches. Empirical observation of the EU suggests that the first path becomes more likely when transnational institutions like the European Commission take an active role in fostering the organizational development of a transnational association. The more successful of these are likely to be those that are direct membership associations at the transnational level rather than peak associations composed of national associations as members. Such logic of membership favours the definition of interests on a regional or even global level, transcending national interests. Conversely, the peak association format appears to favour the pooling of national interests, something difficult to do given the continued important differences between nation states.

As anticipated, the move toward MLG seems to give increasing importance to transnational-expert, somewhat technically-oriented policy communities. This process of change has implications for the constitution of associative orders at the national level. Streeck and Schmitter (1985) have argued that establishment of such an order requires some organizational preconditions: minimizing competition between associations for members, building up the internal resources of associations, constructing horizontal bridges between associations and increasing levels of vertical integration within the associational system. Accordingly, if the interest association system is becoming less capable of maintaining an associative order over time, we might observe this by asking whether this system features increased competition between associations for members, declining internal resources, disintegrating horizontal bridges and weakening vertical integration.

In Part II, I hypothesized that the development a MLG policy environment would destabilize domestic associative orders and trigger new types of associative action at the transnational level. I offer preliminary evidence in support of this hypothesis by focusing on the distinction between comprehensive, general associations seeking to represent the whole of agriculture and more specialized associations that represent producers of a particular commodity.

Over time, the relative importance of these two types of associations changes. The specialized associations become more important and tend to participate more in policy networks at the national level, comprising a vertical production chain, than in ones focused on agricultural commodities alone. In turn, these specialized networks then become nodes in expert transnational policy networks. These changes have an impact on self-identity of farmers, captured in the following quotation taken from an interview in France.

> I am completely convinced that we have lived through a period where all power has been concentrated on sectors (*filières*) and on specialized associations. General farm organizations have difficulty in existing, even the FNSEA and the APCA,[1] because the problems are so sectoralized that these organizations with a more global view have difficulty in coping and having their voices heard. One of the problems of French agriculture today is that under the pressure from economic interests, we have lost perspective on the general interests of agriculture at the expense of milk producers, meat producers and so on. At our meetings, people tend to express themselves by saying that 'I am a milk producer' or 'I am a cereals producer', rather than 'I am a farmer'. With this strong specialization also comes a lack of solidarity. That is to say those who are in the hog sector do not feel affected by what happens in the beef sector and vice versa.

To continue with the French example, this change in the relative influence or power of comprehensive associations versus specialized ones is also complemented by a reorientation of specialized ones, with the assistance of the state. The state has emphasized the importance of vertically organized commodity *filières* which include producers, processors, distributors, exporters and retailers (Coleman and Chiasson 2002). These vertical structures are then encouraged with various financial incentives to integrate further and to cooperate so as to increase their international competitiveness. Hence, internationalization appears to push identity away from a class or producer base of definition essential to maintaining an agricultural associative order to one of a sector more or less oriented to the international economy.

Coinciding with this change in the balance of power between general and more specialized associations is increasing competition for members between alternative general associations. As hypothesized in the section on multilevel governance, to a certain extent, these associations divide along the degree of commitment to participating in a more globalizing agri-food economy. This competition is evident in France between the Confédération Paysanne and the FNSEA, in Germany between *Land*-level associations belonging to the Deutscher Bauernverband (DBV) as well as between the DBV and the Arbeitgemeinschaft der bäuerlichen Landwirtschaft, in the US between the National Farmers Union and the American Farm Bureau Federation and in Canada between the Canadian Federation of Agriculture and the National Farmers Union. This same sort of competition also exists at the specialized or sectoral level, where some commodity groups are more favourable to liberalized trade than others. Accordingly, national-level associations become more ideological and they are drawn more into alliances with non-farmers groups organized along ideological lines, thereby undermining long-standing pacts within agriculture. Ideological differences tend to focus more and more on acceptance of, or opposition to, globalization. Needless to say, this kind of ideological competition places tremendous stress on the pre-existing associative order at the national level, while giving new life to competing international farmers' associations (Coleman 2002b).

In summary, when internationalization takes the path from national autarky to IGN and then to MLG, preliminary evidence exists for changes of the following forms:

- internal reorganization of association functions so as to privilege technical expertise relevant to working at the transnational level;
- a weakening of national associative orders;
- a reorientation of narrow, sectoral associations toward coordination with intrasectoral partners rather than with intraclass partners;
- increasing competition between general comprehensive associations, with degree of acceptance of globalization being an important cleavage line;
- increased vitality of international associations with differences mirroring to some degree those that have intensified at the domestic level.

Case study 2: the movement from national policy environments to self-regulatory private regimes

What distinguishes private regimes from the other two policy environments is the relative absence of state institutions. This path might be taken by sectors of the economy that have globalized very quickly, sufficiently so that nation states cannot keep up to the process nor exercise significant control over what is happening. The path might also be taken by sectors where state regulation has been rather weak at the nation state level as well. We move to private regimes rather than loose couplings when the concentration of economic power in corporate actors appears to be quite high (see Table 9.2). Such a process can be illustrated by the example of derivatives in the financial services sector. This sector has both of the characteristics just noted. It has globalized very rapidly over the past twenty years, and it has operated under self-regulatory, rather clientelist regimes at the nation state level (Coleman 2003).

There now exist large and growing global markets for all principal categories of financial services: bank lending, foreign exchange, money market securities, longer term debt securities, equities and derivatives. Global derivatives markets have very high notional values. A 1995 survey by the Bank for International Settlements (BIS) showed the notional amount of over-the-counter derivatives outstanding was 41 trillion dollars, while 16.4 trillion dollars were outstanding in exchange-traded derivatives. Approximately 35 per cent of these contracts were with counterparties in other countries, giving a rough approximation of the global market in derivatives (BIS-ECSC 1996: 4, 13).

Associated with the growth of these derivatives markets, as well as with the global markets in other areas of financial services, has been the development of 'integrated global financial firms with extremely complex financial and corporate structures' (G30 1997: 7). Various investigations by the General Accounting Office of the US Congress (USGAO 1994), the Group of 30 (G30 1993), the International Organization of Securities Commissions and the BIS (BIS-ECSC 1996) have all shown that the growing volume of business in global financial markets is heavily concentrated in a relatively small number of institutions. These financial conglomerates normally have a universal bank at their core and then various subsidiaries and affiliates specializing in particular markets, often functioning under divergent regulatory systems and cultures.

Derivatives appear to fit better with the concept of globalization (transcending of borders) rather than internationalization (intensification of cross-border relations). Certainly, governance of firms engaged in derivatives markets is difficult to conceptualize in an internationalizing context. Such a context assumes that activity can be located in a given nation state and that transactions will take place across borders. Because derivatives are hedges against various sorts of market risk in particular, their whole purpose is to abstract the risk out of given spatial and temporal contexts. In creating opportunities to protect against losses and other risks involved in conducting business across borders, they are at once coping mechanisms for globalization and contributors to globalization. Where this abstraction process takes place on an institutionalized exchange, that exchange can become a site for regulation and oversight. The majority of derivatives contracts, however, take place over-the-counter which means their location is best understood to be with the transacting parties, who may be operating anywhere in the world.

Private regimes are the dominant organizational form for monitoring and supervising risk in derivatives markets (Coleman 2003). Within these regimes, business associations have assumed an important self-regulatory, governance role. The Basle Committee on Banking Supervision (BCBS) and the International Organization of Securities Commissions (IOSCO) cooperated with firms to provide guidelines on disclosure and risk management in 1994, but these are voluntary in character and are not part of the formal intergovernmental accord on capital adequacy. The same year, the UK and the US reached an agreement on how to oversee over the counter (OTC) derivatives transactions, a minimal intergovernmental step. These efforts are complemented by the Master Agreement on trading that the International Swap Dealers and Derivatives Association (ISDA) promotes among its members. It was first announced in 1987 and was subsequently amended in 1992 and 1998. The Futures Industry Association (FIA), the representative body of the derivatives sector in the US, worked out a series of recommendations on 'financial integrity' in 1995. Derivatives firms also agreed in 1995 upon a 'Framework for Voluntary Oversight' of their own activities that is relevant to credit and operational risk.

Moreover, within financial services more generally, there is an important shift in regulatory philosophy that involves devolving authority on financial services firms. The change in philosophy on the part of governmental authorities was evident in documents released by the BCBS in 1995 in response to criticisms of its initial proposals to control market risk. In response to globalizing conditions, financial services supervisors have decided they will need to rely more on firms' own risk management information systems to protect against losses. Hence their activities have come to focus more on firms' internal procedures rather than on after-the-fact results summarized on balance sheets. In response to this changed situation, the Group of 30 (1997: 12) has urged global financial institutions themselves to take the lead in developing risk assessment frameworks. The Basle Committee has welcomed this advice and has begun to work closely with financial services firms on risk management protocols. Its approach is to identify 'best practice' and to publicize these widely. Reflecting a certain faith in market discipline, it believes that the markets will reward those firms whose practices are up-to-date and come closest to these ideal types (Padoa-Schioppa 1997).

In summary, the governance of cross-border and global financial markets features significantly more self-regulation and delegation of responsibility to financial services firms than was common at the nation state level. As globalization has proceeded, these 'private regime' characteristics of global financial governance have become more, rather than less, prominent. Some of the governance role is assumed by business associations, organized around a global-wide domain of global firms. Other aspects of the role are assumed directly by these global firms themselves.

The adequacy of these arrangements has surfaced as a concern among the world's economic powers, especially after the Asian crisis. Some have reflected on giving the IMF lender of last resort responsibilities (*Financial Times* 1998; Krugman 1998). Others have called for the creation of a global financial services regulatory capability, perhaps housed at the IMF or World Bank (Martin 1998). For now, however, there is no public institution available with the capacity to provide any further guarantees of prudential behaviour. Nor is there sufficient governance capacity to cope quickly and well with a systemic financial crisis on a global scale. In this respect, the arrangements do not conform to the Streeck and Schmitter (1985) notion of private interest government, a notion that presumed some strong state authority keeping the shotgun behind the door, in case self-regulatory organizations became too self-regarding. Rather, in the absence of the equivalent of state authority at the global level, the associations are operating in something resembling global clientelist policy networks.

In summary, in some areas where globalization is taking place very rapidly or where state control and regulation at the nation state level was minimized in favour of self-regulation, self-regulatory and private regimes policy environments appear to be developing at the global level. Moreover, the kinds of pacts and informal understandings that are developing among the various associations and firms conform well to the contingent and strategic interdependence identified by Streeck and Schmitter (1985: 11) as characteristic of an associative order. These environments offer a place for governance to both international associations like the ISDA and even to national associations like the FIA (which has begun to accept non-US members). These environments encourage the development of clientelist policy networks where associations with global membership domains appear to dominate policy making at the expense of state actors. These changes also have impacts on domestic associations. As the example of the FIA shows, some of these will be tempted to open their membership broadly to foreign firms and to remove membership distinctions between domestic and foreign members. As such, they assume a role in these transnational networks. In other instances, domestic associations may lose relevance, if they are not participants in the emerging transnational associative order. Member firms come to rely more on domestic and transnational associations taking on a governance role at the global level.

Conclusion

Based upon this analysis of preliminary data, four tentative hypotheses deserve further study when it comes to globalization and the associative action of business. Each refers to a different effect of the internationalization of policy making.

1. Domestic-level associations will reorganize internal structures in order to increase their knowledge and expertise in areas of global policy making. They will also reorient some of their policy advocacy activities, and the resources devoted to these activities, towards state actors negotiating new frameworks for policy at the transnational level.
2. As ideological and economic conflicts become externalized to international policy arenas, the pacts that gave rise to domestic associative orders will be undermined as understandings of strategic interdependence change.
3. As autonomous policy-making activity develops at the global level in MLG policy environments, and as this activity comes to be framed in terms of international law, associations with international membership domains, particularly those where corporations join directly rather than indirectly through membership in a domestic association, will increase in relative importance.
4. As the preceding changes continue apace, existing associative orders at the domestic level will continue to be destabilized. Some may collapse completely. Under particular conditions to be determined, they may be replaced by associative orders organized at the transnational level.

Each of these hypotheses does suggest that the internationalization of policy making is having potentially profound effects on business associability at the start of the twenty-first century.

Note

1 Fédération Nationale des Syndicats d'Exploitants Agricoles (FNSEA) and Assemblée Permanente des Chambres d'Agriculture (APCA).

References

Bank for International Settlements (BIS)-ECSC (Euro-currency Standing Committee) (1996) *Proposals for Improving Global Derivatives Markets Statistics*, Basle: ECSC.

Coleman W. (1996) *Financial Services, Globalization and Domestic Policy Change: A Comparison of North America and the European Union*, London: Macmillan.

Coleman, W. (2001) 'Policy Networks, Non-state Actors and Internationalized Policy-Making: A Case Study of Agricultural Trade', in D. Josselin and W. Wallace (eds) *Non-State Actors in World Politics*, Houndmills, Basingstoke: Palgrave, pp. 93–112.

Coleman, W. (2002a) 'Policy Networks', in *International Encyclopedia of the Social and Behavioral Sciences*, Oxford: Pergamon, pp. 11608–11613.

Coleman, W. (2002b) 'Globality and Transnational Policy-making in Agriculture: Complexity, Contradictions, and Conflict', Paper presented to a conference on the Reconfiguration of Authority in the twenty-first Century, Technische Universität Munich, 18–19 October 2002.

Coleman, W. (2003) 'Governing Global Finance: Financial Derivatives, Liberal States and Transformative Capacity', in L. Weiss (ed.) *States in the Global Economy: Bringing Domestic Institutions Back In*, Cambridge: Cambridge University Press.

Coleman, W. and Chiasson, C. (2002) 'State Power, Transformative Capacity and Resisting Globalization: An Analysis of French Agricultural Policy, 1960–2000', *Journal of European Public Policy*, April.

Coleman, W. and Perl, A. (1999) 'Internationalized Policy Environments and Policy Network Analysis', *Political Studies* XLVII (4): 691–709.

Cutler, A. C. (1995) 'Global Capitalism and Liberal Myths: Dispute Settlement in Private International Trade Relations', *Millennium: Journal of International Studies* 24: 377–397.

Cutler, A. C., Haufler, V. and Porter, T. (1999) 'Private Authority and Global Governance', in A. C. Cutler, V. Haufler and T. Porter (eds) *Private Authority in International Affairs*, New York, Albany: State University of New York Press.

Dowding, K. (1995) 'Model or Metaphor? A Critical Review of the Policy Network Approach', *Political Studies* 43: 136–158.

Eising, R. and Kohler-Koch, B. (1994) 'Inflation und Zerfaserung: Trends der Interessenvermittelung in der Europäischen Gemeinschaft', in W. Streeck (ed.) *Staat und Verbände*, Opladen: Westdeutscher Verlag.

Financial Times (1998) 'Reforming Finance', 11 May.

Grande, E. (1996) 'The State and Interest Groups in a Framework of Multi-level Decision-making: The Case of the European Union', *Journal of European Public Policy* 3: 318–338.

Group of 30 (1993) 'Derivatives: Practices and Principles', Washington DC: Group of 30.

Group of 30 (1997) 'Global Institutions, National Supervision and Systemic Risk', Washington/DC: Group of 30.

Haufler, V. (1996) *Dangerous Commerce*, Ithaca NY: Cornell University Press.

Held, D., McGrew, A., Goldblatt, D. and Perraton, J. (1999) *Global Transformations: Politics, Economics and Culture*, Stanford CA: Stanford University Press.

Krugman, P. (1998) 'Start Taking the Prozac', *Financial Times*, 9 April: 16.

Martin, P. (1998) 'Statement Prepared for the Interim Committee of the IMF', Speech distributed by Finance Canada, Ottawa, 16 April.

Moran, M. (1991) *Politics of the Financial Services Revolution*, London: Macmillan.

Padoa-Schioppa, T. (1997) 'Market-friendly Regulation of Banks: An International Perspective', in D. Duwendag (ed.) *Szenarien der Europäischen Währungsunion und der Bankenregulierung*, Berlin: Duncker and Humblot.

Pappi, F.-U. and Schnorpfeil, W. (1995) 'Das Ausschusswesen der Europäischen Kommission: Grundstrukturen und Kommunikationsmöglichkeiten für Verbände', in T. König, E. Rieger and H. Schmitt (eds) *Das europäische Mehrebenensystem*, Frankfurt, Campus: pp. 135–159.

Porter, T. (1993) *States, Markets and Regimes in Global Finance*, Basingstoke: Macmillan.

Putnam, R. D. (1988) 'Diplomacy and Domestic Politics: The Logic of Two-level Games', *International Organization* 42: 427–460.

Streeck, W. and Schmitter, P. (1985) 'Community, Market, State and Associations?', in W. Streeck and P. Schmitter (eds) *Private Interest Government*, London: Sage, pp. 1–29.

Streeck, W. and Schmitter, P. (1991) 'From National Corporatism to Transnational Pluralism: Organized Interests in the Single European Market', *Politics and Society* 19: 133–164.

USGAO (United States General Accounting Office) (1994) *Financial Derivatives: Actions Needed to Protect the Financial System*, Washington: USGAO.

Waarden, F. van (1992) 'Dimensions and Types of Policy Networks', *European Journal of Political Research* 21: 29–52.

10 International governance by organized business

The shifting roles of firms, associations and intergovernmental organizations in self-regulation

Karsten Ronit

With the internationalization of the economy over the last several decades, demands for the regulation of business have increased significantly. In this context, a key issue is whether states have surrendered authority to expanding market forces, or whether they have the capacity to control the complex movement of money, goods and services and to develop relevant devices to maintain or improve established regulatory models.

In cases, however, where domestic resources are not available or exhausted, the concerted efforts of states can be wheeled in as an alternative. Given the already existing number of intergovernmental organizations, cooperation between states has been highly institutionalized within many policy fields, and thus, these organizations form a relevant platform for the formulation of new strategies and the adoption of regulations to monitor and influence the operation of international market forces. Although this debate is not focused on the capacity of single states but rather on the processes of negotiation among states – or the creative role of autonomous intergovernmental organizations – the emphasis is still on various forms of public authority. In other words, discourse on the role of intergovernmental organizations in the area of economic issues largely takes place within the framework of a 'state-market dichotomy'.

A third, but less observed possibility is that of international governance through various civil society movements and institutions. However, only a relatively small fraction of those non-governmental organizations that have been studied are concerned with economic problems. Instead, other policy fields, such as humanitarian or environmental issues, have been investigated. Little space is left for the analysis of business, even though the social and political organization of business is an important but underestimated element of civil society that also plays a significant role in the institutionalization of markets. Thus, the international economy does not simply consist of the free and uncoordinated activity of individual firms. Indeed, in many cases, business develops rules within a collective framework, which not only govern the market but also have wider consequences and contribute to societal problem-solving.

There are numerous ways in which business can provide such solutions, but in many domestic and international contexts, business can build upon a rich tradition of associability. Accordingly, associations are the primary candidates for organizing and accommodating different interests among firms. They can develop rules that members comply with in such a way that these arrangements provide a functional equivalent to public authority through states and intergovernmental organizations or the rule of spontaneous market forces. In other words, business can regulate itself within a negotiated institutionalized framework.

Conventional approaches to economics and business administration ignore such arrangements, and tend to claim that this is an impossible exercise given the individualistic creed of the business world. However, there is no reason to exclude the possibility that business harbours this potential, and that such self-regulatory endeavours at the domestic and international levels are welcomed and even encouraged by states and intergovernmental organizations.

In this chapter, we shall first draw attention to the general role of associations in politics. The study of business interest associations has undergone an interesting development, where the original focus on national forms of associability has been expanded to include a comparative and international dimension. This shows that there is a stable organizational basis for political action, including the management of self-regulation as a specific form of associative order at different territorial levels. Other forms of collective action are also available in business and can play a role in private regulation, but associations seem, prima facie, to be best suited to run such arrangements.

In a next step, we shall therefore examine associational models and other formats of business self-regulation in domestic and international settings, where arrangements can be mutually reinforcing. Indeed, international governance appears stronger in cases where some kind of national underpinnings exist. One of the perennial questions of self-regulation in all of these contexts is whether such arrangements can be designed and sustained by corporations and their associations, or whether assistance from relevant interlocutors is necessary to guarantee their survivability – and whether they would crumble away without it. Thus, a key question in international self-regulation is whether intergovernmental organizations have a sufficiently strong public authority to encourage and monitor private regulation, or whether this capacity is only available at national levels. In particular, we shall scrutinize the conditions that make efficient self-regulation feasible and examine which forms of legitimacy support it and make it democratically desirable.

In doing so, we shall also highlight the efforts of some important general organizations like the European Union (EU), the United Nations (UN) and the Organization for Economic Cooperation and Development (OECD) and specific agencies, such as the World Health Organization (WHO), the International Civil Aviation Organization (ICAO) and the International Maritime Organization (IMO) that are relevant for specific sectors of the economy. In the last three cases, emphasis will also be placed on relevant business organizations, such as the International Federation of Pharmaceutical Manufacturers Associations (IFPMA), the International Air Transport Association (IATA) and the International Chamber of Shipping (ICS).

Many intergovernmental organizations today are attentive to the role of alternative governance mechanisms beyond market and state. This group even includes self-regulation by businesses, and shows that there is an increasing general political acknowledgement of organized business as a relevant contributor to international governance. Therefore, in the concluding section, we will critically evaluate the role of business self-regulation through corporations and business interest associations in international governance and discuss the part that intergovernmental organizations play in the creation and maintenance of private regulation across different policy fields.

Domestic, comparative and international studies of organized business

Only a few decades ago, organized business was studied primarily in a national context. The international operations of large corporations were scrutinized in a broad body of literature spanning different social sciences, whereas the organization of business through associations as a specific type of formal organization was sidelined, and only in the best of cases, treated as an issue of domestic politics. In the late 1970s, however, an international comparative project on the organization of business interests was launched (Schmitter and Streeck 1981) and became the most encompassing scheme up to that time to study the organization of business in a cross-national and cross-sectoral perspective. The study was also an attempt to qualify the debate on neo-corporatism. Until then, this debate had focused upon – and was often associated with – labour market tripartism, the design of national institutions of economic policy making and the development of political cultures of compromise at the systemic level.

The project added new dimensions to the study of organized business, where conflicting interests are mitigated and disciplined to represent collective interests. The study dealt primarily with countries in Western Europe – i.e. countries with a distinct tradition of organizing interests in a collective framework – thus indicating that European traditions of associability were not necessarily generalizable to other regions of the world. However, analyses stressed that even in Europe, strong variation existed in the patterns of business collective action, and that cooperation in a regional context had to reconcile different styles of associational behaviour in politics. In other words, international business associations must cope with a high degree of national heterogeneity.

A few aspects of internationalization were integrated into the design and subsequently discussed in empirical analyses. The first aspect was that of the industries or sectors studied. Here, selection criteria were established to include sectors characterized by domestic or international ownership, production and operation – and, to a more limited extent, regulation – of firms. The chemical industry clearly stands out as a paradigm case of an international (or rather, global) sector, but it seems that its global character was first fully recognized in the process of analysing it. Since the analysis of the chemical industry was completed relatively late, it apparently had little impact on the study of other sectors. The second aspect included the territorial levels that were investigated. Primary focus was placed on the national and subnational levels and the role of regions (Coleman and Jacek 1989). However, with a comparative focus, too little space was left for examining other territorial levels beyond the nation state (e.g. Sargent 1985). The European and global levels were mentioned occasionally, but in such cases these levels were rather 'tacked on' and rarely addressed per se. In a number of later works, building upon some of these experiences, the international dimension was treated more profoundly (e.g. Hollingsworth and Streeck 1994).

It may seem a bit ironic today that business – which is a very internationalized interest category – was conceived of mainly as a national or a comparative phenomenon, and that few aspects concerning the international organization of business were considered. Indeed, it is reasonable to ask whether a stronger orientation towards the international dimension was even possible and justified at that time. Such an act of 'self-subversion' is always useful in social science (Hirschman 1995), and may be helpful when tracing the early roots of international business associability.

When pointing to these deficiencies in the so far largest concerted effort to investigate the organization of business, we should bear in mind that in the early 1980s, we were still in the age of 'Euro-sclerosis', which gave little impetus to study the role of business associations in the not very dynamic process of European integration. Although European business associability soon became an important factor in the integration process associated with the Single European Act, scholarly interest was limited, at least until the early 1990s. Since then, our knowledge of European business associations has grown considerably. The flip side of the coin, however, is that much contemporary research into the problem of Europeanization is effectively sealed off from the general question of internationalization. In other words, a significant step has been taken to analyse business beyond the field of comparative politics, but unfortunately, little progress has been made towards analysing associability in a wider international or even global context. This tendency to introduce a kind of Euro-centrism is extremely problematic given the pronounced internationalization of business and the fact that, from a historical perspective, business was thinking in broad categories of internationalization early on, rather than simply in terms of Europeanization.

Ideas and inspiration concerning the involvement of global business associations in politics can, however, be found in studies that do not deal with associations in particular but rather with transnational relations more generally, or with various aspects of international political economy. Transnational relations take a keen interest in the organization of civil society, but in this tradition, the existence of organized business is often ignored or marginalized. In traditions that study the international economy, the economic and political organization of markets is discussed, but business associations have no prominent role in this field of research. Without going into further details on the reasons for this negligence of organized business, we can offer various explanations relating to the state of research and the political scene. One explanation stresses that these new traditions, briefly referred to, originally emerged in North America, where business associations were – and still are – comparatively weak, and where research is therefore inattentive to or not particularly well trained in examining the phenomenon of business associability. Another explanation emphasizes the ambitions of governments and various social movements to monitor the activities of business, especially in the Third World. In this context, large corporations are easily identified, whereas associations generally lead a very anonymous life. Accordingly, international business became synonymous with multinational corporations.

Although the study of global business associations is far less developed than that of domestic or regional (mainly European) associations, there actually is a growing interest in the representation of global industries (Braithwaite and Drahos 2000; Greenwood and Jacek 2000; Ronit and Schneider 1999). Examples show that business is a recognized interest category that is granted consultative status by a number of intergovernmental organizations. All these bodies have a preference for interacting with larger and representative associations and do not establish formal relations with multinational corporations or other actors whose primary objectives are of an economic and commercial nature. At the same time, associations are also being challenged to impose a certain degree of self-discipline in order to become reliable partners.

However, international business associations do not only engage in exchanges with relevant intergovernmental organizations in the formulation and implementation of public policy. Associations carry out private and independent rule-making in a way that is generally recognized, officially welcomed and sometimes even encouraged by intergovernmental organizations. Such practices are not always of recent origin and have not evolved entirely in a global setting; rather, they may predate the most recent processes of internationalization as well as building upon already established forms of national self-regulation. To understand international arrangements and the conditions under which they emerge, we shall first explore the development of self-regulation in a national context and then discuss some cases of international self-regulation.

Self-regulation in domestic and international contexts

Business self-regulation at the national level has been examined both in comparative public policy and in comparative interest group studies. In general, business is seen as being guided by self-interest and consequently, the intriguing question is: under what circumstances can this interest be compatible with or powered by the public interest? It is commonly agreed that various institutional and historical factors play a role, but these factors are not necessarily spelled out in each and every case.

Although the deep historical roots of regulating economy and society have not necessarily been traced (see Black 1984; Wiener 1999), historical traditions are considered important. Accordingly, self-regulation is understood in the overall context of the regulatory traditions that characterize a given country, since there must be a fertile industrial, administrative and political ground for the development of such mechanisms of governance.

Before political and academic interest in self-regulation took an upswing towards the latter part of the 1990s, the role of self-regulatory bodies in domestic settings has been discussed in different historical contexts in modern times (Merriam 1944; McConnell 1966; Ronge 1980). The discussion was developed more systematically beginning in the early 1980s, when a new set of tools was made available under the umbrella term of 'private interest government' (Streeck and Schmitter 1985; Schmitter 1990). These tools were used to analyse the contribution of associations to social order, and thus formed part of a general ambition to further develop the paradigm of neo-corporatism and the emergence of a new or unrecognized form of governance alongside those of the state, market and community. In this body of literature, self-regulation became specifically related to the role of interest groups. In addition, general theories on economic sociology and transaction cost economics were included in order to explain the institutional mechanisms behind self-regulation within organized business (Campbell *et al.* 1991; Hollingsworth, Schmitter and Streeck 1994).

Self-regulation has been explored in different empirical contexts, with a number of interesting analyses being directed towards specific industries. These studies have revealed different capabilities for self-regulation across industrial sectors and countries (Grant 1987; Martinelli 1991; Boddewyn 1992; Knill and Lehmkuhl 2002). However, the information provided is too limited to reach any general conclusions about the advantages of certain sectors or associational structures in fostering such arrangements. But it has been well documented that self-regulation as a specific form of associational order is characterized by some common features. 'Private interest governments' are sustainable in cases where associations fulfil certain basic criteria; thus, some of the key preconditions for establishing and running such arrangements are: a near monopoly in the organization of a given interest category; avoidance of an unacceptable degree of free-riding; the capacity to enforce rules and achieve compliance amongst members; and, last but not least, sufficient power to sanction violations of these rules and – in the best of cases – eliminate problems caused by outside mavericks.

Private interest governments must possess a number of vital properties and manage various associational dynamics, but factors in their environment are also of primary importance. Although associations governing private arrangements are seen as an alternative system of order, in cases where voluntary action is required, they generally need some degree of recognition or licensing from the state. This official delegation of public authority to private actors shows that the state itself is surrendering authority, and that alternative power structures are deliberately being encouraged outside the realm of political institutions.

The ability of states and associations to build domestic arrangements varies across sectors and countries, but it mainly exists in fields with mature traditions of associability as well as an established record of cooperation between state and business associations. In principle, other actors can also participate in such arrangements, but the involvement of interest groups representing – for instance – countervailing groups in society, such as consumers, environmentalists or workers, is generally not considered. Given this pattern, it is no surprise that self-regulation is well documented in the industrialized world, which has a higher degree of associability and a relationship between state and organized interests that is conducive to private governance. Unfortunately, we know little about the relevance and enforcement of self-regulation in other regions of the world.

In most studies the existence of an international dimension and an overarching system of regulation uniting the different national associations is sidestepped or briefly mentioned as something peripheral to the existence of self-regulatory bodies. Even in cases where it would have been obvious to include the international dimension as a possible framework for analysing domestic arrangements (Ronit 2001), this is rarely considered. For example, the highly globalized chemical industry – which actually possesses a strong tradition of national self-regulation – would have been an interesting case. This, however, does not suggest that there is a simple relationship between national and international self-regulation. Although international self-regulation must necessarily be implemented at national levels, whereas national forms of private regulation do not always have an international superstructure, existing national arrangements are not integrated into wider international arrangements in every case. Instead, globalization may erode existing patterns of private authority (Coleman and Underhill 1998). Where linkages between territorial forms of self-regulation can be traced, the specific balance between territorial levels must be carefully examined.

In sum, most studies on national self-regulation emphasize the crucial role of business interest associations that have the organizational capacity to design and enforce rule systems. At the same time, however, a vital role is also attributed to states, in the shadow of which an associative order can be established. Elements of collective action as well as of public authority are deemed decisive to effective problem-solving. What is not included, however, is the international perspective. To understand business self-regulation as a specific form of international governance, we must therefore consult another body of literature.

More than ever, national forms of private authority are not an isolated phenomenon, but rather a development to be placed within the broader framework of international governance. Indeed, private authority at the global level is not quite new – dating back at least to the last century, although at that time it was not as widespread (Ronit and Schneider 2000). In those days, demands for global rule systems were met – at least in part – through the regulatory efforts of emerging intergovernmental organizations (Murphy 1994).

In scholarly work, the idea that private organizations can play a crucial role in global politics was long neglected or doubted, since from a state-centric perspective, the exercise of public functions through self-regulation seemed problematic.

In more and more cases, governance beyond government is analysed and prescribed but still scepticism prevails as to whether self-regulation is manageable with or without the involvement of public authority, and how private and public actors must engage in arrangements where tasks are shared (see Reinicke 1998: 92).

A growing interest in analysing interest group activity in global politics could potentially confirm this view. If the interest groups are merely interpreted as 'pressure groups', they are hardly being recognized as stable players in the policy process, and there is less chance that they will be delegated tasks and become involved in self-regulation. Further strengthening this view is the bias in the study of international interest groups, where the major focus is on relatively weak and under-resourced groups, and where the role of organized business is largely ignored.

Early analyses of non-governmental organizations in international governance concentrated on regulatory developments in specific industries. The shipping industry, for instance, standardized its rules around the globe in order to avoid state intervention – although self-regulation was not always practised through associations proper (Marx 1953). However, few attempts were made to generalize this experience through comparative studies of different industries, and more coherent theories were not formulated.

Today, the variable forms of private authority are scrutinized mainly in relation to regime theory in the field of international relations studies, and in investigations into international cartels and other forms of economic coordination within the international political economy tradition (see Cutler *et al.* 1999). In the first case, inspiration has been sought in the branch of regime theory focusing on interstate cooperation, whereas in the latter case, research has been inspired by studies of networks and alliances in the global economy. However, major emphasis is also placed on the role of multinational corporations that establish their own internal rules and ethics in a global economy (Haufler 2001). Here, we find business self-regulation as a functionally equivalent alternative to public regulation. Problems raised in this line of research are primarily related to the role of international or global organizations, and only occasionally deal with national forms of business coordination (Hollingsworth 1998).

In these traditions, a general search for intermediary structures beyond market and state has begun. Contributions have borrowed from and built upon approaches in management theory, transaction cost economics and economic sociology, where the concepts of markets, hierarchies and networks have been applied, although they are not related to any particular territorial level of regulation. Another source of inspiration has been early historical forms of self-regulation, such as the rules applying to members of national guilds and fairs. In part, studies on global governance make reference to these early forms of self-regulation in the context of the 'new medievalism' (Milgrom *et al.* 1990; Greif *et al.* 1994). Regimes and cartel-like cooperation cannot necessarily be posited as the two extremes of private authority, but they are mentioned here as forms of private coordination that has received attention in the literature. Private regimes seem to be more related to political processes; they are often closely linked to and actively assist intergovernmental organizations and vice versa (Haufler 1993). Cartel-like forms of cooperation are, on the other hand, closer to the market sphere. In this way, the different organizational formats of private authority can be identified between the governance systems of state and market. However, attempts have also been made to show that private authority can be a key feature of global governance but is found in other areas not closely related to business (see for example Hall and Biersteker 2002).

All in all, there is a potential for creating mechanisms for self-regulation in a very broad range of business organizations, so that the ability to regulate is not restricted to a specific group of organizations, such as associations. Contrary to many myths about the individualistic creed and lack of societal perspective in business life, this fact provides evidence that rules are being adopted at the international level – which, perhaps, is not that surprising after all, given the true international nature of many industries.

Research into international self-regulation identifies many of the same features found in the literature on self-regulatory arrangements in domestic settings. Coherent organizations, and the ability to achieve compliance among the membership, sanction non-compliant behaviour and avoid free-riding, are stressed as some of the key conditions of international self-regulation. However, as more formats are generally being interpreted as self-regulating, the conditions for creating and managing efficient self-regulation are also becoming more diffuse. Thus, it is not always clear whether self-regulation is merely a rule system adopted and enforced by private actors, or whether there should necessarily be a public interest dimension involved. If this aspect is missing – and too many cases of private coordination, agreement and control are accepted unquestioningly as 'self-regulation', the concept of self-regulation becomes diluted. In the most extreme cases, exploitative behaviour by large firms or cartels could pass as self-regulation. Consequently, it is necessary to analyse whether and to what extent self-regulation represents collusive behaviour, or whether a public dimension is included that goes beyond simple rhetoric.

So far, the empirical evidence that is available concerning international self-regulation with a public dimension is still rather limited, and only relatively few sectors have been investigated. As a matter of fact, our knowledge of private regulation at this level is still restricted compared to studies on domestic arrangements. Studies on domestic self-regulation have shown that there is considerable variation across industries and countries. It is fully consistent with these experiences to claim that territoriality also matters – in particular because public authority is unequally distributed across territorial levels. A point of departure for studies on international self-regulation is the differing character and quality of public authority and thus, the different conditions for legitimizing and monitoring private arrangements through various intergovernmental organizations.

As yet, there is no systematic evidence as to which branches or industries – or which organizational formats – are best suited to host such international self-regulatory arrangements, or what their limitations are. In sum, however, arrangements seem to be generated to a relatively large extent by voluntary action at the level of single corporations and collective entities.

Although the voluntary element is also important in the study of domestic regulation, public authority is always present. Intergovernmental organizations, however, are not necessarily involved in the process of private regulation: they do not appear to encourage the formation of private institutions in the very same way, nor do they always become involved in active monitoring. Apparently, national and international self-regulation also differ from one another in relation to which actors in the business world have a potential for private regulation. A plethora of actor units are available on the international scene. Unlike associations in a domestic setting, this common form of business collective action is not viewed as having specific advantages in terms of enforcing codes and becoming recognized by public authority. International associations may have specific qualities but are not a key object of investigation.

We have now discussed existing approaches to self-regulation and have found both commonalities and differences regarding the role played by business interest associations and the degree to which arrangements are established by autonomous business initiatives or imposed from above by public authorities. It is now time to explore how self-regulation unfolds at the international level in a period of economic and political internationalization where new forms of governance are required. In the next section, we will focus our attention on the role of intergovernmental organizations and their strategies vis-à-vis the business community, self-regulatory initiatives launched by various industries and which organizational formats have the relevant governance resources to become involved in this specific form of private regulation beyond the state and market levels.

Governance and self-regulation as strategy and practice

Intergovernmental organizations have become increasingly conscious of the resources that non-governmental organizations have at their disposal, to the extent that these are more systematically accounted for in the formation of public policy. On only a few occasions, however, has their self-regulatory potential been examined (see UNCTAD 1996). But in the case of both general and specific agencies, we do indeed find programmatic references to the role of a variety of private actors and their functions in governance. The role of these private organizations was never limited to policy formulation, but greater emphasis is now being placed on their extended role in the implementation of policies.

The European Union – and especially the Commission – and their projects and initiatives have in recent years been criticized for their technocratic and elitist character. In response to this criticism, institutional reforms were deemed necessary to secure participation, transparency, accountability, etc. At the same time, the many economic, administrative and political resources available in civil society should be exploited to enhance the legitimacy of the European integration process. Mindful of these challenges, in 2001, the Commission published its White Paper on European Governance, which envisaged new forms of governance, existing partly outside the established institutional framework of the European Union (EU Commission 2001a).

In this way, and expressed in very simple terms, the European integration process first built on and celebrated the market as the key mode of governance manifested through the Single European Act; this was followed by the public regulation of integration, and manifested increasingly within different sectors. Only more recently has the debate focused on the issue of legitimacy and democratic deficits (Grote and Gbipki 2002). According to the White Paper, European governance should include the stronger participation of voluntary civil society organizations in the policy-making process. However, the Paper does not specify what role is to be attributed to business, but the principle that relevant stakeholder interests should be guaranteed participation basically applies to all groups in society. That the role of organized business is not made explicit in this context is probably due to the fact that business is already an extremely well organized interest category at the European level and that business is generally integrated into public policy-making (Greenwood 2002). Other groups are less self-reliant and resourceful and need assistance from European institutions – which, guided by their own interests, seek to legitimize the integration process by integrating different societal groups. While there is a strong element of rhetoric in the official approaches to European governance, it would nevertheless be wrong to write-off the recent attempts to establish a new governance agenda as nothing more than rhetoric and as having no practical consequences.

A civic perspective also suggests that tasks that cannot be dealt with in horizontal policy-making, where all relevant interests are consulted, may be delegated to organized interest groups at appropriate territorial levels within the European Union. In a few cases, it has been mentioned that self-regulation belongs to the new repertoire of governance, since:

> legislation is often only part of a broader solution combining formal rules with other non-binding tools such as recommendations, guidelines, or even self-regulation within a commonly agreed framework. This highlights the need for close coherence between the use of different policy instruments and for more thought to be given to their selection.
>
> (EU Commission 2001a: 20)

Accordingly, the White Paper carefully considers alternatives to public regulation.[1]

Examples of self-regulation are not always of recent origin, but have evolved without any programmatic background (Greenwood and Ronit 1991). A intriguing problem in the context of business self-regulation is, therefore, whether future arrangements can be designed from above and based upon some of the recently formulated principles, or whether business prefers to run such private regulation independently and without the participation of countervailing powers, such as the environmental or consumer movements. According to the new visions expressed in the White Paper, all affected interests should ideally be involved, but implementation is more complex, and such a practice cannot be taken for granted. To the extent that the European Union insists that private business regulation arrangements include citizens groups, a strong effort is therefore necessary.

Although this document reflects a regional and European debate on various aspects of citizen participation, it also draws on a wider international discussion on governance which is reflected in the programmes and initiatives of many other international organizations. Thus, the problem of governance is central to many international organizations today starting with the United Nations, which launched a major initiative with its report on global governance in the mid-1990s (Commission on Global Governance 1995). At the global level, this report recognizes that the world can neither be governed by the marketplace, nor through the cooperation of states. Other forms of governance must be activated. Enter a variety of civil society institutions and the business sector. In this context, an important role is attributed to international business – which in some cases can be a serious challenge to democracy, but at the same time hosts profound governance potential. In more concrete terms, international business can become a key force in international problem-solving, either at the level of single corporations, or at the level of networks or associations where problem-solving is coordinated.

The UN, however, is not in a position to implement these mechanisms in a top-down fashion across different policy fields and industries. In business, much depends upon relevant international associations and other outlets representing concrete industries, but the debate on governance can impact on various business arrangements as well as on the negotiations between business, various countervailing groups and intergovernmental organizations. It is a rather discursive framework that different actors and interests address, but as such, it has also played an important role and has been linked to other issues such as sustainable development, in which industry-wide self-regulation has become a battleground between the chemical industry and environmental groups.

The United Nations has been concerned with the economic and social responsibility of business for many years. As early as the 1970s, a Code of Conduct on Transnational Corporations was negotiated, and a number of other initiatives for monitoring the behaviour of corporations were launched. For a number of years to follow, however, the role of business played no significant role on the agenda of the organization. But beginning in the 1990s, the regulation of business has found a new role and been rephrased in the discussion on global governance.

The self-regulatory aspect also receives attention in this context. Encouragement given to business to establish and enforce rules of conduct is still rather vague and unspecific, but there is a growing awareness of the social responsibility of business. Accordingly, many international conferences and meetings that followed the report on global governance have emphasized the demand for new rules regulating international business. Indeed, citizens groups can legitimize their claims with reference to UN documents, and at the same time, business groups can argue that private regulation is fully compatible with international standards of responsible business behaviour – at least at the level of individual corporations. In this way, public authority at the global level has again framed the discourse on international business regulation – without, however, taking part in the concrete designing of specific forms of regulation, including norms at the firm level or at the level of international associations. This task has primarily been assumed by other intergovernmental organizations in various policy fields, as we shall see below.

Turning to a third general international organization – but one that is less global in character and outside the UN-family – the OECD is also occupied with various governance problems relating to macroeconomic policy and a range of specific policy fields. This is an organization that has a global outlook, but which is primarily concerned with the affluent regions of the world from where its members come. In other words, the OECD represents countries where international business is strong and well organized, and where there are strong public authorities with a capacity to play an active role vis-à-vis the national and international business community.

In 1976, the OECD adopted its Guidelines for Multinational Enterprises, which were revised in 2000, and which member countries, as well as a group of non-member countries, could apply at the national level. This initiative was aimed at public rather than private regulation, but was intended to affect business behaviour. Some aspects of implementation would nevertheless remain a private affair; however, business did not accede to these guidelines. Apparently, the time was not ripe for such initiatives, and in the business world, attempts to profile corporations with a social and environmental responsibility were not in vogue. Nor were relevant business interest associations at the international level willing to persuade their members to adopt codes under these circumstances.

Like all other intergovernmental organizations, the OECD has, in recent years, been involved in the general discussion on governance. Thus, in May 1999, its ministers endorsed the OECD Principles of Corporate Governance. These principles – which were prepared by various OECD committees and received input from other intergovernmental organizations as well as the business world – emphasize that corporations must work for societal goals and take the interests of broader constituencies into account. To this end, a number of regional round tables has been established, and a dialogue between the public and private sectors has been fostered. However, with a focus on corporations, this dialogue is not aimed particularly at establishing a system of self-regulation within different industries.

It is also worthwhile to take a look at some of the specific agencies that are active in relatively narrow policy fields and examine the ways in which they have addressed self-regulation in the context of international governance. The first example presented here is taken from the area of health policy, where the WHO (World Health Organization) is the leading interstate organization and where the IFPMA (International Federation of Pharmaceutical Manufacturers Association) is the leading producer organization representing the international pharmaceutical industry. Relations between the two organizations have frequently been rather tense; however, they have improved considerably in recent years with the establishment of a new consultation platform with the pharmaceutical industry. Nevertheless, the industry has always been recognized as a key player and one that hosts significant resources and expertise that can be employed for the benefit of world health. Without a doubt, the industry could contribute to problem-solving through partnership and genuine self-regulation in specific issue areas and thereby share the financial burden in health policy with governments and intergovernmental organizations. One example of self-regulation is the Code of Conduct in the marketing of medicines that was first adopted in 1981, revised in the mid 1990s and to which was added a provision on the use of the Internet in 2000. This is managed by the pharmaceutical industry and its global association, the IFPMA, and supported by the internal guidelines of multinational producers of drugs (IFPMA 1994). The WHO has not been uncritical of the efforts of the pharmaceutical industry and has carefully monitored the industry's management of the code. On some occasions, it has even launched supplementary or alternative regulations (WHO 1988). This indicates that the code is not being implemented completely outside of public policy.

The positive experiences with self-regulation in a specific area of health policy do not suggest that the WHO generally supports the efforts of corporations or business associations to provide alternative forms of regulation. The British American Tobacco, Philip Morris and Japan Tobacco companies have tried to develop so-called 'International Tobacco Marketing Standards'. However, voluntary standards in the tobacco industry are seen by the WHO as an attempt to derail reliable and encompassing regulation of the industry, and instead, its member states are negotiating a 'Framework Convention on Tobacco Control'.

In other words, the WHO only encourages and accepts self-regulatory arrangements under specific circumstances, and in these cases, an alternative monitoring capacity is developed. There is a strong preference for industry-wide regulation by representative and recognized associations with which the WHO has an established record of exchange, although the relationship has not been without conflicts. Initiatives by groups of large corporations are rather seen as a kind of collusive activity and are not welcomed and legitimized by intergovernmental organizations, so in the end, they are hardly sustainable. In this context, it is of utmost importance that the pharmaceutical industry – and the generic producers in particular – have a strong tradition of collective action, and that free-riding by large corporations has been reduced to a minimum.

A second example of private regulation in business is taken from the air transportation industry, where the ICAO (International Civil Aviation Organization) is the key intergovernmental organization, and where the IATA (International Aviation Transport Association) organizes most of the world's airline companies. As a private organization the IATA is heavily involved in safety matters, as most recently formulated in the IATA Safety Strategy 2000+ (IATA 2000a), and thereby does more than only implement and complement rules adopted by the intergovernmental ICAO. This is a traditional activity that relates to cargo as well as to passengers. One important issue is the IATA's dangerous goods regulation, which sets standards for the handling of various kinds of potentially hazardous materials (IATA 2000b). To achieve compliance among members, guidelines are issued, manuals published, training is offered and activities are policed by task forces and by the Dangerous Goods Board of IATA (1999).

Passenger safety has always ranked high on the agenda of airline companies, since any violation of rules can have a detrimental impact on the operators as well as on the reputation of the industry as a whole. Thus, the IATA Operational Safety Audit (IOSA) promotes an internationally recognized system to evaluate an airline's level of competence and reliability. Applicant airline companies must satisfactorily clear this audit process in order to become members. In addition, the Operational Quality Standards

(OQS) are mandatory for all new member airlines and for those reactivating their membership. Measures to enhance safety are almost as old as the industry itself, but after September 11 2001, safety has acquired a new dimension, and the IATA has been even more attentive to safety matters. These issues are continually discussed with the ICAO as the intergovernmental organization in the field, but the IATA has also acted independently and launched its own initiatives. Most interestingly, private organizations are here active in the field of security policy – a domain generally thought of in international relations theory as being monopolized by states and regarded as 'high politics' beyond the control of private actors.

In the case of air transportation, a number of institutional conditions facilitate international self-regulation. As a private organization, the IATA is officially recognized by the ICAO as the airline association per se, and private regulation is viewed in the main as a supplement rather than a problematic alternative to traditional public regulation. The IATA also plays a strong role in implementing and monitoring rules, and this makes it a very reliable and efficient partner. Thus, the industry as a whole, as well as the individual airline companies, have very strong incentives to improve safety regulations.

The third and last example of private regulation to be reviewed here is taken from the international shipping industry, where the key intergovernmental organization is the IMO (International Maritime Organization), with the ICS (International Chamber of Shipping) representing shipowners. Much regulation is carried out through international conventions negotiated between states, with important inputs from the ICS and other maritime interest associations, but in some cases regulation is private. The formation of the ICS predates the IMO, and the ICS was, from the early days, an advocate of the private regulation of the seas.

Today, however, examples of self-regulation can also be found in the maritime sector. Thus, the ICS has issued a number of safety guides, such as the Tanker Safety Guides for chemicals and liquefied gas and the International Safety Guide for Oil Tankers and Terminals – co-authored by the International Chamber of Shipping, the Oil Companies International Marine Forum and the International Association of Ports and Harbours – to secure the safe transportation of various types of bulk liquids (ICS 1995, 2002; ICS, OCIMF and IAPH 1996). Together with the regulations provided by IMO, these guides complement maritime regulation and illustrate that private and public regulation can mutually adapt, and that public authority welcomes private action.

We find measures taken by the ICS in other areas of the environmental field as well. An Industry Code of Practice on Ship Recycling has been produced together with other industry organizations for the disposal of redundant ships (ICS 2001). This code is addressed to shipowners and deals with problems related to working and environmental conditions in Third World countries, where most recycling facilities are located today.

These examples are in no way exhaustive and represent just a few instances of the self-regulatory efforts that have been made in the maritime sector.[2] Interest associations at the global level are very important in designing, negotiating and implementing rule systems through the various codes, guides and guidelines; but in most cases, these are all linked to the efforts of states expressed through the activities of relevant intergovernmental organizations in the field – in particular the IMO.

As in the case of the air transportation industry, there is a close and historical relationship between the IMO and the ICS, and public and private regulatory efforts are often of a complementary nature. Although the representation of maritime interests is more complex and fragmented, the ICS holds a monopoly in the representation of the interest category that it seeks to organize. This facilitates the recognition of private arrangements. However, the role of the ICS vis-à-vis its members is not as strong as that of the IATA, and this can make self-regulatory initiatives more fragile. This illustrates that the recognition of self-regulation by intergovernmental organizations is not only a matter of what private regulation can offer, but also a question of the capacity of public authority at the international level.

As these cases have shown, the regulation of international business is highly varied, and practices from other intergovernmental and private organizations representing business interests can further complicate this picture. Self-regulation is, therefore, an element of governance that, under different headings, is considered in many contexts and practised in many different ways. Nevertheless, it is possible to draw some preliminary conclusions and present some tentative answers as to the conditions under which international self-regulation emerge.

Conclusions

Issues of globalization are often framed within the dichotomy of state and market. Alongside the state and the market, however, associations provide an important societal steering system, and many intergovernmental organizations officially recognize business interest associations – as a part of civil society, and as an organization representing interests of the market. Where states and intergovernmental organizations do not have the full capacity and legitimacy to regulate business, and the spontaneous forces of the market do not produce acceptable forms of coordination, business can create self-regulatory arrangements. This kind of alternative problem-solving has been researched in domestic as well as in international politics.

Various forms of business coordination have been identified at the domestic level, but business interest associations are generally seen as the form best suited to design and administer private institutions of governance. Their aim is to organize a given interest category completely and to achieve compliance among the membership. Business associations are noticeable to political authorities and are more likely to become recognized as exchange partners and, consequently, to be held accountable for their actions. At the international level, a somewhat different pattern is observed. Self-regulation is not only linked to associations but also to other collective entities, as well as to corporations. There is no agreement as to the definition of self-regulation, but apparently the associational type of self-regulation is not dominant and – at least according to many studies – no specific organizational format is superior or advantageous.

Another aspect that is treated differently in the literature on domestic and international self-regulation is the relationship between private regulation and public authority. Studies on domestic private interest government stress that the *state* is a key factor in developing associational self-regulation. Under the perceived threat of public regulation, business is challenged to produce its own system of regulation, and the state may license private organizations to develop self-regulatory functions. At the international level, however, public authority through intergovernmental organizations is considered relatively weaker, and under these circumstances, the *market* can become a more decisive factor. Hence, self-regulation will emerge in a somewhat different way.

In the debate on global governance, a new role is also being attributed to business within many intergovernmental organizations. From the large, all-encompassing organizations to the smaller and more specialized agencies, we find references to business as an element in problem-solving. However, it is necessary to stress that the concept and practice of governance has been employed in many different ways. Governance is now a familiar concept within the social sciences, but it is also used as bureaucratic and political jargon to characterize various strategies and practices. In our analysis, it has been interesting to note that self-regulation is also highlighted in these debates; in this chapter, we have discussed which actors in the business world are actually involved in self-regulation, how arrangements become efficient and legitimate and where public authority can be of assistance.

In the very general organizations – such as the European Union, the United Nations and the OECD – it is extremely important that the role of business is integrated into their overall governance strategy. According to these organizations, neither the economic forces in the marketplace nor the efforts of single states or intergovernmental organizations can solve a range of societal problems. Other institutions must be involved, and business – at the single firm level or at the level of industries – must assume a greater social responsibility, broadly defined. These ideas are formulated in a rather general fashion, but large multinational corporations are particularly identified as hosting a strong potential and are encouraged to incorporate a social dimension into their behaviour.

When we shift our focus to special agencies exchanging with specific globalized industries, we find a somewhat different pattern in their governance strategies. There is less rhetoric but more action – and more concrete manifestations of business self-regulation. Organizations such as the WHO, the ICAO and the IMO – all belonging to the UN-family – also address general issues of governance, but in cases where business self-regulation has emerged, little reference is made to grand strategies. Instead, intergovernmental organizations, as well as those business interest associations that manage self-regulation, adopt a more pragmatic attitude. Private arrangements are generally encouraged and welcomed, but specific aspects are criticized if they do not meet expectations, and in some cases it becomes appropriate to introduce alternative public regulation. At the same time, however, it has been interesting to note that there is a strong and independent driving force in specific industries and business associations that do not always wait for the initiatives of public authority, but instead move forward in accordance with internal demands.

These experiences suggest that international self-regulation is a multifaceted thing that is not reducible to associational regulation – although our cases have shown that there is a general preference for such arrangements in some intergovernmental organizations. Indeed, the initiatives of many multinational corporations undeniably possess regulatory qualities: internal corporate standards can have a societal dimension, and when large corporations represent a significant part of a given industry, their rules are applied within a large proportion of the production. Furthermore, multinational corporations apply these rules through their many affiliates across the globe. In this way, private regulation can replace public regulation through intergovernmental organizations. Multinational corporations can set a good example through corporate standards; and they have an incentive to comply with such self-imposed rules, since they are extremely noticeable compared to smaller firms. Consequently, they must demonstrate a much higher degree of accountability – both to the public at large and to those intergovernmental organizations and states that monitor their behaviour.

However, we would sidestep the issue of whether different forms of private business regulation have the same qualities if we were to lump all of them together under the term 'self-regulation'. Thus, corporate self-regulation is distinct from associational and industry-wide self-regulation, which we have also seen in a number of cases. The latter version of self-regulation includes all member firms of a given association, and not just a selection of key players. Various mechanisms are established to monitor their behaviour, and non-compliance with the rules and codes that have been adopted collectively is sanctioned. It is true, however, that free-riders exist and can be very difficult to police and punish; nevertheless, associational rules extend beyond the level of the individual corporation and establish advanced mechanisms of inter-firm pressure that enhance compliance.

Self-regulation through associations is not a watertight system, but it would be wrong to abandon the contribution of organized business to international governance and claim that it is necessarily inferior to traditional public regulation. Private regulation is brought to life in areas where this solution is preferred by private as well as by public actors – and for economic, political and administrative reasons. Furthermore, public regulation produces rules that businesses do not necessarily comply with and which are also difficult to implement. Ample illustration is offered in the cases of health, aviation and maritime policy, where intergovernmental organizations like the WHO, the ICAO and the IMO have been supportive of arrangements provided by the pharmaceutical industry, airlines and shipowners.

Industry has played a leading role, and has the incentives to establish and carry out regulatory arrangements, but none of these are imaginable without the initial and continuous support of – and occasional criticism from – public authority. It is not possible to document the same kind of public involvement in cases where only corporate self-regulation is at stake, and where a mature relationship between business and intergovernmental organizations does not already exist. This indicates that public authority is an important factor in the development of international self-regulation as an alternative form of governance, and that this regulation is embedded in an already established pattern of exchange where relevant associations enjoy a high degree of recognition.

A final factor – and one that is much more difficult to detect and is not well researched in relation to international self-regulation, and will therefore require further exploration – is the role played by organized interests outside of business. In the case of health policy, many professions are extremely well organized at the international level; and although consumers are not organized as a strong, specific group within the field, the general international consumer organizations take a great interest in drug-related issues. There is no strong and genuine interest organization for airline passengers, but there is a general public interest in how safety matters are managed by the companies. Finally, various environmental organizations are concerned about the pollution of the seas, and unions focus attention on safety issues in the maritime sector. Although these countervailing groups have fewer resources than many large corporations and business associations, they also shape the conditions around which international self-regulation is arranged. However, their role varies across policy fields and industries.

Notes

1 For a fuller review of the regulatory instruments, including self-regulation, see: White Paper on European Governance. Work Area No. 2. Handling the Process of Producing and Implementing Community Rules, Report of the working group 'Better Regulation', Group 2c, May 2001. Conferences and meetings with so-called stakeholders have also been organized to discuss the potential contribution of various sectors, but here mainly general principles are on the agenda.

2 In another area, the maritime community is facing challenges that may call comprehensive self-regulation into question in the long run. The IACS (International Association of Classification Societies) holds a key role in coordinating interests

and establishing general standards of classification, but in recent years, larger members in the LAN Group have threatened to leave the association, which has caused resentment among other members. Such a development is problematic for associational self-regulation but does not exclude the fact that the group and its individual members can be involved in private regulation.

References

Black, A. (1984) *Guilds and Civil Society in European Thought from the Twelfth Century to the Present*, London: Methuen & Co.

Boddewyn, J. J. (1992) *Global Perspectives on Advertising Self-Regulation: Principles and Practices in Thirty-Eight Countries*, Westport, CT: Quorom Books.

Braithwaite, J. and Drahos, P. (2000) *Global Business Regulation*, Cambridge: Cambridge University Press.

Campbell, J. L., Hollingsworth, J. R. and Lindberg, L. N. (eds) (1991) *Governance of the American Economy*, Cambridge: Cambridge University Press.

Coleman, W. D. and Jacek, H. P. (eds) (1989) *Regionalism, Business Interests and Public Policy*, London, Beverly Hills, New Delhi: Sage.

Coleman, W. D. and Underhill, G. R. D. (1998) 'Globalization, Regionalism and the Regulation of Securities Markets', in W. D. Coleman and G. R. D. Underhill (eds) *Regionalism & Global Economic Integration. Europe, Asia and the Americas*, London and New York: Routledge, pp. 225–226.

Commission on Global Governance (1995) *Our Global Neighborhood. The Report of the Commission on Global Governance*, Oxford: Oxford University Press.

Commission of the European Communities (2001a) 'European Governance. A White Paper', Brussels 25 July 2001, COM (2001) 428 Final.

Commission of the European Communities (2001b) 'White Paper on European Governance. Work Area No. 2. Handling the Process of Producing and Implementing Community Rules', Report of the working group 'Better Regulation', Group 2c, May 2001.

Cutler, A. C., Haufler, V. and Porter, T. (eds) (1999) *Private Authority and International Affairs*, Albany NY: State University of New York Press.

Grant, W. (ed.) (1987) *Business Interests, Organizational Development and Private Interest Government. An International Comparative Study of the Food Processing Industry*, Berlin and New York: de Gruyter.

Greenwood, J. (ed.) (2002) *The Effectiveness of EU Business Associations*, Houndmills: Palgrave.

Greenwood, J. and Jacek, H. P. (2000) *Organized Business and the New Global Order*, London: Macmillan.

Greenwood, J. and Ronit, K. (1991) 'Pharmaceutical Regulation in Denmark and the UK: Reformulating Interest Representation to the Transnational Level', *European Journal of Political Research* 19 (2, 3): 327–359.

Greif, A. P., Milgrom, P. and Weingast, B. R. (1994) 'Coordination, Commitment and Enforcement. The Case of the Merchant Guild', *Journal of Political Economy* 102 (4): 745–776.

Grote, J. R. and Gbikpi, B. (eds) (2002) *Participatory Governance. Political and Societal Implications*, Opladen: Leske und Budrich.

Hall, R. B. and Biersteker, T. J. (eds) (2002) 'The Emergence of Private Authority in the International System', in R. B. Hall and T. J. Biersteker (eds) *The Emergence of Private Authority in Global Governance*, Cambridge: Cambridge University Press, pp. 3–22.

Haufler, V. (1993) 'Crossing the Boundary Between Public and Private: International Regimes and Non-State Actors, in V. Rittberger and P. Mayer (eds) *Regime Theory and International Relations*, Oxford: Clarendon Press, pp. 94–111.

Haufler, V. (2001) *A Public Role for the Private Sector. Industry Self-Regulation in a Global Economy*, Washington DC: Carnegie Endowment for International Peace.

Hirschman, A. O. (1995) *A Propensity to Self-Subversion*, Cambridge and London: Harvard University Press.

Hollingsworth, J. R. (1998) 'New Perspectives on the Spatial Dimensions of Economic Coordination: Tensions between Globalization and Social Systems of Production', *Review of International Political Economy*, 5 (3): 482–507.

Hollingsworth, J. R. and Streeck, W. (1994) 'Countries and Sectors. Concluding Remarks on Performance, Convergence and Competitiveness', in J. R. Hollingsworth, P. C. Schmitter and W. Streeck (eds) *Governing Capitalist Economies. Performance and Control of Economic Sectors*, Oxford: Oxford University Press, pp. 270–300.

Hollingsworth, J. R., Schmitter, P. C. and Streeck, W. (eds) (1994) *Governing Capitalist Economies. Performance and Control of Economic Sectors*, Oxford: Oxford University Press.

IATA (1999) *IATA Dangerous Goods Regulation*, Montreal: IATA.

IATA (2000a) *IATA Safety Strategy 2000+*, Montreal: IATA.

IATA (2000b) *Operational Quality Standards*, Montreal: IATA.

ICS (1995) *Tanker Safety Guide (Liquefied Gas)*, 2nd edn, London: ICS.

ICS (2001) *Industry Code of Practice on Ship Recycling*, London: ICS.

ICS (2002) *Tanker Safety Guide (Chemicals)*, 3rd edn, London: ICS.

ICS, OCIMF and IAPH (1996) *International Safety Guide for Oil Tankers and Terminals*, 4th edn, London: ICS.

IFPMA (1994) *Code of Pharmaceutical Marketing Practices*, Geneva: IFPMA.

Knill, C. and Lehmkuhl, D. (2002) 'Private Actors and the State: Internationalization and Changing Patterns of Governance', *Governance*, 15 (1): 41–63.

McConnell, G. (1966) *Private Power and American Democracy*, New York: Alfred A. Knopf.

Martinelli, A. (ed.) (1991) *International Markets and Global Firms. A Comparative Study of Organized Business in the Chemical Industry*, London and New Delhi: Sage.

Marx D. Jr (1953) *International Shipping Cartels: A Study of Industrial Self-Regulation by Shipping Conferences*, Princeton: Princeton University Press.

Merriam, C. E. (1944) *Public and Private Government*, New Haven CT: Yale University Press.

Milgrom, P. R., North, D. C. and Weingast, B. R. (1990) 'The Role of Institutions in the Revival of Trade: The Law Merchant, Private Judges and the Champagne Fairs', *Economics and Politics* 2: 1–23.

Murphy, C. N. (1994) *International Organization and Industrial Change. Global Governance since 1850*, Cambridge: Polity Press.

OECD (1976) *Guidelines for Multinational Enterprises*, Paris: OECD.

OECD (1999) OECD Principles of Corporate Governance, Paris: OECD.

OECD (1999) *Principles of Corporate Governance,* Paris: OECD.

Reinicke, W. H. (1998) *Global Public Policy. Governing without Government*, Washington DC: Brookings Institution Press.

Ronge, V. (1980) *Am Staat vorbei. Politik der Selbstregulierung von Kapital und Arbeit*, Frankfurt and New York: Campus.

Ronit, K. (2001) 'Institutions of Private Authority in Global Governance: Linking Territorial Forms of Self-Regulation', *Administration & Society* 33 (5): 555–578.

Ronit, K. and Schneider, V. (1999) 'Global Governance through Private Organizations' *Governance* 12 (3): 243–266.

Ronit, K. and Schneider, V. (2000) 'Private Organizations and Their Contribution to Problem-Solving in the Global Arena', in K. Ronit and V. Schneider (eds) *Private Organizations in Global Politics*, London and New York: Routledge, pp. 1–33.

Sargent, J. (1985) 'Corporatism and the European Community', in W. Grant (ed.) *The Political Economy of Corporatism*, London: Macmillan, pp. 229–254.

Schmitter, P. C. (1990) 'Sectors in Modern Capitalism: Modes of Governance and Variations in Performance', in R. Brunetta and C. Dell'Aringa (eds) *Labour Relations and Economic Performance*, London: Macmillan, pp. 3–39.

Schmitter, P. C. and Streeck, W. (1981) *The Organization of Business Interests. A Research Design to Study the Associative Action of Business in the Advanced Industrial Societies of Western Europe*, IIM/LMP 81 – 13, Berlin: International Institute of Management.

Streeck, W. and Schmitter, P. C. (1985) 'Community, Market, State – and Associations? The Prospective Contribution of Interest Governance to Social Order', in W. Streeck and P. C. Schmitter (eds) *Private Interest Government. Beyond Market and State*, London, Beverly Hills, New Delhi: Sage, pp. 1–29.

UNCTAD (1996) *Self-Regulation of Environmental Management. An Analysis of Guidelines Set by World Industry Associations for Their Member Firms*, UNCTAD/DTCI/29, Environment Series No. 5, New York and Geneva: United Nations.

WHO (1988) *Ethical Criteria for Medicinal Drug Promotion*, Geneva: WHO.

Wiener, J. (1999) *Globalization and the Harmonization of Law*, London and New York: Pinter.

11 Conclusions

Organized Business Facing Internationalization

Wolfgang Streeck and Jelle Visser

Up to about a decade ago, business associations were an overwhelmingly national phenomenon.[1] They organized firms or their owners from one country only, by sector, region, firm size, religious or political sentiment, or generally; lobbied national governments or, in corporatist countries, undertook to perform functions of public policy; negotiated with trade unions from the same country at sectoral, regional or national level – and generally participated in both the construction and the regulation of national markets, in cooperation as well as in conflict with governments and organized labour, pursuing the special interest of capital as well as contributing to the common good of nations, however defined, under capitalism (Cawson 1985; Ziegler 1992).

This picture, which dates back as far as the second half of the nineteenth century, held pretty much true until the 1980s. It dominated the imagery behind the ambitious and influential international research project on business interest associations that was started by Philippe Schmitter and Wolfgang Streeck in the early 1980s (Schmitter and Streeck 1999 [1981]). Twenty years later, it seems clear that rapid and, at the time, more or less unexpected progress in the internationalization of capitalist political economies requires major revisions in how we think about 'the associative action of business'. This, at least, is what the vast recent literature on internationalization and 'globalization' implicitly and explicitly suggests. While there were international associations of business as far back as the early postwar years, there were not many of them and their practical significance was doubtful. There also were multinational firms, but the typical large firm was national, perhaps with subsidiaries abroad. Multinational companies were the exception, not the rule, even in sectors such as automobiles, and they were all directed from their home base. Organized capital was nationally organized, just like organized labour – and what its political role was depended on national traditions and institutions, for example on whether these were more pluralist or more corporatist (on national traditions, see Crouch 1993).

If it is true that in the past, business interest associations were closely intertwined with the structure and functioning of the nation state, then one would expect that their fate under internationalization should be related to that of the latter. Indeed what hypotheses one may hold with respect to the impact of internationalization on business interest associations appears very much driven by what one believes is happening, or expects will happen, to the nation state and the functions of economic governance in which the state has traditionally been involved. As far as Europe and its supranational integration is concerned, many expected for a long time, as a matter of course, that the focus of interest organization and interest politics would shift from the national to the supranational level as integration progressed. Here a new system of interest representation would emerge that would absorb the old, national systems and duplicate them on a much larger scale (Haas 1958; Lindberg 1963; recently Wessels 1997). Later, when European integration was recognized to be tightly coupled to a process of economic liberalization, there was speculation that associations would never recover at the supranational level what they lost at the national level, and that a system of supranational pluralist lobbying, by multinational firms as well as by multinational associations, would replace national lobbying and, importantly, national corporatist cooperation (Streeck and Schmitter 1991). Beyond Europe, economic globalization was believed by many to undercut the nation state and, with it, national business associations. Others speculated about emerging, or for that matter desirable, international arrangements for 'global governance', involving not just states and international organizations but also private non-governmental organizations, including perhaps business interest associations of national or, more likely, international constitution.

The dust of globalization is far from having settled, and this will remain so for a long time. Yet, for those studying business interest politics, there is now enough evidence to conclude that due to the still only vaguely understood complexities of the internationalization process, the pattern underlying the transformation of organized business defies any simple characterization (Wilts 2002). Most students of European integration have now come to understand that the European nation state is not in any way about to be replaced by a European supranational state, and never will be. The implication is that, whatever kind of integration may be in the offing, nation states will continue to play a significant role in the governance of the European economy, although very likely in ways that differ profoundly from the postwar past. If nation states survive, however, national business interest associations might survive, too. Similarly, that free markets do not just emerge, but must be instituted by policy and through politics, could point to a lasting if different role for organized business beyond the end of organized capitalism. Finally, at the global level, while a liberal world market governed by a state-free *lex mercatoria* combined with voluntary codes of practice for large firms might seem an attractive utopia to liberal lawyers and neo-liberal economists, it may in practice not suffice to create the sort of order and confidence that are required for worldwide economic growth and prosperity. Could business associations come in to fill the gap?

Compared to entire states, systems of interest representation and the collective actors that inhabit them are small worlds that are easier, although by no means easy, to traverse and observe. If the response of interest associations to globalization is as closely aligned with that of the national state as one would expect, its study might reveal important insights, not just on the politics of organized interests, but also on the evolution of state governance and state capacities and on the relationship between politics and the economy under internationalization. What is happening to business associations could, as it were, be read like a litmus test for what is happening to the state. As empirical access to a small world is easier than to a large one, the findings this might generate could be more realistic and less speculative – and less driven by wishful thinking – than much of popular writing on 'globalization'. Indeed to the extent that it is possible to study business associations diachronically and trace the trajectory along which they are changing, approaching globalization by studying the transformation of organized business interests might yield major insights on how political institutions are transforming in the present period of worldwide liberalization, and on how institutional legacies influence the gradual but nevertheless fundamental change that seems to be emblematic of the present period of worldwide liberalization.

This volume deals with the internationalization of business interest representation, and indirectly of politics in general, in an actor-centred, bottom-up perspective. Rather than studying emergent supranational business associations and associative orders above the nation state, it begins its approach at the national level where the vast majority of business associations continue to be located, and tries to learn from their behaviour how the rules of the game of interest politics are evolving. Not only does this make it possible to trace the 'path dependence' of change in associations and associative orders, enabling the analysis to take into account the past and the present as important factors shaping the future. It also allows one to relate observed changes in the organizational structures and practices of interest associations – i.e. the corporate actors of interest politics – to changes in the associative orders that constitute the institutional framework of their activities.

The present chapter, which summarizes what we believe are the main conclusions from the empirical analyses presented in this volume, will proceed as follows. Its first part will focus on what seem to be common trends in the development of business associations at national level. While some of these are directly related to internationalization, for others the relationship is more indirect, and yet others are not related to internationalization at all. The main emphasis in this section will be on the 'logic of membership', i.e. the relations between interest associations and the firms that they represent.[2] An important aspect of this will be dealt with in the second section, which discusses the emergence of large firms as independent interest-political actors. Following this, the third section will turn to the role of business associations in the emerging 'Europolity', which we treat as an especially strongly institutionalized example of an international arena of interest politics. As will be seen, the link is the rise of the large multinational firm, not just as a critical constituent of national business associations, but also as a domestic as well as international interest-political actor in its own right. Obviously, the third section will emphasize primarily the 'logic of influence', in that it will explore how the – partial – shift of economic governance to the European level affects the organization and collective action of business. Our main finding is that, rather than being absorbed by supranational associations, many national business associations extend their activities to the supranational, European level, paralleling the efforts of, and sometimes intentionally bypassing, their own supranational associations which remain remarkably restricted in their powers and capacities. By way of conclusion, we relate this observation to the notion of 'Europeanization', both of politics and of political systems.

The national level: business associations under stress

The chapters of this volume depict national associations of business in a period of profound change. As such change has proceeded gradually over two decades without dramatic disruption, its extent, once fully observed, must appear all the more surprising. The same can be said of the fact that a major source of change seems to have been pressures from below, coming from members. This reveals a much higher salience of the logic of membership for business associations than was believed to be possible in the neo-corporatist 1970s. Then, it was widely held that interest associations in advanced industrial democracies were evolving to become something like 'private interest governments', or 'PIGs' (Streeck and Schmitter 1985), governing rather than merely representing their members in a process of political exchange with powerful interlocutors – governments and trade unions – in which interests had to be diluted in return for their limited but securely guaranteed observance in negotiated common policies.

For this, too much member participation was regarded as less than helpful. Of course it was always admitted that given their lower number of members and the considerable resources at the latter's disposal, business associations would likely be somewhat less oligarchic than their trade union counterparts. While for most mainstream trade unions extracting a sufficient supply of resources from their members seemed to be more difficult than maintaining internal discipline, for business associations the reverse appeared to be true. Still, the extent to which the members of national business associations have in recent decades demanded more accountability of their leaders and closer alignment of associational policies to their own perceived interests, refused to continue to provide resources without a visible return for themselves, or even deserted their appointed 'statesmen of industry' and took their case themselves directly to the public and to political authorities, seems remarkable enough to require rethinking of received theories.[3]

To what extent and in what sense the revolt of business firms against the neo-corporatist PIGgery of the 1970s was driven by internationalization is a question that is hard to answer conclusively. A factor that seems to have been highly influential is structural change in the membership base of many business associations, which in turn was partly related to the internationalization of markets and production systems. Among other things, internationalization seems to have caused a sharpening of the traditional division between the concerns of small and large firms (see the three country chapters and the chapter by Lehmkuhl, this volume), which appears to have made the proven methods by which business associations used to manage the conflicts between the two groups of members less effective. Also, increasing international division of labour, together with intensified competition even in previously domestic markets, seems to have caused a wave of mergers that reduced the number of firms in the sectors organized by established associations.[4] Smaller numbers of larger firms are, however, more difficult to manage from above than large numbers of small firms. Moreover, more and more firms are becoming multinational in structure and ownership, and, as we will see below, this posed additional control problems from the perspective of national as well as international business associations.

Another development that seems to have put pressure on national business associations was profound changes in union organization and collective bargaining. This, too, reflected international pressures which often issued in a decline of the industrial sector – the main organizational base of trade unionism – and in different forms of decentralization of wage setting. Due to these and other factors, trade unions seem in recent years to have become less important and less constraining as interlocutors of business associations. This would seem to be behind the tendency, manifested already in several countries, to abandon dual organization of trade and employer interests in separate, independent associations. Postwar industrial relations ideally implied a decoupling of wages and working conditions from the economic situation of the individual firm. Where trade unions were strong this seems to have been conducive to organizational dualism on the side of business. However, as liberalization in the 1980s and 1990s wrought a recommodification of labour and of the employment relationship, it seemed to make sense to business interests to coordinate their collective action in product and labour markets more closely, by incorporating previously separate employers associations into functionally encompassing, general associations of business (cf. Wilts 2002: 103, on the Netherlands).[5]

As the chapters of this book suggest, current developments in different national systems of business interest organization respond to similar endogenous or identical exogenous stress and as a result resemble each other across national boundaries. National differences do not disappear, however, and both national systems and the politics of change and adjustment remain recognizably nationally specific over time, despite similar pressures and adaptive responses. This is a theme in the three country chapters (on the Netherlands, Switzerland and Sweden) and in two of the three comparative sector studies (on the chemical industry in Germany and Britain, and on the logistics sector in the Netherlands and Germany). That convergence does not eliminate divergence and that similar pressures cause reactions that are comparable but not identical may be explained by the fact that common exogenous constraints are mediated by different national conditions and institutions. Also, where responses of national systems are similar, this seems to be due to independent co-evolution caused by endogenous influences rather than to diffusion (see the chapter by Lehmkuhl).[6]

In the following we will discuss three, as far as we can see, rather universal responses of national business interest associations to the ongoing secular changes in their membership base and in the interests emerging from it. We begin with the conspicuous efforts of business associations in almost all countries to rationalize their organizations, not least in response to demands from their members, and cut back on expenses and membership dues. Second, we point to an emerging new style of interest representation, especially by intersectoral business associations, that appears much more 'pluralist' – i.e. conflict-oriented and public opinion-centred – than was deemed politically expedient in the corporatist era. Third, we turn to the already mentioned slow disappearance, or at least the weakening, of the functional division between employer associations and trade associations.

Organizational restructuring

Among the most striking changes we find in almost all countries is that national business associations today experience much more pressure to attend to the perceived interests of their members than they did 20 years ago (see in particular the chapters by Visser and Wilts and by Grote and Schneider, this volume; cf. Boléat 2002). This pertains to the design of their organizational structures as well as to their policies. With respect to both, it seems justified to speak of a slow but effective movement away from a more corporatist towards a more pluralist style of interest representation. Our chapters suggest that this movement has occurred and is occurring above all in response to a significant increase in the heterogeneity of the membership of associations. The result is sometimes intensive organizational restructuring, trying to combine organizational streamlining with increased provisions for member participation, as well as in a different, more aggressive political posture.

Examples of this can be found not only in the three country cases presented in this book. Others come from Germany, where the peak trade association of industry, the Bundesverband der Deutschen Industrie (BDI), under the presidency of Hans-Olaf Henkel waged a public relations attack on corporatism. Similarly in France the rise of Ernest-Antoine Sellière to the top of the Confédération Nationale des Patrons and its subsequent renaming from the CNPF into Mouvement des Entreprises (MEDEF) coincided with an attempt to recover the initiative from the state and the unions, and with a new, more self-confident style of defending the values and spirit of entrepreneurialism in public (Bothorel and Sassier 2002).[7] In Italy, the appointment in March 2000 of Antonio D'Amato as the first leader of Confindustria with a background of small business in the south foreshadowed a far more aggressive and right-wing approach to industrial relations than had been seen in decades.[8] What these events had in common was that they signified a new self-definition of business associations, not as intermediaries, but as a straightforward voice of enterprise and entrepreneurialism. In France and Italy, and in most federations representing small entrepreneurs, such 'insurrections of the bosses' (Helbert 1984) were not infrequent. In corporatist Europe, however, developments of this sort were new, and in fact they are still unstable, contradictory and, going by the Italian example, not irreversible. In the following we will try to account for them as best we can given the state of our knowledge.

The past 20 years have wrought new and sharper divisions in the membership of business associations, especially between large and small firms, between national and multinational firms, and between firms that are nationally and foreign owned. Small firms have often done less well than larger ones in confronting the challenges of internationalization and intensified competition. One consequence was that large firms tended to be willing to maintain good relations with organized labour, whereas small firms felt increasingly unable to continue to pay the high wages and social security contributions that were a legacy of the 1970s (for Germany see Hassel and Rehder 2001). Resentment against large firms rose especially where these used their dominance in employer associations to negotiate wage settlements that secured peace on their own shop floor while the majority of smaller member firms could not afford them. In sectors like the auto industry, where smaller firms did much of their business producing supplies for large firms, more injury, and indeed insult, was added when large firms demanded lower prices from their suppliers because of their increased labour costs, threatening to turn to foreign sources otherwise. In a country like Germany, conflicts like these began to tear apart the powerful employer association of the metal sector, in that they created almost insurmountable difficulties for its leadership in devising a common policy that maintained the integrity of the association.

In the 1990s at the latest, small member firms in a large number of business associations became highly vocal advocates of a political turn towards a policy that was much less accommodating of trade unions and much more insistent with respect to reforms of the welfare state. As small firms became more militant, they often began to doubt whether their changing political interests would be adequately represented by the large firms that had for so long run their associations. Moreover, given their declining satisfaction with associational policies and also their deteriorating economic situation, small firms began to demand lower membership dues, causing a resource squeeze that was to become a growing concern for association leaders. This was all the more so since the larger firms that had always paid the lion's share of associational budgets were less willing now than in the past to fill the gap. Themselves facing more intense competition, many of them agreed with the smaller members in demanding that associations cut expenses, using a rhetoric that was very similar to the general demands by business at the time for a cutback of government expenditures.

Not that associations did not do their utmost to keep their large member firms happy enough to stay on and pay, perhaps, an even larger share of the bill. Some tried to reward continued loyalty by improved opportunities for direct voice, through special forums or direct membership arrangements for large firms along the British and Dutch models and on the example of European peak associations such as UNICE and CEFIC (Cowles 1994: 172ff.; Grant and Paterson 1994: 142). The reason why this was not, however, the ultimate wisdom was that smaller firms, in addition to having become stingier, had grown more suspicious of the motives behind the associational activities of their larger competitors-cum-customers.[9] Also, larger firms had in the course of internationalization often turned multinational, and apparently this affected their attitude towards their business associations at home. From their simultaneous involvement in different national systems of interest representation, company executives especially from corporatist countries learned that firms can sometimes represent their interests on their own or have them represented through lobbying firms, instead of paying dues to a trade association constrained to dilute the special interests of its individual members. They were also likely to have seen business associations in operation that worked with a much smaller staff and focused on a much narrower range of core activities than corporatist associations, as a result costing their members less.[10] It seems that due to these and similar factors, firms throughout Europe developed a growing anti-bureaucratic sentiment in the 1990s against their own associations that culminated in urgent demands for internal reforms quite similar to the sort of reforms that firms themselves underwent in response to intensifying competition, or those that business and political leaders demanded of the public organizations of the welfare state.

Similar problems were caused by the growing number of foreign-owned firms in the domestic political economies of Europe. They, too, increased the heterogeneity of the constituency of national business associations (Grant 1984: 7) and detracted from the, as it were, natural cohesion of their members and potential members that makes for high density of association membership. For Germany, Jacobi (2003: 26) shows that foreign-owned firms are more likely to join German associations if they have been present in the country for a long time. Especially US firms that have set up their

German subsidiaries only recently, tend not to be members of employer associations and instead interact with the unions directly if at all. Still, little is known empirically about how non-national origin affects a firm's attitude towards, and its depth of involvement in, the business associations of a country. Associations themselves seem to have different policies in relation to non-national firms.[11] In any case, however, it is likely that the increasingly heterogeneous composition of their constituencies did not make it easier for association leaders to unite their members behind a common policy (Boléat 2002: 88).

While in terms of internal politics the experience seems to have been similar across national and sectoral boundaries, this does not seem to apply to the resource squeeze, which was faced by some associations but not by others. Especially employer associations in countries like Germany and Sweden, which have centralized collective bargaining systems, had built up considerable funds in the postwar years for supporting their member firms in strikes and lockouts. During the long industrial peace after the end of the 'roaring seventies', these funds and the accumulated interest they had earned became so large that some associations were in a position to finance their operation more or less entirely out of the current proceeds from their invested capital. Clearly this dampened the impact of the pressure from dissatisfied members, at least for a while, and delayed adjustments in organizational structure and practice (Van Waarden 1996: 61). But it also stimulated demands from member firms, not just for rebates on their dues, but also for new kinds of activities to be financed from their accumulated resources. In a number of cases, associational savings were used in part to fund expensive public relations campaigns supporting neo-liberal economic reform (see below). Since it was mostly employer rather than trade associations that held accumulated capital, the position of the former in relation to takeover attempts by the latter was strengthened, counterbalancing the declining importance of organized labour and postwar social partnership.

In the long run, however, it seems unlikely that even large savings can shield associations from member pressures for organizational restructuring. Three tendencies in particular seem to be universal. One is *streamlining of organizational structures*, especially where business associations are fragmented so that especially larger firms have to join several different associations at the same time. This costs them money, but even more so, time, and of this they have less today than was the case in the less competitive environment of the past. The result is a call for mergers between associations, although mergers typically increase the diversity of member firms and member interests. Further below, we will turn specifically to efforts to amalgamate employer and trade associations. At this point it suffices to note that firms, having themselves come under relentless competitive pressures to 'do more with less', seem to have become much less tolerant than in the past of the complicated interlocking arrangements for interest representation that used to exist specifically in corporatist countries.

Second, associations seem to have generally grown more *attentive to the individual needs of their members*, including the smaller ones. This should reflect the fact that exit from associations has become less unthinkable even in corporatist systems; that entry was always less natural for the growing number of firms of foreign origin; and that individual action has become an alternative to associative action for a growing number of strategically important members and potential members. Business associations today seem to be spending more resources than ever on services that accrue directly and exclusively to their membership (see the chapters by Schneider and Grote and by Visser and Wilts, this volume). Of course such 'outside inducements' to membership and participation are by no means new (Olson 1965); but it seems that reliance on them has increased as some of the collective goods provided by business associations, especially the procurement of labour peace, have lost importance. An interesting example for the introduction of new instruments of participation, service provision and communication is Gesamtmetall, the huge employer association of the German metal engineering industry. Faced with desertion by small and medium-sized member firms that would no longer be bound by the sectoral collective agreement, Gesamtmetall created a set of sister organizations, run out of its offices, that formally are not a party to collective bargaining (the so-called *OT-Verbände*; Zimmer 2002: 99ff.). Covering the entire territory of the country, these can be joined by firms from the sector which desire individual services as employers – such as advice in questions of labour law – but not collective representation vis-à-vis trade unions.

Third, organizational restructuring often includes business associations *setting up and owning commercial firms* that provide services, such as consulting, at market prices to members and sometimes also to non-members. Using language suggested by Schmitter and Streeck in the early 1980s (Schmitter and Streeck 1999 [1981]), what one observes here is a tendency for business associations to turn from interest intermediaries into 'interest firms'. This tendency is already evident where associations supplement, as they increasingly do, funding by contributions with various forms of charging for specific services provided. Provision of commercial services may be combined with, and based on the results of, surveys of (panels) of member firms. Together with increased use of the Internet, such surveys seem to have become a regular instrument especially for Dutch associations for tapping the needs and views of the membership, replacing the more traditional forms of associational democracy such as meetings and voting (Wilts 2002: 108; Boléat 2002: 95).

Generally speaking, there can be no doubt that the renewal in the past two decades of the spirit of capitalism has not left the formerly often bureaucratic and sometimes state-like associations of capital untouched. More than ever, business association staff are now expected to behave 'businesslike' and act 'entrepreneurially'. This means not just faster decisions and more visible attachment to modern business ideology, but also a willingness to earn their own income, and that of their associations, in the marketplace rather than as authoritative 'private interest governments' – by developing innovative 'products' that meet the demands of members which, ominously, are now increasingly being referred to as 'customers'.

The post-corporatist politics of liberalization

Liberalization, the dominant theme of political economy since the late 1980s, means disengagement of politics, especially democratic politics, from the economy. It involves a change towards an economic policy that is non-discretionary, rule-based and, above all, shielded from electoral influence. Of course, installing and defending a non-political economic policy is as such a profoundly political undertaking: it requires a difficult and often conflictual dismantling of interventionist institutions and practices, as well as the precarious building of new institutions that protect governments against inevitable temptations to return to non-liberal interventionism. It is in this kind of politics that business associations seem to have increasingly engaged during the past two decades.

In part, the neo-liberal turn of the politics of business interest seems to be a response to changed external circumstances. International, and especially European, prohibitions on 'state aids', instituted to open up national markets for international trade, limit the potential benefits that firms can derive from corporatist insiderism. The same applies to the disappearance of national schemes of corporatist market management, like for example in the Swiss dairy industry (Wagemann 2004). Often internationalization caused a shift from corporatist to state regulation since public government can more easily than private government be held accountable internationally for the opening up of national markets. Thus internationalization may paradoxically strengthen the national state (Lütz 1998). As state-supported associative orders vanished, business associations needed to look for new activities. Public advocacy of economic liberalization partly filled the bill and provided general, cross-sectoral business associations in particular with a new role in which to impress their membership, on the background of a new politics of national political systems in which neo-corporatist self-government was on the retreat. How effective working on public opinion could be was amply demonstrated by the activities of business-funded think tanks and public relations agencies in the pluralist democracies of the United States and the United Kingdom in the Reagan and Thatcher years.[12] Gradually this sort of publicly visible political activity assumed more weight for business associations as the potential gains from neo-corporatist cooperation behind the scenes declined.

Business associations did, of course, not just react to liberalization. In fact many of them were a driving force behind it. With hindsight it can be seen that at some point in the 1980s European business became tired of the corporatist discipline imposed on it by trade unions and social democratic parties in the wake of the labour unrest of the late 1960s. Internationalization sprang from many sources, certainly including technological and economic ones. But it also came to be promoted by business as a way out of the ever more demanding conditions, and the profit squeeze associated with them, to which business had been subjected inside national regimes. The way large firms, acting through their own 'roundtables' as well as through national and European business associations, contributed to the decision to speed up the creation of a Single Market is well-documented (van Apeldoorn 2002: 68). Up to the present day, given the lasting fragmentation of European politics and democracy by an established system of nation states, internationalization remains tightly coupled to liberalization, both within national economies where discretionary intervention is increasingly outlawed as unfair competition, and in the international arena where courts of law and technocratic agencies take the place of popular democracy.

Turning towards pluralist lobbying of domestic publics for liberal reform had a number of virtuous effects for national business associations. Above all, it alleviated their 'policy squeeze' by solidifying their support from increasingly heterogeneous and demanding memberships to whom liberalization represents a collective good that everyone can find desirable. Neoliberal rhetoric tends to appeal especially to the owner-managers of small and medium-sized firms, the constituency that had grown most critical of established business associations in the 1980s and 1990s (Wilts 2002: 105ff.; Zimmer 2002: 99ff.). (Those who still need and actively seek specific government support can agree to the unifying rhetoric while continuing to lobby the state behind the scenes.) Public campaigning for liberalization also offered associations a way to spend part of their accumulated resources, hoping that this would quell demands for the money to be returned to the members. Gesamtmetall, the employer association of the German metal engineering industry, today expends no less than €10 million per year on a highly professional and sophisticated public relations campaign, *Neue Soziale Marktwirtschaft* ('New Social Market Economy'), in which the association itself is hardly visible at all. This effort is all the more remarkable since this sort of activity is not really part of the mission of an employer association, not to mention a sectoral one, and would normally have to be undertaken by an association such as the BDI (the Federal Association of German Industry). Other examples of the same kind are easily found, for instance in France where the renamed Mouvement des Entreprises de France (MEDEF) organized several large gatherings, of up to 3,000 employers, to defend 'the freedom of entrepreneurship'. In the same spirit, the organization launched an annual Summer University in 1999, in an attempt to assert its new role as teacher of a revived capitalist ethos.

Internationalization, one might think, makes firms, and especially the larger firms that are adopting an increasingly international perspective, lose interest in their countries of origin. But this does not seem to be the case at all. Here our Dutch, Swiss and Swedish case studies are particularly instructive as they deal with small countries whose economies have long been among the most international ones. In all three countries, and in Switzerland and Sweden in particular, national peak associations of business have devoted and continue to devote enormous resources to influencing public opinion in favour of opening up and liberalizing the domestic economy, apparently with the full support of their highly internationalized large member firms.[13] The explanation seems to be that precisely as firms venture across national borders into the international economy, they develop a strong interest in a favourable business environment at home, including a public opinion that accepts the domestic restructuring necessary for international competitiveness. Very likely, firms also feel they need the support of their home state in the politics of the international marketplace. National associations, in particular cross-sectoral trade associations, obviously continue to be important instruments for business in creating and securing conditions at home that are supportive of their growth into the world economy. Moreover, large and multinational firms, if they want to be effective in democratic politics, seem to need associations that also represent a fair number of small firms.

The decline of dual organization

For a long time dual organization of business interests in trade and employer associations was typical of corporatist countries, where trade unions were strong and industrial relations were largely autonomously governed by the organized 'social partners'. Dual organization remained alien to Britain and Ireland, despite some early attempts at functional differentiation, as well as to southern Europe. In the first case business associations served mainly as lobbyists and, to some extent, as providers of services, while industrial relations remained under the control of individual firms and a large number of small, often competing unions. In the second case business associations were always highly politicized, and relations between capital and labour were mediated through social movements, political parties and the politics of the state. In neither case were business associations involved in centralized industrial relations, and hence functional differentiation was a luxury that they could do without.

One of the most striking developments in recent years was that separate employer associations at the national peak level disappeared in a great number of countries, including Denmark (1991), Norway (1989), Finland (1993), Switzerland (2000) and Sweden (2001), which followed the early lead of the UK (1965) and the Netherlands (1968). This seems to have left Germany as the only country where dual organization at the peak level survived.[14] At *sectoral* level separate employer associations continue to exist, just as they have for a long time in the Netherlands. In many countries, however, again excluding Germany with its generally frozen institutional structures, there were numerous mergers between employer and trade associations also in individual sectors, resulting in functionally mixed associations of one sort or other. We have already touched on what we think are some of the reasons for this. More detailed discussion is found in Traxler's chapter and in the three country chapters in this volume. What follows is a brief review of the main points that seem to be relevant here.

For one thing, the integration of employer and trade interests in one organization appears to be part of the ongoing streamlining of business associational systems. As we have seen, firms seem to have become less tolerant in the 1990s than they were in the past of what they increasingly perceive as duplication of effort, leading them to demand reductions in the time and money association members are asked to contribute. Internationalization of firms has added to this as it has undermined the sectoral and national basis for collective agreements which, in an internationalizing economy, can no longer take wages out of competition. Employer associations, but also the industrial relations sections inside general business associations, are therefore increasingly less able to serve as instruments of collective market governance. It is true that the need for associations lobbying against European or national social legislation may have grown, just as associations may have to play a role in inspiring and servicing firms and their human resource managers in local negotiations with unions and employee representatives. That role, however, seems to be better performed, from a business point of view, by organizations placing social and employment issues in the context of the general economic interests of firms.

Another factor seems to be increases in firm size due to mergers, which force the remaining firms to bear a larger share of the burden of collective action, while at the same time requiring them to coordinate their simultaneous involvement in several associations and, where they exist, in several sectoral collective agreements. As has been seen, the only country that thus far escaped the trend towards merger of trade and employer associations is a large country, Germany – which is also, together with Japan, the only large country featuring an elaborate institutional organization of its market economy. German exceptionalism with respect to the trend towards functional de-differentiation may indicate that small absolute size of associations – and perhaps a secular increase in the minimum size required for associations effectively to provide services to their members – may have contributed to the decisions in smaller countries to abandon functional differentiation.[15] Similar factors may also explain why dual organization disappeared so early in Belgium and the Netherlands even though these are corporatist countries. Both are not just small, but in addition they are also divided by religion and, in the Belgian case, regions. When dual organization was abandoned in the Netherlands in 1968, this was partly in response to pressure from large firms dissatisfied with having to pay dues in general as well as in denominational organizations.

Perhaps the main force enabling business interests to abandon dual organization was the general weakening of organized labour in the 1990s and the attendant tendency towards decentralization of collective bargaining. The Swedish case is highly instructive here. Growing cost-consciousness of members of business associations coincided with demands by firms for a reorientation of activities towards lobbying, public relations, direct services to members and more effective presence on the European and international scene, building up pressure to end dual organization and double membership. That such pressure was actually heeded was due to the decline of the economic clout of the unions. But it was probably also strategically aimed at contributing to that decline, as had been the withdrawal of Swedish business at the end of the 1980s from the corporatist labour market policy boards (Martin 1997: 278ff.). Not only do weaker unions require fewer resources on the part of business associations for negotiations and, in particular, conflict insurance. Dismantling or, for that matter, refusing to create a specialized employer association also makes capital unavailable for union and government attempts at 'concertation' and prevents unions from establishing or defending an institutionalized role in regulating the labour market.[16]

In the Swedish case, there are reasons to believe that in withdrawing from centralized bargaining and national corporatism, employers killed two birds with one stone: regaining the support of those member firms that had grown most critical of associational policies, as well as denying the trade unions the political power that had become the undesirable side-product of decades of centralized bargaining. Where employers are still prepared to participate in national forums and make pacts with the unions and the government, agreements tend to be non-binding, making expensive negotiation and governance machinery dispensable and allowing for the functions of employer and trade associations to be carried out by one organization. The same applies at the sectoral level. When sectoral agreements turn into non-binding recommendations, this is, as the case of the British engineering industry shows, likely to be the beginning of the end of separate employer associations.

Generally, we have already noted that today, social policies are more difficult to separate from economic policies and must prove their economic usefulness. The same applies to working conditions in relation to the economic situation of the individual firm. It is widely accepted that this is behind the trend for a conversion of industrial relations into 'Human Resource Management', accompanied by deinstitutionalization of industrial relations as a separate policy sector or 'subsystem'. As this process advances, as it has in western Europe in the past decade, separate employer associations are likely to be seen as redundant by business firms, and their reduced tasks may be taken over by functionally amalgamated associations, with the benefit of potentially significant organizational economies of scale.

The rise of the large firm

Business associations have always been particularly responsive to the special interests of large firms. Without their financial and personal contributions, most associations, whether employer or trade associations, would not have the resources they need to perform their mission, including representing and servicing their small and medium-sized members. It is not surprising, therefore, that business associations are more often than not run by their large member firms. Frequently the president of an association comes from a large company, or the secretary-general is selected by the large member firms, or only with their consent. Many associations also provide arrangements for their larger members to meet separately, in round tables or special committees, to articulate their specific interests and impress them on the association's leadership. In return, large firms may, in addition to paying their regular dues, sponsor special projects either financially or by temporarily seconding staff to the association's office. Obviously where this happens, associations become even more dependent on their large members and are even more constrained to do their utmost to maintain and, if possible, increase the satisfaction of the latter with their policies and services.

In many ways, binding large firms seems to have become more difficult for business associations. A variety of authors have noted the emergence of large, mostly international firms as independent interest-political actors, on the national as well as the European and the global level (Coen 1997; Coleman, this volume; Cowles 1994; Ronit, this volume). Rather than letting themselves be represented by business associations – and necessarily allow the latter to aggregate their individual interests into a common group interest – firms have more than ever begun to lobby political institutions and decision makers directly, either through newly created special departments for 'political relations' or by employing professional lobbyists. This practice was always well known in pluralist countries with weak business associations and sectional trade unions, and with governments that were traditionally highly accessible to individual firms as distinguished from representatives of entire sectors or industries. Even here, however, Wyn Grant (1984) observed as early as the 1980s a tendency for large firms to expand their political relations operations and begin on an unprecedented scale to take their interests into their own hands. Today it appears that large firms in corporatist countries have followed their lead and act much more frequently than they used to in the past as interest-political 'free agents'.

This does not necessarily mean that large firms are giving up employer or trade association membership. In fact they do not normally resign from associations even if they are extremely critical of how they are run. Typically large firms prefer voice over exit, putting pressure on the leadership or moving their own staff into leading associational positions. This is because exit may cut them off from information and informal networks essential for exercising influence. In national systems with centralized collective bargaining, like Germany, large firms even have a vital interest in belonging to an employer association as this protects them from wage demands that would reflect their superior ability to pay. In fact, even international companies normally do not discourage membership in national business associations. Apparently they leave it to local management, and headquarters may often not even know (Grant 1984: 7; Greenwood 2003). Few multinational companies seem to look at membership in business associations in a strategic way, from the perspective of whether to concentrate resources on particular national, European or global associations (Boléat 2002: 93). Of course, this may change and more firms may follow the example of McDonald's, which is among the very few international companies that have a general policy of not becoming involved in national business associations.

It is therefore not primarily a problem of membership that most business associations have with large international firms, but rather one of discipline. As small and medium-sized firms have lost confidence in the intentions of large firms, the extent to which associations can cater to the special interests of the latter would appear to have become more limited.[17] As we have seen, one way in which this conflict is being resolved is associations focusing more than before on public lobbying for neo-liberal policies in general, like the German BDI in the 1990s under the leadership of a representative of a very large multinational company (Hans-Olaf Henkel of IBM).[18] But the less specific the polices of business associations become, for internal or external reasons, and the more their public pronouncements celebrate the virtues of free markets in which there is no place for special political favours to national champions or ailing firms, the more of a need large firms may feel to open up additional avenues for themselves to make their particular interests heard. This, we believe, is a main reason why so many of them, including firms from corporatist countries, have begun to develop, in addition to their still carefully cultivated capacity to organize and direct collective action through associations, a variety of instruments of direct intervention with policy makers on their own behalf, such as exclusive Business Round Tables of selected national or international corporations, or representative offices in national capitals or in Brussels.

Several of the forces that have propelled this development have already been mentioned. Internationalization is one of them, as it may offer firms from corporatist systems opportunities to observe and imitate the weaker collective solidarity and the more aggressive individual lobbying of their competitors or subsidiaries under pluralist regimes. Similar to general managerial practices, indications are that internationalization of firms de facto often means Americanization. Both multinational and national firms alike seem to learn the same lesson, of less discipline and more political individualism, as they begin to represent their interests at the European level in Brussels where the style of relations between decision makers and industry differs from the corporatist model and comes much closer to the pluralist,

Anglo-American pattern (for an example from the early 1990s see Cowles 1994: 182).

Second, cross-national mergers and takeovers may produce large 'disembedded firms' (Pestoff, this volume) that may be less comfortable with, or care less for, the traditional 'clubbiness' of national business associations, again especially in corporatist countries or institutional arrangements. It is true, as the Dutch case in particular shows, that associations can adjust to the demands of large multinational firms and may, with innovative practices, manage effectively to integrate them. Still, as pointed out by Traxler (this volume), cross-national mergers disturb sectoral and national identities and loyalties, and while this may not make firms resign or abstain from membership, it is likely to change their attitude towards it. Large firms, which increasingly tend to be multinational, may opt more than before to locate parts of their activities in other countries. Very likely, their attitude towards national interest intermediation will be more instrumental and noncommittal and will include a general readiness to 'go it on their own' if associational policies are not to their liking. The more often this happens, the more one would expect corporatist cultures of associative action to be modified in a pluralist direction.

Third, it seems that corresponding changes are taking place in the practices and habits of the political interlocutors of business in national governments and international agencies, which constitute the opportunity structure of business interest politics and define its logic of influence. Increasingly, even in corporatist countries, politicians and public officials seem to be willing to speak to representatives of large firms directly, especially if these happen to be prominent. Publicly visible contacts with the leaders of big firms, unlike corporatist-style closed-door meetings, bestow on politicians an aura of entrepreneurialism, which they today believe they need for creating an attractive image of themselves and the entire political enterprise. Direct contacts between business interests and political decision makers, instead of relations mediated through associations or corporatist institutions, gain importance in national polities also due to deregulation weakening collective representation; to the rise of new sectors without established sectoral organizations, such as information and telecommunications technology; or the expectations of and the attention given to foreign firms. Push and pull come together as top managers learn at business school and from their, increasingly Anglo-American, role models how to build direct relations with politicians and governments. Both opportunities and temptations for large firms to bypass associations have increased in the national as well as the international arena; one might think of the Davos gatherings and similar forums. This implies, incidentally, that the very firms whose resources are most needed by associations are becoming less dependent on them and, as a result, are less available to be drafted into contributing to their organizational capacities. This point, which has been made regarding the relationship between large firms and European-level business associations (Coen 1997; Cowles 1994), applies certainly at the global level (see the chapters by Ronit and Coleman) and is also true at the national level.

The emergence of large firms as independent interest-political actors inevitably gives rise to a new kind of duplication of effort, this time between associations and their most potent members. But, unlike in the case of imperfect functional differentiation between employer and trade associations, there are few complaints to be heard. Associations, of course, might resent that their large member firms spend growing amounts of resources on pursuing their special interests, instead of contributing to the general interest of the industry or of capital as a class. Association officials know, however, that they have no choice but to take what is given to them, and continue to do their utmost to serve the interest of their large members in whatever they can still offer in return. That large firms flexibly and opportunistically shift between a variety of modes of making their interests heard, from individual lobbying to collective action, from national to supranational action and back, and if necessary from one national arena and associational system to the next, is now more or less taken for granted (Greenwood 2003: 119). 'Solidarity' is often demanded of business firms by their associations, but it is generally understood that it is only rarely supplied. After all, business firms are supposed to be pursuing their individual interests, and their associations are there to ensure that they can do just that. Small firms, too, know where the money is. In times of economic turmoil, when their large competitors are getting ready to cut their throats, they may dream of organizing separately in a *Poujadiste*-style movement of their own. But reality being as it is, it usually offers them a choice only between having little influence in associations with much influence dominated by large firms, and having much influence in associations of only small firms that have only very little influence.

The European level: new complexities

Economic internationalization in Europe was from early on and continues to be accompanied by supranational integration of political institutions. The past two decades saw the slow emergence of a new, Europe-wide political system *sui generis*, one that exists on top of and in addition to the national systems. Together with these, it forms an international multilevel system of political–economic regulation, which greatly adds to the complexities of interest politics in European countries. In the following we will briefly summarize, first, what we know about the institutional and organizational structure of interest representation in the European Union. Second, we will in particular look at the consequences of multilevel interest representation for national business associations. Third, we will briefly explore the relevance of our findings for what could reasonably be meant by that much used concept, Europeanization.

Interest representation at European level

Early integration theory, developed in the mixed economy world of the 1950s and 1960s, expected business associations to be among the driving forces of European integration, with functional representation preceding and pulling forward territorial representation through parties and parliaments (Haas 1958: 9ff., 16; Lindberg 1963: 101). More or less, the imagery informing neo-functionalist perspectives on integration was one of a supranationally organized 'modern capitalism' (Shonfield 1965), with an orderly, essentially corporatist system of supranational interest intermediation absorbing and in the long run replacing the national systems of member states.

By the end of the twentieth century, it had become clear that this was not the direction in which united Europe was moving. The logic of influence for organized interests that had over the decades established itself in Brussels differed profoundly from that of postwar neo-corporatism (Streeck and Schmitter 1991). In the 1970s at the latest, the European Community had turned into a site of extensive lobbying in the Anglo-American style. This was reinforced with British accession, when British firms extended their domestic practice of direct relations with government agencies to the supranational authorities of what was soon to become the European Union. European business associations, which began to be created as early as the mid-1950s, soon had to share access to European authorities with representatives of large firms and professional lobbyists, often American law firms. As mentioned above, while it is widely assumed that the European Commission tried to encourage the formation of strong sectoral and intersectoral associations of business, it was unable to establish a corporatist culture limiting access to collective organizations and withholding it from firms. Also, trade unions were and continue to be present at European level only as lobbyists. Due to the weakness of the European quasi-state and the refusal of employers to take part, there is no collective bargaining in Europe above national systems in which, in addition, it is slowly eroding or weakening in a number of countries, especially at the sectoral level (Marginson and Sisson 2004).

Brussels, however, must not be regarded in isolation. As pointed out, rather than a political system like any other, the European Union is the upper layer of a unique multilevel-cum-multinational governance arrangement and is adequately understood only as such, i.e. in its interaction with the growing number of national polities that continue to form its base. For interest representation, this means above all that the European Union offers many more and different access points than a normal polity, not just in Brussels with its complex institutional set-up but also through the national polities, with the relationship between the two levels being much less well-defined and much more in flux than in any national federal system. In part, the complicated logic of influence that derives from this is to do with the fact that it continues to be the Council that is the – nationally divided – political centre of the Union. Council decisions may be influenced via the Commission or the European Parliament but also, and sometimes more effectively, through national governments (Greenwood 2003: 39ff.). This holds certainly where European-level decisions require unanimity. In this case it is enough for a group interested in preventing a given decision to avail itself of the support of just one member state – which for business interests first was Thatcherist and, later, Blairist Britain.[19] While with majority voting a Council veto requires more than one country, it may still be expedient for interest groups to access European Union decisions in national capitals putting together a multinational veto coalition.

The structure of European business associations reflects the complexity of, and the continuing significance of national states within, the de facto constitution of the European multilevel regime. UNICE, the peak association of European business, organizes national peak associations, not European-level sectoral associations. European business associations at the sectoral level exist apart from UNICE and are structurally unrelated to it. Indeed lack of coordination between UNICE and the various European sectoral associations represents a lasting problem for business interest representation at European level (Teuber forthcoming).[20] Moreover, while sectoral associations differ considerably in their resource endowment, many are under-resourced and nearly all are far less well endowed than their national members.[21] If the allocation of resources between different levels of organization can be taken as a proxy of the relative significance of the latter, it shows that in spite of all the talk of globalization, internationalization and Europeanization, the national level has remained central for organizing economic interests.

The weakness of business associations at the European as compared to the national level may also have to do with the fact that national traditions of interest organization are very different within the European Union (Grande 2003: 53ff.; Platzer 1984: 166). This seems to make it difficult if not impossible politically to integrate national organizations closely into a common supranational format. One expression of national differences in traditions of associative action is differences in the amount of resources associations have available. Rich and well-established associations from corporatist countries thus may enjoy an important advantage when it comes to the distribution of influence and power in European associations. That advantage may enable them to protect their own freedom of action, just as it may make weaker national associations reluctant to give up their independence in favour of an organization inevitably dominated by much better endowed member associations from other countries.

Empirical research and theoretical reasoning also suggest that national differences of interest continue to exist and may even increase within sectors, regardless and perhaps precisely because of the completion of the 'Internal Market'. Thus a given industry may turn out to enjoy comparative advantage in some countries while losing out in others, which may result in its increasing geographical concentration. In this case, with prospering and declining firms located in different countries, it would seem difficult to combine their interests and, in particular, their national interest organizations in an integrated supranational trade association. More likely, the evolution of such an association would be blocked and the different national associations with their different interests would try their European luck on their own – unless the national association of the country winning the *Standortwettbewerb* would either take over or de facto turn into the sector's European association (for an instructive example see Teuber, forthcoming).

Interest organization at the European level, to sum up, is much more fragmented and much less institutionally settled than at the national level (Grant 2002: 56ff.). The number of independent actors is higher, and there is less space for authority from above to impose coherence by coordination. This is further exacerbated by the fact that UNICE itself is far from sectorally all-encompassing and has difficulties organizing small and medium-sized firms as well as commerce and trade (Greenwood 2003; Platzer 1984). Most importantly, however, European business associations, including UNICE as well as the sectoral associations, have to come to terms with the independent and often highly sophisticated lobbying activities of large firms. Some of these appear to expend sums on their Brussels offices that exceed the budget of many trade associations (Grant and Paterson 1994: 143). There are even cases of large firms luring experienced staff away from their sectoral trade association to hire them as their own European lobbyists.

Large firms also organize their own business round tables, which exclude both smaller firms and the representatives of business associations (Greenwood 2003: 119ff.). The latter have little choice but to organize themselves around their ever more powerful large members. In return for staying on, large firms tend to demand opportunities for direct membership in what otherwise are European associations of national associations. They may also want to form special committees, which inevitably creates tensions with small and medium-sized firms envious of their influence.[22] Generally, as Coen (1997) and others have shown, many large firms tend to use the Brussels business associations opportunistically as footholds in the European capital if they believe they need one; if not they circumvent them and act on their own.[23] Add to this, as observed already by Streeck and Schmitter (1991), that even member states and subnational regions appear on the Brussels scene as active lobbyists defending their interests, making for a political environment that is extremely diversified and pluralist. This offers a great variety of opportunities for political access and coalition-building that was quite unknown in the more sedate settings of west European nation states after 1945.

National business associations in the European multilevel polity

From the perspective of theories of organization and institutional change, it was always unrealistic to assume that national business associations would happily transfer their resources and decisional autonomy to supranational associations, only because European integration would shift decision-making power from the national to the supranational level. The inherent tendency of organizations to strive for their reproduction even in the face of changing external conditions, and generally the path dependency of social institutions, would inevitably have resulted in delayed rather than accelerated adjustment of the organization of collective interests to the progress of European integration. Now that such progress has been slower and, most importantly, in a different direction than originally expected, the persistence of national business associations and their continuing strength in relation to their supranational extensions should not be seen as surprising any more.

In fact, it is not just their established control over their resources, their well-oiled organizations and the costs sunk in them that protect the position of national business associations in, and in spite of, a more integrated Europe. Another condition militating against the weakening of national associations and their eventual absorption by European ones is the problematic compatibility of different national traditions of interest organization and interest politics. Corporatist and pluralist organizations function differently and cannot easily be merged. As the result of attempts at merger is uncertain, it is less risky to reserve one's own proven capacities and operate if necessary through two channels. In addition, there are at least three other factors that have prevented and are likely further to prevent a decisive weakening of the national level of interest politics in the European Union.

First, as stated above, among the many points of access the European Union offers to actors interested in its decisions are the national capitals, whose representatives continue to be the dominant players in the governance of the Union. As a consequence, European business associations, including UNICE and the various sectoral peak associations, more often than not depend on their national affiliates to intercede with their national governments,[24] so that the Council gets an impending decision 'right' from the perspective of European business.[25] It is obvious that such dependency strengthens the role of national associations within their European peak associations, mirroring the strong position of national governments inside the Union.

Second, economic sectors continue to differ in structure and performance between countries, even in an integrated world economy. To the extent that different institutional and other conditions in different countries make for differences in the competitiveness of firms, the interests of the latter in relation to supranational decision making may be too heterogeneous to allow for joint representation through a unified European association. Competition may also lead to specialization within and between sectors. In the former case, firms in one country may specialize on subsectors that may have very different interests with respect to legal or political regulation than other subsectors (for the retail industry, see Teuber forthcoming). For example, if bulk chemicals are produced in some countries while fine chemicals or pharmaceuticals are produced in others, national sectoral interests with respect to environmental policy may differ so much that they cannot be represented by one and the same association.[26] Finally, specialization between sectors may result in concentration of a particular industry in one member state, or a small subset of member states. This would make it very difficult for a European association to prevent its respective national member associations from bypassing it and entering into direct relations with European Union agencies.[27]

Third, not only do European-level associations often find it hard or impossible to represent a common supranational view. In addition, European authorities are willing to speak, not just to individual multinational firms, but also to national associations from individual member states. As these are in contact with their governments, which in turn are dominant actors in Brussels, this is not surprising. Often European associations cannot deliver the quality of expertise that national associations can provide. Moreover, if nationally-based interests are too diverse, European associations cannot produce a coherent non-trivial policy position, and consultation with the relevant national players will be required for meaningful decision making. Direct national access also reflects the openness and multiple accessibility of the Brussels machinery of governance, which leaves a lot of space for interest-political entrepreneurialism, not just of professional lobbyists and large individual firms, but also of associations of less than full European scope.

Rather than going away, national business associations, sectoral as well as cross-sectoral ones, have expanded their – inevitably national – strategies into the European arena. Here they act, not according to a European ideology, but in pursuit of nationally based interests interpreted in a European context. National business associations often and, if they command enough resources, typically do this through European offices of their own that liaise with all sorts of other actors, from the Permanent Representation of their home country to the different levels of the Commission, the European Parliament, the lobbying establishments of large firms and, importantly, the head offices of the very same European-level peak associations to which national associations are affiliated. Moreover, European action of national associations includes the selective formation of, as it were, horizontal alliances with other national associations outside the purview of European peak associations, even those of which all parties are members. If anything, it is the increased capacity of national actors for international action that is emblematic of that multifaceted process referred to in the academic literature and in everyday parlance as 'Europeanization'.

The 'Europeanization' of interest politics

In the history of research and theorizing on European integration, Europeanization has come to mean a great number of things. Originally it seems to have meant the expected dissolution of national institutions and identities into a more or less federal, but in any case unified, European political system (Haas 1958). More recently, the concept is used to refer to a gradual restructuring of national polities and policies from above, by European legislation, court decisions and 'benchmarking', issuing in a reorganization of national regimes according to norms originating at the upper level of the European multilevel system. The end result of this process is supposed to be convergence of national, political and administrative systems on a common European template. To us, looking at the ongoing transformation of systems of interest representation in Europe, this image of European integration seems by far too top-down and mechanistic.

Given what we have observed in this book and elsewhere, if Europeanization as a concept is to be useful at all, it must be reformulated once again and become more actor-centred. By this we mean that it must reflect the strategic dimension that is essential to the adjustment of originally national collective and individual actors to the progress of European economic and institutional integration, i.e. to the specifically European version of internationalization. Far from passively receiving and obeying decisions of the new agencies that have arisen above the nation state, and changing their views and ways accordingly, national actors as we see them respond to the growth of international transactions and institutions as to an additional parameter for their strategic action and, ultimately, self-definition. As they experience increasingly frequent transactions across national borders and perceive growing opportunities in taking part in them, national firms, associations and governments adopt an international perspective and begin to conceive of their location in an increasingly transnational context as a defining characteristic of themselves: they become national players on a playing field, Europe, that extends beyond the borders of their own country. How they move in this environment, and what goals they choose to pursue in it, is not something that they will allow others to determine, not even, and perhaps precisely not, a supranational agency or peak association of which they are simply one client or member among others.

Europeanization, as we see it happening, does not in principle preclude that actors may at some point rescind their national constitution and dissolve into more encompassing, denationalized collectivities, provided they find these better suited for containing the risks and opening up the opportunities of internationalization. But this is far from the only possible response, and indeed now it seems to be among the least likely. A concept of Europeanization that accords the national actors undergoing it an active capacity would lead one to expect not uniformity but difference: driven by different national starting points, structurally-based interests and strategic choices. The changes that will result from this must be empirically traced rather than theoretically predicted. The extended strategic reach that accompanies internationalization may undo old constraints, such as obligations to participate in corporatist interest intermediation. But it may also create new ones, like those associated with supranational competition law, just as it may open up new opportunities, for example possibilities for strategic and tactical alliances with actors outside one's own country that previously seemed to be without practical significance. Old goals may become unrealistic, but then some of the new possibilities that are gradually being discovered may be turned into new goals. Similarly, proven means may cease to be available, but others may turn up that may usefully be deployed in pursuit of old or new objectives.

In other words, for Europeanization of interest politics to be a reality, it is not necessary at all for the resources of European business associations to exceed the combined resources of their national constituents – and the fact that they do not, and very likely never will, is no proof of national parochialism or of ignorance of the consequences of internationalization. Nor is there reason to treat as an anomaly – or as a transitory condition on the way towards 'real' Europeanization – what has long become a normal and stable feature of business interest representation in Europe, namely the presence in Brussels of bureaus of national sectoral or intersectoral trade associations that operate separately from the bureaus of their respective European-level associations. The same is true for the fact that there are and continue to be major differences in the European presence of different sectors, and especially in the way national and European organizations relate to one another, and it holds similarly for the absence of an intersectoral European peak association organizing the European-level sectoral peak associations. That integrated Europe is not an integrated polity on the model of national polities does not imply at all that actors do not take the reality of integration into account when pursuing their interests; it only means that they do this in their own way, proceeding from where they are instead of from where 'theory' tells them they will have to be.

Notes

1 We wish to express our gratitude to Jörg Teuber for competent research assistance.

2 For a more elaborate presentation of this concept and related ones, see the Introduction, this volume.

3 An interesting parallel exists on the side of trade unions. Here, too, it seems that the literature on neo-corporatism has underestimated the demand of members of interest organizations for political participation, while overestimating the capacity of established associations to generate member commitment without a minimum of organizational democracy. See Baccaro (2002).

4 Mergers, according to Boléat (2002: 87), are bad news for trade associations. Among other things, mergers tend to lower an association's subscription income. Usually subscription scales are capped. When two member firms

merge, the new firm will likely pay less than the two had paid together before the merger. Associations must react to this by reducing expenditure or seeking to increase revenue from other sources. They may also on their part try to merge with associations in the same or an adjacent sector.

5 Interestingly in the 1970s it seems to have been the other way around. Where mergers between trade and employer associations were considered, they were basically conceived as a takeover of the former by the latter. This may have reflected the strength of the trade union movement at the time which resulted in an increase of national labour market regulation, by law or collective agreement. This in turn gave primacy to the labour market interests of employers over the product market interests of producers, especially since firms were less exposed to international competition than today (see Bührer 1989: 157ff., on the attempted merger of the German peak associations BDI and BDA).

6 Independent parallel evolution in response to similar pressures in the absence of cross-national diffusion or joint action was also found with respect to organizational changes in postwar trade unions in Germany and the Netherlands (Streeck and Visser 1998). This testifies to the continuing importance of national borders and legacies. Given the manifold international contacts and the increasing internationalization of business, the national embeddedness of its organizations may seem more surprising than in the case of labour.

7 Sellière's motto, frequently repeated in his notorious press conferences, was 'dire sans prudence ce que pensent les entrepreneurs français'.

8 D'Amato's appointment by Confindustria's General Council deeply divided the organization and did not have the support of the large industrial firms and the powerful federations of large industry. He was not given a second term and in 2004 the organization elected Luca di Montezemolo, who is close to the Fiat dynasty and not himself an entrepreneur. This was widely seen as an attempt to repair the damage in the relationship with the unions and put a distance between Confindustria and the Berlusconi government.

9 The French intersectoral business and employer association, MEDEF, was able to introduce direct membership of large firms in its most recent constitutional reform because in most sectors small firms had already established strong peak associations of their own. This holds for the Netherlands as well, although the separate organization of small firms may also be seen as the *result* of direct membership and the consequently enhanced influence of large firms in confederations representing small firms as well.

10 This is a point made for example by Pestoff and by Grote and Schneider in this volume. A contrasting view is that of Greenwood (2003), who claims that no one in an international firm knows what the local subscription fees are, and that association membership is one of the last areas of the activities of firms where hard-headed cost-evaluation methods are not used. But this may apply more to the low cost European associations than to the more expensive national associations, especially in the case of employer associations or associations with dual functions.

11 In the automobile industry foreign-owned producers are often only informally or not at all involved in national or European-level trade associations. They are most firmly integrated in the German association whereas in Britain, US multinationals have abstained from membership (Teuber forthcoming).

12 The equivalent at the European level was the Centre for European Policy Studies, which was founded in the 1980s by large companies (Cowles 1994: 168).

13 Dutch peak associations and multinational firms have unwaveringly promoted the same cause, but somewhat less aggressively and publicly. Presumably this

was because they were well served by the liberal market policies of their government that had the backing of the unions during the successful phase of Dutch 'supply-side corporatism' in the 1990s.

14 There is also a separate trade association of industrialists in Austria. It plays only a minor role next to the all-embracing Chamber of Industry and Commerce, which has obligatory membership and represents both trade and employer interests.

15 As noted above, the resilience of German employer associations, especially in the metal sector, may also be explained by their enormous wealth. The national peak association of German employers, BDA, receives approximately one half of its revenue from Gesamtmetall. In part this reflects the relatively slow deindustrialization of Germany, which in turn is due to the high international competitiveness of its exposed industrial sector. Note that in Sweden, a smaller country which, in addition, progressed much faster on the road to a service economy, the similarly rich financial endowment of national employer associations did not save these from consolidation.

16 As we will argue further on, this is how it has worked on the European level.

17 This has interesting consequences even for the mobilization of associational resources (Boléat 2002: 86). More often than not, business associations are constrained by their smaller member firms to place a ceiling on the financial contributions large firms are allowed to make, so as to protect the association from becoming overly dependent on them. The contradiction between this and the strong desire of the small firms for the large ones to subsidize collective action and individual services is obvious.

18 In France, Mr Sellière, who came from one of the largest financial holding companies with stakes throughout industry and services, provides another example.

19 As has often been stated, the great strategic advantage of business in European politics is that its interest is more in preventing than in shaping the building of European-level institutions, especially as regards industrial relations, employment policy and social protection.

20 In other words, the architecture of the functional representation of business interests in Europe remains open at the top, indicating the weakness of the European polity as a reference point for political organization at the class level. One might also speak of an unresolved pluralism of national and sectoral interests existing next to each other at the level of the European Union. Something like this is also found within sectors. The Council of European Employers of the Metal, Engineering and Technology-based Industries (CEEMET), formerly the West European Metal Employers (WEM), finds it difficult to prevent independent associations in subsectors such as shipbuilding, aircraft production or car manufacturing from dealing directly with the Commission or with national governments and trade unions.

21 Greenwood *et al.* (1999) observe that almost half of all European associations have no more than two staff members. 'Most EU business associations remain chronically under-resourced and are thus ill-equipped to perform the tasks demanded of them' (Tyszkiewicz 2002: 171). The same applies to the trade unions.

22 In peak associations, tensions also arise with member associations. In the late 1980s, the influence of large multinational firms in UNICE was institutionalized by the creation of the UNICE Advisory and Support Group, which is funded by the participating firms themselves and directly. Especially British, Dutch and American firms make use of this platform. The national peak associations, which are the formal constituents of UNICE, agreed to the formation of the Group only after some firms had threatened to reduce their national

membership fees (Cowles 1994: 179ff.). Especially the German and the French national peak associations fought to defend their monopoly of representation inside UNICE. After the reform they tried to make their domestic firms channel their contributions to UNICE through their national associations (Cowles 1994: 181).

23 'Thus according to the issues, the big company will wear the EU trade association's hat when it has an interest in doing so. Conversely, it will undertake its own lobbying actions when this is to its advantage' (Guéguen 2002: 51).

24 Even here, according to a knowledgeable source, 'much essential work is left undone and the political potential of concerted and timely action at national level is left unexploited' (Tyszkiewicz 2002: 171).

25 The same game is often played by multinational firms trying to coordinate the lobbying activities of their national subsidiaries in the interest of the firm as a whole. Firms may also make themselves available to associations for this sort of coordinated European lobbying of national capitals.

26 A similar case would be the auto industry. British firms now produce exclusively supply parts rather than whole automobiles (which are produced in Britain by foreign subsidiaries). The interests of suppliers may differ from those of final assemblers of automobiles. Where subsectoral divisions come to coincide with geographic or national divisions, unified supranational interest organization seems difficult to achieve, and national associations may have to begin to play a supranational role.

27 Thus German chemical industry associations are aware of the fact that the European chemical industry is essentially concentrated in only four countries whereas the European sectoral peak association, CEFIC, encompasses the entire European Union as well as other countries. While in the postwar decades German interests could effectively be articulated at an international level only through multilateral channels, today this is no longer necessarily the case. As a consequence German national associations increasingly rely on independent European action, sometimes in variable alliances with associations from countries that happen to have identical interests on a particular matter.

References

Baccaro, L. (2002) 'The Construction of "Democratic" Corporatism in Italy', *Politics and Society* 30 (2), June, 327–357.

Boléat, M. (2002) 'The Changing Environment for Trade Associations and Strategies for Adaptation', in J. Greenwood (ed.) *The Effectiveness of EU Business Associations*, Houndmills: Palgrave.

Bothorel, J. and Sassier, P. (2002) *Seillière, le baron de la république*, Paris: Laffont.

Bührer, W. (1989) 'Unternehmerverbände', in W. Benz (ed.) *Die Geschichte der Bundesrepublik Deutschland*, vol. 1, Frankfurt: Fischer.

Cawson, A. (ed.) (1985) *Organized Interests and the State. Studies in Meso-Corporatism*, London: Sage.

Coen, D. (1997) 'The Evolution of the Large Firm as a Political Actor in the European Union', *Journal of European Public Policy* 4: 91–108.

Cowles, M. G. (1994) *The Politics of Big Business in the European Community. Setting the Agenda for a New Europe*, PhD Thesis, Washington DC: The American University.

Crouch, C. (1993) *Industrial Relations and European State Traditions*, Oxford: Oxford University Press.

Grande, E. (2003) 'How the Architecture of the EU Political System Influences EU

Business Associations', in J. Greenwood (ed.) *The Challenge of Change in EU Business Associations*, Houndmills: Palgrave.

Grant, W. (1984) 'Large Firms and Public Policy in Britain', *Journal of Public Policy* 4: 1–17.

Grant, W. (2002) 'The Importance of Institutions to Associations: Evidence from the Cross-National Organisation of Business Interests Project', in J. Greenwood (ed.) *The Effectiveness of EU Business Associations*, Houndmills: Palgrave.

Grant, W. and Paterson, W. (1994) 'The Chemical Industry: A Study of Internationalization', in R. J. Hollingsworth, P. C. Schmitter and W. Streeck (eds) *Governing Capitalist Economies. Performance and Control of Economic Sectors*, New York: Oxford University Press.

Greenwood, J. (2003) *Interest representation in the European Union*, Houndmills: Palgrave Macmillan.

Greenwood, J., Stanchich, L. and Strangward, L. (1999) 'The Capacities of Euro Groups in the Integration Process', *Political Studies* 47: 127–138.

Guéguen, D. (2002) 'Governance and the Role of Associations in Economic Management: A Response from an EU Public Affairs Practitioner', in J. Greenwood (ed.) *The Effectiveness of EU Interest Associations*, Houndsmills: Palgrave.

Haas, E. B. (1958) *The Uniting of Europe. Political, Social, and Economic Forces 1950–1957*, Stanford: Stanford University Press.

Hassel, A. and Rehder, B. (2001) 'Institutional Change in the German Wage Bargaining System. The Role of Big Companies', MPIfG Working Paper 01/9, Max Planck Institute for the Study of Societies. Online, available at: www.mpi-fg-koeln.mpg.de/pu/workpap/wp01-9/wp01-9.html.

Helbert, J.-P. (1984) *L'Insurrection des Patrons*, Châteaugiron: Samon.

Jacobi, O. (2003) 'Renewal of the collective bargaining system?', in W. Müller-Jentsch and H. Weitbrecht (eds) *The changing contours of German industrial relations*, Munich: Hampp.

Lindberg, L. N. (1963) *The Political Dynamics of European Economic Integration*, Stanford: Stanford University Press.

Lütz, S. (1998) 'The Revival of the Nation-State? Stock Exchange Regulation in an Era of Globalized Financial Markets', *Journal of European Public Policy* 5: 153–168.

Marginson, P. and Sisson, K. (2004) *European Integration and Industrial Relations: Multi-level Governance in the Making*, Basingstoke: Palgrave Macmillan.

Martin, A. (1997) 'The Swedish Model: Demise or Reconfiguration?', in R. Locke, T. Kochan and M. Piore (eds) *Employment Relations in a Changing World*, Cambridge: MIT Press.

Olson, M. (1965) *The Logic of Collective Action: Public Goods and the Theory of Groups*, Cambridge MA: Harvard University Press.

Platzer, H.-W. (1984) *Unternehmensverbände in der EG – ihre nationale und transnationale Organisation und Politik. Dargestellt am Beispiel des Bundesverbandes der Deutschen Industrie, der Bundesvereinigung der Deutschen Arbeitgeberverbände, der deutschen industriellen Branchenverbände und deren EG-Verbandszusammenschlüssen*, Kehl: Engel.

Schmitter, P. C. and Streeck, W. (1981; 2nd edn 1999) 'The Organization of Business Interests: Studying the Associative Action of Business in Advanced Industrial Societies', MPIfG Discussion paper 99/1, Cologne: Max Planck Institute for the Study of Societies.

Shonfield, A. (1965) *Modern Capitalism. The Changing Balance of Public and Private Power*, London: Oxford University Press.

Streeck, W. and Schmitter, P. C. (1985) *Private Interest Government: Beyond Market and State*, London: Sage.

Streeck, W. and Schmitter, P. C. (1991) 'From National Corporatism to Transnational Pluralism: Organized Interests in the Single European Market', *Politics and Society* 19 (2): 133–164.

Streeck, W. and Visser, J. (1998) 'An Evolutionary Dynamic of Trade Union Systems', MPIfG Discussion Paper 98/4. Cologne: Max Planck Institute for the Study of Societies.

Teuber, J. (forthcoming) 'The Europeanization of Organized Interests in Selected Industries: Case Studies in the Automobile and Retail Sector', Doctoral dissertation, Cologne: Max Planck Institute for the Study of Societies.

Tyszkiewicz, Z. (2002) 'National Members and their EU Associations', in J. Greenwood (ed.) *The Effectiveness of EU Interest Associations*, London: Palgrave.

Apeldoorn, B. van (2002) *Transnational Capitalism and the Struggle over European Integration*, London: Routledge.

Waarden, F. van (1996) 'The Organizational Power of Employers' Associations: Cohesion, Comprehensiveness and Organizational Development', in C. Crouch and F. Traxler (eds) *Organized Industrial Relations in Europe: What Future?*, Aldershot: Avebury.

Wagemann, C. (2004) 'Private Interest Governments are Dead. Long Live Private Interest Governments? Lessons from Swiss Cows', Badia Fiesolana: European University Institute, EUI Working Paper SPS No. 2004/13.

Wessels, W. (1997) 'An Ever Closer Fusion? A Dynamic Macropolitical View on Integration Processes', *Journal of Common Market Studies* 35: 267–299.

Wilts, A. (2002) 'Strategies of Business Interest Associations in the Netherlands and Germany: European Priorities or Domestic Concerns?', in E. Grossman and S. Saurugger (eds) *Les Groupes d'Intérêt et l'Union Européenne, Politique Europeenne*, No. 7, spring 2002.

Ziegler, H. (1992) 'Interest Groups', in M. Hawkesworth and M. Kogan (eds) *Encyclopedia of Government and Politics*, vol. 1, London: Routledge.

Zimmer, S. (2002) *Jenseits von Arbeit und Kapital? Unternehmerverbände und Gewerkschaften im Zeitalter der Globalisierung*, Opladen: Leske und Budrich.

Index

For Product Safety Concerns and Information please contact our EU representative GPSR@taylorandfrancis.com
Taylor & Francis Verlag GmbH, Kaufingerstraße 24, 80331 München, Germany

www.ingramcontent.com/pod-product-compliance
Lightning Source LLC
LaVergne TN
LVHW011117300926
849160LV00008B/419

* 9 7 8 0 4 1 5 6 4 8 0 9 7 *